DREAM CITY

DREAM CITY

CREATION, DESTRUCTION, AND REINVENTION IN DOWNTOWN DETROIT

CONRAD KICKERT

THE MIT PRESS   CAMBRIDGE, MASSACHUSETTS   LONDON, ENGLAND

Illustrations in this book were funded in part or in whole by a grant from the SAH/Mellon Author Awards of the Society of Architectural Historians. Color reproduction of this book was supported by the University of Cincinnati, School of Planning, Orville Simpson II Endowment Fund.

This book was set in Minion and Trade Gothic by The MIT Press. Printed and bound in the United States of America.

Library of Congress Cataloging-in-Publication Data

Names: Kickert, Conrad, author.
Title: Dream city : creation, destruction, and reinvention in downtown Detroit / Conrad Kickert.
Description: Cambridge, MA : The MIT Press, 2018. | Includes bibliographical references and index.
Identifiers: LCCN 2018019052 | ISBN 9780262039345 (hardcover : alk. paper)
Subjects: LCSH: Central business districts--Michigan--Detroit--History. | Detroit (Mich.)--History. | Detroit
    (Mich.)--Economic conditions | Urban renewal--Michigan--Detroit--History.
Classification: LCC F574.D46 D665 2018 | DDC 977.4/34--dc23 LC record available at
https://lccn.loc.gov/2018019052

10   9   8   7   6   5   4   3   2   1

CONTENTS

PREFACE

We Europeans change within changeless cities, and
our houses and neighborhoods outlive us; American
cities change faster than their inhabitants do, and it
is the inhabitants who outlive the cities. ...For us a
city is, above all, a past; for them it is mainly a future;
what they like in the city is everything it has not yet
become and everything it can be.

Jean-Paul Sartre[1]

This is a book about an anomaly. In a city known for discarding anything it deems obsolete, from last year's car model to entire neighborhoods, downtown Detroit has always stood out as an unavoidable reminder of the past. Downtown is different—it's slower. Perhaps that's why it piqued my fascination as a young European urbanist over a decade ago. Downtown Detroit challenged my Dutch upbringing that hinged on viewing the past as an asset and public authority as benevolent and inevitable. Downtown Detroit's tangible failure to embrace the past and the public became the starting point of the journey that has led to this book—a journey that would soon challenge my notion of the American urban condition.

This work would not have been possible without the support of the countless archivists that hold the key to Detroit's past, most notably the staff at the Burton Historical Collection at the Detroit Public Library, the Walter P. Reuther Library at Wayne State University, the University of Michigan Clark and William L. Clements Libraries, and the United States Library of Congress. I would also like to thank my dissertation committee members Robert Fishman, Linda Groat, June M. Thomas, and Henco Bekkering for helping me lay the groundwork for this book. In Detroit, I am very grateful to Keith Harder Cavazos, Paul Szewczyk, Dan Austin, Mark Nickita, Dorian Moore, Michael Hauser, and John Gallagher for their input. I would like to thank my colleagues at the University of Cincinnati for giving me feedback, space, and resources to pull this off. And I would like to thank my graduate assistants for helping with graphics and management. Last but not least, I would like to thank my family and friends for their moral support, most notably my parents for encouraging me to keep asking questions, and Kelly Gregg for tolerating my spiritual absence in writing this book.

0.0
Street names in downtown
Detroit throughout history

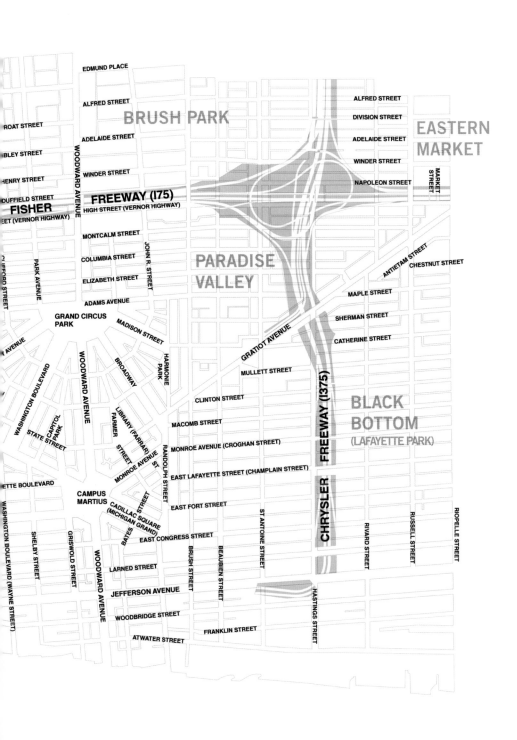

INTRODUCTION

0.1
Campus Martius in downtown Detroit.
Image by author, 2014.

If you visit downtown Detroit today, you could easily witness a remarkable rebirth. Streets are bustling with people, streetcars rush by, well-manicured patios and carefully renovated buildings are filled with lively restaurants, busy offices and luxurious dwellings. Cranes dot the skyline again for the first time in decades, replacing the wrecking balls of only a few years ago.[1] Where vacancy pervaded the buildings and despair echoed in the streets of downtown, life and wealth seem to have taken their place. A new generation of Detroiters and aspiring Detroiters has arisen to rediscover the virtues of downtown's unique urban qualities, left to linger since the lights went out in stages between the 1929 stock market crash, the 1950s urban renewal crisis, and the 1967 civil disorders. Where else in the region or even the state can one find such a uniquely dense and historic environment of Art Deco skyscrapers, Beaux-Arts retail palaces, lush plazas, and an international riverfront? For many young professionals, empty nesters, and tourists, downtown Detroit makes a dream of urbanity come true.

But turn the corner from downtown's hub of activity at Campus Martius, the breathtaking lobby of the Guardian Building, or the cheerful tunes of Greektown, and the downtown dream soon makes way for a nightmare of gravel, rust, and debris. Turn another corner and find yourself walking along barbed-wired fences, blank concrete walls, and empty parking ramps. Latte-sipping millennials make way for cars speeding past the homeless. Boutique fashion shops make way for check cashers, grimly barricaded liquor stores, or plywood-shuttered storefronts. The sidewalks start to crumble and go missing in places. The dream city of today seems but a stone's throw away from the urban nightmare of the previous decades. Is it all just a mirage?

It is easy to become fascinated by the material experience of this paradox. Why is one downtown building immaculately renovated while its neighbor crumbles? Why is downtown's buzzing historic core surrounded by underused parking lots, aloof

0.2
Only a few blocks away, downtown
Detroit turns into an entirely different
landscape. Image by author, 2017.

corporate campuses, and secured entertainment complexes? And why on earth are there so many highways circling downtown, seemingly empty most of the time? The very visible contrast between growth and decline has attracted the interest of local historians who tell a story of lost opportunities,[2] photographers eager to portray the ruins of a lost city,[3] and architects who describe the erosion of downtown in ominous series of maps and graphics, warning teetering peer cities that "Detroit is everywhere."[4] Sometimes shocked, often fascinated, most authors, artists, and architects have focused on the unique outcomes of downtown Detroit's fall and rebirth without questioning *why* this has happened.

It is also easy to view downtown's rebirth as part of Detroit's urban promise, a vanguard of prosperity in a sea of blight. As written thus far, most of Detroit's story concerns its neighborhoods. Scholars and journalists have keenly described the spiral of decline that has overtaken much of Detroit as either a reflection of postindustrial and social failure or an omen of bottom-up urban reinvention.[5] Downtown has always stood out as a different animal altogether. Detroit's many homes may have been built at an accelerating pace across the Michigan plains, but nothing topped the vertical fever of its downtown skyscraper boom. When downtown grew, it grew faster than any other part of the city. And when downtown declined, it declined differently. Detroiters could shut down inner-city factories and leave entire neighborhoods to wither, but they were unable to avoid the hulks of their ancestors' dreams in downtown—even if they tried. Instead, downtown's central role in Detroit's image and imagination forced it to continuously reinvent itself. Downtown had no choice but to reconcile its past and its present, public authorities and private interests, creation and destruction, success and failure, and its local and global role. Downtown's contemporary landscape of contrast is the result of this confinement of compromises.

This book investigates how these compromises have crystallized into today's dichotomous downtown landscape, by focusing on several dialectics that have shaped downtown. To begin with, it deepens the insight into downtown's visible tension between creation and destruction by focusing on the underlying process of reinvention. Downtown had no choice but to transform to keep up with Detroit's fever for innovation and ultimate survival. By uniquely combining Detroit's changing notion of progress with a series of detailed maps of the physical shape of downtown, this book will demonstrate that downtown showed its first signs of decay decades before Detroit's midcentury peak. When the much-maligned federal bulldozers arrived during the 1950s, much of the damage had already been done. Interestingly, in its rebound downtown has also preceded the rest of the city. After urban renewal left a shattered downtown in the late 1960s, a slow process of physical growth began, and at the dawn of the twenty-first century downtown is bigger than it had ever been. More importantly, downtown is different from before, breaking new ground for peer cities across the nation.

This transformation reflects how downtown has been in constant battle with its own offspring: the automobile, and the suburbs that it enabled. Disconnected from Detroit's four-wheeled raison d'être, downtown has been fighting a rearguard battle with uninterested industrialists, parking lot barons, and overzealous highway builders for almost a century. More than any of its radical but surprisingly futile modernist urban renewal plans, downtown modernized *itself* through a slow but steady process of parking attrition and land consolidation. And beyond its eclipse by the suburbs, downtown's desperation has fueled a process of self-suburbanization, materializing in a ring of neon lights, corporate campuses, and parking structures. In succumbing to its descendants, Detroit often predated national trends on peripheral decline and large-scale renewal, a path-breaking role it scarcely fulfilled with flair.

These highly transformative processes were able to wreak havoc on downtown, as it typically had little regard for its past. Relentlessly looking toward a brighter future, from next year's car model to the newest suburban mall, Detroiters frequently struggled to come to grips with downtown's vertical repository of previous dreams and failures. In the city's restless cycles of growth and decline, downtown's building stock mostly served either as an obstruction to growth or an embarrassing monument to failure. This book will trace the slow change in the city's perceptions of preservation, from marginalized philanthropic endeavors and overwhelmed individual acts of sentimentalism to an economic driver that has the potential to lift up the entire city.

Even with the best intentions, urban planners, politicians, and aspiring developers were surprisingly powerless to change downtown's fate. Instead, today's downtown landscape has been shaped by those who possessed the right balance of land, money, and political power—yielding a surprising cast of downtown players, from the car body salesman whose parking lot empire would eat through downtown's periphery by the

1920s to the pizza tycoon family and mortgage billionaire who control downtown's fate today. Ever since Detroit's refusal to comply with Judge Augustus Woodward's street plan in 1805, two centuries of wishful but mostly impotent downtown plans have demonstrated the ongoing hegemony of market forces over governance, of short-term solutions over coordinated efforts. Without agency, aspiration was futile—a plight that especially befell downtown's African American population.

Downtown Detroit is a prototype for downtown America. While downtown's roller-coaster history may seem unique to Detroit, it is an amplification and a precursor to the American postindustrial downtown. The trail it blazed was often ominous. When cars were becoming commonplace in American cities during the 1920s, Detroit had been battling congestion for over a decade. When American downtowns were peaking at the onset of the Depression, downtown Detroit had already eaten itself from the outside in. When the first urban renewal plans came to most American inner cities, Detroit had already cleared the land for its own. Downtown Detroit wouldn't wait for federal highway subsidies before slashing the first urban freeway through its brittle fabric. And when downtown America was hanging by a thread, the lights in downtown Detroit had long gone off. Then again, as America is refurbishing its downtowns, Detroit's urban core is now prospering like no other—for those who can afford it.

In four stages of growth, blossoming, decline, and stagnation, this book will take the reader through downtown Detroit's landscape of steel, brick, and tarmac, glistening neon and crumbling concrete. This book will mainly take a morphological approach to the historiography of downtown Detroit, augmenting the social focus of most other books on the city. Urban form is analyzed as the outcome of social, economic, political, and cultural forces. Two centuries of downtown creation, destruction, and reinvention will connect the dreams and nightmares that have created this landscape today and may preface America's tomorrow. As downtown Detroit is undergoing a remarkable rebirth to some, and sets a dangerous precedent to others, downtown's unique urban condition may once again guide Detroit and its North American peers into the future.

I SPRING

1   FROM OUTPOST TO DOWNTOWN: 1805–1884

The town of Detroit exists no longer.

The Intelligencer, August 7, 1805[1]

Downtown Detroit as we know it started with an act of complete destruction. On June 11, 1805, almost the entire dense and fortified settlement of Detroit burnt to the ground, most likely due to the mistake of a baker's apprentice. Just over a century after being settled as a fur trading outpost by French pioneer Antoine de La Motte Cadillac, and in the same year as it was designated the capital of the new Territory of Michigan, Detroit was left hanging by a thread as most citizens lost all their belongings and their homes.[2] Even in the face of adversity, Detroiters kept up hope. Witnessing the ruin, local priest Father Gabriel Richard pronounced "Speramus meliora; resurget cineribus"—"we hope for better, it shall arise from the ashes." This mixed message of hope and restlessness would pull the city up by the bootstraps in the decades to follow, and is still the city's apt motto today.[3] The year 1805 marked only the first time that the city would reinvent itself.

While Detroit was still smoldering, Augustus Brevoort Woodward was on his way to the city, newly appointed as judge of the new territory as a favor from his close friend Thomas Jefferson.[4] In the eyes of some, well-educated Woodward was a hopeless dreamer; for others, he was a visionary.[5] To the holdouts in smoldering Detroit, he was all they had—for better and for worse.[6] Upon his arrival there, he announced to Detroit's baffled citizens that instead of letting them rebuild as they liked, he would design a new city according to the principles of "scientific town planning" of European cities he had visited and the recent layout for his hometown of Washington, D.C.[7] In the buoyant spirit of the nation's capital and its European predecessors, Woodward forwent the simple grid in favor of a grandiose vision for a region he foresaw "thriving with people, characterized by industry and abounding in the productions and arts which minister to the

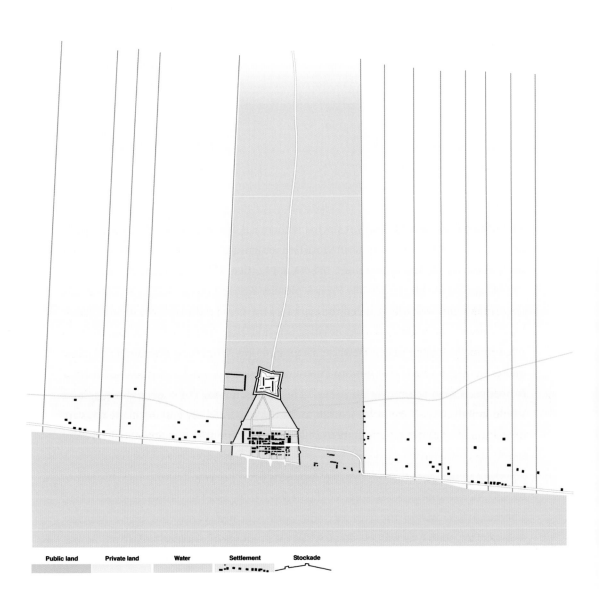

1.1

Detroit before the 1805 fire: a fortified riverfront settlement, surrounded by narrow French farm fields with farmhouses clustered along a riverfront path.

convenience and comfort of man."[8] Woodward's bullish words highlighted his belief in the power of entrepreneurialism unleashed on the sheer infinity of the Michigan hinterland, as he prepared Detroit for a prosperous future in which "the interior recesses of these pleasant and fertile regions are laid open to the irresistible energies of American enterprize."[9]

True to this enthusiasm, Woodward planned an elaborate radial city, built on a modular interplay between large "circuses," wide radial boulevards in all directions, and squares that connected them. The plan's unprecedented 120- to 200-foot-wide streets stood in stark contrast with the narrow thoroughfares of the old French settlement, an act of fire prevention as much as formalist hubris.[10] This put his work in close alignment with the Charles L'Enfant plan for Washington that he was intimately familiar with, although his layout avoided some of the awkward lots resulting from L'Enfant's sharply angled streets.[11] Michigan's virgin prairie allowed Woodward to rethink the city on a blank slate, with only the flow of the Detroit River and the cardinal systems influencing his vision.[12] Woodward envisioned his geometric carpet as no less than an infinite prototype for the new territory, expandable "whenever the growing city or public interest might require it."[13] Woodward's Detroit plan was far larger than the town it aimed to replace, resonating poorly with many citizens mostly yearning to rebuild.[14] While convinced of the value of his vision, even Woodward understood citizens' urgency, and he allowed them to resettle in a regularly gridded settlement between the riverfront and Detroit's east-west main street, later renamed Jefferson Avenue. His progressive radials would only start north of this street, well out of the way of current affairs.[15]

Legal issues, chaotic bookkeeping, and regular fights between Woodward and fellow Jefferson appointee Governor William Hull prevented the quick realization of the plan.[16] Especially Woodward was despised, as citizens viewed him as a stubborn dreamer choosing to lay out his white elephant settlement on Detroit's empty hinterland rather than help them rebuild the struggling riverfront town. The naming of the main north-south street after himself only added insult to injury.[17] Bit by bit, Hull would chip away at Woodward's plans, despite the latter's frequent protests. Five years after Woodward's plan was drafted, only 750 people lived in Detroit, which reached a new low point when Hull surrendered the city to the British at the first sign of trouble

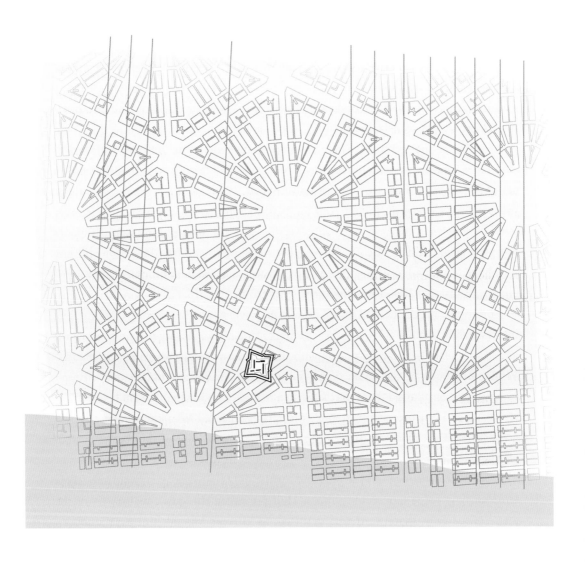

1.2
Woodward's radial plan superimposed on the former settlement of Detroit, with only the fort and farm strips remaining.

in 1812. Once again, Detroiters were left homeless and penniless.[18] In less than a year, the American army reconquered Detroit from the British and restored order under new Governor Lewis Cass, a former army general.[19]

Governor Cass was far more expedient in breathing life back into the city and the territory than his rather feeble predecessor, successfully kick-starting Michigan's economy through an assertive investment strategy. By colonizing Detroit's hinterland, he shifted Michigan's reputation from a worthless swamp to a land of agricultural opportunity, bolstering the city as a trade port.[20] The growth of commerce was reflected in a construction boom in the city, with the 1816 opening of a public market at the foot of Woodward Avenue laying the foundation of Detroit's first commercial district.[21] The arrival of the first steamship in 1818 regularized water access and bolstered trade.[22] Unlike his predecessor, Cass was assertive enough to fully sweep aside Woodward's control over the city's layout, which he increasingly considered a roadblock to Detroit's expedient expansion. Many landowners adjacent to downtown, including Cass himself, understood that Woodward's wide boulevards would obstruct easy land sales and subdivisions. Cass allowed an 1818 auction of public lands to deviate from Woodward's elaborate plan, and a subsequent citizen vote superseded the plan altogether. Detroit's expansion would be gridded from then on.[23] A few years later, a bitter Woodward was relieved from his duties as territorial judge and returned to Washington, almost as penniless as he had arrived.[24] Cass also embarked on a massive road improvement project for Michigan in the 1820s, understanding the economic and military benefits of good land access, especially as Michigan's waterways froze up for months each year.[25] Ironically extending his project from the Woodward plan he had snubbed, Cass would construct radial roads to Toledo (improving and extending Jefferson Avenue), Chicago (now Michigan Avenue), Fort Gratiot (now Gratiot Avenue), soon followed by a road to the Grand River (now Grand River Avenue).[26] The roads were a resounding success as they opened up Detroit's hinterland to new settlers, bolstering the city's commerce and enabling the first inland settlements like Pontiac and Rochester.[27]

While Detroit certainly grew as a result of Cass's expansion strategy, most of the inland radials of the plan that Woodward was able to execute still lay fallow in the late 1820s, and most streets in the plan weren't even named until around 1830.[28] Woodward's baroque streets still comprised the "upper part of the city," and for good

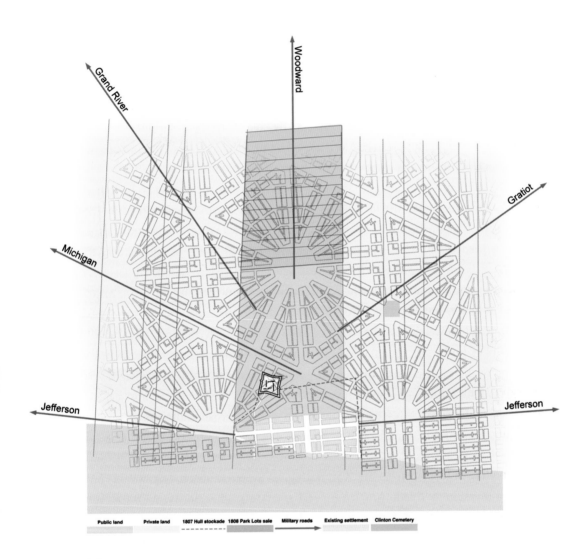

Grand River

Woodward

Michigan

Gratiot

Jefferson

Jefferson

Public land   Private land   1807 Hull stockade 1808 Park Lots sale   Military roads   Existing settlement   Clinton Cemetery

1.3
Woodward's grand plans were tamed between 1807 and
1827 by a stockade constructed in 1807 by Governor Hull,
various gridded land sales, Cass's radial streets, indifferent
settlers, and antagonistic adjacent landowners. In the end,
Woodward was only able to realize his vision on the publicly
owned Commons.

reason. The vast majority of Detroiters lived no more than a few blocks away from the river, and business growth still mostly occurred around Jefferson Avenue.[29] Detroit's business community grew rapidly around this street, with taller and more elaborate buildings soon replacing their frontier predecessors in the city's first wave of building obsolescence, fueled by land and capital accumulation. As citizens built their wealth through trade, some opted to invest in a commercial block bearing their name, renting out auxiliary space to other tenants while often remaining in the building themselves.[30] Detroit's first real growth spurt came in the late 1820s because of the opening of the Erie Canal and Welland Canal, drastically improving the city's connectivity to key ports on the East Coast and Canada.[31] Now accessible within days from North America's main economic hubs, Detroit matured as a maritime trade city and frontier destination.[32] By the end of the decade, Detroit had reinvented itself once more—the last building constructed directly after the 1805 fire was demolished by 1830.[33]

Detroit's commerce and population continued to grow during the 1830s, attracting the first foreign immigrants to the city. A small working-class neighborhood grew west of Detroit's core, attracting some of the city's first Irish immigrants—and was soon aptly named Corktown.[34] Simultaneously, Germans had formed their own neighborhood eastward.[35] African American immigration to the city grew with the abolition of slavery in Michigan in 1837, mostly fueling growth in the lower east side of downtown.[36] While most newcomers saw Detroit only as a waypoint on their path to prosperity, the city was abuzz from the resulting commercial activity. An early Detroiter boasted: "Every steamer that lands at our docks is over-burdened with its freight of living, moving, human beings, and they arrive some two or three each day. … The hotels are thronged with an eager, excited crowd of strangers, all rushing about as if afraid Michigan would be bought out ere they had a chance to buy an acre."[37] Unleashed from the ties of the Woodward plan, the city began to expand beyond its former boundaries of the Commons. One by one, the city annexed French farm strips adjoining the existing built-up area and subdivided them into new neighborhoods, expanding laterally before going inland.[38]

Expansion was feverish, as described by author Caroline Kirkland in 1835: "log houses and mansions were standing side by side. Unworthy as the crude, uncomfortable log abode might be from the architectural standpoint … it nevertheless

1.4
Comparing the skyline of Detroit in 1820 and 1836 demonstrates significant growth.
(Both images cropped from the originals.) Top image by the Calvert Lithograph Company after
a sketch by George H. Whistler, courtesy of the Yale Art Museum. Bottom image from an oil
painting by William James Bennett, courtesy of the Detroit Institute of Art.

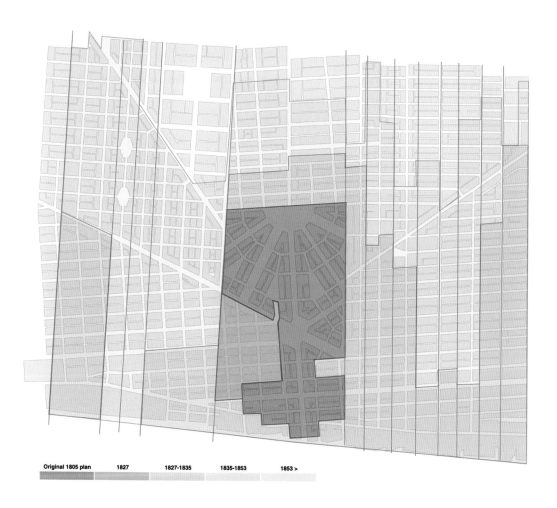

Original 1805 plan   1827   1827-1835   1835-1853   1853 >

1.5

Growth of Detroit between 1827 and the 1850s. As land-owners gridded their subdivisions, they generally ignored Woodward's 1805 aspirations, leaving his baroque vision heavily truncated amid a jumble of grids.

harbored temporarily the spirit of refinement which would eventually better itself."[39] Just in the next year, the city added another third to its building stock as it became the first capital of the newly admitted State of Michigan, marked with a state house in what is now Capitol Park.[40] The Bank of Michigan was constructed on the corner of Jefferson Avenue and Griswold Street by 1837, marking the start of the city's financial district in the blocks to the north.[41] By the end of the decade, Detroit hosted one of the first rail lines west of the Appalachians, with a northern line to Pontiac and the western Michigan Central line toward Dearborn and ultimately Chicago, both initially terminating near Campus Martius before finding permanent stations near the river, to allow for the easy transfer of goods to a growing array of warehouses along the city's waterfront.[42] Here, railroad goods and passengers could also embark on steamers crossing Lake Erie to reach Buffalo, bringing commercial and storage activity to the city—especially when water navigation shut down for the winter months.[43]

Detroit's growth from a trading outpost to a key hub in Michigan's growing agricultural economy continued to accelerate during the 1840s. Despite an 1848 fire and several cholera outbreaks, a local newspaper boasted by the end of the decade: "Pulling down and building up. In every part of the city we see unmistakable signs of progress and improvement."[44] The entire cityscape had a very ephemeral nature, as many buildings were still "constructed as to be easily removed; and it is a common occurrence to see one or more buildings moving from one part of the city to another, as the convenience of their owners require."[45] The city's population boom resulted in increased foot traffic on its most central streets, prompting retailers to improve their premises to lure in potential customers.[46] Jefferson Avenue solidified as the main commercial district of Detroit, though this was confined to only a few solid blocks. Local entrepreneur General Friend Palmer recalled: "around these four corners—Jefferson and Woodward— and in the immediate vicinity for many years ebbed and flowed the life of the city. It was its business center, and to be located from it, even in a small way, meant disaster."[47] The commercial activity around Jefferson Avenue was reflected in the increasing number of taverns and hotels in this central district, correlating with the growing number of visitors arriving at Detroit from the river.[48] Visitors and Detroiters alike were entertained at the city's first purpose-built but modest theater on Jefferson Avenue, which later reopened as the Metropolitan Theatre.[49] Less above-board entertainment was on offer closer to the river, with the lower east side increasingly known for vice and gambling.[50] Fortunately, a veritable row of churches along Woodward Avenue offered redemption a few blocks to the north.[51]

Despite this rapid growth, the town's extent certainly remained confined. The first detailed and comprehensive map of post-fire Detroit was drawn by Henry Hart in 1853, showing a city of over 26,000 inhabitants and almost 5,000 mostly wooden buildings containing over 500 stores.[52] The map shows a dense strip of commercial buildings lining Jefferson Avenue (1), with an increasing number of buildings along Woodward Avenue up to Campus Martius (2), forming a central node where the two axes crossed. One didn't have to venture far from this commercial district to find sparsely built-up residential streets, and the edge of the city was still within walking distance even from its center. Woodward's radial plan was mostly occupied by dwellings, and several speculative subdivisions had sprouted in various directions, depending on the desire of farmers to sell off their land. Especially at the western end of the city, this led to a rather hopscotch pattern of urban growth, with fully developed blocks surrounding farmland (3). Most residential growth, however, was still limited to less than a dozen blocks from the riverfront, and many inland blocks remained vacant, some not yet even subdivided. Most Detroiters had no choice but to live within walking distance of their riverfront jobs, and while a private company had initiated a system of horse-drawn omnibuses to outlying districts by the 1840s, it initially had little success.[53]

Detroit's growth paled in comparison to many of its Midwestern peers like Chicago, Cincinnati, or St. Louis, which strongly benefited from their status as gateways to the west.[54] Especially Detroit's lack of easy eastward railroad connections would hamper its industrial growth in the decades to follow. While the city had constructed direct railroad service to Chicago by the early 1850s, service to New York was forced to make a cumbersome river crossing by boat and travel through Canada, while a direct route from booming Chicago to New York along the southern shore of Lake Erie in 1855 bypassed Detroit and had no need to transfer goods to a boat.[55] Unhindered by any major body of water blocking it from the East Coast, Chicago was the greatest beneficiary of the railway revolution and the opening up of the Great Plains, its 1860 population already double that of Detroit. Over the next decades, Detroit's industries benefited from the Civil War and newly opened copper mines in northern Michigan, but manufacturing would continue to trail Midwestern neighbors until the end of the century.[56]

1.6

Downtown Detroit's blocks, buildings, parcels, open spaces, parks, and river in 1853. Map by author, based on 1853 map of Detroit by Henry Hart.

Industrial growth mostly occurred on the fringes of the city, as manufacturers sought river and rail access at either end of downtown along Jefferson Avenue. Nevertheless, the city's economic growth was reflected in downtown, as its most central blocks transitioned from a fine-grained mixture of dwellings, retailers, and offices into an exclusively commercial district. Many of the remaining wooden structures had already been replaced by multistory brick commercial blocks, like the Merill block at Detroit's main corner of Jefferson and Woodward avenues, which was built in the late 1850s and would survive for almost a century after.[57]

By the next decade, the downtown business district began to shift northward from this corner as Detroit grew inland and the city's Central Market and City Hall on Campus Martius grew in importance.[58] As a result of the area's prosperity and the city's general growth, inland land values skyrocketed during the 1860s.[59]

Campus Martius grew as an entertainment and retail center, as Detroit opened its first grandly designed Opera House in 1869 on the square that would serve as an incubator to multiple retail emporia in the following decades.[60] New England retailers Cyrenius Newcomb and Charles Endicott founded the state's first department store as the first tenants of the modestly sized retail nooks abutting the entrance of the Opera House. Benefiting from Detroit's population growth, Newcomb and Endicott outgrew their confines and relocated northward near the corner of Woodward and Grand River avenues in 1881, in "the most massive and elegant [building] as yet erected by private enterprise in this city," built by seed magnate D. M. Ferry.[61] Soon after opening their initial store, Newcomb and Endicott faced competition from the clothier Christopher R. Mabley who located in a nearby storefront in 1870, expanding in subsequent years into several buildings on either side of Woodward Avenue just south of Campus Martius and becoming the largest store in Michigan by the late 1880s.[62] English-born retailer Joseph Lowthian Hudson, a former employee of Mabley's, took the space left by Newcomb and Endicott in the cultural venue in 1881—the start of an empire that would outgrow all others. Reflecting the increasingly sophisticated palette of merchandise on offer, the value of foreign imports increased twentyfold in Detroit between 1850 and 1870 alone. While many inland retail pioneers initially failed to survive,[63] increased commercial activity at last broke the invisible northward barrier of Campus Martius by the 1870s, as "the tide of business has swept past."[64] Retail growth would soon also reach the radial Michigan and Gratiot avenues, increasingly leaving the Jefferson Avenue retail core to wholesalers and warehouses.[65]

Improved transportation and communication technology bolstered office construction in today's financial district around Griswold Street, which hosted Detroit's first dedicated private office building in 1852. This building prompted the federal government to open Detroit's first purpose-built United States Custom House and Post Office nearby in 1860, in turn spurring more nearby private office construction.[66] The opening of the Moffat Building in 1871 brought the first elevator to the city, allowing it to

Population over time

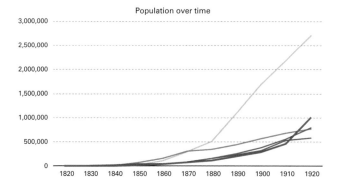

1.7

Comparison with Detroit's main Midwestern peers demonstrates that Detroit was a late bloomer in urban population, especially eclipsed by Chicago during the railway age.

1.8

Advertisement for Detroit Stove Works, located on a ten-acre lot along the Detroit River east of the city, demonstrating a reliance on water and rail transportation. The Stove Works had its headquarters and sales office on Woodward Avenue in downtown. Its factory (pictured here) was located in Hamtramck before the land was annexed by Detroit in 1885. More information on the Detroit Stove Works is in Farmer, *History of Detroit and Wayne County and Early Michigan*, 809–813. Image courtesy of the Burton Historical Collection, Detroit Public Library.

receive two extra floors to accommodate more offices, spurring a subsequent wave of nearby taller office buildings.[67] The upward cycle of growth in the financial district solidified with the location of Detroit's initial telephone switchboard in 1877 in the area, allowing offices to benefit from statewide communications by 1881.[68] Already by the 1860s, the most desirable downtown plots had seen at least one reconstruction, with some parcels on Campus Martius in a state of almost constant flux.[69]

The residential quality of downtown began to decrease amidst this commercial fever, prompting an outward shift and a stratification of Detroiters along lines of class, race, and ethnicity. At first, residents who had only recently built their homes along downtown's leafy streets would refuse to give way to commercial buildings,[70] and were lamented as staunch obstructers of commercial progress: "men of means who had an attachment to their landed patrimony that outweighed their desire to see Detroit become a metropolitan city."[71] But mostly, Detroit's business elite simply had no choice but to live close to their place of business, as the infrastructure outside of the city's most central streets was too cumbersome for daily travel.

Nevertheless, their desire to move out of downtown grew by the day. The elite had to bear with a massive influx of new neighbors as Detroit more than doubled in population in the 1850s alone. The bulk of the city's newcomers lived in a growing and hardly appetizing array of hotels and boardinghouses in downtown, with almost 200 such establishments recorded by 1868. Downtown's temporary housing stock varied widely in price and quality, from higher-end houses run by respectable widows to backrooms of riverfront saloons. Their residents formed a subculture of "men in motion" that spawned an industry of entertainment in downtown—one of highly variable reputability. Transient workers fueled the growth of "vice districts" in Detroit's lower east side, correlating with a concentration of boardinghouses in the area.[72] Housing an impoverished mixture of European and African American immigrants, the Potomac Quarter, one of Detroit's oldest riverfront districts close to the docks, suffered from rising crime and deteriorating living conditions.[73] As racial prejudice began to heighten tensions in the city, Detroit's growing African American population became mostly confined to the city's lower east side, and were only allowed to move northward from there.[74]

1.9

The transformation of downtown from residential to commercial life and architecture materialized as a juxtaposition of French Détroit and American Detroit, exemplified by this late nineteenth-century image of the Campau residence on Jefferson Avenue, named after one of Detroit's earliest settlers. Image courtesy of the Burton Historical Collection, Detroit Public Library. Cf. Farmer, *History of Detroit and Wayne County and Early Michigan*, 373; Burton, Stocking, and Miller, *The City of Detroit, Michigan*, 139.

Other newcomers had more choice, with many foreign immigrants settling in large ethnic enclaves which surrounded downtown, comfortably surrounded by people of similar class, culture, and language. Detroit's growing ranks of German immigrants brought a vibrant industry of beer halls and breweries to the city, as well as community centers such as Arbeiter Hall in 1868.[75] Others moved to Dutchtown and Polacktown—quite direct descriptions of their tenants.[76] A growing number of African Americans found their domicile in "Kentucky," an area north of Gratiot Avenue named after the origin of its new tenants, with saloons, dance halls, and brothels soon following. A significant wave of Italian immigrants settled north of Kentucky, with the near east side continuing its role as the first port of entry to newcomers.

Detroit's wealthiest residents ultimately moved into the west side of downtown, settling in ornate mansions along the leafy Fort, Congress, and Lafayette streets.[77] While these areas were somewhat removed from the eastern slums, they were near enough to the city's poorest and most crime-ridden districts to create significant struggles for morality and order—especially as the city's elite realized that disorder was an immediate threat to their own well-being.[78] The close proximity between classes and cultures in Detroit prompted the rise of centralized crime control as a perceived matter of necessity. Early voluntary night watches and law enforcement patrols were fleeting and did little to curb crime or maintain the peace.[79] The mass immigration of European newcomers in the 1840s and 1850s further increased tensions between races and ethnicities. Between 1849 and 1863, there were more than 20 major and minor riots in the city, mostly among immigrant groups. Despite the instatement of various volunteer police forces and the construction of a city jail on the near east side, crime continued to increase.[80] After the 1859 creation of a private "Merchants' Police" to protect downtown businesses from nighttime crime and vandalism, the city's first professional police patrol arrived in May 1865 to alleviate Detroit's "crisis in law and order."[81] Increasingly, the wealthiest Detroiters found at least temporary relief from the urban struggle for order in weekend and summer homes on the former French ribbon farms east of Detroit in Grosse Pointe, which they could visit when business didn't beckon.[82] By and large, however, Detroit's social classes were destined to share the same confined city.

This forced proximity was relieved with the arrival of the first streetcar line in 1863 and the maturation of the network in the following decade, opening vast tracts of land

1.10

Opulent residences on West Fort Street, belonging to Governor Henry
Baldwin (top) and merchant Allan Shelden (bottom), both built in 1875.
Images courtesy of the Burton Historical Collection, Detroit Public Library.
Cf. Farmer, *History of Detroit and Wayne County and Early Michigan*,
396, 399.

to development to feed the city's hunger for space and distance.[83] Detroit's elite eagerly benefited from this new spatial paradigm, looking to escape from the city's rising social tensions and displaying their wealth accumulated with the city's industrial growth.[84] Upper-class residential architecture was opulent and eclectic, with stately mansions regularly depicted in news media and guides as if they were located in a rural setting. An observer noted, "the city outside the business centre ... has the appearance of a dense forest with many heaven-pointing spires towering above the trees, justifying that Detroit is a park city."[85] The streetcar system prompted an acceleration of the city's inland growth over riverfront expansion, drawing the city's elite into new parklike neighborhoods. Two neighborhoods were at the forefront of the city's first wave of sub-urbanization: Brush Park and Cass Park, named after their original land owners.

The first new elite neighborhood to benefit from the streetcar system was Brush Park, a district to the northeast of downtown that had been slowly growing since the early 1850s. For the next three decades of its maturation, large lots and strict building quality and size standards set by the Brush family that owned the land resulted in opulent mansions, often with French-inspired mansard roofs, soon earning the district the title of "Little Paris."[86] To the west of Woodward Avenue, General Cass donated a central parcel of land to the city from his farm to erect "Cass Park" in 1860. While Cass's altruism was questionable and his gift certainly not uncontroversial, the central park helped boost land values for the subdivision he subsequently wrapped around it.[87] Benefiting from its location on the elite-preferred west side of Detroit, the area soon became one of the city's finest residential districts, comprising a mixture of mansions, churches, and cultural institutions.[88] The largest and most expensive lots of both districts faced Woodward Avenue, where some of the city's most elaborate Victorian residences were constructed, resulting in an avenue with "no superior on the continent."[89]

As Detroit's elite started to leave the city's oldest streets, the streetcar soon enabled the middle class to follow, accelerating the city's ethnic, racial, and class segregation. The city's growing real estate industry aggressively promoted new streetcar subdivisions to a growing middle class, promising the exclusion of "undesirable" land uses and tenants in sales contracts.[90] Among the first to climb the social ladder, the original German population of the east side moved out and began to rent their homes to the city's growing Jewish population, which soon established Hastings Street as their main business corridor. As the pressure for affordable housing grew, former upper- and middle-class homes were subdivided into "lodging houses," the cheaper successors to boardinghouses, offering the poorest transient population daily rentals without meals.[91] A growing cohort of Detroiters was able to benefit from the streetcar's growing catchment area by constructing their own homes in new suburbs, with cheap land and construction costs putting homes even within the reach of day laborers.[92] As a result, the majority of Detroiters were now able to combine spacious living with easy downtown accessibility. As East Coast cities cramped their residents into increasingly dense tenement blocks between 1860 and 1880, a majority of Detroiters were able to live in relatively spacious homes within easy reach of downtown, earning the city its late nineteenth-century slogan "Detroit, where life is worth living."[93] By then, that life had already mostly moved away from downtown.

The streetcar system had cemented the city's desire to separate work from home, commerce from family life, and downtown from the residential front yard. While increasing strata of Detroiters were now able to escape downtown's dwellings, the radial streetcar system ensured that residents still frequented the shops and theaters along Woodward Avenue, worked in offices in the financial district and along the riverfront, and regarded Campus Martius as the civic core of their city. The growth of Detroit's population and prosperity continued to be reflected in the city's expanding civic infrastructure. An impressive new four-story City Hall, designed by James Anderson after fierce competition, opened in 1871 across from its 1835 predecessor, now finally in the city's center of gravity on Campus Martius. Locals praised the new building as having "probably no superior" in the country as it filled Detroit's most prominent block and even required the purchase of part of the Campus.[94] From the top of City Hall, Detroit increasingly looked like a forest of homes, although the Michigan wilderness was still easily visible.[95] East of the Campus, old City Hall was replaced by a much larger Central Market building to feed the growing city.[96] More space-intensive market functions began to be pushed outside the urban core, as the city's hay market was moved to the current site of Eastern Market.[97] Besides civic infrastructure, Detroit's educational system also expanded with the city's first purpose-built public library in Center Park and with Detroit College, which rapidly expanded on East Jefferson Avenue.[98] As in many

1.11

Dwellings in Brush Park marked a leap in spaciousness, allowing owners to express their wealth in eclectic architecture, exemplified by the residence of lawyer Elisha Taylor constructed in 1871 on Alfred Street. Image courtesy of the Burton Historical Collection, Detroit Public Library. Another image of the residence can be found in *History of Detroit and Wayne County and Early Michigan*, 444.

other American cities, the core of downtown Detroit hence began to take shape as the city's exclusive civic and commercial district.

By 1884, Detroit's greater downtown was almost fully built out with a mixture of residential, commercial, civic, and manufacturing buildings. The various residential districts that surrounded downtown clearly displayed class differences through various sizes of buildings and lots, from the city's oldest and most densely developed homes in the near east and west side (1) to the lush mansions of Cass Park (2) and Brush Park (3). Detroit's haphazard development pattern had created a multitude of grids that jogged

1.12

The old City Hall in the centerline of Woodward Avenue is dwarfed by the new City Hall to the right from 1871. Image courtesy of the Burton Historical Collection, Detroit Public Library. More information is in Burton, Stocking, and Miller, *The City of Detroit, Michigan*, 361.

along the lines of the French agricultural parcels they had filled. As the city's residential districts were now fully developed, they were able to support commercial activity along most of the radial avenues that entered the city, where residents could also catch a streetcar to downtown. With commercial development now mostly located inland along Woodward Avenue (4), Jefferson Avenue anchored a riverfront district of warehouses, wholesalers, and manufacturers (5). Downtown had established itself as the heart of a growing urban area that comprised over 200,000 inhabitants in 1884. In the city alone, hundreds of new buildings were going up each month, and exports to the rest of the country had grown steadily.[99] While Detroit's industrial output still trailed most of its peers by the end of the decade, its downtown had laid the foundation for the revolution that would put the city on the national and international map in the next decades.[100]

1.13
Downtown Detroit's blocks, buildings, parcels, open spaces, parks, and river in 1884.
Map by author based on 1884 Sanborn Fire Insurance Atlas of Detroit.

2 GOING UP AND OUT: 1884–1911

At the end of the nineteenth century, Detroit's path to progress would drastically alter with the coming of the automobile, an invention that transformed it from a sleepy trade city bypassed by most of its peers to an industrial powerhouse of half a million inhabitants. Detroit's fame as the locus of mass-produced automobility had its roots in downtown, but the car would soon turn against its place of birth. The modernity and progress brought by the automobile simultaneously bolstered downtown as a reflection of the city's dazzling growth in prosperity while hollowing it out as a viable destination for growth. The paradox of downtown as a place of both innovation and inertia would become a centerpiece of its history from then on.

While the rise of the automobile industry was sudden and powerful, it was firmly rooted in Detroit's long industrial history, which provided the wheeled newcomer several unique circumstances in which to thrive. Firstly, the city had experience in the manufacturing of machines for movement as it had a tradition of building maritime internal combustion engines, bicycles, railroad cars, and locomotives. The skilled labor pool easily transitioned to automobile manufacturing, and after the waning of lumbering and railroad manufacturing they were eager to find new work. Detroit's existing plants were also easily adapted to car manufacturing.[1] Furthermore, Detroit had significant prowess in iron, steel, and copper and brass manufacturing, as well as in paints. These were essential parts of early automobiles, and again they were easily transitioned toward this new industry. But perhaps most importantly, the city had a significant amount of investment capital. The extraction of raw materials from the Michigan hinterland had concentrated significant capital in the city, and the nouveaux riches were eager to invest their wealth in perhaps a somewhat riskier venture than "timidly aloof"

East Coast money would have agreed to.[2] By 1900, Detroit's elite had no clear other industry in which to invest, like textiles in New England or steel in the Appalachians. For example, the lumber industry had run out of raw materials, the carriage and railroad car industry faced stiff competition, and the stove industry was hardly growing. This investment vacuum benefited the relatively untested automobile industry.[3]

Initially, car manufacturing had little impact on the city. In his time off from working at the Edison Company, young mechanic Henry Ford developed his first "quadricycle" in a barn behind his downtown Bagley Street townhouse in 1896, inspired by the car that his friend Charles King rode through Detroit about a year before.[4] While Ford was focusing on racing cars, Ransom E. Olds first manufactured cars at a scale that made them accessible to a wider market by 1899, taking them "from the classification of a rich man's toy to that of every man's servant."[5] Olds's Detroit production grew more than tenfold between 1901 and 1904, fueling a growing cohort of parts suppliers and attracting others like Cadillac and Packard to enter the field.[6] Ford soon took the same approach to car manufacturing and started the Ford Motor Company in 1903, launching the Fordmobile before the wildly successful Model T.[7] As car manufacturing became more efficient and lucrative, more manufacturers came to Detroit, or consolidated from smaller companies as General Motors did in 1907.[8] Detroit thus began to establish itself as "the center of the automobile industry of the world," with car factories growing their output from just over $6 million in 1904 to $60 million in 1909. By the end of the decade, automobile plants had become the dominant employer in the city and supported a slew of suppliers.[9] Manufacturers were beginning to take pride in their city, and "Made in Detroit" became used in advertising in export journals.[10]

The growth of the automobile industry also marked another leap in the suburbanization of jobs. During the 1880s, Detroit's industries were still mostly tied to the historic riverfront for access to raw materials, reinforced by the first railways that paralleled the river.[11] But as industries grew by the next decade, they moved further inland and to the edge of the city in search of larger parcels of land, lower property taxes, and easier accessibility to the reliable rail system that had formed a belt around the city.[12] In turn, these factories sprouted adjacent worker housing, ultimately growing into almost self-sufficient live-work clusters around major railway junctions, with neighborhoods and business districts of their own.[13] At a railroad crossing three miles west of Campus

Martius, the settlement of West Detroit grew around industries, followed by a growing settlement at "Milwaukee Junction," another railroad crossing between the city's belt line and the railroads leading to downtown and the river.[14] Perhaps the most notable example was the decision of Ford to move his manufacturing operations inland, first to Midtown Detroit, followed by a new plant in the suburb of Highland Park in 1910 that enabled a massive increase in efficiency thanks to Taylorization and the introduction of the conveyor belt.[15] Increasingly, the city's commuter pattern began to bypass downtown, reflected in the number of east-west retail streets and streetcar tracks that ran miles inland.[16]

2.1

Bird's-eye view of Detroit in 1889, showing the beginnings of a ring of factories on the periphery, although a significant amount of riverfront manufacturing remained in the foreground. Calvert Lithographing Company, *Birds Eye View—Showing about Three Miles Square—of the Central Portion of the City of Detroit, Michigan* (Detroit, 1889). Image courtesy of Library of Congress Geography and Map Division.

Nevertheless, the growth of Detroit still fueled the growth of downtown at the turn of the century. If anything, the city's newfound industrial prowess accelerated the transformation of the urban core, prompting the *Evening News* to exclaim, "the present generation is tearing down the work of the past and replacing it with buildings of its own. Every 25 years the city is entirely built anew."[17] The pace of change certainly reflected the transformation of Detroit thus far, as the older stock of Detroit's most centrally located buildings would increasingly give way to elevator-enabled skyscrapers by the 1880s. The urge to replace buildings in Detroit's business district was a simple by-product of the city's rapid growth, which increased the pressure on downtown land due to the continued centralizing effect of the city's infrastructure. The radial layout of the city and its growing streetcar network ensured that while Detroiters and their jobs were spreading throughout the city, they would continue to meet downtown.[18] Most Detroiters saw demolition and reconstruction as a sign of progress. When one of the city's oldest hotels was torn down for a taller successor, a local judge cheered: "we no longer need [the old hotel]. Tear it down! … Like all other things that stand in the way of progress it is doomed. … What do we care for the past? It is nothing to us. We have only the present and the future."[19] Perhaps the best example of the creative destruction that this centrality would spur was the growth of Detroit's retail district in the blocks around Campus Martius. As all the city's eyes, feet, and wallets passed these precious few acres, they grew into Detroit's department store district, the scene of some of the fiercest competitions for survival and prosperity as the city entered the twentieth century.

Especially Woodward Avenue became the thriving commercial main street of Detroit, running almost a mile from the riverfront to Grand Circus Park.[20] Retailers continued to move their premises inland, and by 1896 the *Detroit Journal* boasted: "All the way along Woodward to the Grand Circus are great establishments doing an immense volume of business."[21] Along the avenue, remaining midcentury commercial buildings gave way to three-to-six-story brick- or terracotta-clad retail palaces, inspired by peer cities like Chicago and New York. Woodward Avenue slowly transformed from a diverse commercial district into the regional destination for luxury shopping.[22] No longer fitting in his Detroit Opera House confines and a temporary abode on Woodward Avenue, retail magnate Joseph Hudson commissioned architect Mortimer Smith to build an eight-story retail palace at the location of Detroit's First Presbyterian church off Woodward Avenue, to provide his growing clientele with "maximum commercial efficiency and convenience."[23] Although the location was off the main retail street, the store opening in 1891 proved a smashing success, and in its first year the new store would already generate four times its construction cost in sales volume, almost single-handedly creating "one of the most bustling and thriving localities to be found in the city."[24]

Hudson's success was certainly not unique, as the department store competed with numerous powerful competitors such as Newcomb-Endicott, Taylor and Woolfenden, and Kresge's new five-and-dime. Detroit's most central blocks also attracted newcomers that quickly rose in the city's commercial ranks. Just south of Hudson's growing emporium at the busy corner of Woodward and Gratiot avenues, German-born retailer Ernst Kern Sr. and his wife commissioned a five-story building for their growing textile firm, while maintaining a foothold at their old location a few blocks east.[25] More

2.2

Hudson's eight-story department store on the left of the image eclipses its nearby competitors. Image courtesy of the Burton Historical Collection, Detroit Public Library.

competition came from the east in 1909, where wholesale and retail experts Joseph Crowley and William Milner had taken over the recently built but already ailing department store of Pardridge and Blackwell. Crowley, Milner & Co. aggressively modernized the massive block-long, six-story building to include new fashion departments and a restaurant, aiming to make the department store no less than "the strongest establishment of its kind in this section of the country."[26] These giants were surrounded by a variety of smaller and larger shops, differentiating themselves with extraordinary levels of service, ever-larger offerings of merchandise, or specialization.[27] The retail growth of the avenue prompted the construction in 1901 of the elaborate Washington Arcade connecting Woodward Avenue to Washington Boulevard, which had entered the sights of retailers looking to escape the congestion and cost of Woodward Avenue. While the *News-Tribune* claimed this expansion as part of downtown's organic growth, as "the business center of Detroit is like a swelling seed, enlarging, widening and deepening its displacement of earth," the boulevard would not see any significant growth for another decade.[28] Similarly, downtown's invisible northern boundary had simply moved up Woodward Avenue to Grand Circus Park.[29]

Beyond the feverish growth of Detroit's retail core north of Campus Martius, perhaps the most visible expression of the city's modernization was the construction of downtown's first skyscrapers on the southern side of Detroit's road and streetcar hub. As the state's elite accumulated wealth in transportation, commerce, and technologies, their buildings would challenge the religious spires of Detroit's churches and the cupola of its City Hall by the end of the nineteenth century. Meatpacking magnate George Hammond commissioned Chicago architect George Edbrooke to construct a ten-story building named after himself in the financial district, opening in 1890.[30] While it garnered criticism for its rather spartan exterior and foundation issues, the local press and the public soon embraced the building as a landmark of progress, elevating Detroit among its Midwestern peers. The building housed various legal professionals and companies, benefiting from its proximity to the city, state, and federal buildings and nearby financial institutions, as well as hosting various retailers on the ground floor.[31] Only a few years later, the business heirs of department store magnate Christopher Mabley commissioned another Chicago architect, Daniel Burnham, to design a fourteen-story skyscraper right across the Hammond Building.[32] Nearby on Griswold Street, the ten-story Union Trust Building and twelve-story Chamber of Commerce Building opened in 1895, anchoring Detroit's established financial district.[33] As the federal government significantly upgraded its presence in Detroit with a new post office and federal building in 1897, the financial district grew further with the opening of the Burnham-designed eighteen-story Ford Building in 1909.[34] While Detroit's first skyward rise was drafted in Chicago, the rapid growth of new construction in downtown soon fueled Detroit's local architecture industry, and bolstered a growing industry of real estate developers.[35]

Downtown's commercial growth was also reflected in the construction of elaborate new hotels, which continued their predecessors' roles as social centers. The Pontchartrain hotel opened in 1905 on the site of the former Russell hotel at the prime corner of Campus Martius and Woodward Avenue. While the hotel's rooms and lobby were rather spartan, the "Pontch" gained its place in the history books for its illustrious marble and mahogany bar that brought together the city's movers and shakers. Frequent visits by public officials earned the bar the title of "City Hall Annex," but it became most famous as a haunt for Detroit's automobile manufacturers. Anyone and everyone who mattered in motoring discussed new inventions and made deals there, with the likes of Dodge, Durant, Chevrolet, and Ford huddling around bar tables scattered with blueprints and machine prototypes. Within a few years of its opening, the Pontchartrain's owners had already added five more floors to the building.[36] The thriving hotel business prompted residential developer Lew Tuller to extend downtown further north in 1906 by constructing his largest project yet, the nine-story Tuller Hotel at the still-swampy Grand Circus Park. While ridiculed by some of his peers, the hotel was an instant success and received a five-story addition less than five years after its opening, resulting in the same type of odd architectural collage that adorned the Pontchartrain—yet Detroit grew too fast to care.[37] Hostels grew as well, as the YMCA constructed a nine-story complex of dormitory rooms east of Tuller's hotel on top of recreational and educational facilities.[38]

Monroe Avenue and Farmer Street near Campus Martius began to solidify into the city's entertainment district with the construction of many theaters, including the Wonderland Building containing the vaudeville Temple Theatre and Wonderland Theatre, opening in 1901.[39] The Wonderland clearly followed the inland growth of Detroit and the proximity to the successful Opera House on the Campus, recently rebuilt after a large fire.[40] The theaters were among the first of many to grace Monroe Avenue, soon thronging the wide street with evening crowds who enjoyed everything from high-class opera to vaudeville and burlesque shows. The Casino, Detroit's first dedicated "nickelodeon" movie theater, was retrofitted into a nearby storefront in 1906.[41] While moving pictures were thus far usually shown only before or after main shows, the success of the Casino was feverishly followed by neighboring theaters such as the Bijou, the Star and later Theatre Royale, the Family Theatre, and more than a hundred storefront theaters in the city's growing neighborhoods.[42] The growth of movie entertainment allowed local entrepreneurs like John Kunsky to build out their cinema empires in the decades to follow.[43] While to a much lesser extent than east of Campus Martius, the Lafayette Boulevard entertainment district still grew, as an old church was converted into the Folly Theatre, followed by the Orpheum Theatre in the 1910s.[44]

Meanwhile, the growth of rail transportation anchored downtown as the city's main port of entry for passengers. The Michigan Central Railroad opened a Romanesque depot west of downtown near the waterfront in 1884, connecting passengers with the still-thriving ferry system on the river to bring them via Lake Erie to destinations such as Cleveland and Buffalo. While initially leasing space in this new Michigan Central station, several railway companies combined forces and opened the Union Depot in a similar architectural style a few blocks to the north at the corner of Third and Fort streets in 1893, reinforcing the west end's role as a passenger transportation hub and gateway to visitors.[45] Benefiting from the newfound centrality afforded by the railroad terminals, the Wayne Hotel opened between the stations and the Detroit River. The grand hotel eventually constructed its own riverfront pavilion, sunroof, and spa and hosted daily orchestra concerts.[46] Yet the vicinity of the railroad stations was not just a scene of grandeur, as the termini transformed much of the formerly wealthy Fort Street into a more down-market area of "celluled roominghouses and railroad hostelries."[47]

The transformation of Fort Street was exemplary of the pressure that the remaining downtown elite felt from the expansion of central business functions, prompting them to abandon downtown as a place to live by the end of the century. When Detroit was in the early stages of industrialization in 1880, almost half of the city's white-collar workers lived within a mile of the landing of Woodward Avenue on the Detroit River, especially along Jefferson Avenue and Fort Street and in the Brush and Cass Park neighborhoods.[48] Cass Park was still advertised as "a section free from unsightly structures, disorderly houses and everything that a founder of a home most desires to avoid … where men of wealth seek the sights of beautiful homes."[49] The city's first public art museum opened in 1886 among the mansions on Jefferson and Hastings Street, but elite neighbors would soon make way for commerce and working-class housing.[50] As a result, the museum and other civic institutions followed their clientele northward to Midtown. As downtown's elite continued to move inland, an increasing number of their mansions were converted into boardinghouses for Detroit's growing transient population, mixing with the staunch few old residents who remained.[51] The exodus of elite residents prompted the demise of institutions like the First Presbyterian Church, which Joseph Hudson eagerly purchased for his first dedicated department store.[52] In turn, the overwhelming mass of Hudson's new store and its draw for other businesses to follow provoked the Detroit library in the adjacent Centre Park to seek greener pastures. Judge Woodward's plan for "civic dignity and grandeur" seemed likely to succumb to its own success, as rampant commercial development displaced stately homes and temples to knowledge, governance, and divinity.[53]

At the dawn of the twentieth century, as downtown's elite residential streets succumbed to commerce, Detroit's close-in upper-class neighborhoods would rapidly change into more diverse and cosmopolitan areas. The elite Brush Park neighborhood was among the first to make this transition.[54] The demographics of Brush Park shifted as it became a Jewish center, with African American residents soon to follow; the original residents increasingly left for the greener pastures of the Boston Edison district or departed the city altogether for Grosse Pointe. They were easily able to do so, as infrastructure had vastly improved. The introduction and rapid rollout of electric streetcars in the 1890s enabled people to live further away from their place of work.[55] Urban observer Friend Palmer described Brush Park's remaining social mix in 1895: "in their faces are portrayed all characteristics of the human race. All sorts of occupations are represented and all classes of society."[56] As had happened in downtown's elite streets in previous decades, many Brush and Cass Park mansions were subdivided into apartments or boarding rooms. Others were cleared from their spacious lots to make way for opulent buildings comprising "flats" that offered generous floor areas while benefiting

2.3

The Alhambra Flats, located in Cass Park and designed by John Gentle in 1895, was among the first apartment buildings in the city, its 24 units aimed squarely at the well-off. Image courtesy of the Burton Historical Collection, Detroit Public Library.

from centralized maintenance and services.[57] While drastically altering and densifying these neighborhoods, such buildings had little impact on Detroit's overall housing stock, as the middle class hardly developed a penchant for inner-city living, and was easily able to follow the elite further inland for a vast offer of affordable subdivisions.[58] As a result, the flats of Cass and Brush Park never grew into the veritable apartment house districts that sprouted in many cities of the same size. The growth of central businesses and of traffic along Woodward Avenue further hampered the quality of these neighborhoods as elite residences.[59]

The near east side continued its downward spiral into a slum district, containing "some of the worst dens of infamy existing in Detroit—the purlieus of vice and debauchery and the resort of criminals … resorted to by the most dangerous of the criminal class and their concomitant depraved women." The area's housing stock was in poor shape, but even here high-density brick tenements like those found in New York at the end of the nineteenth century were rare. Instead, "nearly all [dwellings of the poor] are of one-story wood, generally occupied by two families. … A considerable number of these tenements are located in alleys; three-fourths of the entire number are in bad condition."[60] The growing African American community in this district established a business cluster around St. Antoine Street by the turn of the century, with an increasing number of services and hotels augmented by social institutions like churches and social clubs. At the other end of the spectrum was a growing array of saloons, which began to function as social hubs and offered a range of legal and illegal activities. The police tolerated these establishments within the confines of the African American district, but they aggressively raided any outliers.[61] While white European and North American immigrants were able to select ethnically homogeneous districts on either end of downtown, African Americans were forced to remain in the city's near east, decreasing their social mobility in the city.[62] As crime and prostitution continued to spiral in the area, residents even asked the city to have their street names changed so as to be dissociated from their "undesirable fame."[63]

The rise of commerce in downtown spurred a debate on the urban core's continuing role as a civic center, inspired by the national City Beautiful movement that aimed to balance commercial growth with civic and aesthetic values. While the movement ultimately had much less impact than in Chicago, it fueled a debate that would prompt some of the first concerted planning efforts to beautify and order downtown Detroit. City Beautiful planning in Detroit focused on improving the role of civic buildings and the quality of public spaces in downtown's rapidly transforming milieu, with the fear that while commercial growth had given Detroit a "metropolitan air," buildings like City Hall had become "lost in a wilderness of commercial structures."[64] When the Wayne County government outgrew its offices that were still located in City Hall, early proposals sought to clear the less than three-decade-old building and replace it with a grander structure. Instead, a new county courthouse was constructed in 1902 on the other end of a newly improved Cadillac Square, where the Central Market Building had been cleared in favor of the Eastern Market and Western Market on the outskirts of town. The courthouse's location across the square from City Hall was a pragmatic implementation of City Beautiful urban design, synthesizing simultaneous civic construction and public space improvements into "the attractive scene of which [they are] part."[65] The removal of the Central Market was hardly an altruistic gesture of civic pride or aesthetic sensitivity, as the market had simply outgrown its location and sharply rising adjacent land values warranted a "higher and better" use than its rather messy daily trade.[66] Lacking the catalyst of new government buildings, the transformation of Washington Avenue into a boulevard with a landscaped median was more difficult to sell to the public; it took years of bickering before the transformation was finished in 1896.[67] At the turn of the century, the city government simply did not have enough power to make significant changes to the downtown landscape—its only tool to regulate construction was the fire code.[68]

The City Beautiful movement closely interlinked with Detroit's milieu of progressive politics at the turn of the century, exemplified by the election of Mayor Hazen S. Pingree in 1889 on a platform of public reform. Despite his success with on-the-ground urban improvements such as street paving, sewer construction, and municipalizing utilities, Pingree was ultimately unable to lay stronger foundations for comprehensive urban planning in the seven years he held office.[69] As the mayor tried to greatly enlarge Grand Circus Park and create a riverfront park between the foot of Third Street and Orleans Street, the press criticized his plans as "fantastic and ruinously extravagant," and they were subsequently killed. Instead, the oldest part of downtown continued its decline as water-based transportation lost importance.[70] Similarly, his calls to replace the twenty-three-year-old City Hall with a structure more "in keeping with the progress of the day" went unheeded.[71] Frustrated by the lack of concerted action to improve downtown, Detroit's Board of Commerce commissioned Charles Mulford Robinson and landscape architect Frederick Law Olmsted to draft a follow-up plan for the city's downtown and riverfront in 1905, with riverfront beautification and the expansion of civic buildings around Campus Martius returning as focal points. These plans similarly fizzled.[72]

The progressive City Beautiful movement soon realized that it could make the greatest gains away from the commercialism, congestion, and high land values of downtown. City leaders abandoned the central business district's plans for a cultural center with an art museum and a municipal library on Grand Circus Park, instead choosing a location a few miles north in the growing Midtown area by the dawn of the twentieth century.[73] The most successful implementation of the City Beautiful movement in Detroit occurred even further outside of downtown, with the construction of an eleven-mile Grand Boulevard circling the city by the late nineteenth century. Initially proposed by a nearby landowner in the mid-1870s, the boulevard proposal gained momentum in subsequent decades when it was linked with plans to purchase and improve Belle Isle Park a few miles east of the city—the eastern anchor of the proposed boulevard.[74] However, the ultimate success of the boulevard had more pragmatic roots. The rise of the automobile, and its ability to traverse the city in any direction without entering downtown through the still mostly radial streetcar system, prompted Detroiters to traverse and settle along Grand Boulevard as Detroit's first major tangential road.[75] Benefiting from the city's outward growth and independence from its congested downtown, a new commercial district sprouted at the intersection of the new boulevard and Woodward Avenue, more than three miles north of downtown.[76]

The automobile would soon leave its physical mark on downtown as well. The city's first automobile showroom was opened by William Metzger at the corner of Jefferson Avenue and Brush Street in 1902, followed by Detroit's first drive-in gas station by Central Oil on the corner of Fort and First streets in 1910.[77] A group of car dealerships organized the city's first auto show in 1907, and the Wayne Hotel became the home to annual shows between 1909 and 1912.[78] As cars added to the already crowded downtown Detroit streets, the first proposals for street widening popped up, and the first proposal for a subway system surfaced and fizzled in 1906.[79] Instead, the city resorted to improving traffic management by instating a downtown speed limit of eight miles

2.4

Detroit's first drive-in gas station, owned by Central Oil. Image from "No Bitter Garage Competition in Detroit," *National Petroleum News*, August 1915.

per hour and installing a rudimentary traffic light at Campus Martius by 1909.[80] Detroit soon realized that it needed a more concerted planning effort to rescue the city from its congestion and overcrowding.

Inspired by the Chicago Plan of 1909, Detroit installed its first City Plan and Improvement Commission that same year. The commission's main mandate was to beautify the city by focusing on public art, parks, and boulevards, but it also sought to improve traffic arteries and the riverfront.[81] Starting with only $1,000 and a shared office at the Park Department, the commission began its task by commissioning City Beautiful icons Daniel Burnham and Edward Bennett "to draw up plans for the general betterment and beautification of Detroit."[82] The plan would materialize over the next decade as the 1915 "Preliminary Plan of Detroit," a rather disorganized and incoherent proposal for a new Midtown cultural center, two downtown alternatives, a series of diagonal streets to alleviate the congestion caused by Detroit's radial layout, as well as a new beltway further outside the city.[83]

With the popularization of the car, Detroit's growth spurt had finally begun. While the nineteenth century had brought steady but unspectacular growth to the city, especially compared to its Midwestern peers, the city's population almost doubled between 1900 and 1910 to over half a million inhabitants, fueled by the rise of manufacturing jobs.[84] Over the course of merely half a decade, Detroit had become virtually synonymous with the nation's automobile industry. Only three years after Ford began producing the Ford Model T at his new Highland Park plant, Detroit housed almost 300 establishments that either built or maintained cars, employing about 40,000 people and producing over a quarter billion dollars' worth of cars per year. Meanwhile, the city remained an industrial powerhouse in sectors like tobacco, railroad cars, iron, and copper, benefiting from its location along North America's busiest inland waterway.[85] Compared to its status as a frontier waypoint less than a century before, Detroit had become a destination for those in search of a better life. The local convention bureau boasted: "Detroiters do not seek new locations, they stay."[86]

Cheered on by the local press, Detroit's growth transformed downtown from its makeshift roots to a mature commercial center, which was reflected in its physical transformation.[87] Moving away from the central axis of Woodward and Jefferson avenues, commercial growth had spread inland throughout the area of the Woodward Plan, with large commercial buildings transforming Washington Boulevard (1), Cadillac Square (2), Monroe Avenue (3), and the financial district (4). Commercial buildings now almost fully lined radial avenues such as Michigan Avenue (5) and Gratiot Avenue (6), while others like Grand River Avenue (7) and Woodward Avenue (8) were still transitioning from residential to commercial. Yet business was growing rapidly along these radials, "fast outgrowing the boundary lines of its business district of a decade ago."[88] The city covered the Eastern Market in the northeast corner of downtown (9) with two shed roofs in 1891 and 1898, as the market had become Detroit's major destination for farmers to sell their produce and other goods.[89] The area south of Jefferson Avenue (10) had fully transitioned into a warehouse and manufacturing district which focused on trade from the Detroit River while still benefiting from rail access via terminals that were located adjacent to the river. The completion of a rail tunnel between

Detroit and Canada two miles south of downtown in 1910 would soon supersede the downtown riverfront symbiosis between rail and water transportation.[90] Despite this challenge, warehousing and manufacturing activities from this district had percolated into surrounding residential areas (11), harming their residential qualities and sowing the seeds for a "zone of transition" with vacant lots and factories that severed the link between the commercial core of downtown and its residential periphery. With the growth of downtown over the next decades, this zone witnessed its greatest transformation.

2.5
Downtown Detroit's blocks, buildings,
parcels, open spaces, parks, and river
in 1911.

II SUMMER

3 DOWNTOWN IN TRANSITION: 1911–1921

While Detroit's character as the Motor City was born during the previous fifteen years, it matured in the 1910s, permanently changing the physical, social, and economic landscape of Detroit and its core. As a result, downtown Detroit came closest to reaching its dreamed-of potential over the decades to follow. The city was already responsible for most of American car production by the beginning of the decade, and car manufacturing increased twentyfold between 1908 and 1917. By the end of the decade, the car industry employed the vast majority of Detroit's industrial workers and produced over two million cars and trucks a year.[1] The onset of World War I brought significant government orders to Detroit, boosting industrial production in the city even more and attracting a wave of African American workers to the city.[2] Detroit had become a destination for those seeking a better life, "a land flowing with milk and honey and opportunity."[3]

The spectacular growth of car and wartime manufacturing continued to benefit Detroit and its urban core. Factories remained scattered throughout the city; in the late 1910s, the city had "hardly what one may call a factory section."[4] However, a new trend was set by those industrialists who sought to leave the city altogether, which began to affect the vitality of Detroit and its downtown. Industry's lack of rootedness in Detroit is best exemplified by the travels of Henry Ford's growing empire. Though one of the region's largest car barons, Ford had a very ambiguous relationship to his Detroit milieu. Coming from a rural background, he lamented modern cities as "a pestiferous growth" and sought to take his manufacturing and his workers out of the city.[5] His disdain is reflected in one of his most famous quotes: "We shall solve the city problem by leaving the city."[6] His first dedicated factory was located north of downtown in 1902, but Ford soon left the city for the low taxes and low land values of Highland Park, locating his new factory along the newly constructed Detroit Terminal Railroad. This railway was built as a belt line around Detroit for new suburban factories to plug into the nation's railway network. An array of other car manufacturers followed suit and located along the line.[7] In his quest for control and independence, Ford also organized his own subsidiary bank to loan money to Ford car dealers, bypassing downtown's financial institutions. Thus, both the production and the financing of the famed Model T, revolutionizing by democratizing personal transportation, took place outside of Detroit's city limits.[8] What had started as a downtown trend of industrial decline was threatening to become a citywide issue, with riverfront factories among the first to close. Their decline did not automatically result in vacancy, as the rapid growth of new companies in the city prompted the renovation of former factories or their replacement by bulk goods warehouses to benefit from the water connections.[9]

Furthermore, less and less of the wealth that the automobile industry was creating accumulated downtown. Successful automobile entrepreneurs began to outpace Detroit's old aristocracy who had amassed their fortunes in trade, agriculture, and raw materials—activities that hinged on long-term investments and passed through the urban core of the city.[10] Instead, the new wealth came from modern enterprise, mostly built on independence from the city and the past. Automobile wealth came fast and seemed to know no bounds, as described by contemporary author Julian Street: "The wheel of commerce has wire spokes and rubber tires, and there is no drag upon the brake band."[11] As car manufacturers rose in stature, they withdrew from downtown public life, shifting their stomping grounds from the public Pontchartrain bar to the private Detroit Athletic Club, a venue constructed in the northern part of downtown in 1915 "to get the men of the automobile industry out of the saloons on Woodward Avenue." Furthermore, automobile industrialists were far less keen to invest their wealth in downtown real estate.[12]

Perhaps more important than the wealth it created for its owners, the automobile industry created an explosive mixture of mobility and wealth for its workers, allowing a growing cohort of middle-class Americans to abandon their cramped streetcar commutes and live farther from downtown than ever. Ford's famed decision to hire employees at an unprecedented $5 a day in early 1914 brought thousands to the city but hinged on employees' compliance with his vision of rural living, favoring homeownership over inner-city rooming.[13] Between 1910 and 1920, more than 500,000 people moved to

Detroit from rural areas in the Midwest, the South, and a growing number of European countries, making Detroit the fourth largest city in the United States by 1920.[14] While many newcomers would initially seek a home near downtown, the vast majority would eventually settle along the city's growing periphery. Beyond Ford's homeownership mandate, this suburbanization was mainly an issue of capacity, as Detroit's existing urban area simply couldn't cope with the sudden influx. As Detroit was short an estimated 30,000 homes by the end of the 1910s, the city's rail yards became filled with household goods belonging to families in search of a home, tent camps were constructed at the city's edges, and rents rose to among the highest in the country. Over the past two decades, Detroit's oldest neighborhoods within Grand Boulevard had almost doubled in population.[15] The inner city was bursting at the seams, as the limited supply of homes prompted property owners to subdivide their homes, starting a downward cycle of overcrowding, social decline, and profiteering.[16]

For the first time in history, a majority of Detroiters would be able to escape this vicious cycle, following the elite's decades-long exodus into the Michigan prairie.[17] Enabled by the growth of disposable income and wealth and pushed by Ford's policies, the city's homebuilding industry leapt in scale to rehouse the city's middle class in affordable, suburban homes.[18] During the 1910s, the city added almost a billion dollars in real estate property value, an investment that prompted not skyscrapers but "a steady growth in every section of the city. Where a year or two ago one could go out and wander in what was then veritable country without a real estate sign, one now sees block after block of comfortable homes."[19] In 1912, almost half of new construction was for single-family homes, followed by duplexes, with multifamily housing taking up less than ten percent of granted permits. Detroit's homeownership rate was the highest of all large American cities, especially surpassing those on the East Coast.[20]

Rather than purchase and demolish an existing inner-city building and construct new higher-density housing in its place, Detroit's homebuilders found new construction far easier and more profitable on virgin land on the city's outskirts. Such suburban communities were more than happy to be annexed to Detroit afterward.[21] In the city's booming market, all a developer had to do was run streets through a farm lot, with zoning not yet applicable and public works left to the authorities. At the higher end, developers would construct parks, boulevards, and streetcar lines to raise land values.[22] Every day, new subdivisions were advertised in the local newspapers, focusing on transit accessibility, property restrictions, and affordability—while touting their removal from the grime and vice of the city. As a result, Detroit, like many of its industrializing peers, experienced a growing trend of inner-city overcrowding and suburbanization of wealth.[23] Upward mobility had become synonymous with outward mobility, and those who were able to climb the social ladder were now also able to afford a new, suburban house.

Yet the continuing suburbanization of Detroit had little effect on the growth of downtown—if anything, the city's population boom strengthened the commercial growth of the urban core. Downtown became ever less central as the border city had no choice but to grow inland, but a prominent local real estate trader commented that with the city's main arterials "running toward a central point as they do, the main business section will remain just where it is now."[24] Furthermore, the vast majority of factory workers still relied on the city's streetcar system that reinforced downtown's centrality, as the expanding network mostly continued its hub-and-spoke pattern into downtown. Despite ongoing political battles and persistently poor service, the city had an extensive streetcar network by the end of the 1910s, connecting downtown with its surroundings along about 780 miles of tracks. Despite the length of the network, downtown could be reached from the edge of the city in less than an hour.[25] Furthermore, an extensive network of frequent and electrified interurban lines carried over 260 daily passenger cars between Detroit's downtown termini and towns within a 75-mile radius in southeast Michigan.

This extension of the reach of the city benefited downtown retailers, who siphoned off trade from smaller towns. Downtown offices were accessible to a vast hinterland of workers and business peers.[26] As a result of Detroit's extensive transit network, passenger numbers and revenues shot up in line with the city's growth, with rides per capita increasing over 70 percent between 1904 and 1913.[27] At the hub of these rides still stood Campus Martius—Detroit's central square envisioned more than a century earlier. The continued hegemony of Campus Martius and the restless nature of downtown's creative destruction are aptly demonstrated by the start of construction for the 25-story Albert Kahn-designed First National Building in 1920, replacing the Hotel Pontchartrain constructed only 13 years earlier. The owners of the National Hotel, built in 1836 on what was then the marshy edge of the city, could not possibly have fathomed that their land would house Detroit's tallest and most central skyscraper, its land worth thousands of times what it was less than a century before—while bearing a similar name.[28]

As a result of the symbiosis between suburbanization and centralization, commercial building activity continued to accelerate in downtown. Amazed at Detroit's pace of growth, an out-of-town observer noted, "there is not another city in the United States

3.1

The reinvention of downtown's most central block on Campus Martius. Left to right, top to bottom: National Hotel, opened 1836; Russell House, opened 1857; Hotel Pontchartrain, opened 1907; First National Building, opened 1922. Top left image from Silas Farmer, *The History of Detroit and Michigan, or, the Metropolis Illustrated* (Detroit: S. Farmer & Co., 1884), 534. Top right and bottom right images courtesy of the Burton Historical Collection, Detroit Public Library. Bottom left image by the Detroit Publishing Company, courtesy of the Library of Congress.

so far as I know and I doubt if there is in the world, where building operations are being conducted on such a proportionate scale as they are here."[29] His observations reflected an acceleration in the number and size of new office skyscrapers, most of which were constructed close to Campus Martius and the growing financial district in the south-west portion of downtown. The crowning skyscrapers of the 1910s were constructed almost simultaneously in the financial district, with the Burnham-designed Dime Bank Building and the Donaldson and Meier-designed New Penobscot Building (an addition behind their earlier building on Fort Street) vying for the title of Detroit's tallest structure at 23 stories each. Downtown also continued its northward expansion, with pioneer Lewis Tuller's lonely hotel building on Grand Circus Park soon standing amid an emerging high-rise district, completely transforming its formerly residential character. Tuller's initially ridiculed bet on downtown's northward growth trend had clearly paid off, as he gloated: "nowhere in the city … has real estate made the sensational spurts in price that it has along the Grand Circus Park." He saw the unique quality of the park: "Nowhere else downtown today can you get the light and breathing space that the park provides." This pastoral quality dovetailed with the still-leafy streets of the Cass and Brush Park districts right north of the park, which lent the area an aristocratic air.[30]

Tuller continued along the same lines, building several apartment buildings in the blocks north of Grand Circus Park and doubling his hotel on the park itself with a fourteen-story annex. He soon received competition from the Statler Hotel, completed in 1915 as the largest and arguably most elaborate hotel in the Midwest.[31] The Whitney family continued the growth of their estate by replacing the Grand Circus Building with the Burnham-designed David Whitney Building, its fourteen office floors constructed on top of an elaborate "exclusive shopping center of Detroit," a four-story upscale shopping arcade topped by a glass dome. The building opened in 1915 as the northern anchor to the buzzing Woodward Avenue retail strip. The new building was heralded by the local press as "a forerunner of the day when the park will be girded round with towers of stone and steel and Woodward Avenue will be a canyon hemmed in by skyscrapers. In that day the center of the city's life will have moved from the Campus [Martius] to Grand Circus Park."[32] The growing Kresge retail empire constructed its headquarters on the northern end of the park, followed by Fyfe's, the world's largest shoe store, in 1919.[33]

3.2

Dime Bank Building under construction behind City Hall in
1912. Image by the Detroit Publishing Company, courtesy of
the Library of Congress.

No builders exemplified the early twentieth-century faith in downtown's growth more than the Book brothers. Springing from the wealth and strong downtown land-holdings of former Michigan governor Francis Palms, James Burgess Book Jr. started an empire of buildings named after himself along Washington Boulevard. At a time when most of the boulevard was still lined by residential buildings and rather haphazard commercial development, Book recognized the strategic location of the street he was born and raised on as a connection between the growing shopping districts on Michigan and Woodward avenues.[34] With his significant family fortune, and following extensive travels in Europe, the local press saw J. B. Book as likely to "make Washington Boulevard one of the famous retail shopping streets of the world. What Fifth Avenue is to the great city of New York, Washington Boulevard seems destined to be to Detroit."[35] Despite a near standstill in construction after the onset of World War I, Book joined forces with his two brothers to construct the first Book Building on Washington Boulevard in 1917. The Louis Kamper-designed Italian Renaissance building combined three floors of "the finest shops to be found on this continent" with ten upper floors of offices.[36] The development was an unprecedented example of Detroit's belief in progress and modernity—the Book Building alone drew as much electricity upon its completion as the entire city had slightly more than two decades before.[37] The Book brothers continued their expansion on the boulevard with the purchase of the ailing Cadillac Hotel in 1918, prefacing larger plans ahead.[38] Eventually, the Book family controlled more than half of the properties on Washington Boulevard.[39] Their success prompted them to expand their holdings to Cadillac Square, with the twenty-story Real Estate Exchange Building to house the city's growing real estate industry opening in 1919, close to the county courts and their records.[40] The Book buildings didn't just exemplify the growth of Detroit in its skyline, but also the continued emphasis in downtown commercial buildings on ground-floor commerce, as they catered to passerby with shops, bars, and restaurants visible through large plate glass windows.

The continued focus of the Book brothers on active ground-floor tenants reflected downtown's growing importance as a citywide and regional retail hub.[41] While the city had dispersed the Cadillac Square market's activities to the Western and Eastern markets, a new downtown market hall opened on Broadway in 1912, which prominently presented its wares to passersby behind a total of 1,834 feet of counters.[42] Woodward Avenue solidified its role as the main retail street in the city with the construction and renovation of several large retail palaces for illustrious tenants like Kresge's and Heyn's department stores, the F. W. Woolworth Company, and the anchor of the street, the rapidly growing J. L. Hudson Company.[43] In 1911, Hudson's store on Farmer Street made its grand entry on Woodward Avenue through the construction of a ten-story "annex," providing shoppers on Detroit's main retail street with a shortcut to its larger store at the back of the block.[44] Soon realizing the value of presenting its merchandise

3.3

Left image: Book Building on the left of the rendering, with the later addition of the Book Tower to the right. Right image: Book Building rotunda providing access to several levels of shops. Both buildings designed by Louis Kamper. Both renderings taken from *Detroit Saturday Night*, December 30, 1916.

to a growing audience on Woodward Avenue, Hudson's slowly but steadily bought up smaller competitors on the avenue, replacing their relatively narrow buildings with its coherent, tall facades. Most holdouts wouldn't stand a chance against Hudson's superior purchasing power, marketing, and research budget, aided by the store cooperating with major department stores in other cities.[45]

Hudson's expansion reflected a trend of consolidation along Detroit's main retail street. Between 1913 and 1915, Kern's department store bought up several neighbors to construct a vastly larger store, and Crowley and Milner expanded similarly feverishly. After rather clandestinely topping up their original building with two extra sales floors, Crowley and Milner bought out all the remaining tenants on its block and construct a near facsimile of its original building to fill the block and double its floor space.[46] In their battle for the consumers' gaze and income, Detroit's most central retailers lured passersby with large display windows in richly decorated tall structures, with several arcades constructed to draw customers into several floors of independent shops. Beyond their function as retail stores, the buildings on Woodward would also house community events and exhibits, fashion shows, banks, and repair services, serving as a cultural hub of the city.[47]

The entertainment area around Campus Martius and Monroe Avenue continued its growth, as the vaudeville and early movie theaters were joined by the Columbia Theatre in 1911, the first large purpose-built movie theater in Detroit, providing over 1,000 patrons with seating, a theater pipe organ, and its own orchestra. Within two years, the success of the Columbia was followed by the nearby Cadillac Theatre, Comique Theatre, and the Liberty Theatre, which was fitted into a former church.[48] The first theaters also started to appear along Broadway, marking its birth as an entertainment district.[49] By 1916 there were almost a dozen movie theaters in operation around Campus Martius and Monroe Avenue, not to mention the countless theaters that were being constructed throughout the city.[50] Meanwhile, the National Theatre built by Albert Kahn and the Palace Theatre by Howard Crane continued to focus on vaudeville. A growing cohort of theaters like the Gayety also hosted burlesque shows, despite public outcry on their perceived lack of "public decency and morality" and mayoral threats to shut them down.[51] More active nighttime entertainment options also grew downtown, as Detroit joined the national ballroom dancing craze with the construction of four ballrooms along its main arterials, as well as regularly hosting dances on its riverboats.[52]

As in previous decades, downtown Detroit would again run into its limits of growth. Apart from Tuller's apartment buildings, commercial growth north of the Grand Circus Park skyscrapers never took hold. Similarly, westward growth beyond the financial district failed to materialize. The opening of a modest new Board of Commerce building on Lafayette Boulevard prompted feverish land speculation, but failed to generate significant new office construction in this relatively remote district.[53] Compared to its East Coast or even Midwestern industrial peers, Detroit's economy and identity were relatively independent of typically centralizing service industries such as finance and legal services, with office development notably lagging as a result.[54] Detroit's growing governmental apparatus also didn't generate significant new building activity, as City Hall itself was increasingly derided for its cramped and unsanitary conditions.[55]

Further afield, the urban core's remaining mansions continued their decline into a tattered fringe of rooming houses occupied by "people whose names will never adorn the page of a blue book"—often transient workers in the downtown industries and traveling businessmen.[56] The growth of these (often illegally operated) rooming houses and the various businesses scattered between them initiated a cycle of decline by depressing the value of the surrounding single-family homes that remained. This cycle of decline was seen as a prelude to future growth, and intervention was regarded as a "fight against unequal odds, a lost cause from the very outset. Detroit was destined to grow." In the meantime, the fringe was left as a "score of massive houses in varying stages of unkemptness."[57] Rooming houses continued to be a source of social problems for the city, with reports of prostitution, crime, and drug use emanating from houses on the near east and west side districts.[58] In the inner city, more than 500 brothels were in operation—more than there were churches. Entire east end downtown streets were renamed to cleanse their poor reputation, Croghan Street becoming the extension of Monroe Avenue and Champlain Street becoming East Lafayette Avenue. By the end of the decade, Detroit's police commissioner vowed to curb the downtown vice districts—to the dismay of many nearby business owners who saw their trade diminish.[59]

The near east and west side districts saw the most rapid decline in living conditions yet, as the influx of southern and foreign immigrants exacerbated overcrowding, resulting in over 300 people living per acre in some cases.[60] Especially African Americans had no other place to go than the near east side, as racial segregation and a dearth of housing made other districts unavailable to them. While the African American population increased more than sevenfold between 1914 and 1920, the middle-class suburban property ladder that enabled most others to escape the inner city was closed to them. Even attempts by African Americans to locate elsewhere in the inner city were stopped by surrounding residents, often with violence. Due to their confinement, African Americans were forced to pay some of the city's highest rents for its worst housing stock, as rents tripled between 1915 and 1920. Some of the city's bars even started charging rent for sleeping on the pool tables overnight.[61] Some workers' housing was constructed by the Detroit Housing Association, an agency of the city's Board of Commerce. However, the organization was woefully underfunded, employing only six people by 1913.[62] Labor market and housing discrimination prompted the start of the Detroit chapter of the National Urban League in 1916, helping African American newcomers adjust to city life.[63]

The discrimination against African Americans in downtown retail establishments led to the growth of an analogous business district along Hastings and St Antoine streets, with around 350 black-owned businesses counted in Detroit in 1920, ranging from banks and dentists to grocery stores and bars.[64] This pattern was quite common in many other American cities, as downtown businesses shunned the growing African American clientele.[65] African Americans were similarly considered second-class citizens in most downtown Detroit theaters and ballrooms, prompting them to start an entertainment cluster of their own around St. Antoine and Adams streets in Black Bottom. This cluster spawned the beginnings of the African American musical culture that would later put the near east side on the national map.[66]

The districts around downtown also suffered from the success of the nearby central business district, as land values skyrocketed and property owners waited for a grand sale to a commercial buyer rather than investing in their properties. A lack of zoning also allowed the further intrusion of commercial and industrial properties into these districts.[67] Central business interests ensured that proposals to instate official zoning continued to be rebuffed, as they were afraid that regulations might limit the height and profit on downtown construction. Zoning was also opposed by many landowners in the deteriorating ring around downtown, as they saw zoning as limiting their potential to accommodate the lucrative commercial downtown growth they expected.[68] Districts like Cass Park saw the growth of large apartment buildings, prompted by its relatively large lots, its proximity to downtown, and the continuing housing shortage. Despite

3.4

The contrast between inner-city overcrowding in the near east side, with rooming houses constructed with no access to light, air, and sanitation housing up to a hundred boarders, and a newly constructed subdivision near Ford's Highland Park factory. Left image from 1942 by Arthur S. Siegel, courtesy of the Library of Congress Farm Security Administration—Office of War Information photograph collection, roll 12, frame 1298. Right image courtesy of the Burton Historical Collection, Detroit Public Library.

high-profile land sales along the park itself, most new apartment buildings in the district catered to a decidedly lower-end market than their upscale predecessors. Unhindered by zoning, the newer buildings also often filled their entire lots save for small light wells, significantly altering the leafy suburban setting of the original neighborhood.[69] Commercial businesses also crept into the district, especially along the busy Cass and Woodward corridors. The 1916 *Guide to Detroit* described Woodward Avenue north of downtown in a clear state of transition: "within ten years most of the houses have been replaced by automobile showrooms, garages, department stores, and shops ... one by one, [old residences] are being crowded out to satisfy the ever increasing demand for business sites."[70]

The new typology of car-dependent architecture marked the other problem that downtown was facing: the growth of car traffic, most of which was caused by the city's own leading industry. The increasing affordability of mass-produced cars enabled a growing echelon of Detroiters to avoid public transit altogether, fueling the growth of parking garages, service stations, and traffic jams, especially downtown.[71] To some, the rise of the automobile was a sign of progress—at least initially. Observer Julian Street commented that it "has not only changed Detroit from a quiet old town into a rich, active city, but upon the drowsy romance of the old days it has superimposed the romance of modern business," transforming the Village by the Straits into "Detroit the Dynamic." As owners parked their cars haphazardly throughout downtown, a local automobile industrialist gloated that "our wide streets lend themselves to it, and our Chief of Police ... lets us leave our cars about the streets because he thinks it a good advertisement for the town."[72]

The love affair was short-lasting, as on-street parking capacity was soon outstripped by demand, even when scarce downtown green spaces like Cadillac Square's newly landscaped median were turned into excess parking lots. In 1913, the *Detroit Tribune* featured a page-long article on "The Parked Automobile, Detroit's latest problem arising out of her unparalleled prosperity," in which it lamented that "our finest streets [are] lined on either side with vehicles so closely crowded together as to make the use of the curb practically impossible for other purposes than the parking of automobiles." City leaders began to acknowledge the parking issue, but they initially felt indebted to the automobile's role in the city's growth.[73] Their first step was to enforce parking regulations, with the arrival of Police Commissioner James Couzens—ironically a former

Ford executive—marking the end of the unregulated heyday of the automobile.[74] With cars subsequently looking for off-street parking, the first private parking lots appeared in the city. In response to the increased demand for car parking, car supply salesman Max Goldberg opened a parking lot to offset losses to his ailing adjacent business on Lafayette Avenue and Cass Street in 1917—assumed to be the nation's first commercial parking lot. Inadvertently, Goldberg had started an empire with drastic consequences for downtown.[75]

Moving cars also tested the limits of downtown. A 1911 *Detroit Free Press* article mentions the problem of Woodward's original radial plan with avenues that "converge to a common center and draw the entire traffic of the city into a vortex."[76] As in many other cities like Chicago and Los Angeles, management of traffic within the existing right-of-ways was the first step toward alleviation. To help the flow of traffic through some of downtown's most central and narrow streets, one-way streets were introduced in 1916.[77] The next year, Detroit installed its first "crow's nest": a traffic tower with a police officer overlooking the city's busiest intersection on Campus Martius to choreograph traffic.[78] Despite these palliative measures, citizens expressed outrage at the "tyranny" of cars downtown, prompting elaborate proposals such as multilevel streets to alleviate congestion—to no avail.[79] By 1920, the downtown corner of Woodward and Michigan avenues had become the nation's busiest intersection, and new car registration continued to skyrocket.[80]

Despite downtown's growing pains, public interventions failed to take hold. Unlike other major American cities, downtown Detroit never had recourse to a successful rapid transit system. Instead, the city had to make do with its overstretched streetcar network, which suffered from severe overcrowding and was managed by a newly conglomerated private monopoly almost universally reviled for high fares and unreliable service. As the network hadn't seen any serious investment since the turn of the century, despite a near tripling of passenger numbers, Detroiters had to fight for a spot on a streetcar, and downtown streets became clogged with overfilled streetcars. While a number of downtown bypass lines were constructed to alleviate this congestion, downtown streets were nearing transit gridlock by the mid-1910s.[81] The situation prompted an initial plan for three subway lines along the Woodward, Gratiot, and Michigan Avenue radials in 1914, followed by a more elaborate 1915 proposal drawn by Barclay Parsons & Klapp, the Manhattan transit engineers that created New York City's initial subway system. This plan presented Detroit with two alternatives: either a long subway line under Woodward Avenue to connect downtown to Ford's new Highland Park plant, with cross-town streetcar lines feeding the line, or a shorter tunnel routing existing Woodward Avenue streetcars underneath downtown's most congested streets below Grand Circus Park at a fraction of the cost. Despite the two options at various price points, a lack of urban density, the outbreak of World War I, and continued public opposition to anything proposed or endorsed by the city's streetcar monopoly prevented City Council from taking action: just like its 1906 predecessor, the plan died.[82] A subsequent proposal for a hybrid subway and elevated line along Detroit's five radial arterials and two tangential routes in 1918 was rejected by Mayor Couzens, as the tail end of World War I and other local matters took precedence.[83] Alternative proposals by local architects and developers, including an elevated monorail proposal for rapid transit, went similarly unheeded.[84] Detroit's failure to implement transit set it apart from larger East Coast peers and Chicago, but mirrored the failure of transit to gather traction in many other rapidly growing cities like Los Angeles.[85] As in the latter city, the lack of rapid transit's centralizing force would soon challenge downtown Detroit's monopoly as the regional hub of activity.

Comprehensive urban planning remained similarly ineffective during the 1910s. An increasing number of Detroiters realized that the challenges of transit overcrowding and downtown congestion warranted a strong and feasible plan for renewal. The 1915 City Beautiful plan by Chicago architect Edward H. Bennett proposed to extend Woodward's radial avenues throughout the city to relieve congestion from the existing avenues, as well as to move some of Detroit's civic functions to Grand Circus Park and Midtown. Nevertheless, the plan was never fully implemented, as it lacked popular, legal, and political support.[86] A new city charter in 1918 provided Detroit with more power to tackle traffic, downtown fringe decline, and intrusion of undesirable uses into residential districts, making the thus far mostly powerless City Plan Commission a more powerful part of the city government, further benefiting from state legislation in 1921.[87] The new commission immediately set to its task by proposing a Building Zone Plan for Detroit, citing the importance of "insuring a more stable and hence more desirable form of development," proposed by petition from residents surrounding downtown.[88] The zoning plan focused on order and predictability, separating business and residential sections and preventing the further intrusion of multifamily dwellings

3.5

Congestion on Campus Martius in 1915. Image cropped
by author. Photograph by the Detroit Publishing Company,
courtesy of the Library of Congress.

and industrial buildings in residential neighborhoods.[89] Like its predecessors, the zoning proposal was not well received by the downtown business community, as it continued to regard land use control as restricting development and suppressing land values by its proposed height limits; the plan was subsequently rejected by City Council.[90]

With transit and zoning off the table, car traffic remained the only issue that the public seemed to agree was worthy of public investment. The city hence embarked on its only successful planning mission in the decades to follow: making way for more cars.

Acting commissioner of Detroit Public Works Porter J. Murphy named Detroit "the most poverty-stricken city in the country with respect to thoro arteries of travel."[91] The first large proposal to alleviate downtown traffic was by the City Plan Commission in 1917 to connect and widen existing streets into a downtown bypass.[92] An 80-foot-wide and 12-mile-long road just north of downtown aimed to alleviate congestion by allowing increasing east-west traffic to pass from Michigan Central Station to Eastern Market without entering the urban core. The city would take it upon itself to condemn $3 million worth of properties to facilitate the street widening, selling the remainder of these lots back upon completion. Part of the condemnation and construction costs would be paid for by levying a special assessment fee on the properties along the new thoroughfare, assuming their property would increase in value due to the street's improved connectivity.

The contentious proposal soon pitted downtown business owners, the Detroit Automobile Club, automobile manufacturers, the Detroit Real Estate Board, and most of City Council against adjacent property owners who feared insufficient compensation and an increase in taxes with unclear results.[93] The argument that city traffic had become congested to the point of "traffic blockade" and that several other cities, from Paris to London and—perhaps most sensitively—Chicago, had successfully undertaken similar large infrastructure works ultimately prevailed.[94] After City Council approved the project in 1920, followed by public approval of an amendment in favor of the project in 1921, the widening started in the early 1920s for the new Vernor Highway.[95] Ironically, the widening project ended up costing about the same amount as the recently rejected rapid transit proposal would have, a clear sign that Detroiters preferred to use their own product.[96]

In the face of wavering public support, downtown's hegemony met its first major challenge by the end of the 1910s. In response to downtown's congestion and high land values, the president of the newly conglomerated General Motors announced in 1919 that he would locate his new headquarters—the world's second largest office building thus far—roughly three miles north of downtown, near the rapidly growing intersection of Woodward Avenue and Detroit's main east-west rail line. The building would house not only executive offices but also the company's research laboratories and car showrooms on the lower floors and an underground parking garage—amenities meant to make the headquarters "the most modern and complete private office building in the world."[97] The project signaled not just a move away from downtown, but also a move closer to the constellation of General Motors plants along the multitude of rail lines that circled the city. Many downtown retailers and banks had already established their first branches in this growing area in the preceding decades, and for good reason.[98] Bordering Canada to the south, Detroit could only grow toward the north, placing its downtown further away from the geographic center of the city. By the end of the 1910s, the new geographic center of the rapidly northwestward-expanding city was around the company's new head offices, earning the area its new name of New Center.[99] General Motors' decision prompted many other magnates to follow, growing into the nation's first edge city and demonstrating to downtown businesses that the historical location of the urban core did not guarantee an eternal monopoly of central functions.[100]

New Center's offices joined other formerly downtown landmarks on their way out, as the Michigan Central railroad had opened its new station two miles west of the city in 1913—a feat of superlatives with its elaborate marble, bronze, and mahogany central hall leading to twelve tracks on 50 acres of land, topped by a fifteen-story office tower making it the tallest station in the world.[101] On the other end of an envisioned radial street, the Detroit Municipal Arts Commission had decided to move downtown's cramped art museum toward Midtown to accommodate its expansion plans.[102] Nearby, the Detroit College also decided to move out of downtown to a suburban campus in the northwest of the city in 1922, as growing enrollment forced the institution to abandon its crowded Jefferson Avenue confines.[103] After dwellings and factories had already moved away from downtown, offices, infrastructure, and civic institutions had now followed. For the first time, downtown's commercial future became less shaped by what happened inside its perimeters than by what happened around it.

■ Remove
■ Add
■ Remove and add on the same site

3.6
Downtown Detroit's blocks, buildings, parcels,
open spaces, parks, and river in 1921.
Total square footage: 57.3 million square feet
Added since 1911: 18.1 million square feet
Removed since 1911: 6.5 million square feet
Percent of downtown that is vacant or parking lot: 3%

As Detroit had doubled its population to over 1.1 million during the 1910s, downtown had similarly boomed, as figure 3.6 shows. By 1921, almost a third of downtown had been newly constructed over the past decade. This marked increase in building density mostly reflected commercial development, as Detroiters increasingly chose to live elsewhere in the city. The displacement of residents by large commercial buildings can be seen on the previously residential Washington Boulevard (1) and Broadway (2) radials within the Woodward plan, and the mansions of Woodward (3) and Jefferson avenues (4) were also quickly being replaced. As the financial center and the retail core of downtown continued to solidify, most land in Detroit's central blocks had become covered by buildings. At the same time, the first small gaps (5) began to appear in nearby blocks, some indicating a holding pattern before more construction, but most reflecting the introduction of the off-street parking lot in Detroit. Conveniently placed close to the city's largest buildings, these initial lots presented the first gaps in the city's central urban fabric.

4 GROWING PAINS: 1921–1929

The 1920s marked another decade of unprecedented growth for Detroit, as the city had entered into the "Machine Era" of mass manufacturing. Growing car production fueled the growth of every imaginable characteristic of Detroit: population, size, wealth, and mobility. By 1920, Detroit produced $1.5 billion worth of goods each year. From cars and trucks to stoves, spectacles, ice cream, or pickled vegetables, Detroit was the top manufacturing center in the nation.[1] Yet the returns of this manufacturing prowess for downtown would markedly diminish over the decade. The city's quest for growth and prosperity continued to move into the hinterland, bypassing the urban core. While downtown experienced its peak at the end of the 1920s, the seeds of its decline were firmly planted in its bloom. As a result, the decade brought a paradox of growth and decline to downtown, the two sides often expressed within close proximity. While downtown's most central blocks experienced their largest-ever building boom of offices, retail palaces, and theaters, Detroit's rising suburbanization prompted the first inner-city population decline. The explosion of car ownership swelled the already troublesome trickle of automobiles of the 1910s to an uncontrollable torrent of moving and stationary metal, prompting drastic measures to drag the urban core into the automobile age. While proposals for rapid transit surfaced in a more mature form and with more political backing than ever before, they were once again defeated by the allure of Detroit's own offspring. The 1920s was the moment when Detroit's greatest product and the city's relentless spirit of progress would finally turn their back upon their cradle—at the moment citizens least expected it.

It is impossible to describe the growth of Detroit or its downtown during the 1920s without describing the source of its prosperity—the car industry, whose phenomenal growth ushered in an era of superlatives for the city. Between 1919 and 1929, production more than doubled to around 5 million cars and trucks per year, putting more Americans than ever on wheels. Ford sold more than any other manufacturer due to its continuing efficiency and standardization improvements, prompting other manufacturers to follow suit.[2] The *New Republic* described the fever of immigration that accompanied this industrial growth: "Tens of thousands of men and women come annually to Detroit; they come to make money. ... Detroit's people are restless, living for excitement."[3] The *New York Times* described the citizens of "Detroit the Dynamic" as "the most prosperous slice of average humanity that now exists or ever has existed."[4] America's frontier had shifted from the West toward industrial powerhouses like Detroit, providing newcomers the opportunity to earn some of the nation's highest wages with relatively few required skills. As a result, population increased by another 600,000 during the 1920s, many of the newcomers having migrated from the South, significantly raising racial prejudice and tensions.[5]

As in previous decades, most of Detroit's residential growth occurred on the city's fringe, enabled by the city's own popularization of the automobile.[6] The *New York Times* described the result of Detroit's continuing decentralization as a veritable chaos: "The city has been, one might say, assembled rather than manufactured. ... When Detroit goes to work in the morning the effect is as if some one had poked a stick into an ant hill and had temporarily lost their sense of direction. There is no general stampede toward a centralized workshop district. The traffic flows all ways at once." The suburban boom in Detroit increasingly coincided with the rise of the motor vehicle, allowing citizens to travel in all directions and expanding the city beyond recognition. Yet this was certainly also seen as a sign of progress: "The city has expanded as a city on wheels must."[7] While most suburban growth thus far had occurred within Detroit's city limits, the growth of surrounding suburbs first began to outpace the city as it ran out of undeveloped land by the mid-1920s. While the elite had been leaving the city for decades, middle-class suburbanization drastically accelerated by the 1920s.[8] By 1930, 25 percent of the overall metropolitan population already lived outside of Detroit's boundaries, following the accelerating pace of job suburbanization.[9] The industrialization of homebuilding contributed to the affordability of suburban homes, with almost 60,000 acres of subdivisions built around Detroit during the 1920s.[10] By the end of the decade, the subdivisions around Detroit covered a larger land area than the city itself.

The pace and magnitude of suburban growth began to break the symbiosis between downtown and surrounding residential areas. Many new suburban neighborhoods had plenty of commercial amenities to make them self-sufficient, at least for daily needs.[11] Furthermore, the suburban answer to Detroit's housing shortage caused the first inner-city population losses. Some areas near downtown lost over 30 percent of their population in only four years, as more Detroiters were able to move "away from the filthy alleys, congested and dangerous traffic arteries, and the undesirable element always found loitering in the fringe of the downtown section."[12] Detroit's City Plan Commission became fully aware of the threat of suburbanization and the slowing growth of Detroit by the late 1920s, as it cited a warning by German philosopher Hermann von Keyserling in its 1929 annual report: "Owing to the fact that all modern town-planning and building has been carried out under the assumption that everybody owns a motor car, there is no limit to the extension of suburbs."[13]

Detroit's car manufacturers started to leave the city themselves, as the industry's feverish quest for efficiency threatened to pass the city by. Much of Detroit's industrial growth during the 1920s occurred outside city limits, with newer plants located in suburban municipalities to avoid city taxes and regulations, but also because the city was running out of space to house the ever larger factories.[14] Perhaps the most vivid example was Henry Ford's decision to move most of his manufacturing to the new River Rouge Complex west of Detroit, where he could control every aspect of the production chain. As a result, nearby Dearborn's population catapulted tenfold to 50,000 during the 1920s.[15] Due to the growth of the US population toward the west and increasing congestion of Detroit's manufacturing corridors, some large industrialists had even started to move some of their operations out of the region altogether.[16] Meanwhile, the automobile market began to reach saturation. As manufacturers attempted to induce demand with annual model changes and advertisement, the unemployment rate in Detroit swung wildly due to retooling cycles and plant shutdowns.[17] In this roller coaster pattern, returns on real estate investments were inevitably measured in months, not years. This economic boom-and-bust cycle made large investments in the high-density residential and commercial real estate that comprises downtown districts a rather risky affair.[18] The stable prosperity that a growing downtown required began to falter, and in the eyes of the automobile industry, Detroit and its downtown were growing into a liability rather than an asset.

At first, these cracks in the symbiosis between Detroit's industry and its downtown were hard to see in the groundswell of new construction during the 1920s. While the local press sensed that Detroit was decentralizing,[19] the hegemony of downtown was not yet questioned. The consensus seemed to be that even though newcomers settled outside the urban core and often beyond the city limits, "every additional resident in Detroit adds to the prosperity of the city and indirectly is responsible for the phenomenal growth of the downtown section."[20] The downtown retail core grew steadily into "a highly sophisticated shopping and hotel district" as the retail palaces on Woodward Avenue feverishly expanded to keep pace with prosperity.[21] Especially Hudson's growth accelerated during the 1920s, usurping almost the entire city block its store occupied as surrounding stores fell to Detroit's leading retailer. One by one, Hudson's purchased and demolished competitors' buildings, consolidating into a twenty-five-story, almost 2-million-square-foot retail emporium, second only to Macy's in New York in size.[22] As a result of its aggressive expansion strategy, Hudson's sales increased almost twentyfold between 1912 and 1929.[23] Nearby Crowley-Milner vied for the title of largest department store in the state by adding a new eleven-story tower for home goods that connected to its main store.[24] While Kern's department store never reached this size, it did construct a new ten-story building in 1928, crowning a tenfold increase in floor area since 1913.[25] Nearby, Detroit's jewelers clustered in the fifteen-story neo-Gothic Metropolitan Building completed in 1925, housing almost 200 different establishments at its peak.[26] However, the breakneck speed at which surrounding shops renovated and constructed new premises on the Avenue during the 1910s was markedly slowing, as retailers started to set their sights elsewhere.

The 1920s marked the decade in which retailers truly began to follow the suburbanization of Detroit's middle class, as small suburban shopping clusters expanded from only supplying daily needs to challenging the breadth of merchandise on offer in downtown. By 1928, Sears, Roebuck and Company opened anchor stores in two secondary business centers on Grand River and Gratiot avenues in northwest and northeast Detroit respectively. The stores expressly focused on "favorable location and easy accessibility" by cars, streetcars, and buses, with street-facing storefronts adding to their suburban "splendid location, unobstructed by any closely adjacent buildings." Parking was provided in large free lots directly adjacent to the buildings, and air conditioning provided comfort to customers—two advantages that downtown stores struggled to match.[27] Similarly, after starting in a small downtown storefront in 1929, Federal Department Stores soon expanded to locations across the city as it aimed to "bring closer to the buyer the variety of merchandise, the service, and the hundreds and hundreds of brand name products, that are not usually found in smaller neighborhood establishments."[28] Kresge's five-and-dime had already established ten branches outside of its downtown locations by the end of the decade, and competitor Woolworth's had double that number in the city's neighborhoods.[29] Downtown retailers realized that they had to organize themselves to plan, lobby, and negotiate for continued growth. Hudson's department store had hosted the first meeting of the Central Business District Association in 1922, and the organization doubled its efforts to promote the interests of downtown business owners.[30]

Downtown also grew as an office and entertainment center. The Book brothers' bet on Washington Boulevard was starting to pay off as they completed the Book-Cadillac Hotel in 1924, replacing the late nineteenth-century six-story Cadillac Hotel they were born and raised in and later became the owners of.[31] Upon completion, the twenty-nine-story Book-Cadillac was the tallest hotel structure in the world, but it was soon surpassed by the thirty-eight-story Book Tower which was added to the existing Book Building in 1927, with grand plans to add even six more skyscrapers to the boulevard.[32] After installing decorative light posts, the former "cow pasture of Detroit's pioneer days now boasts [the] brightest lights of any city in [the] world."[33] Downtown's northward push toward Grand Circus Park solidified with the construction of a 34-story tower by the Eaton family estate, containing five floors of retailers with mostly medical offices above, crowding the several other office skyscrapers around the park.[34]

Nevertheless, the northern part of downtown became mostly known as a place of entertainment rather than work, a trend that had been started by the northward expansion of theater operator Kunsky's downtown movie empire, as he opened his Madison and Adams theaters on Grand Circus Park in the late 1910s. To hedge his investments, the theaters were wrapped by office buildings—if one venture failed, the other could soften the blow. The new theaters marked a leap in scale—at 2,000 seats, the Madison was twice as large as any of its predecessors—and they were part of a trend of growth and decentralization. A slew of ever larger and more opulent movie palaces followed in this direction, many still designed by local architect Howard Crane and operated by Kunsky, although national companies such as Paramount and Fox gained a foothold toward the end of the decade. During the 1920s alone, almost 20,000 seats were added in palaces such as the Capitol, State, Michigan, Fox, United Artist, Wilson, and Gem theaters, each with their own specific clientele, entertainment offerings, and layout. Grand openings wowed the local press and patrons alike as they gawked at marble-filled lobbies, baroque domed ceilings, grand staircases, extravagant art pieces, and elaborate amenities such as powder and smoking rooms. The theaters allowed even working-class Detroiters to spend a night amidst architectural grandeur and first-rate entertainment. Perhaps the crowning achievement of the northern theater boom was the opening of the Fox Theatre on Woodward Avenue in 1928, Detroit's largest with over 5,000 seats, "a wonderland of continental treasure … [which] will reverberate around the architectural world."[35] Another local group of entrepreneurs envisioned an entire district for living, working, and entertainment west of Grand Circus Park around Bagley Street. Over the course of a few years, various developers including Kunsky constructed the twenty-two-story Leland Hotel, the United Artists Theatre, and the opulent Michigan Theatre, with the theaters both situated at the base of large office buildings.[36]

As a result of the northern competition, many of the original theaters in the Monroe Avenue area resorted to burlesque shows to survive.[37] While most downtown theaters offered popular entertainment, classical music and opera were only on offer in Mid-town's growing entertainment district, and outside observers noted that highbrow cultural life in Detroit paled in comparison with cities of a similar size.[38] Ballroom dancing remained popular in the city, with several new ballrooms constructed in and around downtown. African Americans continued to be shunned by downtown establishments and chose to expand their own entertainment offerings, hosting early blues, big band, and jazz music to increasingly national audiences in Black Bottom venues like The Kopping on Gratiot Avenue. The rising popularity of African American music brought in significant numbers of white patrons in mixed-race "black and tan" establishments

4.1

The Michigan Theatre on Bagley Street opened in 1926.
Kunsky's flagship theater hosted over 4,000 seats and was
housed within a thirteen-story office building. Image courtesy
of the Burton Historical Collection, Detroit Public Library.

like the Palms, and brought African Americans to play at white-owned ballrooms.[39] Entertainment was also offered in the city's many bars, restaurants, and saloons. Despite the prohibition of alcohol instated in Michigan in 1918, nightlife in the city was thriving as smuggled Canadian liquor flowed freely in gang-controlled "blind pig" establishments—often on the near east side.[40] A significant underworld of smugglers and widespread police corruption earned the city a reputation as "a flagrant example of a wide-open booze town."[41] Illicit drinking certainly wasn't the only vice that could be found downtown. The continued overrepresentation of single men in the city also supported a wide variety of sexual services, most of which were found within easy walking distance of the city's above-board entertainment district.[42]

Detroit's skyline especially grew in the financial district in the mid to late 1920s, as Detroit's banks prospered due to the growth of the credit economy and beneficial federal regulations.[43] A series of skyscrapers would cement the reputation of local architecture firms, perhaps best exemplified by the work of head architect Wirt C. Rowland of Smith, Hinchman & Grylls. In 1925, the Buhl family commissioned Rowland to design a twenty-six-story skyscraper on Griswold Street, finished in a rather transitional style between its Romanesque and Gothic details and a more modern stepped-back floor plan to allow for light and air to enter.[44] The thirty-one-story Barlum Hotel and forty-story Barlum Tower were finished by another local firm, Bonnah and Chaffee, on Cadillac Square in 1927, the latter standing as the tallest skyscraper outside of New York and Chicago.[45] Rowland took back this title only a year later with the opening of the Greater Penobscot Building in 1928, its forty-seven floors crowning the two earlier similarly named skyscrapers constructed on the block between Griswold, Congress, Shelby, and Fort streets. While the building contained an ornate entrance, lobby, and ground-floor shops as in Rowland's earlier designs, the detailing of the upper part of the building had become far more streamlined, "emancipated from the shackles of historical styles."[46] Nearby, the Union Trust building, named after the bank that commissioned Rowland to design it, was completed as an elaborate "cathedral of finance," specifically following the wishes of the Union Trust director Frank Blair to reflect the Trust's concept of warmth, accessibility, and personal care combined with strength, security, and dependability.[47] The financial district skyscraper boom concluded two

4.2

Postcards of the Greater Penobscot Building (left) and Guardian Building (right) on Griswold Street, both designed by architect Wirt C. Rowland, depict the skyscrapers towering over their urban context. Left image by United News Company; right image publisher unknown. Both images courtesy of the Burton Historical Collection, Detroit Public Library.

blocks to the north in 1929, when local industrialist David Stott opened his thirty-eight-story building designed by Donaldson and Meier.[48]

The local realtors' association boasted of the massive investment in downtown's skyward leap: "Confidence in the sound and amazingly rapid growth of Detroit has led the country's keenest business men and financiers to invest millions in the city's future. And every dollar invested in these great buildings not only increases the value of downtown property, but assures the future increases throughout the entire city."[49] Visiting artist and architect Hugh Ferriss was struck by the burst of Art Deco growth in the city and complimented: "Here in Detroit, I see a great city of the future. Already your great buildings rise majestically against the sky."[50] Amid the rising frames of over $100 million worth of new construction, the *Detroit News* heralded "that the great vested estates of Detroit—corporations that have millions at stake on the growth or decline of Detroit, have faith that Detroit has a future even greater than its past."[51] Nevertheless, the Stott building would be the last skyscraper to be constructed downtown until the 1950s.

While this post-Depression hiatus was common in American cities, Detroit's pre-Depression boom had been smaller than those of cities of the same size. The growth may have expressed "rich men's faith in Detroit," but only a certain type of wealth was willing to invest in downtown—the "vested estates" that the *News* had praised.[52] Almost all downtown buildings had been constructed by the city's old elite who had gained their wealth from downtown-based trade. Lumber tycoon Simon Murphy built the Penobscot Building, flour tycoon David Stott was behind his namesake skyscraper, and downtown-based institutions such as the Chamber of Commerce and the financial industry finished the list. The generation of automobile barons who helped put Detroit on the world map were notably absent. After General Motors settled in its recently finished New Center headquarters and even expanded into the nearby Argonaut Building in 1927, its newly purchased supplier Fisher Body similarly opted to build its stunning Art Deco headquarters in Detroit's second business district. One of Fisher Body's directors acknowledged the changing geography of the growing city: "Detroit was startled some years ago when General Motors decided to erect its mammoth office building on Grand Boulevard … it has seen this section develop into an important one commercially. … This section is, as a matter of fact, from a geographical standpoint and elapsed time in travelling point, the very heart of Detroit"—an advantage that the building wouldn't hesitate to advertise.[53] These three iconic New Center buildings constructed during the 1920s totaled almost as much floor space as all downtown office buildings built in the same decade. As a result, New Center's newfound centrality attracted residential development such as Lee Plaza, a seventeen-story apartment building.[54]

Other industrialists continued to avoid Detroit altogether. Notably opposed to cities, Ford commissioned Albert Kahn to construct new company offices next to his River Rouge plant in Dearborn in 1923, the first part of what would become Ford Motors' corporate campus in the mid-twentieth century. The Chrysler Corporation, emerging from what had been Maxwell Motors in 1925, decided to stay in the Highland Park office complex that had housed its predecessor, before Walter Chrysler decided to build the Chrysler Tower in New York to house the company's headquarters in the late 1920s. Detroit's major auto manufacturers also didn't conduct much of their financial business in the downtown banks: General Motors and Chrysler mainly worked with banks close to their offices in New York, and Ford financed his own bank as he deeply distrusted the finance industry.[55] As a result, 1929 bank clearings in Detroit per capita were the lowest of the ten largest cities in the United States; Detroit's banks cleared less than half of Chicago's money per capita and a quarter of New York's.[56] The other typical downtown staples of governance and legal services couldn't compensate for the lack of financial centralization. As one of the few American downtowns not directly connected to the city's raison d'être, downtown Detroit fared much more poorly than its peers, and many downtown offices were underoccupied for years after completion.[57] As the dust of the roaring twenties settled, per capita downtown office construction in Chicago had been more than twice as high as in Detroit during the decade, and seven times higher in New York.[58]

More worrying than the modest growth in the core of downtown Detroit was the spiral of decline that had gripped the surrounding fringe. The direct vicinity of Detroit's newest skyscrapers began to solidify into what Chicago School sociologist Ernest Burgess called a *zone of transition*—at best an area that served the parking, wholesale, and logistical needs of a more demanding downtown, and at worst a blighting holding pattern for a downtown that was unlikely to grow.[59] As seen in figure 4.9, entire blocks west of the financial district and north of Grand Circus Park were given over to parked cars,

4.3

While the growth of Detroit's financial district had drastically expanded the city's skyline by 1929 (top), it was dwarfed by the growth of Chicago's Loop during the same decade (bottom; printed by Kaufmann & Fabry Co. after a painting by William Macy, parts of which are aspirational). Images courtesy of the Library of Congress Prints and Photographs Division.

severing the links between the commercial core of downtown and its residential periphery. Max Goldberg's first parking lot had grown to an empire of 23 lots, mostly on land leased from landowners looking to eventually benefit from downtown growth. From his desk thirteen floors up on Washington Boulevard, the self-crowned "parking lot king" oversaw his holdings, amassed by convincing struggling peripheral building owners to tear down their properties and fill them with tarmac, augmented by billboards and the odd lunch room—lowering their tax bills and returning their land to profit.[60] As the population pressure on Detroit's inner city subsided, parking lots became more profitable than most remaining downtown rooming houses, with the hulks that once housed Detroit's urban elite on Fort Street and Jefferson Avenue consequently paved over. Goldberg's business model could succeed unhindered by any zoning, and the resulting peripheral erosion proved in turn disrupted the stability of surrounding properties, especially in residential districts.

Automobile-oriented commerce also began to become a staple in downtown. Detroit's first Auto Row formed north of Cass Park along Cass and Woodward avenues from the isolated establishments of the mid-1910s, filling the large lots of former stately mansions with showrooms, garages, and gas stations. The city constructed its Convention Hall in 1925 a few blocks north of Cass Park to host large automobile shows, cementing the area as an automotive center, with the construction of car-related businesses accelerating in the neighborhood during the subsequent years. Low land values also attracted corporate offices and cultural landmarks such as the Standard Accident and Kresge headquarters, the eight-story Cass Technical High School, and the massive neo-Gothic Masonic Temple facing the neighborhood's namesake park by the late 1920s.[61] Other, smaller businesses soon followed, and the back streets of Cass Park soon contained a curious hodgepodge of offices, apartment buildings, workshops, tin, and tarmac.[62] Remaining properties with deed restrictions on business construction succumbed to the growth of downtown, as property owners admitted defeat and sold their land to the highest bidder.[63]

The encroachment of business not only deteriorated the residential character of Cass Park but also obstructed other opportunities for high-end downtown growth. Emboldened by his success with the Tuller Hotel and joining forces with the newly formed Park Avenue Association, Lewis Tuller aimed to continue downtown's northward growth trend by constructing three new residential hotels along Park Avenue in the heart of the Cass Park district, all opening in less than a year between late 1924 and 1925. Tuller and the Association aimed to develop the area further as a shopping and entertainment area, but Tuller's hotels in the declining district soon proved a bridge too far and ultimately sank his empire.[64]

Cultural and retail activity followed the residential decline of downtown's fringe. As residents left Detroit's downtown-adjacent districts, their churches closed or transitioned to serve as social institutions to a growing number of working-class and transient patrons—a precursor to the various homeless shelters that would be constructed in Cass Park in later decades.[65] Corner shops in the residential districts similarly started to thin out, their departure accelerated by the invention of the refrigerator that allowed households to buy their food in larger quantities and from larger shops and fledgling supermarkets farther from home.[66] Housing conditions in the near east and west side districts also continued to worsen, with the City Plan Commission warning in 1928 that "housing conditions in some sections of our own city are almost intolerable."[67]

Urban planners still had relatively little agency in this downward spiral. Housing and zoning proposals continued to be obstructed by downtown business interests and were shot down by voters and politicians, and the City Plan Commission's limited budget was mostly spent on coping with growth in the city's outskirts.[68] Furthermore, the city planning milieu in Detroit was still enthralled by the aesthetic and civic focus of the City Beautiful movement, exemplified by a 1924 proposal by Eliel Saarinen to transform the city's declining industrial riverfront into a civic center. Sponsored by the local press and the local chapter of the American Institute of Architects, Saarinen embedded a memorial and convention hall into a coherent ensemble of civic buildings surrounding a riverfront plaza, punctuated by a new city hall tower, routing traffic and rapid transit below.[69] Despite strong support from prominent citizens, the City Plan Commission, and Mayor Lodge and subsequent approval by Detroit voters, a shortage of funds and political will to purchase land for the elaborate ensemble killed the plan in 1925—marking another in a long series of failed riverfront proposals.[70] In many ways, the civic center proposal could be seen as the end phase of the City Beautiful movement, which focused on aesthetics over practicality—a priority for which most Detroiters had neither time nor patience.[71]

More pragmatic planning efforts were far more successful, especially those that addressed the pressing need to improve Detroit's growing automobile congestion problem. Inspired by their predecessors the 1910s, these infrastructural plans exacerbated the decline of downtown, especially in its fringes. But in this case, inaction was not an option. As an increasing number of Detroiters were able to afford a car, and were increasingly compelled to use it to commute to work and visit downtown, the number of cars on Detroit's streets and parking lots skyrocketed during the 1920s.[72] The municipalization of the streetcar system prompted the creation of the Detroit Rapid Transit Commission, which was tasked to study the alleviation of the city's traffic woes.[73] The

4.4
Waterfront rendering of Eliel Saarinen's 1924 plan for a civic center in Detroit, with City Hall tower on the left and a convention and civic hall in the center of the image. The two columns between the buildings reflect the foot of Woodward Avenue and mirror the columns that mark the foot of Piazza San Marco in Venice. Image from Eliel Saarinen, "Project for Water Front Development, Detroit, Mich," *American Architect* 129, no. 2495 (1926), 481.

commission produced a master plan, adopted by Detroit in 1925, that focused on infra-structural interventions to accommodate public and private transportation.[74]

Unfortunately, the public transit portion of the proposals soon faltered. Streetcar trips per person decreased by more than 50 percent during the 1920s, even after the city finally gained control over the much-maligned streetcar monopoly in 1922. Due to near-constant battles over ownership since the late nineteenth century, the system hadn't received any significant improvements since that time and continued to fall behind Detroit's growth.[75] Similarly, over half of the interurban rail lines had gone into receivership as Detroiters embraced automobility.[76] At the other end of the cycle, new middle-class neighborhoods were constructed without public transportation in mind as most owners had gained access to a private car.[77]

Ten years after the last such plan failed, the Rapid Transit Commission proposed a plan in 1926 for four subway lines, connecting downtown with factories along two radial routes while now also acknowledging the city's dispersed pattern of manufactur-ing with two tangential routes that bypassed downtown.[78] The proposal's list of sup-porters was long, strong, and kaleidoscopic. The usual combination of downtown merchants, the Board of Commerce, and the Detroit Real Estate Board pushed for the adoption of the subway system, as they sought to keep wealth and spending central-ized.[79] More unusually, major industrialists like Henry Ford joined in, as he recognized that only efficient mass transit could provide plants with a reliable and efficient supply of workers, many of whom still didn't own private cars.[80] On the other hand, City Council, the local press, and the general public were hardly enthusiastic about the cost of the proposal—which had ballooned to $280 million from 1916's $16 million—even if over half was proposed to be paid by directly adjacent landowners. Detroit's existing Department of Street Railways, which would be bypassed by the plans, was also against its new competition. Nor were the plans helped by the fact that Detroit had reached its bonded debt ceiling, and that Detroit's economy had entered a downturn by 1927. Even after the proposals were scaled back to two and ultimately just one line and some down-town streetcar tunnels, a 1929 referendum killed the system.[81] The defeat of rapid tran-sit in Detroit is not unique to the city; nationwide public and professional sentiment had swayed against major transit investments by the mid-1920s as cars had become more popular. If anything, the transit proposals had simply come too late to be taken seriously in the Motor City.[82]

SUPER-HIGHWAY 204 FEET WIDE
DESIGNED BY
RAPID TRANSIT COMMISSION·· DETROIT
DANIEL L. TURNER· CONSULTING ENGR.
JOHN P HALLIHAN· ENGR. IN CHARGE

4.5
Proposed suburban superhighway with rapid transit
in highway median. Rapid Transit Commission,
"The Relation of Individual to Collective Transportation"
(Detroit, 1928).

With rapid transit wavering, only road improvements remained on the table. The Rapid Transit Commission equated the two: "the one is rapid transit on rails, while the other is rapid transit on rubber."[83] Together with the City Plan Commission, they proposed a system of 204-foot-wide "super-highways" for Detroit's suburbs: an innovative system of grade-separated highways that initially contained a center median of rapid transit lines surrounded by several lanes of fast car traffic—an apparent symbiosis of individual and mass transportation.[84] The city of Detroit and Wayne, Oakland, and Macomb counties cooperated in Superhighway Commissions to buy the land for the road widenings. Outside of Detroit's city limits, where land was cheap and readily available, state gas taxes supported the swift purchase and construction of the envisioned highways.[85] Widening roads was a lot more difficult within Detroit's city limits, especially as outer municipalities refused to chip in for inner-city projects.[86] The master plan recognized the expense of breaking wide roads through existing urban areas, as it pared down the width of thoroughfares to 120 feet within a six-mile radius of downtown. The resulting required width was equal to most boulevards in the original Woodward Plan more than a century ago, which was considered an act of "vision and courage" that warranted a modern successor.[87] Widening was an express act of modernity; the new Rapid Transit Commission president Sidney Waldon mirrored Swiss modernist Le Corbusier's narrative of breaking with the past to make way for the future: "We must lay aside our ox cart and horse and buggy yardsticks of right-of-way and adopt new ones that adopt the motor vehicle."[88]

Akin to the widening of Vernor Highway—which was still ongoing during the 1920s—existing streets were to be widened by condemning property on one side, setting back the build-to line, and selling off the reduced plots at a later stage. While much of the cost of widening was to be paid for by city funds, a significant part was to be borne by the property owners along the widened street, under the assumption that their property would increase in value as a result of the better connectivity of the street.[89] This local assessment wasn't unique to Detroit, as nearby landowners had successfully funded over half of Wacker Drive's decking in Chicago, and the improvement in fact had resulted in a significant increase in land values and densities. Furthermore, local assessments for infrastructure improvements were common throughout the nation, and were recommended by the federal government.[90] Quite differently from the

Vernor Highway bypass, in this case the choice was made to widen the existing radial avenues that led into the heart of downtown Detroit, containing some of the highest-priced land in the city as these streets were lined by retail businesses. A "traffic belt" of widened roads was also proposed around downtown, running right through the near east Black Bottom neighborhood. The location of the belt was close enough to downtown to relieve through traffic, while the cost of land acquisition in this declining area was deemed low enough to be feasible, with the belt "protecting and in a very large manner stabilizing [the] conditions in the center of the city."[91] The belt widenings were also likely inspired by the success of Chicago's widened traffic belt around the Loop by 1926.[92] The proposal to run a traffic belt through Hastings Street, the growing main street of African American Detroit, reflected the racial prejudice in Detroit's culture and politics at the time, with racially motivated violence and KKK membership drastically increasing, influencing even mayoral elections.[93] At best, City Hall regarded the demolition of Detroit's African American hub as collateral damage in improving downtown. In the end, however, the city opted not to pursue the widenings for the traffic belt, approving instead a belt of one-way streets around downtown by 1926 to route traffic without the need for condemnation.[94]

As the cost and effort of these large-scale widenings were unprecedented in the city and subject to citizens' approval, the construction projects needed to be sold to the public. The rhetoric of road widening hinged on three concepts. The first two arguments went hand in hand: the rapid, seemingly endless growth of the city and its traffic needed to be tackled before the rapidly growing land values along the major avenues to be widened made them become too costly for public purchase. In other words, growth warranted urgency. For road widenings, it was claimed, it was now or never: "opportunity [knocks], hand in hand with necessity."[95] Furthermore, if roads weren't widened soon, growth might pass by downtown in favor of "the development of other districts which do afford capacity"—with New Center serving as a case in point.[96] Sidney Waldon realized the power of this narrative of urgency, harnessing "the passage of time [as] an ally of immense power."[97] While the symbiosis of growth and expediency justified the widening of roads at a regional level, the third and final argument focused on the local benefits of wider roads, arguing that "the pavement invites traffic and enhances the value of the land adjacent and served. Traffic creates business and encourages the

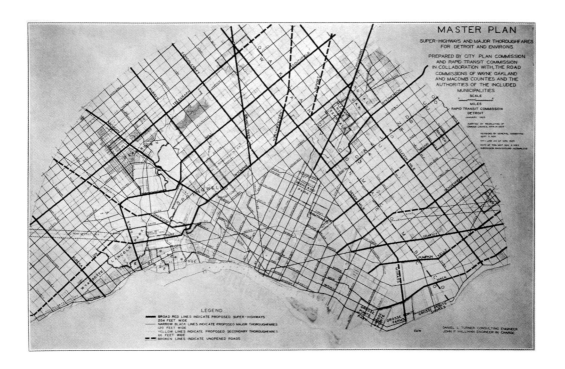

4.6

Master plan of superhighways and major thoroughfares for Detroit and environs, January 1925.
Superhighways 204 feet in width shown in thick black lines; 120-foot thoroughfares in thin black
lines. Image by Rapid Transit Commission.

4.7

Left: proposed downtown traffic belt in 1925, curiously missing the Woodward and Gratiot Avenue
widening schemes. The belt was proposed to be 150 feet wide. Right: one-way traffic belt around
downtown. Left image: Rapid Transit Commission, "Carrying out the Master Plan" (Detroit, 1925).
Right image: Sidney D. Waldon, "How Wider Streets Here Will Mean Better Rapid Transit Facilities,"
Detroit Motor News 6 (March 1926).

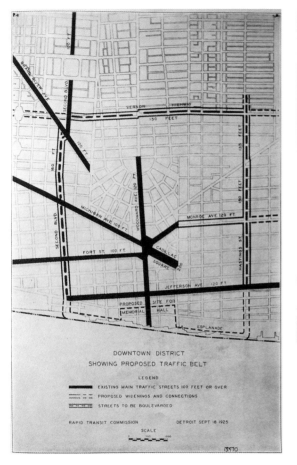

DOWNTOWN DISTRICT

SHOWING PROPOSED TRAFFIC BELT

LEGEND

▬▬▬▬ EXISTING MAIN TRAFFIC STREETS 100 FEET OR OVER

- - - - PROPOSED WIDENINGS AND CONNECTIONS

▬▬▬▬ STREETS TO BE BOULEVARDED

RAPID TRANSIT COMMISSION   DETROIT SEPT 18 1925

SCALE

erection of buildings which hug the narrow right-of-way."[98] In other words: wider roads were good for business. This argument was paramount in gathering support for widenings from adjacent landowners, as they were asked to finance the widened streets through a local assessment, a similar financing structure to the one used in the widening of Vernor Highway.[99]

As the wider streets were seen as supporting the continued prosperity of the central business district, they were strongly supported by downtown business interests, such as the Detroit Board of Commerce and the Detroit Retail Merchants Association led by Oscar Webber, the new vice president of Hudson's department store. In a 1928 article in the *Detroit Times*, Webber stated: "How are we going to get people downtown if we don't have the thoroughfares?"[100] Perhaps less surprisingly, car manufacturers like Edsel Ford also supported the widening, as it would make automobile trips through the city more expedient and comfortable.[101] The local Real Estate Board also expressed its support for the widenings as they "will mean giving the automobile the maximum usefulness which was originally intended for it"—doubtless improving the land value of the subdivisions its members were laying out across the region.[102] With a powerful narrative and a similarly powerful alliance backing the proposals, all that was left was to convince the citizens of Detroit, who were to vote on each widening project separately. A propaganda leaflet to vote for the widening of Woodward Avenue sums up the rhetoric of widening proponents in Detroit, with an image of the development boom that would occur on the new, wider boulevard. The campaign was successful, as Detroiters approved the widening of Woodward, Gratiot, and Michigan avenues in October 1925.[103] The widenings would take over a decade to finish, with costs and priorities constantly adjusted according to the political milieu.[104]

The initial results of Detroit's road widenings soon disproved their claimed benefits. As the first widenings were completed along Vernor Highway, business owners began to realize that wider streets actually *hurt* their property values, complaining that "many persons hesitate to cross the widened street with its speeded traffic and that the business zone is thus cut in two."[105] At the eastern end of Vernor Highway, the Eastern Market's president complained that his business had dropped by 50 percent, as the "widening has merely created a speedway, which in no way benefits our property or business."[106] While automotive traffic increased on the newly widened roads, footfall

_A_ Wider Woodward _Now!_

from Adams Avenue to Highland Park Limits

will save Detroit Millions _of_ Dollars _in the near future_

MAMMOTH BUILDING BOOM, will be started by the widening of Woodward avenue (Adams Ave. to Highland Park Limits.)

$100,000,000 WORTH OF NEW SKYSCRAPERS will rise on the vacant lots of Woodward avenue to take the place of tin shacks, peanut stands, used car lots, etc., between Adams avenue and Highland Park limits.

THOUSANDS OF MEN WILL BE EMPLOYED in the erection of these magnificent buildings that will start construction following the widening.

HUMAN LIVES WILL BE SAVED and traffic congestion will be relieved if Woodward is widened out to the Highland Park limits.

DETROIT WILL SAVE MILLIONS OF DOLLARS BY WIDENING WOODWARD because $100,000,000 worth of new buildings on Woodward will pay $2,000,000 in taxes annually. The city is losing this much and more each year the widening is put off.

4.8

Advertisement promoting the widening of Woodward Avenue through a ballot proposal, ca. 1925. Image source unknown; from the local history files in the Burton Historical Collection, Detroit Public Library.

decreased and business owners began to realize that their newly raised property taxes and special assessments were footing the bill for an improvement that mostly benefited others. The widening of Detroit's arterials mostly seemed to help the further expansion of Detroit's edges, as an array of advertisements promoted subdivisions along the newly widened roads. A local business owner protested: "the only fair thing for the city to do, as I see it, is to place the cost of this wide street, which has made a nice, convenient race track for motorists, on the general tax roll." The city eventually and partially gave in to this argument.[107]

As a result of the "false premises" of road widenings, business failures mushroomed along the radial streets leading into downtown. The glacial pace of widenings exacerbated the problems, as businesses lost neighbors and sometimes faced over a decade of road construction. Vernor Highway was still being widened at the end of the 1920s, and looked "as though the World War had been shot out on the street."[108] Furthermore, cleared parcels along the newly widened arterials were difficult to sell, and if purchased, most were filled with automobile-oriented land uses such as gas stations, drive-ins, car shops, and parking lots—transforming the downtown periphery into a suburban commercial strip, only blocks away from central department stores. As the stock market crashed in 1929, the struggle to rebuild properties along the newly widened streets ground to a complete halt. Instead of the anticipated boom in property values and density, the road widenings had created the first traces of planners' blight in downtown, fueled by the same combination of public naivete and private lack of interest that would plague many succeeding public interventions. Instead of the envisioned building boom, strips of vacant land had cut the critical mass of business on downtown Detroit's peripheral arteries, worsening the divide between a stable downtown core and a declining fringe.

The map of Detroit in 1929 illustrates the rapid growth of new construction during the 1920s, especially in the financial district. At the same time, the map illustrates the first erosive effects of cars on downtown Detroit. West of the financial district and north of downtown the first gaps had appeared in the urban fabric of downtown— parking lots. In certain areas, parking had already taken over the majority of peripheral urban blocks (1). By the end of the decade, cars had eroded the edges of downtown far beyond the ragged arterials: over a million square feet of land accommodated almost 10,000 parking spots, feeding a veritable industry of private lot operators. The rise of the automobile also manifested itself in Detroit's first infrastructural renewal. The northern half of Vernor Highway, the southern half of Gratiot Avenue, and the eastern half of Woodward Avenue were practically cleared of any major buildings, ready for the roads to be widened (2). Little did planners know, these vacated lots were not just "taxpayer" holdovers waiting for a developer to come along;[109] the Depression and the subsequent downturn of Detroit's downtown and city economy had created the first permanent holes in the Motor City's urban tissue. Despite the ravaging effects of the car on the inner-city landscape, Detroit relentlessly looked forward, regarding its urban tissue as a vessel for progress, easily discarded in times of despair, reinvented in times of hope. Journalist Matthew Josephson aptly summed up Detroit's feverish spirit of growth in a 1929 magazine article, praising the Motor City as "the most modern city in the world, the city of tomorrow. There is no past, there is no history. ... One day, thousands and thousands of human beings turned themselves over and found that they were in the huge metropolis of Detroit."[110]

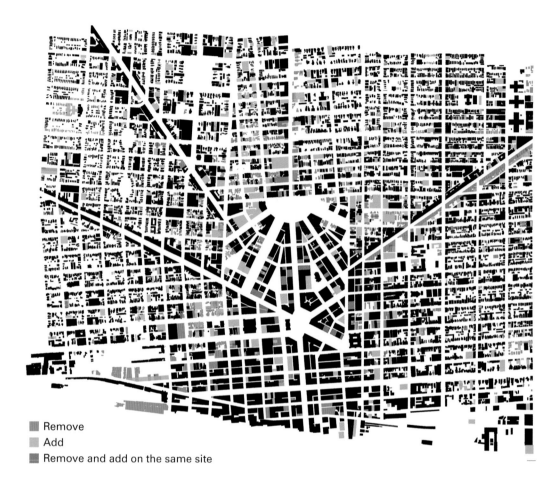

Remove

Add

Remove and add on the same site

4.9
Downtown Detroit's blocks, buildings, parcels, open
spaces, parks, and river in 1929.
Total square footage: 65.2 million square feet
Added since 1921: 15.7 million square feet
Removed since 1921: 7.8 million square feet
Percent of downtown that is vacant or parking lot: 10%

III   FALL

5 EARLY EROSION: 1929–1937

In November 1930, downtown Detroit again stood in the center of the region as local notables opened the world's first international tunnel to Canada near the foot of Woodward Avenue.[1] The joy was fleeting, as Detroit and its downtown had little other cause for celebration. The stock market crash of October 1929 announced a decade of deep economic depression for Detroit, arguably hitting it harder than any other major city in the country. Auto production plummeted more than 75 percent between 1929 and 1932. By the summer of 1931, Ford had even decided to suspend production altogether until the end of the year. Many were forced to follow suit—some indefinitely.[2] By 1933, almost half of the city's automobile workers were unemployed. Knowing that no other work was available, many Detroiters left, and building permits plummeted by 90 percent between 1926 and 1933.[3] As in previous instances of economic instability, the city's African American population was among the hardest hit. The Depression reminded Detroiters of their "feast or famine" economy, employing anyone with a pair of hands in high times, laying thousands off in low times. And these were low times indeed.[4]

Beyond its social repercussions, the Depression introduced a devastating new physical trend to downtown, as progress increasingly meant demolition rather than creation. Instead of the next tall skyscraper or elaborate retail palace, as in the previous decade, the highest and best land use for many downtown parcels went from marble and steel to tarmac and tin. Urban planning and design efforts to counter this cycle hardly materialized, as the planning apparatus was decimated due to dwindling city property and business taxes. To avoid bankruptcy, the city was forced to drastically cut staff and wages, first focusing on reducing public works in districts with high tax delinquencies. This especially hurt the city's oldest districts adjacent to downtown, as their relatively low-skilled residents were among the hardest hit by layoffs. By 1931, all public improve-ment projects in the city were halted.[5] Without proper staff and budget, strong legal and political backing, or any investment to guide, the City Plan Commission mostly retreated to a reactive role, not even able to make full use of federal investments during the Roosevelt era. Instead, most citywide planning effort was left to the newly instated Detroit Housing Commission, overseeing the slow start of public housing develop-ments under Roosevelt's administration.[6] During most of the Depression, the shape of downtown Detroit was left to the market, which mostly followed prompts by down-town's only steady visitor—the automobile.

Retail customers were among the first to abandon downtown. As the spending power of impoverished Detroiters plummeted, they especially put off buying durable goods of the sort traditionally bought in downtown stores.[7] Hudson's sales halved between 1929 and 1930 and Crowley-Milner's sales dropped by almost 75 percent.[8] Although both had created bargain basements during the previous decades, the reduc-tion in disposable income would drive many Detroiters to discounters such as Sam's Cut Rate store, which had opened in the now closed Detroit Opera House, soon expanding into adjacent buildings.[9] The nearby Temple Theatre wasn't lucky enough to find a new tenant, and decided to tear down its building for its "highest and best" land use—a parking lot, leaving one of the first voids right in the heart of downtown.[10] Despite efforts to modernize facades with federal subsidies, the number of stores in downtown declined by more than 25 percent during the Depression.[11] Pedestrian traf-fic measurements in 1936 showed a marked decline in footfall on Woodward Avenue compared to 1925, with other downtown streets even less traveled by pedestrians.[12] Along with footfall, business was slowly retreating from peripheral streets, concentrat-ing around the Woodward Avenue anchors to stay alive.[13]

The office market fared no better. Real estate appraisers initially argued that the city had simply overbuilt during the previous decades and that a correction was taking place, but matters would soon take a turn for the worse. Book's bold vision for a line of skyscrapers along Washington Boulevard was among the first to be taken off the table in 1929.[14] Many other projects would follow. The low point for Detroit's financial center came in 1933, when the impending bankruptcy of the Guardian Detroit Union Group prompted the governor to declare a two-week bank holiday, ultimately starting a second national wave of financial turmoil.[15] Stunned by the unannounced shutdown, the city fell into silence, downtown into darkness. While both Ford and General Motors soon funded new banks out of the ruins of their predecessors,[16] office vacancy soared to over a third of Detroit's downtown stock, and the consistently high taxation of now empty buildings prompted many owners to cut their losses and demolish their premises. As shown in figure 5.1, downtown building demolitions rose sharply during the Depression, exacerbated by inflated local tax appraisals and the federal Works Progress Administration's aid to remove "obsolete and unsafe" buildings.[17] Even City Hall only narrowly escaped the sledgehammer despite an onslaught of proposals to replace it.[18] Some private building owners decided to clandestinely burn down their buildings for insurance money, as returns were fixed at vastly inflated pre-Depression rates.[19]

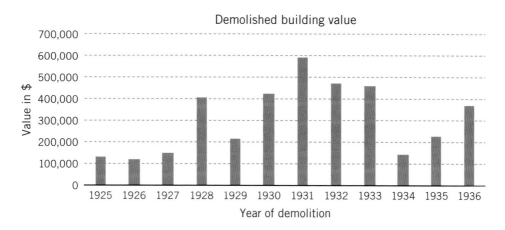

5.1

Value of buildings demolished in downtown Detroit for each year between 1925 and 1936. Redrawn from Orin F. Nolting and Paul Opperman, "The Parking Problem in Central Business Districts," ed. Public Administration Service (Chicago: R. R. Donnelly & Sons, 1938), 3.

After more than a century of rapid growth, downtown Detroit had begun to shrink. This contraction wasn't even, but exacerbated the divide between the densely built-up core of downtown Detroit and the fringe that had rapidly eroded since the 1920s. As office and retail tenants had many choices of where to locate, they increasingly retrenched to central business blocks, leaving the downtown fringe to wither. City valuation records substantiate that while land values sharply decreased in downtown as a whole, they especially plummeted in districts that were right outside the business core. Among of the first victims of this contraction were the hard-hit blocks northwest of Grand Circus Park.[20] Pushed by declining land values, level taxes, and rising vacancy, more and more peripheral building owners began to understand Max Goldberg's rationale for parking devised in the previous decades. With building tenants leaving in droves, parked cars remained the landowners' only viable source of income: while the total number of downtown commuters had declined sharply between 1928 and 1935, the number of commuters by car actually increased.[21] Parking made increased sense as a stand-alone enterprise, even prompting the demolition of relatively young and valuable commercial buildings.[22]

One building's loss could mean another's gain, as demolished buildings' open lots helped provide parking for holdouts. As a result, "bald spots" of parking began to amalgamate into a ring of parking around downtown by the end of the 1930s.[23] By the middle of the decade, Goldberg's firm held 36 of these lots, and had been joined by several other parking lot chains.[24] The sheer number of lots, most of which were unpaved, was enough to cause veritable dust storms by the mid-1930s.[25] While many Detroiters lamented the erosion of their downtown, some praised the demolition of the "scores of cancerous buildings that had made the town hideous" and the promises it brought for beautification.[26] The city even considered condemning more lots to ease downtown's parking shortage and "enhance the appearance of the City by clearing out many of these unsightly structures and also to boost the value of substantial structures nearby."[27] By the end of the decade, car parking had permanently transformed the downtown landscape, as described in a *Life* magazine article: "Detroit probably has more parking lots than any other big city in the world. Even in the downtown section, there is a parking lot on almost every block and the sun glistens on the tops of mile upon mile of parked cars. … But [downtown] Detroit was not designed for the motor age."[28]

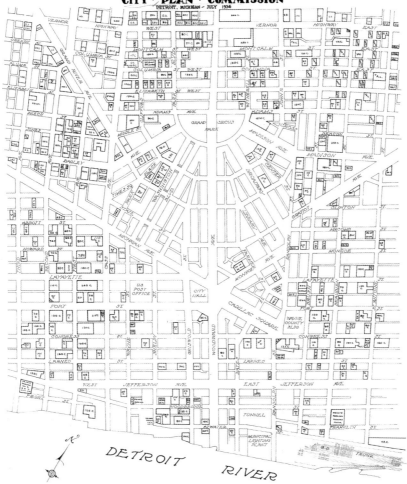

5.2

Parking lots pervaded the downtown periphery by 1936, as demonstrated in this City Plan Commission map. Map by Detroit City Plan Commission, 1936; image courtesy of University of Chicago Library.

Besides observing the rise of parking downtown, the *Life* article identifies a main underlying force behind the caustic cycle of increased car traffic and decreased downtown demand: decentralization. "Instead of having one business center, the city now has half a dozen, well out from the downtown area."[29] The underlying element was transportation: the cars that Detroit built were starting to radically alter the city's configuration, as downtown-accessible land was no longer limited by short walking radii or streetcar systems. Real estate appraiser Walter Kuehnle noted in nearby Chicago: "These changes [in transportation] are increasing our supply of land … within a reasonable time limit of the center of the city … to an almost unlimited supply."[30] Admittedly, Detroit's job base was already scattered throughout the region as factories located around railway transportation and easily assembled peripheral land, spawning factory settlements with their own retail and business centers. But for the first time, downtown functions weren't just being replicated elsewhere; they were actively moving out.[31]

The consensus in City Hall was still that infrastructure investments would reverse this cycle of decentralization, and the road-widening projects started in the 1920s continued. Yet progress was painfully slow, as the cash-strapped city had no money to pay for any of the approved widenings, which could only continue when the state and county stepped in and offered to pick up most of the funding.[32] Even then, the road widenings remained highly controversial. Especially in the higher-priced sections near downtown,[33] ongoing protests of local landowners along the widened streets frustrated condemnation proceedings and special assessments on finished projects.[34] For example, Woodward Avenue owners refused to agree to their offered compensation until 1934, nine years after the approval of the avenue's widening.[35] The widening would only take another year, and by 1935 a parade was held to celebrate the "city's salute to progress," with Detroiters expressing that "broad, light, straight ways will continue to open leading progress to prosperity."[36] While the local press touted the benefits of the newly widened avenue for Detroit's image, Depression-era single-story "taxpayer" buildings would strongly diminish its architectural character.[37] Furthermore, local realtors agreed that the widening had effectively killed the retail viability of the avenue, while mostly benefiting passing traffic.[38] By the mid-1930s, Detroit had lost its appetite for road widenings, approving Michigan Avenue as the last to be widened in 1935.[39]

Detroit's avenue widenings had not only proved arduous to implement and counter-productive to local business; they were also quickly obsolete, the widened roads simply filling up with traffic as soon as they opened. At a 1930 national highway convention, Rapid Transit Commission director Sidney Waldon acknowledged his department's rearguard fight, and first took the concept of the suburban superhighway a step further by focusing on completely grade-separated express lanes.[40] The car did not just need more space in the existing city, it needed its own environment altogether. By 1930, the preliminary 1925 proposal for a traffic belt of widened boulevards cutting through the downtown fringe had matured into a full-blown superhighway proposal by Wayne County, calling for an extension of the superhighway plan of the previous decade into the city itself, "entering the very heart of Detroit or as nearly so as possible, practically and economically." Although it would take decades before these plans were implemented, they proved an interestingly accurate prophecy of the traffic structure which still surrounds downtown Detroit today.[41] The new freeways cutting through Detroit's near west and east side surpassed any of their incremental predecessors, not only due to their vastly increased width and consequent demands for clearance, but also with the realization that a symbiosis could form between traffic relief and slum clearance. The future highways of Detroit were no longer envisioned as wider business streets, but as a separated environment for fast traffic, opening up the crowded city to light, air, and speed. Local real estate developers almost instantly picked up the opportunity to couple highway construction and urban renewal. In an article in the *Detroit Realtor*, the vice president of a local bank applauded the bold highway plan for clearing the "blighted area" surrounding downtown and transforming it into "proper housing and residential sections."[42]

The location of the new expressways in the near east and west side of the city was no coincidence, reflecting the growing racial and class division between central business district and inner-city residential interests.[43] While low property values and rising vacancies allowed an increasing number of African American Detroiters to escape the crime- and disease-ridden near east side, most were still concentrated in a few districts, living in tremendously overcrowded dwellings.[44] The result of this overcrowding and underinvestment by the city and private landlords was a spiral of decline aptly described by historian Conot: "The [inner] city, quite literally, was rotting."[45] As the clamor over

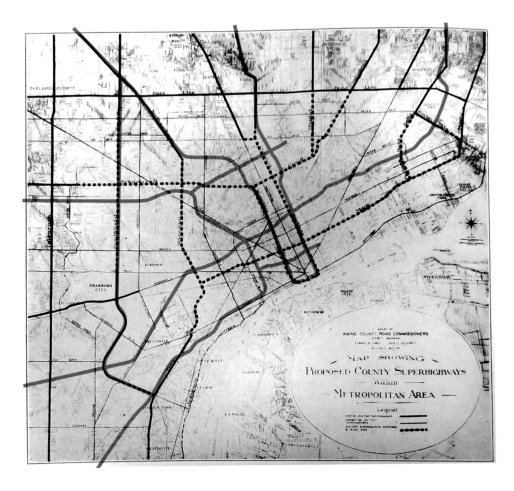

5.3

Map showing proposed superhighways within Detroit as dashed lines, 1930. The current freeway system is overlaid in red. Map modified by author, based on background map from Board of Wayne County Road Commissioners, "Proposed County Superhighways," *ATS Review* 9, no. 9 (1930).

the poor housing conditions and the growth of slums intensified during the 1930s, the city attempted to respond within its means. Sponsored by the federal Works Progress Administration, the extent of the poor housing conditions surrounding downtown was unveiled by Detroit's Real Property Survey that documented the physical, socioeconomic, and hygienic conditions of the city's housing. The results were disturbing but unsurprising: directly east and west of downtown, vast slum districts had formed that contained the city's oldest and most dilapidated structures, housing the poorest and most socially distressed residents.[46] The only difference was that the west side remained mostly white, while black residents were still mostly forced to remain east of Woodward Avenue—a result of ongoing racial restrictions on housing.

This pattern of racial segregation continued to be fiercely defended by white property owners and tenants in the city of Detroit, either through violence or through organizations like the Central District Protective Association or the Wider Woodward Association. The latter explicitly fought the growing momentum of the Detroit Housing Commission that materialized in a proposal for a racially integrated public housing development in the near east side, fearing that displaced African Americans would cross over into the west side. Instead, early housing commission leader Josephine Gomon achieved a compromise of an all-black public housing development, the Brewster Homes, a series of elaborate superblocks and communal spaces northeast of downtown. This 1,500-home development was located on several blocks of slum properties northeast of downtown and aimed at African Americans; it broke ground two years later with a ceremony led by Eleanor Roosevelt.[47] Despite this initial success and an ongoing federal funding stream, the housing commission's limited budget, competition with the City Plan Commission, and its frequent lack of local political support simply could not counteract the continued overcrowding of affordable housing in the city, especially for its poorest and most constricted African American residents.[48] The efforts of public housing proponents were especially frustrated by Detroit's simmering culture of racial prejudice, especially prevalent among frightened white homeowners and downtown business owners. This prejudice would significantly influence the course of inner-city redevelopment over the next decade, fueling an agenda of reintroducing the values and presence of the white middle class next to downtown Detroit.

Condition of residential structures

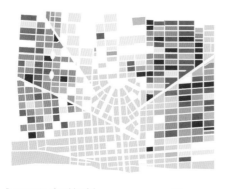

Race of household

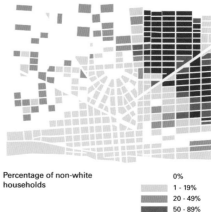

Percentage of residential
structures in need of major
repairs or unfit for use

0%
1 - 9%
10 - 19%
20 - 29%
30 - 39%
40 - 59%
60 - 79%
80 - 100%

No data

Percentage of non-white
households

0%
1 - 19%
20 - 49%
50 - 89%
90 - 100%

No data

5.4
Condition of residential structures and race of households for the downtown area, adapted by
author from the 1938 Detroit Real Property Survey. Note that the racial makeup of the west side
is completely different from that of the east side.

As the Depression came to a close after the mid-1930s, the landscape of downtown Detroit had altered significantly. Initial patterns of core stability, fringe erosion, and residential deterioration that had surfaced during previous decades of growth had intensified to form three distinct rings that can be recognized in figure 5.5. The Depression mostly left the solid financial (1), retail (2), and civic (3) core of Detroit intact. The city's most central dozen blocks suffered from a lack of construction activity or maintenance during the Depression but did not see any significant demolitions. Conversely, the scattered parking lots of the 1920s had grown into a ring of empty blocks directly adjacent to the core (4). The accelerating growth of parking lots had deteriorated many of the blocks in this ring to a point where some blocks hardly had any buildings left, leaving a twilight zone that was neither residential nor commercial but blighted both— a "creeping paralysis that gradually is encircling the downtown business district."[49] The ring of parking effectively cut off downtown from its surrounding residential districts (5), which were themselves in increasingly poor condition, illustrated by increasing vacancy and building inactivity. Walking from home to downtown was no longer a viable option, let alone an exciting experience. Street-widening projects (6) removed the majority of downtown Detroit's peripheral businesses, replacing them with tarmac or vacant lots. Furthermore, the deteriorating business climate had caused significant storefront vacancies, especially outside the main retail core on Woodward Avenue. Alarmingly, as the city's economy picked up during the late 1930s, these businesses did not return. The recovery revealed that the deterioration of downtown and its fringe was not just a cyclical phenomenon.

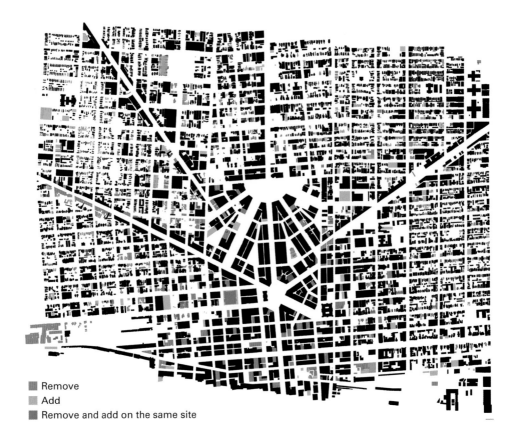

Remove
Add
Remove and add on the same site

5.5
Downtown Detroit's blocks, buildings, parcels, open
spaces, parks, and river in 1937.
Total square footage: 61.3 million square feet
Added since 1929: 2.9 million square feet
Removed since 1929: 6.8 million square feet
Percent of downtown that is vacant or parking lot: 16%

6 BATTLING BLIGHT: 1937–1951

As Detroit emerged from a turbulent decade of economic depression by the late 1930s, its urban planning apparatus arose again to find the city in bad repair and trending downward. While World War II would prompt a brief frenzy of activity, Detroiters realized that the future of their downtown and much of the inner city that surrounded it could no longer rely on market forces for growth, but would need concerted public action to bolster infrastructure, housing, and economic development. The 1940s marked a paradigm shift in how the city saw its downtown and planned for its future, shaping the large-scale interventions of the decade that followed.

Detroit's attitudes toward growth had first changed during the Depression, as the breakneck speed of physical growth in the region slowed almost to a halt.[1] Internally, the slowdown exacerbated the divide between Detroit and its surrounding suburbs. As middle- and upper-class families continued to leave Detroit for greener pastures, their departure resulted in vacancies or their replacement with people who had little choice of where to live, often African Americans. While suburbs grew during the 1930s, the downtown population declined, and the ring surrounding downtown fared even worse.[2]

By the end of the decade, it had become time to take stock. The economy had gathered steam again, with the auto industry mostly recovering to pre-Depression levels of economic output and employment, but downtown was increasingly left by the wayside.[3] Before the onset of World War II, Detroit had cemented its position as the nation's leading car manufacturing center. However, the typical downtown employment base of service, finance, insurance, civic, and real estate jobs occupied the lowest percentage of total city workers of any major American city.[4] By 1940, metropolitan Detroit had already become the second-fastest suburbanizing region in the United States, with more than half of its manufacturing jobs located outside the city limits.[5] This trend would only accelerate during the following decade, as World War II transformed Detroit from car to war manufacturing virtually overnight. Employment boomed, the number of manufacturing jobs increasing 40 percent just between 1940 and 1947 and unemployment dropping 97 percent between 1940 and 1943.[6] Yet again, this shift mostly occurred outside of downtown, and increasingly outside of the city altogether. As many factories shifted from car to war production at record pace, entire swaths of the region transformed into surprisingly self-sufficient "linear cities"—rapidly constructed settlements of factories, homes, and amenities around railway lines, constructed and managed with a machine-like efficiency that earned Detroit its title of "Arsenal of Democracy."[7] All construction effort in the city shifted to wartime demands, with drastic restrictions for any nonessential project like downtown repair and renewal.[8]

The drastic shift in the type and scale of wartime manufacturing prompted a leap beyond the contiguous urban growth that Detroit had seen thus far, as Henry Ford constructed a bomber airplane plant almost thirty miles west of downtown in Willow Run, connected by one of the nation's first grade-separated highways.[9] As workers sped from home to their shift on the new tarmac of the Willow Run and Detroit Industrial Expressway from 1941 onward, a new era of suburbanization loomed for the city and its core. The desperate need for wartime labor resulted in a decade of rapid growth in the region, which mostly occurred in rapidly constructed tract housing on the urban periphery.[10] As historian Arthur Pound describes in 1940: "The result is spaciousness— a charming and impressive spaciousness at some points, a fuzzy and slovenly spaciousness at others, with the two often in sharp, immediate contrast. … Detroit, you see, is so spacious that it does not have to use land thriftily. Fussy citizens can always move farther out on several hundred square miles of nearly level plain."[11] The density and verticality of downtown and the inner city gave way to the horizontal spread of Detroit's industrial suburbs: "The decentralized factory is surrounding itself with houses built along the one-story lines of the plant itself. Nearby is the modern supermarket where production-line selling is on a one-floor basis. The one-story school is there, too, with horizontal communication. All these are offspring of the modern factory."[12] Detroit's frontier had moved beyond its city limits, as the modern factory worker "frequently lives 40 miles or more from his job. He lives where he chooses, and works where he chooses."[13]

Many of those who moved out still frequented downtown for work, shopping, or leisure. Especially during the fuel-strapped war years, downtown experienced what would be its last hegemony. Retailers modernized and expanded their premises to retain customers and attract new ones. At street level, facades increasingly reflected the cleaner lines and more expansive window displays of the modern era.[14] Similarly, hotels and offices modernized their interiors, exemplified by a revamp of the Statler Hotel in 1937 and the inevitable follow-up by the nearby Tuller Hotel after a change in ownership in 1944.[15] In the sky, Hudson's added yet another few floors to parts of its building. Large military victories were celebrated downtown, and the bicentennial and upcoming 250th birthday of the city were lavishly celebrated in downtown storefronts.[16]

Yet the modernization of downtown's building stock did little to alleviate its structural challenges. Visitors continued to clog Detroit's most central streets with moving and parked cars, with no alleviation of automotive congestion in sight. Transit use continued to decline, with buses increasingly replacing the downtown-centered streetcar system.[17] Parking lots had become a common sight in downtown Detroit, as the battle for survival continued between older and newer buildings. Historian Pound praised the modernization of downtown for the car, "a crude drawing of the city of the future," which provided more daylight for offices and breathing space for visitors. Yet the modernity forced upon downtown by the automobile also intensified its sense of impermanence, typified by "the ugliness of the average parking lot and of the back-walls, never built for public gaze, that surround it. Such scars cloy the near view of business Detroit, even though the beholder rejoices that so many minor structures have been cleared away, permitting better vision of the more important buildings."[18]

More worryingly, an increasing cohort of middle- and upper-class émigrés didn't return downtown on a regular basis; the number of people visiting downtown Detroit decreased 16 percent between 1925 and 1940.[19] Rental income in the central business district had even dropped by half between 1929 and 1940.[20] A 1940s federal guide to Michigan noted: "There are crowds of pedestrians downtown, as in any big city, but these crowds soon thin out. Where, then are all the people? A vantage point near one of the large factories at the end of a working shift will provide the answer. Here is the

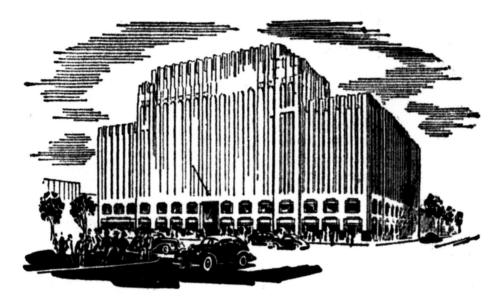

6.1

The rendering of the Saks Fifth Avenue store in an advertisement by the Fisher Brothers prominently features space for moving and parked cars. Charles T. Fisher, "Fisher & Company Announce That Saks Fifth Avenue Will Open a Store in the New Center Building," news release, March 26, 1940; "Saks Fifth Ave. to Open in City," *Detroit Free Press*, March 26, 1940.

most exciting spectacle in all Detroit."[21] Many former residents no longer needed to shop downtown: in the early 1940s more than twenty major outlying shopping centers had already been scattered throughout the city, many of which approached downtown in their scope and breadth of merchandise offerings. While daily needs had been met by countless minor shopping centers for decades, districts like Seven Mile and Livernois had grown into veritable "Avenues of Fashion," enabling their nearby patrons to avoid shopping downtown altogether.[22] When upscale retailer Saks Fifth Avenue wanted to open its sixth American branch in Detroit, it opted to bypass downtown in favor of the car-accessible New Center, right at the fourth-busiest traffic intersection of America.[23]

These businesses catered to the growing percentage of Detroiters who owned a car, 40 percent more than in the average large American city.[24] Growth clearly trended outward—the further away these centers were located from downtown, the more likely they were to increase in size.[25] Downtown entertainment also suffered from suburbanization, with an increasing number of downtown theaters resorting to burlesque shows, turning Monroe Avenue's entertainment district into "a street on which decent persons are loathe to pass."[26] While the local press acknowledged the growing decentralization of wealth, it downplayed the declining role of downtown that resulted. As long as plans were implemented to cater to those who had left downtown Detroit as a place of residence, they would at least continue to visit, and some could even be lured back to stay: "Downtown may have been overbuilt in the halcyon days of the twenties, but it is not by any means on the way out."[27]

As the middle class departed, the inner city saw a different type of growth. For the first time since the Depression, significant numbers of new, well-paying wartime jobs were accessible to African Americans, attracting a new wave of mostly Southern blacks eager to find work.[28] The newcomers were forced to live in the same few neighborhoods east of downtown that accepted African Americans, as they had been for over a century. The resulting population boom prompted a veritable explosion of new entertainment and cultural venues, some of which clustered along Hastings Street, others along St. Antoine Street in Paradise Valley, a new African American entertainment area that had grown from the establishments that settled between Black Bottom and downtown in the 1920s.[29] Dozens of black-owned hotels, theaters, cabarets, and nightclubs like the Club Plantation, Band Box, and Harlem Club hosted jazz and blues artists like John Lee Hooker, Ella Fitzgerald, and Count Basie, nourishing the following generation of Motown stars Diana Ross, Marvin Gaye, and Stevie Wonder.[30] Paradise Valley grew to an analog of downtown Detroit for African Americans, counting around 300 businesses at its peak in the early 1950s, some of which made millions in annual revenue. The district had started its own newspaper, the *Michigan Chronicle*, in 1936, and even informally elected its first mayor that same year: Roy Lightfoot, a popular local nightclub owner.[31] White Detroiters continued to visit the black and tan establishments in the Valley, and blues artists like Hooker reached an international audience. By the late 1940s, Hastings Street had reached such a status that it featured in popular songs like "Hastings Street Opera," "Hastings Street Woogie Man," and "Boogie Chillen."[32] Former resident and later mayor Coleman Young described the district as "a thrilling convergence of people, a wonderfully versatile and self-contained society. It was degenerate, but not without a lofty level of compassion. It was isolated, but sustained by its own passion. It was uneducated, but teeming with ideas. It was crowded, but clean. It was poor, for the most part, but it was fine."[33]

The growth of black culture in Detroit may read as one of flourishing, but can just as easily be interpreted as one of necessity. While Paradise Valley's black and tan entertainment venues continued to cater to mixed-race audiences, African Americans remained unwelcome in many downtown establishments and still had to live in or near the district.[34] A growing number of African American wartime workers arriving in an unwelcoming city faced severe limitations on where they could live and were forced to take the lowest-paid jobs in the war plants, if they were accepted at all.[35]

Especially the African American housing situation became increasingly untenable. The near east was at a boiling point, with its vast swaths of overcrowded and undermaintained dwellings resulting in significant social and hygienic distress.[36] By the late 1940s, the *Michigan Chronicle* reported on the inferior housing conditions for most black Detroiters, concluding that "the Negro pays more for less."[37] The neighborhoods to the west and north of downtown underwent similar overcrowding and social pressure, but catered to a different audience. The Cass Park neighborhood was flooded with southern white workers ("hillbillies" in common parlance) due to its affordable apartment housing, excellent connectivity to urban employment and long-distance bus lines, ample entertainment venues, discrimination against their moving into other neighborhoods, and their own discrimination against African Americans, who still lived mostly east of Woodward Avenue. Most new residents of the newly named "Tennessee Valley" were single, male, and poorly educated—rapidly becoming a class of "forgotten people." Some returned unsuccessfully to the South, some climbed the social ladder to the suburbs, others lacking social mobility remained in the area.[38] As a result, Cass Park spiraled into decline. By the mid-1940s, the district's once stately mansions had become a "blighted area" of "dismal structures … in bitter need of paint and repair."[39]

While the Detroit Housing Commission was able to construct wartime housing for white workers, it was mostly unable to relieve African American housing pressures, as white Detroiters fiercely resisted any African American public housing entering their neighborhoods—or any African Americans, for that matter. Detroit's existing over-crowded African American districts had no room for more clearances to make way for public housing, preventing an easy expansion of the Brewster Homes, which remained the only African American public housing project at the dawn of the 1940s. The lengths to which white homeowners would go to maintain racial segregation is demonstrated by their intimidation and assault of African Americans who attempted to move into the suburban Sojourner Truth public housing project. The federal government already feared this would happen, ultimately allowing African Americans to settle in the neighborhood after several flip-flops and significant local pressure from the city, labor and civil rights activists, and the Sojourner Truth Citizens Committee. It took thousands of city and state police officers and guardsmen to protect the first half dozen African American families who moved into the neighborhood.[40] African Americans who wanted to escape their near east side confines by buying a home also faced an uphill battle, as the federal government refused to insure mortgages in integrated districts, mapped for their Home Owners Loan Corporation in the late 1930s. Realtor complicity and overt racism in suburban cities like Dearborn, Ferndale, and Grosse Pointe further limited African American housing mobility.[41]

The feverish competition for jobs and housing between whites and African Americans in wartime Detroit prompted federal officials and the national media alike to warn that the city had turned from Dynamic to Dynamite.[42] Their fears came true as a race riot erupted in 1943. Starting with a scuffle on a hot summer day on Belle Isle, anti-black violence soon spread to downtown and the near east side. Spurred by unsubstantiated rumors, white Detroiters began to assault African Americans across the inner city, prompting retaliation. One of the worst battlegrounds was on Woodward Avenue just north of downtown, as the street had become a dividing line between races in the city. Despite various warnings, police were woefully underprepared for the situation, and the mostly white force suffered from its own bias against African Americans, killing seventeen black and no white Detroiters.[43] When federal troops had to be called in to restore order, the damage had been done. Dozens of people, mostly African American, had been killed, and the widespread media coverage of racially motivated murders on familiar downtown street corners had forever changed the perception of Detroit's urban core.[44] The aftermath of the 1943 riots exacerbated racial prejudice and accelerated the flight of mostly white middle-class Detroiters from the city. This left African Americans among the city's only growing demographic, with over 62,500 African Americans arriving during World War II alone. As white Detroiters left the city, African Americans were finally able to move into new districts, with especially the growing black middle class now able to move out of Black Bottom and Paradise Valley. This relieved population pressure on these districts but also prompted the decline of their African American entertainment offerings in favor of newer clubs to the north and west. Many downtown venues remained inaccessible to African Americans well into the 1950s, and Detroit's "golden age" of jazz occurred in far-flung clubs like the Blue Bird Inn, over four miles west of downtown.[45]

After decades of social, economic, and physical signs of trouble, downtown Detroit faced a critical juncture by the 1940s. Central business owners were increasingly perturbed at the loss of suburbanized customers and workers, most of the central building stock had seen no maintenance beyond fresh paint since 1929, traffic came to a daily standstill, and deteriorating social and physical conditions around downtown had created a literal and figurative tinderbox. The steady deterioration of Detroit's oldest residential districts, only blocks away from the city's main retail and office skyscrapers, was aptly described by a Detroiter in the early 1940s, for whom downtown had become a "desert island in a swamp of blighted areas."[46] A low point was the condemnation of City Hall itself in 1940 after a section of its balcony fell off a year before.[47] The consensus was that something had to be done; but while the problems facing downtown were socially loaded and multifaceted, the response was technocratic and heavy-handed—at least initially. Over the next two decades, downtown Detroit would be radically transformed by a unique mixture of deep public pockets, political willpower, and a genuine desperation and drive to modernize.

A paradigm shift in thinking about reshaping the city came with the election of Mayor Edward Jeffries on a platform of modernization in 1940. Jeffries launched a

$730 million capital improvement program to repair almost two decades of neglect.[48] This infusion of money allowed the City Plan Commission to awake from its Depression-era dormancy, receiving a boost in staffing budget to enable it to venture beyond its most basic daily duties.[49] Together with the still-powerful Housing Commission, it set the gears in motion to reshape Detroit's urban landscape. Within a year of Jeffries's inauguration as mayor, the City Plan Commission had drafted a zoning ordinance based on the modernist urban tenets of a five-part separation between dwellings, workplaces, commerce, recreation, and traffic.[50] Where earlier zoning ordinances had failed to launch, City Council enacted such zoning in 1940.[51] Partly this success was the result of Jeffries's popularity at the beginning of his term, but a deeper reason can be found in the acceptance of zoning by citizens and business interests in light of the city's social and physical deterioration. Residents and politicians blamed the lack of proper zoning for the encroachment of incompatible land uses such as manufacturing plants, car garages, and multifamily dwellings into otherwise stable residential neighborhoods, decreasing their land values and increasing the chance of spreading deterioration.

For central business interests, a main reason for this change of view about zoning was the realization that downtown was not going to grow any further, so that zoning was no longer perceived as a threat to growth.[52] Instead, central business owners focused on the beneficial effects of zoning in stabilizing the downtown fringe and improving the residential inner city as an act of self-protection.[53] In reality, however, much of the damage had already been done, especially in the neighborhoods close to downtown. Existing conflicting land uses were granted exemptions, and new intrusions were easily permitted by the Board of Zoning Appeals—especially if they could be justified on economic or military grounds. As a result, the new zoning ordinance did relatively little to stem the erosion of downtown by parking lots, and of its nearby districts by the familiar sprinkling of workshops and factories.[54]

Mayor Jeffries soon took a much more powerful step that would lay the groundwork for most of the present-day urban form of downtown: the preparation of a comprehensive master plan. Gaining the political, popular, and financial power to enact a drastic transformation of Detroit's existing urban fabric required a strong narrative of urgency and growth. A key element of this narrative was the identification of "blight" as the enemy of urban order and prosperity—a term that had gained traction in American

6.2

The Detroit Housing Commission deemed most areas around downtown blighted in 1940. Redrawn by author after Carl S. Wells, "Proposals for Downtown Detroit" (Urban Land Institute, Washington, DC, 1942), 16.

planning discourse since the 1930s. Taking its information from the 1938 Real Property Survey, the City Plan Commission had concluded that one-third of Detroit was blighted, a condition that hinged as much on the condition of homes and residents as on the perceived burden these areas placed on the city's tax revenue. While blight was difficult to define, it was characterized by the commission as "old dilapidated buildings crowded together on narrow lots, lacking adequate light, air and sunshine … marked by unusually high rates of disease, crime and delinquency."[55] As was to be expected, blight seemed to concentrate around downtown: a vast majority of the area within the Grand Boulevard ring directly surrounding the urban core was considered blighted (see figure

6.2). A staggering 38 percent of dwellings in this inner-city area were considered substandard by the Detroit Housing Commission by the 1940s—with a slightly higher rate still to the east of Woodward Avenue.[56] Planners feared blight would spread to "invade and destroy every neighborhood in the community," not least including downtown.[57]

The popularization of the concept of blight coincided with the realization of many business owners in Detroit and others that the deterioration of downtown-adjacent districts resulted in more than just a worse view from the central office and department store towers. A "dirty collar" of slums was threatening to suffocate business, and its clearance became a matter of commercial self-interest, not just the rather altruistic improvement of working-class lives that underlay the 1930s public housing projects. As downtown acknowledged that it was not going to grow much further, surrounding slums transformed from temporary conditions that would give way to further growth into threats to downtown's continued prosperity.[58] Especially this realization would drastically accelerate urban renewal during the postwar era. After years of standing on the sidelines or even obstructing slum clearance projects (in the case of the Brewster Homes housing project by the Wider Woodward Association), a curious coalition of central business interests, housing reformers, and public bodies were preparing for action against this newly coined enemy.

Acknowledging the importance of countering inner-city deterioration, Jeffries convened a "blight committee" in the first year of his tenure that consisted of downtown business interests and civic leaders. Besides surveying blight, the committee recommended the development of a master plan and focused on legal frameworks for countering urban blight, as Jeffries called for "a comprehensive outline for the future physical development of the city," arguing that "proposals to rectify 'blighted' areas cannot proceed without such a plan."[59] In 1943, a newly organized committee started work on the first master plan in almost two decades.[60] Where they had foreseen continued vertical growth in the 1920s, planners now took a far more regional approach that took cues from the horizontality of Detroit's growing suburbs. City planner George Emery went so far as to acknowledge that Detroit's ongoing suburbanization was but an expression of "the escape from the congestion of the city for the relief of the openness of the country," adding that "the transfer of city dwellers into the country, with its accompanying urbanization, must at the same time involve a degree of ruralization of the congested core of our city."[61]

Emery's statement marked a startling twist in the still-ongoing dual view that downtown should learn from or even emulate the suburbs, and that downtown's progress didn't necessarily mean extra density. The new approach aimed to encourage middle- and higher-income groups to return to the central city by wholesale demolition and replacement of the blighted districts surrounding downtown, bolstering the income of downtown retail stores and the hegemony of downtown offices as a workplace, countering their "decline as an inevitable concomitant of the decentralization of business."[62] Furthermore, redevelopment was mostly to be financed by private investors as "private capital should do its part towards meeting the blight problem of cities as a matter of self-preservation and enlightened self-interest as well as sound investment."[63] Other funds would come from the expected increase in property tax revenue after low-rent slums were converted to higher-class areas. Financially, the city hardly had an option, as federal subsidies were still in an early stage and city coffers were running low. Despite the rapid worsening of the African American housing shortage and vehement opposition by civil rights activists, the city set a redevelopment machine in motion that would replace thousands of African American residents with suburban housing and infrastructure. While city officials like Mayor Jeffries and his successor Van Antwerp sympathized with the predicament of African Americans, attempting to build public housing for this demographic, they also felt fiscally obligated to stem the beginning middle-class exodus from the city.[64] The election of conservative Mayor Cobo in 1949 ended this sympathy, as he was expressly elected by white homeowners on a platform of continuing confinement and segregation of African Americans. After replacing defiant public housing advocates with willing subordinates from the private sector, he canceled all public housing projects in the city's suburban areas where much of his voter base resided. The few remaining projects were concentrated in the inner city around downtown, worsening the divide between city and suburb.[65]

In the early 1940s, Mayor Jeffries effectively set in motion an almost three-decade-long era of drastic urban renewal that would alter the face of inner-city Detroit forever. Of urban renewal's two strong pillars of slum clearance and highway construction, slum clearance came first. After two brief detours on the west side of the city and a private proposal to raze most of Corktown for apartments,[66] a "slum territory" just east of downtown Detroit was chosen as a representative pilot site to test the mayor's and the blight committee's approach to redeveloping the inner city. Joining other deindustrializing cities like Pittsburgh and Philadelphia, Mayor Jeffries announced the redevelopment as the Detroit Plan in 1946, "a program for Blight Elimination" as well as for countering suburbanization—white flight, in other words.[67] The chosen area was at the heart of African American Black Bottom, which was mainly targeted for renewal in order to stabilize the land value and development potential of downtown, with the rehousing of existing Black Bottom residents only a secondary consideration.[68] The Detroit Plan was originally mainly concerned with attracting higher-income residents to protect downtown, as "surrounding the central commercial district with an increasing number of [low-income] inhabitants of subsidized housing would not be conducive to the maintenance of that district."[69]

This aim was fiercely debated by various government organizations, builders, and politicians, and was ultimately settled under Cobo's conservative administration in favor of mixed-income and mixed-density housing—expressly rejecting any public housing.[70] His vision led the *Michigan Chronicle* to denounce Cobo's version of the Black Bottom redevelopment as a "Jim Crow Project." The NAACP similarly condemned the process.[71] Yet by the late 1940s, Black Bottom's economic, political, and population base had already significantly weakened, as African Americans were able to leave the district and the Paradise Valley entertainment district had reached a state of "financial paralysis." As a result, the district's residents were unable to stop the condemnation of land, which started the year after the Detroit Plan was published. Detroit's radical clearance strategy predated the expansion of federal support for urban renewal with the Housing Act of 1949, which only helped alleviate the ballooning land purchase costs during the latter part of the project. When the neighborhood's last 43 blocks were condemned by 1951, the city had spent almost twice as much for the land as originally envisioned. With Black Bottom erased, the Gratiot Project was born.[72]

The second challenge a downtown revival had to overcome was chronic car congestion, which persisted even during the fuel-strapped wartime years. The rapid growth of Detroit's suburban population during World War II and the streetcar strike of 1943 fueled Detroiters' love of automobility, with per capita car ownership the second highest in the nation after that of Los Angeles. A continuing problem was how to park this growing number of cars. For decades, public and private authorities had floated various ambitious plans to raise parking capacity, but a shortage of spaces persisted downtown, with estimates of the shortfall varying between 3,000 and 20,000 spaces.[73] While the municipality continued to operate park-and-ride lots via its Department of Street Railways in the periphery of downtown, it had not yet entered the core parking market in the early 1940s. Instead, the city continued to focus its efforts on constructing a ring of parking lots surrounding the "business heart" around Woodward Avenue, even though private interests were perfectly able to chisel out parking lots on their own in this area.[74] The main issue for downtown was that it could only compete with car-accessible suburban rivals by locating parking closer to the heart of the city, as Hudson's acknowledged in constructing a multilevel parking deck a few blocks from its downtown store.[75] After finally convincing downtown business interests of the need for government intervention in providing parking in 1948, Hudson's treasurer became the first leader of the newly created Municipal Parking Authority.[76] Private parking lot interests fought the municipal efforts tooth and nail, initially securing legal victories—demonstrating that they were a maturing industry.[77]

Beyond car parking, downtown's access roads remained congested, despite the opening of the wider Michigan Avenue in 1938, the city's final widened arterial.[78] Almost from the outset, the widening schemes had proved obsolete. Firstly, the widenings were unable to cope with Detroit's postwar explosion in car ownership, while transit continued to wither due to a lack of political backing and funding.[79] Rather than implementing proposals for underground rapid transit, Detroit's last remaining streetcars were replaced with cheaper buses, despite warnings that this neglect would exacerbate downtown decline.[80] The widened arterials also failed to bring any of their advertised benefits to surrounding landowners, instead burdening them with assessments to the point of bankruptcy. By the end of the 1930s, a local real estate broker concluded that Vernor Highway, the city's first major road widening, "is now a street of vacant lots and rundown buildings … the heavy traffic on a widened street kills its value."[81] By the late 1940s, Detroiters acknowledged that the widenings had failed to achieve any of their original promise.[82] They were ready to take more drastic steps to accommodate traffic.

CHAPTER 6

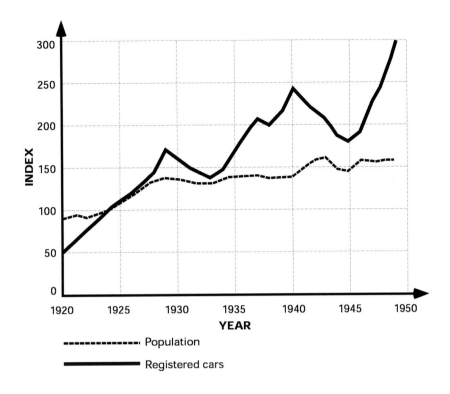

6.3
Detroit's population and number of registered cars indexed
to 1923 values demonstrates a rapid growth of car
ownership after the Depression, with only a brief respite
during World War II. Image by author, from "Detroit's
Critical Transportation Needs" (City of Detroit, 1950).

Acknowledging defeat, the state decided to abandon the remaining street widenings and instead focus on a new project: an east-west crosstown superhighway between downtown and New Center, following the line of what is now Interstate 94.[83] Freeways were not new to the city, as Detroit had already gained experience in suburban limited-access highway design in its 1925 master plan, and the wartime construction of the Willow Run and Detroit Industrial Expressway for factory workers and cargo had proved that highways were a highly effective vessel for large amounts of car traffic. But all these highways were conveniently located outside of the urban area. In order to reconnect downtown to the expanding universe of customers and workers, the highway had to reach right into its core.

From the beginning, the concept of urban freeways hinged not only on traffic improvements but also the other urban renewal pillar of slum removal. Inspired by the initial 1930 proposals for an urban freeway system (thwarted at first by the Depression), in the late 1930s then-city treasurer Albert Cobo proposed two north-south highways cutting through the city's near east and near west districts, implying a block-wide "clean sweep of all structures" in their path. The Detroit Real Estate Board agreed, especially supporting the plan's potential to "do away with some of our blighted areas."[84] Downtown business interests soon joined the chorus, as they realized that freeways could reconnect them to suburban workers and customers.[85] As the federal government was slowly warming to the prospect of funding these massive improvement schemes, Detroit and Wayne County leaders dusted off their proposals by 1939.[86] The state came on board the next year.[87] With this strong backing, Mayor Jeffries appointed a Street Improvement Committee which in 1943 advised the construction of an extensive expressway system, the first piece of which would run from downtown northwestward and was named after former mayor and Council member John C. Lodge in 1944.[88] City Council soon approved the entire network. The approved system that was published in a report in 1945 comprised almost the same highway ring around downtown that was drawn in 1925 and in 1930, with spurs into the entire region. Highway routes consciously avoided "blasting through an established neighborhood" and instead ran through struggling Corktown and Black Bottom, considered "belts of depressed property."

The plan clearly proposed combining expressway planning with "genuine, large scale slum clearance," which in the case of the Hastings Expressway through Black

Bottom would "invite and justify private development of wide scope along it." Expressways aimed to "stabilize" residential areas by buffering them from other land uses such as commercial and industrial areas, further legitimizing their construction between the central business district and its surrounding neighborhoods. Furthermore, they were to be sunk below ground level to minimize their presence in the city,[89] and their landscaped medians were even touted as assets to surrounding districts.[90] Reality proved much harsher, as completed highways, even when sunken, severed neighborhoods from one another and from downtown. Vibrant business districts like Hastings Street fell to the highway engineer, displacing thousands of residents and businesses in the path of progress. Some Black Bottom residents argued that the choice of running a freeway down their main street was an express act of political aggression. Hastings Street resident Mark Mitchell recalls: "When they broke up Hastings Street, they broke up the power. They broke the black power. Because of all the money was staying [in Black Bottom]."[91] The African American community did not have the political power to halt construction. To make matters worse, the expressway only served those who drove, despite a promise of a major public transit upgrade to accompany road construction, including several subway lines under downtown and express lines following the new sunken expressways.[92] Especially the difficult financing at the local, state, and federal levels continued to put transit at a great disadvantage to the automobile expressways outlined in the same document.[93] As had happened with past plans, the master plan's car infrastructure would be realized while the transit portion was left behind.

The first highways to be constructed were the Edsel Ford Expressway (an extension of the Detroit Industrial Expressway into the city, named after Henry Ford's son) and the John C. Lodge Expressway.[94] Ground was broken on both projects in 1947 after the federal government, state, county, and city agreed to jointly finance them, even before large-scale federal money became available. Detroit deemed its traffic crisis to be of such urgency that it even paid for the early construction out of pocket, with bond issues following to speed up construction.[95] A new Department of Streets and Traffic was formed in 1951 to expedite the design and construction of more expressways in search of solutions to the traffic "crisis."[96] Despite the confident press statements and broad local support for urban expressway construction, the expressways were quite a big gamble for the city's future. Ominously, Mayor Jeffries would state in a U.S. House Committee hearing that he wasn't sure whether the expressway plans would help

Detroit by bringing people back to downtown or ultimately ruin the city by allowing even more residents to move to the suburbs, aided by the fast links to downtown—a fear shared by some contemporaries that ultimately proved well-founded.[97]

The zoning amendment and plans for slum clearance and expressway construction were ultimately consolidated in the city's first comprehensive master plan, completed in 1951—itself a product of more than a decade of planning and public vetting.[98] While still framing the city along lines of transportation like its 1920s predecessor, the document also provided guidance for land use as well as recreational, educational, and public service amenities, ultimately providing a "basic pattern for the guidance of normal change and growth within the city's legal and financial capacity" for the following twenty-five years. Inspired by the work of Finnish architect and urbanist Eliel Saarinen at the nearby Cranbrook Academy of Art, the main structuring element of the 1951 master plan was the neighborhood unit, balancing "the individual citizen's family life and his work in the city" through a nested system of neighborhoods and communities.[99] A system of relatively self-sufficient districts of roughly 100,000 inhabitants each that still fed into downtown acknowledged Detroit's decentralization while continuing to seek the integration of neighborhoods into a hierarchical system that reinforced the hegemony of the urban core.[100] The master plan also directly shaped the form of downtown as it provided guidance on redevelopment sites around the urban core, a combination of public housing, infrastructure, and civic projects. The ring around downtown was to be freed of any dwellings, as the fringe and Corktown were designated as light industrial areas. Only northern Brush and Cass Park and eastern Black Bottom remained as residential districts.

The modernist vision for Detroit had crystallized in this master plan document, shaping the city as a coherent settlement with neatly separated land uses, furnished with public amenities, connected by an extensive network of highways, and most importantly free of the dirt, congestion, and blight that had characterized the city thus far. A master plan for Detroit's renewed downtown riverfront was integrated into the document as a concrete microcosm of this vision, clearing the formerly grimy riverfront warehouse district for a campus-like setting of "harmony and a high degree of architectural excellence" with a mixture of cultural, civic, and government buildings grouped around a central plaza dedicated to the veterans of both world wars. Detroit's oldest riverfront district had lost further relevance due to dwindling water-based

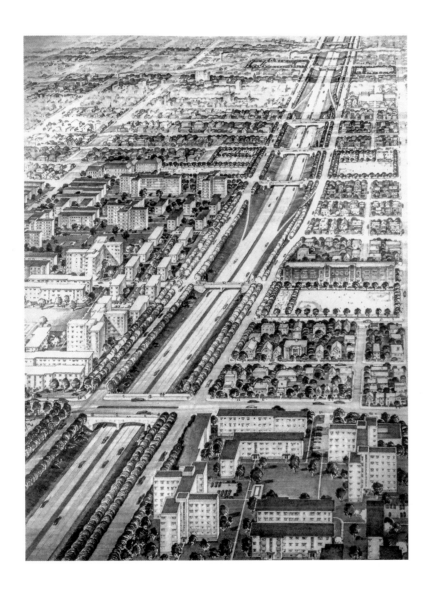

6.4

The vision for a modern Detroit as expressed by sunken expressways, modern housing, and recreational areas. W. Earle Andrews, "Detroit Expressway and Transit System" (Detroit Transportation Board, 1945), 16.

6.5

The 1951 master plan segmented the city into districts and zones. Image from City Plan Commission, "Detroit Master Plan" (Detroit, 1951).

transportation, prompting debate about its new purpose. In Detroit's pragmatic spirit, it was the pressing need for a larger convention hall that prompted the revisiting of the riverfront improvement.[101] It was this pragmatism that had enabled the City Plan Commission in 1939 to shake off its roots as a public organization "interested primarily in esthetic and ornamental physical features," while ironically still proposing a mainly physical plan for the riverfront civic center.[102]

The Ottoman-born Armenian architect Suren Pilafian, who had recently won a competition for the Wayne State University campus, was commissioned to draft a preliminary design for the waterfront center. An initial plan to have a downtown expressway loop run in a trench between downtown and the riverfront was quickly dismissed in favor of government offices north of an at-grade Jefferson Avenue.[103] Recommended by the Detroit chapter of the American Institute of Architects and following in his father Eliel's footsteps, Eero Saarinen finalized the design of this *Gesamtkunstwerk* of architecture, urban design, traffic engineering, and landscape architecture, instilling a much-needed dose of civic pride.[104] The project symbolized the drive started in the 1940s to clear Detroiters of their "inferiority complex" and convince them that "Detroit is a good city to live in."[105] In 1947, the Veterans Memorial Hall (the middle left mid-rise in figure 6.6) began construction as the first building of this ensemble. Across the street, one of the main elements was the City-County Building, built right on top of the Potomac District, which was still one of downtown's sore spots.[106] By 1951, Detroit's oldest main corner at Woodward and Jefferson avenues came down in the name of progress, with the jumble of commerce and entertainment of the illustrious Merrill Block making way for the marble and steel of modern governance.[107]

6.6

The Civic Center on Detroit's riverfront offers a unique sense of urban and architectural order.
Image courtesy of the Burton Historical Collection, Detroit Public Library. Original image at Yale University Library.

Remove
Add
Remove and add on the same site

6.7
Downtown Detroit's blocks, buildings, parcels, open
spaces, parks, and river in 1951.
Total square footage: 59.3 million square feet
Added since 1937: 3.0 million square feet
Removed since 1937: 5.0 million square feet
Percent of downtown that is vacant or parking lot: 24%

The 1940s was an era of hope and anticipation for a more modern future for down-town Detroit. Reality almost inevitably proved harder, and not all would benefit from downtown's progress. While the outlines of the modern city were certainly visible on the drawing boards, and while the bulldozers were preparing the way for new high-ways, housing, and institutional buildings, most new construction was still in the future in 1951 (figure 6.7). To the west of downtown, the first land clearance for the John C. Lodge Expressway is visible as a strip of scattered vacancies (1). Meanwhile, the land clearance for the public Jeffries (2) and Douglass (3) Homes had been almost com-pleted in the northwest and northeast portion of downtown. African American Black Bottom was still mostly intact, as land clearance for the Gratiot redevelopment was progressing slowly, marked only by the removal of scattered buildings and a single block (4). In downtown, the first building of the new Civic Center, the Veterans Memo-rial Hall (5), was finished, and the land for the next project, the City-County Building, had been cleared (6). Yet the grand plans for downtown had already had repercussions on existing businesses in the near east side. Especially on Hastings Street, the former main retail strip of the Black Bottom neighborhood, the consequences of planners' blight had forced businesses to abandon the area in droves (7). Furthermore, the blocks directly downtown continued their erosion into a ring of parking lots. Overall, the 1951 map shows as yet only a faint outline of the transformation that was envisioned for downtown. World War II had halted almost any new construction in Detroit, and even after the war most construction activity was taking place outside the city. The planners' determination to clear the districts around downtown may not yet have resulted in removals of buildings, but they did prompt a halt of any investment in this fringe, exacerbating its physical and social decline.[108] While the traces of transformation were drawn, they only solidified into steel, concrete, and tarmac in the decade that followed.

7 THE CITY OF TOMORROW: 1951–1961

At first sight, 1951 was a proud year for Detroit. As the Motor City celebrated the 250th anniversary of its founding, its population peaked at just under two million.[1] Almost a million eager visitors flocked downtown to witness about 20,000 parade participants reenacting important episodes of the city's history, with Hudson's unfurling America's largest flag on its Woodward Avenue facade. President Truman and Secretary of State Acheson joined the parade, and for good reason. Detroit was still a symbol of industrial prowess and military might; factory jobs were on the rise, as the close of World War II had spawned vastly increased consumption and the Korean War continued to fuel Detroit's war industry, despite a short recession in 1949. In 1951, the *New York Times* observed that "never in its history has Detroit been busier." Yet while the city still provided the central identity to its surroundings, the *Times* also observed that "almost half of Detroit lives outside Detroit," and the local press warned that "Detroit is rapidly becoming a city overshadowed by its offspring."[2]

Especially white middle-class Detroiters continued their exodus from Detroit, while industrial employers such as Ford, General Motors, and Chrysler were moving their operations to larger suburban plants in search of more space. Boosted by federal programs such as the GI Bill, VA mortgages, an expanding mortgage interest deduction, and accelerated depreciation programs, the metropolis moved out.[3] Detroit would lose 10 percent of its population in the 1950s, even as the metropolitan population and manufacturing job count continued to increase.[4] With Detroit past its peak, downtown was more aware than ever that the time for action had come. The 1950s marked the first decade when the sea of plans hatched over the past decades were able to come to fruition. Under new leadership, downtown would reinvent itself in a whirlwind of smaller and larger interventions that have shaped its form to the present day. Some of those would fall in line with the bold visions of the midcentury; many would not.

Time was running out for inaction. After the dust of World War II had settled, downtown clearly understood that the combined effects of decentralization, blight, and congestion were becoming permanent and beginning to intensify. The total assessed valuation of downtown properties had dropped by around 40 percent since 1929 because of deteriorating land and building values and continued building demolitions.[5] For over two decades, no noteworthy new construction had taken place in the downtown area, partly as a result of the restrictions on nonessential construction during World War II, partly also as a result of the overbuilding of office space during the 1920s. As new offices and stores were constructed in the suburbs, downtown's building stock looked tired in comparison.[6] A quarter of downtown's land was "going to waste as open lots" according to a local survey by the City Plan Commission, comprising parking and an increasing number of vacant lots.[7] Downtown was losing its luster as Detroit's cultural heart as well. The advent of television had significantly weakened the central entertainment venues, with over half of Detroit's movie theaters seeking tax relief and over a third having closed over the previous decade, including in downtown.[8] An old-time Detroiter lamented the loss of downtown's entertainment options: "Go to town any night now. The lights are out and the gayety is gone, and you are even frightened by the hollow echo of your own footsteps on a deserted highway."[9]

Retail had gone down a similar path. The neighborhood retail clusters that had formed around downtown Detroit over the past decades had grown into what retail geographer Richard Nelson recognized as "interceptor rings" of department store chains like Sears, Montgomery Ward, and Federal, challenging downtown not just for daily purchases but for a comprehensive variety of merchandise;[10] downtown sales dropped over 10 percent between 1948 and 1954 alone.[11] To counter the pressures of these suburban competitors, Hudson's department store ventured to build one of America's first suburban mall anchors in Southfield, just outside Detroit's city limits and about twelve miles northwest of their downtown flagship store. Detroit's middle and upper classes were increasingly moving in this direction, and Hudson's saw no option but to follow their disposable income. The result was Northland Mall, opened in 1954 as a fully designed environment that provided the—often female—suburban consumer with a safe, comfortable, and most importantly convenient shopping experience, "a model of enlightened planning and of social co-operation between merchants, architects, sculptors, artists and civic minded citizens ... entirely the creation of private enterprise."[12] Victor Gruen, the nationally renowned retail architect who designed Northland, warned Detroit that it would need to come up with a similarly strong and integrated plan for its downtown if it was to compete with his new center.[13]

Gruen's warning would soon be heeded. Perhaps the most important force in shaping downtown in the postwar era was planner and architect Charles Blessing, hired in 1952 as the director of the City Plan Commission. The choice seemed clear. Blessing was educated at some of America's top universities, he had a distinguished record of accomplishment as a leading planner in Boston and Chicago, and he served on planning committees for the American Institute of Architects and the American Society of Civil Engineers and for two terms as the president of the American Institute of Planning. A well-traveled man, Blessing was also a product of the modern era of urban design, valuing physical interventions over social concerns and technocratic solutions over political handwringing.[14] Arriving in a peaking city, Blessing wasn't fond of the layered history of Detroit nor of its impoverished inner-city residents. "We may now consider downtown Detroit as almost raw land,"[15] as he found the urban core to be held back by the "inertia of the horse and buggy pattern," a thoroughly modernist viewpoint that reflected his alignment with the views of the CIAM movement. In Blessing's eyes, downtown streets were unsafe due to heavy traffic, inner city parks were absent, and housing conditions unsanitary. Instead of fixing up the existing urban fabric, he wanted to propel the city into the automobile age, using the skills of architects and urban designers but also learning from the fast-paced creativity of Detroit's automotive designers. "The modern, automobile city would be in the blueprint stage now, not a distant hope, if we had use of just a small part of these [automotive design] brains and skills over the last 50 years." The car industry's growing attention to the cycle of obsolescence and reinvention resonated with Blessing's proposal for "restyling the very environment in which we live."[16] Within the inner-city ring of Grand Boulevard, Blessing wanted nothing short of a "New City," almost completely rebuilt according to modernist design standards of separated land uses in green settings, connected by

7.1
Middle-class Detroit's new downtown in the 1950s: Northland
Mall, a consumers' paradise, surrounded by ample parking.
Image courtesy of Walter P. Reuther Library, Archives of Labor
and Urban Affairs, Wayne State University. Image from *Detroit
News*, August 11, 1965.

expressways.[17] Blessing's linking of urban and automotive design would prove far less symbiotic than he imagined.[18]

Detroit planners had acknowledged for over a decade that their city was being over-taken by suburbia, and had reacted by seeking to emulate suburban design concepts. The suburban "freedom from noise, dirt, confusion and blight" was assumed to have taken the middle class out of the city, and by hiring Blessing, Detroit was aiming to bring them back.[19] By using "ultra-modern principles of townscaping," he sought to provide "plenty of light, air, and greenery around buildings" that would emulate the qualities of suburbia in the city's heart.[20] Planning for downtown Detroit would specifi-cally take cues from newly constructed suburban shopping malls such as Northland and its successor Eastland for sales and tenants.[21] Blessing was especially enamored of the separation of pedestrians and car traffic in Northland, as well as the intricate arrangement of parking and servicing for the mall's many tenants and visitors in a superblock setting. His plans would take these elements from Northland's design and implement them in and beyond Detroit's downtown, as he aimed to make the entire city as "safe, humanized, efficient and beautiful" as any suburban community.[22] More than in previous decades, Detroit understood the need to make radical changes within its current urban fabric, as the city had run out of room to grow and had to improve its current assets if it was to retain value. The editorial board of the *Detroit News* described the sentiment: "The built-up city can continue to grow by making better and more intensive use of its land. ... Barred from growing in space, Detroit is not barred from growing better."[23]

The shift from progress by expansion to progress by reinvention was well suited to the modernist paradigm of the time, personified by the courage if not downright radi-calism of Blessing. His arrival in Detroit came at an opportune time, as the federal government was ramping up its funding for urban renewal and highway construction, with Detroit ready to receive hundreds of millions of dollars to redevelop thousands of acres of urban land.[24] Blessing also enjoyed strong local support for his drastic visions for downtown renewal, as the newly reformed Central Business District Association of downtown banks and retailers vowed to "get into the battle ... right up to our necks" to gather support for his vision of a more modern downtown,[25] joined by the Detroit Board of Commerce. Blessing also enjoyed the support of Mayor Cobo, who ordered all city departments to focus on halting the trend of commercial decentralization and gathered a panel of experts to plan for downtown improvements, as "the future of the entire metropolitan area is dependent on an efficient, prosperous downtown Detroit."[26] Cobo stressed the loss of downtown's tax value and its repercussions for Detroit's balance sheet, a fiscal argument that resonated with city planners and federal lawmakers, as downtowns often accounted for more than a quarter of a city's tax revenues.[27] Calling downtown "the taxpayer's friend," Cobo argued that "its billion dollar investment in business … must not be allowed to deteriorate."[28] The local mainstream press was also in support of drastic action, and organized several committees to think about the future of downtown.[29]

Taking and improving on the advice from these various organizations, and building on the growing number of ongoing urban renewal projects, Blessing developed one of the nation's first three-dimensional urban designs for a complete central city, akin to Edmund Bacon's ambitious plans for central Philadelphia. Renderings and later models depicted a completely new "City of Tomorrow" within the Grand Boulevard area, with barely any existing structures left standing. Local leaders and Hudson's department store sponsored a massive $250,000 model of Blessing's vision for downtown, which was proudly displayed in the department store for its 75th anniversary in 1956, displaying Detroit's dream of a "city center rebuilt."[30] The work drew national attention, with Blessing and Mayor Louis Miriani proudly posing with the model for a *Life* magazine article on national urban renewal trends.[31]

The model accompanied a more detailed study of downtown in which Blessing divided Detroit's core into distinct rings, each of which warranted a different approach.[32] First, he recognized a healthy downtown core: an "area of tall buildings, intensified uses" that consisted of Detroit's retail, entertainment, institutional, and financial district, which was to be strengthened by a mixture of public interventions such as the growing Civic Center on the riverfront, but also by plans for a pedestrian mall on Woodward Avenue connecting the city's main retailers along an "atmosphere of calm and beauty."[33] Seeking to emulate Northland's consumer environment, Blessing designed a themed mall between Grand Circus and Campus Martius in which shoppers could enjoy fountains, greenery, a merry-go-round, and carnival-themed sculptures to emphasize the "carefree and gay pulse of the city."[34] While the local press

7.2

Detroit Mayor Louis Miriani (background) and planner Charles
Blessing (foreground) next to the three-dimensional model
of downtown Detroit, with existing buildings in gray and new
buildings in white. Image by Joe Clark, *Life*, August 25,
1958.

supported converting Woodward Avenue into "a downtown Northland" and the Central Business District Association was cautiously in favor, several larger retailers along the avenue opposed the idea for fear of losing customers, and traffic concerns stalled the proposal.[35] Blessing did effect several other public space improvements[36] which were often accompanied by traffic enhancements, such as the widening of Woodward Avenue between Campus Martius and the riverfront to make an "attractive approach to the [Civic Center] Plaza Area." Like the widening projects from the 1920s, this project displaced yet another cohort of small downtown businesses, but this time large new office construction was actually lined up to take their places. A "rather dingy, unimpressive sector" of nineteenth-century buildings including the Hammond Building, Detroit's first skyscraper, made way for the reflective modernist facades of the National Bank and Michigan Consolidated Gas buildings.[37] Mayor Cobo expressed Detroit's ongoing desire for progress: "This pleases me no end. It's nice to envision that you're going to tear down some old buildings and replace them with something that Detroit needs—a new, modern building."[38] Similarly, Washington Boulevard was extended and widened to the riverfront, accompanied in later years by the modern design of a twenty-six-story skyscraper for the Detroit Bank and Trust Company, set in its own landscaped plaza.[39]

Downtown's core was surrounded by what Blessing called the Intermediate Area, consisting of "parking areas and other uses serving the core." Here the Municipal Parking Authority was gathering steam, as the private parking industry failed to meet Detroit's demand for parking spaces, especially in central locations.[40] As downtown businesses clamored for more spaces at lower prices, City Council approved the construction of a centrally located municipal garage under Grand Circus Park in 1954, followed by a significant number of nearby lots and garages.[41] These efforts were very successful as parking continued to be in high demand, and the Parking Authority regularly floated plans for further expansion, perceiving parking as a key element of downtown's revitalization.[42] Private stakeholders would continue to raze peripheral buildings to construct parking lots or garages at a rapid pace, furthering the deterioration of this zone. A 1954 report stated that more than half of the lots in most blocks surrounding the downtown core were in use as parking lots, and by 1957 downtown counted more than 20,000 parking spaces. No end was in sight, as the demand for parking seemed

7.3

Renderings of Woodward Avenue's proposed pedestrian mall illustrate a pleasurable setting, filled with public art, entertainment, and greenery. Image from Detroit Tomorrow Committee, "Detroit Tomorrow Committee Report and Review" (Detroit, 1958).

insatiable.[43] Blessing certainly didn't shed any tears over the growing disconnection between downtown and its immediate periphery. As he considered most buildings in this ring obsolete, he ultimately planned to raze most of them and construct a "distributor loop" to ease access to parking lots.[44] This use would turn downtown into a retail core surrounded by parking lots—mirroring the shopping malls that Victor Gruen had designed around the city.

Next outside the ring of parking was the Fringe, an area of "blighted and obsolete structures, inadequate transportation facilities, and poor layout." Vermin infestations earned this area the dubious title of the "Rat Belt." Not only did the physical condition of the downtown fringe not fit into Blessing's vision of a modern downtown, but its weak social conditions were seen as an increasing threat to central business. The City Plan Commission squarely blamed a significant part of the decline of downtown on its context, as "the CBD has felt the repercussions of the blight in the fringe."[45] Hence, a significant portion of the city's effort to stabilize downtown would be through wholesale fringe clearance and redevelopment. This pattern reflected national trends of distinguishing between a productive downtown core and a dwindling surrounding frame of marginal businesses and slum dwellings, ripe for redevelopment.[46] Among Detroit's top priorities for this area was the completion of expressways that simultaneously bolstered downtown by providing connectivity to the suburbs while shielding central businesses from the rest of the deteriorating inner city. The local Real Estate Board praised the new expressways for defining downtown as a "new inner quadrangle," providing for "a downtown area moated on three sides."[47]

As in previous decades, the construction of expressways would take preference over the still-remaining rapid transit dreams. The American Society of Planning Officials warned that neglecting transit would accelerate the departure of businesses from downtown, stressing the essential fact that "it's people we want to move downtown, not cars." The majority of City Council agreed, but Mayor Cobo held that transit had simply proven too expensive and unfit for Detroit's low density.[48] The editors of the *Detroit News* concurred, stating that "we are deeply and enthusiastically committed to our expressways and to the rubber-tired transportation the people everywhere prefer. This is a preference with which an automobile city, mindful of the side on which its bread is buttered, is not disposed to quarrel."[49] Even though the newly opened Lodge and Ford expressways were as congested as the widened radials of the 1920s when they opened, Detroit's expressway program coordinator Glenn Richards argued this was only a sign of success as Detroit answered to the needs of its automobile citizens: "The day of subways and other rail services is past."[50] When a flood of federal funding for freeway construction became available under the 1956 Federal-Aid Highway Act, Detroit doubled its bet on freeway construction.[51] Along with the expressways, a complete ring of redevelopment areas was projected to be constructed around the central business district. With federal funds from the increasingly flexible Housing Acts of 1949 and 1954, a full-scale assault on blight in the downtown fringe would commence in the mid-1950s.[52]

The first wave of fringe redevelopment came through residential renewal. The Detroit Plan had established a beachhead in the 1940s, which continued in the next decade as the Gratiot Project. Demolition started in 1950 and displaced almost 2,000 mostly African American families by 1956, many of whom struggled to find alternative accommodations in the already overcrowded and highly restrictive housing market. Most residents ended up in dwellings that were as bad as or worse than those left behind.[53] While original residents clamored for space, the Gratiot Project ironically suffered from a lack of demand: when the land was offered for auction in 1952, no developer bid on the site as they loathed the strict sales conditions, feared the bureaucracy, and found it impossible to achieve the desired mixed-race housing in what was considered an African American district. In 1953, a first bid failed to meet the demands of city and federal regulators. The bid was canceled in 1954, and silence ensued.[54]

Under the effort of labor union leader Walter Reuther and the sponsorship of J. L. Hudson and the Big Three car manufacturers led by Henry Ford II, a Citizen's Redevelopment Committee was formed in the following months to break the stalemate.[55] The committee proudly presented its new vision for the area in 1954, "an integrated residential community of the most advanced design [that] can attract back to the heart of the city people who are finding their housing in the outlying sections of the city and its suburbs."[56] The committee subsequently joined forces with a private developer, who appointed German-born modernist architects Ludwig Mies van der Rohe and Ludwig Hilberseimer to redesign the district as a neighborhood that provided middle- and upper-class professionals "good city living close to their work"—signifying another upward shift in the target audience. High-rise structures and low-rise townhouses were integrated into a green environment that separated pedestrian and car traffic and centered on a central park with amenities for families, a residential version of Blessing's desired suburban downtown that broke with the past.[57] While a minimal amount of affordable housing was integrated into the plan, the main target audience for Lafayette Park (as the development was branded) was well-off professionals, as "their purchasing power will refinance the area." Ten years after the initial Gratiot project had been devised, construction finally started in 1956, and the first residential building, the high-rise Pavilion Apartments, opened two years later.[58]

Lafayette Park was almost universally praised in the professional and popular press, but the project had undeniably transformed from a low-income housing project, through a mixed-income community, into a refuge for the well-off, as leadership shifted between political denominations and development shifted from public to private.[59] Some of Detroit's African American elite like Motown director Berry Gordy and Congressman Charles C. Diggs Jr. did settle in Lafayette Park, but most non-whites were simply priced out, forced to move into the Twelfth Street corridor northwest of downtown. Many of Black Bottom's social issues simply shifted to this district, and were exacerbated by the move. While urban renewal and freeway construction drastically worsened the already tenuous housing conditions for African Americans, southern blacks continued to move to Detroit in search of opportunities.[60] A very small number of impoverished African Americans were able to move to the newly finished Frederick Douglass public housing project that was completed north of downtown in the mid-1950s.[61] Yet the project's federal mandate to house only the poorest Detroiters, combined with underfunded maintenance and a haphazardly designed tower-in-the-park format, soon turned this site and the nearby Jeffries Homes into socially problematic "concentrated foci of poverty." Furthermore, the project hardly made a dent the waiting list of tens of thousands of African Americans in search of replacement housing for the city's renewal ambitions.[62]

Next up were commercial redevelopment sites, enabled by the Housing Act of 1954, whose expanded allocations allowed for the funding of more nonresidential urban renewal projects. On the west side of downtown, a Skid Row had grown around Michigan Avenue over the past decades that housed most of the city's sizeable transient population.[63] City planners loathed the area's poor living conditions, high crime rates, and the financial burden it placed on the city by its high use of city services and low land value for such a central site.[64] Perhaps more than the living conditions in Skid Row, the city worried about the poor first impression for visitors entering downtown from the new John C. Lodge Expressway as they drove past run-down pawn shops, liquor stores, and bars.[65] The City Plan Commission therefore aimed to raze the 94-acre district and redevelop it for high-density housing and offices, a proposal that strongly resonated with downtown business interests.[66]

7.4
View of Frederick Douglass Homes. Image courtesy of the
Burton Historical Collection, Detroit Public Library, and
Rauhauser Photographic Trust.

Not everyone agreed with the removal of Skid Row.[67] While Skid Row inhabitants were commonly perceived as alcoholics and transients, the director of a local rescue mission argued that "not all of our people are victims of alcohol, some are workers from other states lured here by fancy advertisements, looking for jobs or waiting for their first pay check." The district also housed many day laborers and seasonal workers, arguably the lubricant in Detroit's ebb-and-flow industrial machine.[68] Furthermore, Detroit's Chinatown was located in the middle of Skid Row, and protested its annihilation.[69] More importantly to the downtown power structure, the removal sparked fears that displaced residents and the associated social issues would simply settle elsewhere.[70] Indeed, when clearance of the district began in the mid-1950s, Skid Row moved northward into Cass Park.[71] Already weakened by decades of social and physical decline and rising crime rates, that district became the new location for Detroit's transient population, served by charitable organizations that provided shelter and substance abuse counseling.[72] Cass Park's worn-out apartment buildings were further subdivided and leased to the highest bidder, or abandoned and left to squatters. By 1960, more than half of its residents were single and male, and fewer than half had a high school degree.[73]

Further west, redevelopment was taking an entirely different form. In an effort to retain industrial jobs in the city and to relocate some of the wholesalers and small manufacturers that were displaced from the Civic Center redevelopment area, the City Plan Commission proposed to clear a large part of Corktown for the "West Side Industrial District," fitting into its master plan vision of industrial corridors running throughout the city.[74] While the removal of homes in favor of space-extensive warehouses might seem like a drastic downgrade, Corktown was described as one of Detroit's oldest and most blighted areas whose land could much better suit the needs of industrial and wholesale uses due to the proximity of rail lines to Chicago and Toronto and the new Lodge Freeway. The 1958 report on Corktown's redevelopment summarized this argument: "The very factors which make it unfit for homes … make it an excellent location for small industries, warehousing and related activities." Streamlined renderings of a logistically efficient low-rise district conveyed a sense of order and cleanliness that stood in great contrast to the existing conditions of Corktown.[75]

Unlike the marginalized and dispersed African American population of Black Bottom, the residents of Corktown refused to go down without a fight. The district had a

7.5
Detroit's Skid Row: a mixture of dilapidated buildings, urban poor, and alcohol.
Image courtesy of Walter P. Reuther Library, Archives of Labor and Urban Affairs,
Wayne State University. Image from *Detroit News*, August 18, 1953.

7.6
Proposed redeveloped Michigan Avenue in the Skid Row area. Image from
Detroit Tomorrow Committee, "Detroit Tomorrow Committee Report and Review"
(Detroit, 1958).

history of successful defiance, as local government officials had already fruitlessly proposed to replace much of the district with public housing in the late 1930s.[76] What planners saw as a slum two decades later, residents considered a valuable community worth saving. Led by local resident Ethel Claes and Reverend John Mangrum, Corktown residents persuaded councilmembers to vote against the plans, successfully contacted their congressional representative, set up a study to prove that Corktown wasn't a slum under the city's own definition, and attended city hearings in large numbers. Residents even set up a district renovation program to prove that "Corktown may be old, but paint takes as well to houses here as elsewhere."[77] While this opposition was able to delay the renewal process, it ultimately failed to halt the redevelopment of a significant portion of Corktown, starting in 1957. The *Free Press* concluded that the city had simply run out of land to retain its industries, and praised the decision while acknowledging that "progress is not without sacrifices."[78] The *Detroit News* agreed: "residents quite naturally are resentful … [but] to stand tall is to die. Progress always has been at the expense or inconvenience of a few."[79] After its buildings were condemned and razed, the district's parcels were sold to manufacturers and wholesalers, with an office and hotel among the first to locate close to downtown.

By the mid-1950s, the outlines of Blessing's City of Tomorrow had been solidly drawn on the map of Detroit. As the federal government funded 90 percent of new freeway construction under the 1956 Highway Act, Detroit's highway program sped up even further. A 1957 traffic study alarmingly concluded that Detroit's metropolitan traffic was projected to increase by more than 75 percent by 1980; the study suggested an unprecedented plan for a 250-mile expressway system in the region, estimated to cost $1.5 billion.[80] Local politicians and Detroiters began to question the value and direction of further freeway construction; as a Councilmember put it, "I'm tired of being told we have to dig these ditches all over Detroit for people who don't pay any taxes here … it begins to appear as if we'll have to tear down the whole city to make room for the traffic."[81]

However, Blessing's vision for the automobile-led reshaping of downtown would soon find a powerful ally. Newly elected on a platform of urban transportation improvements, state highway commissioner John C. Mackie pressured Detroit decision makers by threatening to withdraw state funding if City Council couldn't agree on routes and designs. Downtown business interests such as Hudson's department store also ramped

CHAPTER 7

Innocent Bystander

7.7
Detroit Free Press cartoon on the
razing of Corktown, July 11, 1957.
Image © Detroit Free Press/ZUMA.

7.8
A bird's-eye rendering of the
Corktown industrial area illustrates
a modernist urban order of ware-
housing and broad streets, a far
cry from Corktown's former fine-
grained urban tissue. Image from
City Plan Commission, "Industrial
Development; West Side Industrial
District" (Detroit, 1958).

up pressure, arguing that the congested city threatened to become "a classic instance of the American community whose least accessible point is its own center."[82] After the north-south John C. Lodge Freeway and east-west Edsel B. Ford Freeway were finished in the mid-1950s, Mayor Cobo promised to mirror this mostly western investment in Detroit's east side by prioritizing the Chrysler Expressway over the old route of Hastings Street, combining the relief of traffic from Woodward Avenue with slum clearance and completing the outlines of downtown's freeway loop.[83]

The subsequent demolition of Hastings Street ripped out the last pieces of the African American east side, forcing hundreds of businesses to relocate or close. While the highway demolitions hastened its demise, Hastings Street's vitality had been waning for decades as surrounding residents had left and the jazz scene had followed to newer and more upscale clubs throughout the city. By the late 1950s, only one jazz club survived.[84] Right before demolition, many businesses on the street lay vacant.[85] It was estimated that for the complete freeway system to be constructed, thousands of families were forced to move—most of which were African American, with hardly any choice of a new home.[86] Adding insult to injury, the Automobile Club of Michigan discovered that the time savings of the newly completed freeways during rush hours were negligible compared to surface streets.[87] Commuters had little choice but to sit in traffic as transit withered. Streetcar ridership dropped about 90 percent between 1946 and 1956; for the first time, more people entered downtown by car than by all modes of transit combined between 1950 and 1952. Detroit's last streetcar retired in 1956.[88]

The extensive public investments did lead to the first significant uptick in building activity in decades, transforming certain areas of downtown such as around the Civic Center, the lower Woodward Corridor, and the block around Campus Martius. Mayor Cobo predicted no less than a billion dollars in private investment flowing into downtown as a result of his urban renewal efforts, and the *Detroit News* boasted that the transformation was "but the springboard for what is yet to come in Detroit in the next 10 years."[89] While building activity was certainly on the rise, the new buildings hardly contributed to the street-level vibrancy of downtown, transforming the area from a chaotic but vibrant marketplace to a corporate realm of concrete, steel, and glass.[90] Especially in the fringe of downtown, many new buildings hardly addressed pedestrians at all anymore. Increasingly, modernist Detroit projected an architecture of automobile convenience, "clean lines and functional approach," toward visitors and potential suburban remigrants.[91] The crowning achievement of automobile architecture was surely the Convention Center, named after its fervent supporter Mayor Cobo, which aimed to attract major trade shows and their lucrative spinoff business to Detroit.[92] Spectacularly built over the new John C. Lodge Expressway, Cobo Hall was seen as an exemplar of an "arena for the auto age." Visitors were able to arrive by car, park on the roof deck of the center, and enter their exhibit without ever setting foot on a downtown Detroit street.[93] The massive building sat squarely atop Jefferson Avenue, one of Detroit's oldest streets, making a clear statement that Detroit did not look back on its path to the future—and that this future had wheels.

Most development in Detroit's downtown fringe was far less coordinated than Cobo Hall, straying from the clean lines of Blessing's peripheral plans and continuing in the haphazard manner of the preceding decades. At an accelerating pace, the small-grained urban tissue that remained from the pre-automobile era was being replaced by the tarmac and steel of new automobile showrooms, gas stations, and motels—if not for freeways or more parking lots. An array of challenges made the redevelopment of Detroit's fringe a lot more cumbersome than the high-profile success stories of downtown.[94] The redevelopment of Corktown progressed far slower than expected, with most downtown wholesalers losing patience and moving elsewhere. Land values were too high for space-hungry industrial uses, and discussions flared on whether to halt further public investment in the project.[95] In the Skid Row redevelopment project, a developer proposed to construct an "International Village" with various commercial establishments reflecting cultures across the globe, but investors hardly lined up for the opportunity.[96] A vast mixed-use project west of Cobo Hall on a former railway yard similarly fizzled.[97] The press was beginning to wonder whether the desired public-private partnerships in urban renewal were working as well as promised by Detroit's leaders and planners. The private financial base of Detroit's redevelopment efforts was weaker than anticipated, a problem that plagued many other American cities.[98] Furthermore, continued opposition from increasingly organized community groups in neighborhoods like Corktown were disrupting the blank-slate proposals that Blessing and his team were proposing for most of inner-city Detroit.[99]

Beyond its physical condition, Detroit's inner city was also deteriorating socially. The destruction wrought by urban renewal further destabilized the struggling neighborhoods that surrounded downtown. While inner-city residents received assistance

7.9
Detroit's City-County Building replaced the city's oldest commercial corner of Woodward and Jefferson avenues with a modern structure, propelling the city into the automobile age. Rendering by Harley, Ellington and Day Architects.

7.10

Cobo Hall with the John C. Lodge Expressway in the foreground, parking ramp to roof deck to the right, and convention arena in the background. No surrounding buildings other than the modernist Veterans Memorial Hall were included in this unattributed rendering. Image from Report and Information Committee, "Detroit, the Newest Convention City" (Detroit, ca. 1959).

when their neighborhoods were condemned in order to build housing projects, those displaced by highway projects got much less support. Thousands of mainly African American inner-city families were forced to leave their homes, move into the few, already crowded districts they were still confined to, and pay some of the city's highest rents for the worst housing stock. City leaders remained mostly indifferent to their plight.[100] Conversely, continuous white flight caused a quarter of all homes within Grand Boulevard to lie vacant by the end of the 1950s. The downward spiral accelerated as the city failed to invest in inner-city schools, worsening the fate of nearby residents and diminishing the convenience of living near downtown.[101] Inner-city African Americans' disproportional suffering from low income and high unemployment rates intensified as Detroit's economy began to sputter. During the 1950s, Detroit's already volatile industrial economy intensified its traditional roller coaster pattern, with no fewer than four recessions over the decade resulting in over 100,000 manufacturing jobs lost, prompting the first full closure of factories in Detroit.[102] Even manufacturers that had stable or growing output began to replace their older urban factories with spread-out suburban complexes following the latest assembly line and automation technology.[103] Others moved jobs to cheaper, less regulated and unionized regions like Ohio, Indiana, and southern states.

In both cases factories in the inner city were hardest hit—often mostly employing African Americans.[104] Slowly they became part of a new underclass of the long-term unemployed, living in districts that had lost their reason for being.[105] As a result, inner-city crime rates steadily rose during the late 1950s, and crimes were widely covered by the media, further weakening downtown's reputation as a retail center.[106] Frightened by crime and presented with an increasing number of suburban alternatives, Detroit's middle class chose to shop elsewhere, as the number of people entering the downtown area continued its decline between 1950 and 1960.[107] While Hudson's leadership continued to maintain that "the central business district will retain its position as the foremost center," downtown retailers were forced to branch out or lose out, as suburban shopping malls mushroomed in the city's outskirts, increasingly followed by office developments that bled well-paid workers from downtown.[108] One of the first major casualties was Kern's department store, which hadn't followed Detroit's middle-class wealth by opening suburban branches during the 1950s and was forced to close in 1959,[109] prompting a wave of smaller nearby retail failures in its wake.

Perhaps more worryingly, the city's capacity to turn the tide was starting to reach its limits. Upon Mayor Cobo's sudden death in 1957, it dawned on Detroiters that he had funded his grand visions for downtown and his reputation as "the big builder" with significant city bonds, which had become unsustainable in the face of the city's declining population and job base by the late 1950s. His successor Louis Miriani inherited the vicious financial cycle of an exodus of residents and jobs and the cost of building a Dream City which itself displaced even more residents and jobs. Miriani's tax increases and service cuts hardly helped, and his more liberal successor Jerome Cavanagh was only able to balance the books by imposing an income tax on residents and nonresidents of the city—ultimately accelerating Detroit's middle-class exodus.[110] Despite Cavanagh's tight connections with the Kennedy and Johnson administrations in Washington, D.C., federal funding hardly offset Detroit's fiscal plight.[111] Meanwhile private support for the grandiose interventions in downtown continued to falter, as demonstrated by the great lengths that Detroit had to go to secure financing for Lafayette Park, with much of the development for Corktown and the riverfront still up in the air. By the end of the 1950s, the already sputtering public-private machine behind Detroit's modernization was threatening to grind itself up, leaving downtown and its surroundings as collateral damage.

As the next decade dawned, downtown had reinvented itself faster than ever before, as reflected in the drastic changes shown in figure 7.11. Through Blessing's radical plans, the "zone in transition" that started to ring downtown in the 1920s had materialized as a full separation between downtown and the rest of the city, and the bulldozers were only getting started. Downtown Detroit had become a solid core of retail buildings and offices surrounded by a sea of parking, infrastructure, public buildings, and an increasing number of vacant lots and buildings. To the west of downtown, the Lodge Freeway had been finished (1), as had the first phase of Lafayette Park to the east (2) and most of the Civic Center on the riverfront (3). However, most other modernist public interventions were in their early stages. The path for the Chrysler Freeway to the east of downtown is most clearly visible, with most buildings on Hastings Street removed (4). Land clearance in Corktown (5) and the various downtown redevelopment sites (6) was beginning to carve vacant lots and blocks. Downtown Detroit stood at a clear crossroads between tradition and modernity, demolition and hope, fighting for its life and relevance amid a struggling city.

Remove
Add
Remove and add on the same site

7.11
Downtown Detroit's blocks, buildings, parcels, open
spaces, parks, and river in 1961.
Total square footage: 56.2 million square feet
Added since 1951: 8.4 million square feet
Removed since 1951: 11.6 million square feet
Percent of downtown that is vacant or parking lot: 35%

8 BOILING POINT: 1961–1967

The 1960s dawned as the high point of Detroit's downtown renewal, with modernism's nearly blind faith in the future evidenced by an accelerating flurry of large-scale urban renewal projects. Charles Blessing defied the growing objection to the determination of Detroit's planners to turn downtown's tide through bulldozing and rebuilding: "there is no room for defeatism in our fight against the gray areas, our fight against the pessimists, the forces of decay, the despoilers, the men of little vision."[1] Nevertheless, the warning signs continued. Detroit was gaining a national reputation for urban decline; an article in *Time* magazine on the social and physical ills of the city named it as suffering from unemployment, white flight, and "blight … creeping like a fungus through many of Detroit's proud old neighborhoods."[2] With public support, private investment, and political backing running dry, Mackie and Blessing's bulldozers would perform a last round of radical reinvention before they themselves were deemed obsolete.

One couldn't hear the renewal machine's sputter in the roar of downtown demolition, which took Detroit's beleaguered 1871 City Hall after 90 years of service. In a feverish quest for progress, Mayor Miriani agreed to sacrifice the building for parking to entice the local First Federal Savings and Loan to add a few extra floors to their plans for their modern headquarters a block to the north—which itself would replace the Majestic Building from the late nineteenth century.[3] Columnist Judd Arnett of the *Detroit Free Press* agreed with the deal: "City Hall? Rip it down! … The past belongs to yesterday; today is ours." Arnett specifically railed against the various organizations and leaders that had attempted to preserve the building, backed by a majority of Detroiters looking to save their ties to the past, accusing them of "apathy to progress."[4] The city prevailed, and its former home was demolished for Kennedy Square, an underground parking garage with a rather underutilized plaza on top.[5] For the first time, Detroiters seemed to realize that progress also meant loss. While supporting the removal of City Hall, the *Detroit News* asked historian and journalist Russell Lynes and architect Minoru Yamasaki to address whether "Detroit's landmarks [were] worth saving." Lynes derided the mentality of automobile leadership that led Detroit to "[pour] down the expressways like the torrents of spring, and as the flood of cars rises the banks give way, little by little, and destruction spreads across city and suburb and open country." Yamasaki countered that "the preservation of too many buildings in a particular center can tend to stifle the creativity and vigor of a people. ... When Detroit is vigorously building a greater city, should nostalgia and sentimentality stand in the way of real progress?"[6] The drastic downtown transformation in the decade to follow sided with Yamasaki's sentiment.

While popular support for controversial demolitions was indeed waning, urban renewal was still generally supported in the early 1960s. And while private investment was hard to come by, federal highway and urban renewal money allowed planner Blessing and his highway counterpart Mackie to expand and accelerate their overhaul of downtown, making it "very possibly the most extensive center city redesign assignment currently under study in the nation."[7] A 1961 Ford promotional video on Detroit praised the city for its innovation, not least in reinventing itself. "The old gives way to the new, yet all that is good is cherished and contributes to the dream of the future for Detroit. The city of contrasts looks toward tomorrow, confident that its great goals will be gained through the vision, cooperation and energy of all its people."[8] Newly elected liberal Mayor Jerome Cavanagh went even further, proclaiming in his 1963 New Year's greetings that "our city is striking out at blight and other stifling factors of urban life. Detroit is becoming a better place to live."[9]

At first sight, the efforts were paying off: tax revenue in renewal areas rose significantly, and federal money generously supported further expansion. In Lafayette Park, one single redeveloped building generated more taxes than the entire cleared area the district replaced.[10] While its construction had been embarrassingly slow, the "little bit of suburbia in the city" was praised by residents, architects, and planners alike when construction was completed in the mid-1960s.[11] The feverish building activity in the downtown core was noted as "the biggest building boom since the '20s," transforming the city's skyline in the "Soaring 60s."[12] Gleaming new office buildings rose along newly widened lower Woodward Avenue, crowned by the Yamasaki-designed Michigan Consolidated Gas Building and the new Pontchartrain Hotel along a freshly opened riverfront park.[13] Existing buildings like the Statler and Madison-Lenox Hotel and Whitney Tower received extensive modernizations to keep up.[14] Postwar urban design and planning in Detroit was generally respected in the field and Blessing received numerous accolades, including an American Institute of Planners Honors Award in 1964.[15] Detroit was touted—at least by the local press—as a "pilot city for the nation in its redevelopment, watched nationally and internationally in its onslaught on the problem of decay."[16] Due to an uptick in automobile manufacturing, it even seemed for a while that Detroit's population decline had halted and might reverse.[17]

At the helm of it all stood a proud Mayor Cavanagh, hailed by national and international press as "the mayor who woke up a city." Cavanagh received the most recognition for his efforts to repair decades of racial prejudice in City Hall by focusing on improving the lives of Detroit's African American population, but he was also well respected for his persistence in spurring downtown development. Some even foresaw a federal career for him, as he had achieved the seemingly impossible and transformed Detroit into a self-proclaimed "City of Promise."[18] A significant part of this reversal of fortunes occurred in downtown, as Cavanagh stated in a speech to the Central Business District Association: "In great degree, the reputation, the prosperity and the future of Detroit depends upon the appearance, the vigor and the plans affecting the central business district. ... Downtown *is* Detroit."[19]

Despite the public praise, Detroit's urban renewal efforts came increasingly under fire behind the scenes, as financial and political support for radical clearance and redevelopment continued to erode, and nongovernmental interests such as business leaders and growth coalitions were slow to step up.[20] At the root of the crumbling support was the growing realization that urban renewal wasn't producing the revitalization it had aimed for. Detroit's modern shapers simply couldn't build their way out of the city's adversity, as a lack of market enthusiasm continued to plague most renewal projects, especially in the periphery of downtown. Making matters worse, cities were required by federal guidelines to anticipate demand and clear land before approaching developers, which asked public officials rather than private investors to accurately gauge the market.[21] While central business district office vacancy was still relatively low during the late 1950s, downtown employment actually dropped by a third during the decade that followed, and new office construction in the 1960s often simply shifted tenants from older buildings in a zero-sum game, with downtown's older office stock undergoing drastic renovations to stay afloat.[22] Detroit had one of the nation's lowest percentages of metropolitan office space located downtown, as office jobs moved to new edge cities like Southfield and Dearborn.[23] Instead of buying into the planners' radical vision for the future, downtown business leaders sought tax relief just to remain in their existing properties, earning scorn by the city for a lack of enthusiasm.[24]

Instead of glistening new buildings, most renewal areas only sprouted weeds, mostly because demand simply wasn't there.[25] A "city within a city" of connected residential towers west of the Civic Center, proposed by the developer of Chicago's Marina Towers, never materialized as the federal government withheld its support due to the trouble other large residential projects had had in filling their units.[26] Able to find less than a third of the mere $3 million sought in private investment, the failed International Village proposal for the former Skid Row site was eventually replaced with mostly government buildings—a bailout trend that pervaded American renewal sites.[27] The western edge of downtown was turning into a curiously suburban office park, replete with parking lots and security fences—"a sort of garden of new buildings."[28] As urbanist Jane Jacobs had presaged in her 1961 book *The Death and Life of Great American Cities*, urban renewal in Detroit was creating "border vacuums" in which adjacent land lost value and vitality, instead of the gains promised by city planners and leadership.[29] Furthermore, the fear of becoming part of an urban renewal area caused many owners to stop investing in their properties around downtown, accelerating the fringe's spiral of decline.[30]

The retail market in downtown Detroit fared even worse than offices did. While large department stores like Hudson's still sold more than half of their merchandise downtown in 1960, the numbers soon took a turn for the worse. With Detroit's continuing socioeconomic downturn and growing image problems, downtown stores faced the double pressure of losing wealthy suburban clients who were afraid or reluctant to come downtown, and increasing losses of merchandise due to theft.[31] The statistics were dire. In the decade after Northland opened, the proportion of downtown sales in metropolitan Detroit dropped by almost half, with downtown department store floor space decreasing while suburban branches quadrupled in size. By the late 1960s, more than 85 percent of metropolitan Detroit's department store floor space was located outside downtown, and more than three-quarters of new commercial space was being constructed outside the city limits.[32] Although one could argue that the downtown merchants had doomed their own downtown stores by branching outward, Kern's failure to survive and the success of suburban chain stores like Sears and Federals demonstrate that department stores like Hudson's and Crowley's had no choice.

Part of downtown's retail decline can be attributed by the poor adaptation of central retailers to the city's changing racial makeup. Businesses like Hudson's still had no African American sales staff by the mid-1960s, and African Americans were frequently shunned by higher-end stores. Those businesses that did adapt fared better in the longer run, with Grinnell Brothers Music House on Woodward Avenue becoming a staple in the city's growing African American music scene. As movie theater business relocated to suburban shopping malls and remaining downtown spaces resorted to horror flicks to stay in business, the Fox Theatre successfully adapted to Detroit's changing demographic by hosting the highly successful Motown Revue. This was the exception, however, as most downtown venues continued to avoid African American entertainment, prompting the vibrant jazz, blues, and soul scenes to evolve into the Motown sound in Midtown and beyond.[33] Economist James Ticknor further ascribed the decline of downtown retail and entertainment to an inevitable suburbanization process that underlay Detroit's blue-collar culture: "the supermarket, the new car lot, and the suburban Sears store are more typical symbols of Detroit's postwar affluence than Saks, art galleries, or Lincoln Center."[34]

The lack of clear results prompted further doubts that urban renewal policies were effective in reversing the decline of the city and its downtown. Following a growing national opposition to urban freeway construction, Detroiters began to question the merits of radical infrastructural interventions.[35] A series of *Detroit News* articles on urban renewal illustrated these doubts, as "much of the aging city's fading strength has been drained away into disorganized, inefficient and often planless suburbs [causing] a near-vacuum at the center." Charles Blessing, given space to respond, stated that Detroit's existing street pattern was "basically obsolete. ... We are therefore using the freeway and major thoroughfare plan as the major structural element in the master plan of the city."[36] City Council's resistance to freeway construction grew, but Mackie's state-propelled steamroller was difficult to stop.[37] By the mid-1960s, the final parts of the expressway loop around downtown were under construction. Despite its sunken construction and avoidance of major buildings, the east-west Fisher Freeway introduced another barrier between downtown and Cass and Brush Park. Running on the path of Vernor Highway of four decades previous, the freeway had a similarly deteriorating effect on adjoining blocks.[38] Hemmed in by freeways, pockmarked by vacant urban renewal land, the downtown fringe had turned into an unwalkable wasteland of parking garages, parking lots, vacant lots, and blighted buildings. Moreover, even as the fringe was recast as "a huge parking lot," it was still unable to provide parking at the level of suburban office and retail parks.[39]

While Blessing sacrificed downtown's fringe as collateral damage to save its core, even his visions for Detroit's most central blocks failed to launch. Two iterations of pedestrianization proposals for Woodward Avenue came and went, and a more entertainment-focused pedestrianization proposal for Broadway similarly fizzled.[40] The renewed spaces would have led to fewer storefronts than ever before. The lack of market demand for downtown properties was most starkly demonstrated by the failed renewal of Detroit's most central block north of Campus Martius. After greatly suffering from the closure of Kern's department store, the remaining largest landowner on the block proposed to clear the block and build a seven-story building in 1961 with two stories of shopping, underground parking, and pedestrian bridges linking to nearby department stores, a project meant to "turn the tide and make it easier for shoppers to come downtown."[41] The city successfully applied for federal funding to clear the block in 1965, putting significant faith in the return of middle-class residents and workers through urban renewal projects like Lafayette Park and the reconstruction of lower Woodward Avenue and the riverfront.[42] While initial developer interest in the block seemed high, multiple proposals for its construction stalled due to lack of financing and legal issues, leaving the "city's most expensive vacant lot" untouched for decades to come.[43] Within the span of a few years, some of Detroit's oldest remaining buildings on Campus Martius had been replaced by tarmac, tin, or nothing at all.

8.1

Aerial view of the cleared Kern's block (renamed as Kern's Common, bottom right) and former City Hall site (renamed as Kennedy Square, top left), with the new First Federal Savings and Loan building located in between. Image courtesy of Walter P. Reuther Library, Archives of Labor and Urban Affairs, Wayne State University. Image from *Detroit News*, July 27, 1967.

Some grassroots downtown revitalization proposals were more successful, as they focused on downtown as a leisure destination. East of Woodward Avenue, Greektown was suffering from illegal gambling activities and other crime, but decisive action by the Central Business District Association and the newly formed Greektown Businessmen's Association significantly aided its recovery as a retail and entertainment destination.[44] Northwest of downtown, a local high school teacher and real estate developer teamed up to buy properties on Plum Street near Elton Park, one of two remaining oval parks in the increasingly gutted area between the Lodge and Fisher freeways. Following examples of themed shopping and entertainment districts in Chicago and St. Louis, they wanted to start "a thriving center of interesting shops, a theater and restaurants" aimed at downtown workers and tourists.[45] Rather than attracting the targeted suburban clientele, the area soon became a center of Detroit's hippie scene, with a mixture of bars, shops, and cultural venues. Historic preservation was still in its early days, benefiting from the city's first Historical Commission, started in response to federal guidelines in 1966 to start documenting the city's landmarks.[46]

Despite these small victories, no matter what plans were drawn or investments were made, downtown's fate had become almost impossible to turn, as the surrounding inner city had entered a seemingly irreversible and accelerating decline. The combination of successful integrational housing policies spearheaded by civil rights advocates and less scrupulous "blockbusting" practices by realtors led to a further relaxation of the confinement of African Americans in the near east side. As a result, those who could moved out. While this led to an improvement of generally overcrowded living conditions, it also resulted in a separation by class if not by race, as Detroit's oldest districts became the city's refuge for the poor.[47] By the early 1960s, almost a third of the residents within the Grand Boulevard ring were unemployed, and almost a fourth of families received public assistance. Almost three-fourths of homes needed major repairs or more, as plummeting home values disincentivized landlords from making any investments. A majority of the families in the area had one or more adult members with chronic illnesses; almost a quarter had adult members with mental health issues, and medical care was far below par.[48] The arterial streets that led through these districts into downtown had plunged into a crisis of vacancy and disrepair.[49] Riddled by crime, vacant storefronts, car lots, and vandalism, the formerly vibrant Grand River Avenue was described by the *Detroit News* as an "avenue of broken dreams," "dying of cancerous blight."[50] Similarly, Cass Park quickly slid from a port of entry for southern white immigrants to a last resort for the city's poorest during the 1960s. The area had lost almost half of its population since 1940 and suffered from unemployment, infectious diseases, and homelessness.[51]

An increasing number of Detroiters became disillusioned by Detroit's modernizing urban planning, and their power grew as they organized. Many citizen protests against

8.2

Clearance along Jefferson Avenue for the Chrysler Freeway. Image courtesy of Walter P. Reuther Library, Archives of Labor and Urban Affairs, Wayne State University. Image from *Detroit News*, February 4, 1964.

urban renewal had a significant racial component, as planning proposals were often viewed as the imposition of white elitist visions on African American neighborhoods— "Negro Removal," as many activists put it. Despite Cavanagh's efforts to improve the city's racial relations, tensions continued to mount in the city. In 1963, a group of about 125,000 African Americans and allies joined a march by Martin Luther King Jr. and several city leaders down Woodward Avenue to Cobo Hall, where King first elaborated on his dream for an integrated America. While the march was inspired by frustration at the slow progress of African Americans, its arrival in downtown marked a shift in the role of this traditionally white power center from which so many urban renewal plans had hatched. A local NAACP official commented on the transformative power of the march's destination at Cobo Hall: "This venue, named after a racist mayor, was transformed by a man who would become the iconic voice for racial justice."[52] Unlike the bitter reception of King and his message in many other cities, Mayor Cavanagh welcomed him and joined as one of the march leaders. While conciliatory, this show of support came too late for many marchers, who had seen their homes and places of worship leveled by Cavanagh's predecessors.[53] Despite decades of activism and official housing integration, African Americans continued to be confined to some of the worst districts of the city, a segregation pattern that was still violently guarded by white homeowners and neighborhood associations.[54] Furthermore, the city's police force increasingly militarized in response to Detroit's worsening crime rates and socioeconomic conditions, and continued to disproportionally target African Americans.[55]

The final nail in the coffin of urban renewal was struck when Detroit's political and downtown business leaders began to withdraw their support. By 1967, Mayor Cavanagh acknowledged the self-defeating nature of the physical determinism of the city's modernization. Besides the obvious social problems renewal had created, Cavanagh especially criticized the vicious cycle of Detroit's freeway construction: "We built freeways and parking which bring more cars and people into the core city, and this creates the need for more freeways and parking."[56] City planners slowly changed their tune and planned to save certain neighborhoods from the wrecking ball by "conservation," although this program ultimately failed to retain residents, alleviate racial prejudice, or bolster civic participation and pride.[57] Unfazed by the growing opposition to his physical and technocratic approach to urban planning, Charles Blessing doubled down on his visions for pedestrian malls, parking garages, and plazas, complaining that local business owners should demonstrate more commitment. The Central Business District Association countered that Blessing's visions were "nebulous," demonstrating an increasing schism between city planners and local business interests.[58] As a result, downtown fell to its smallest size since 1929, caught in a limbo of half-finished urban renewal projects, as demonstrated by figure 8.3. Almost a million square feet of downtown floor space had been demolished each year in the 1960s, and there was relatively little to show for it in return. Lafayette Park (1) was mostly completed, but Corktown's transformation into the West Side Industrial District (2) was still under way, the transformation of Skid Row (3) had mostly led to empty lots, downtown's Kern Block (4) was vacant, and the Fisher (5) and Chrysler (6) freeways were still under way. This vacancy reflected the nationwide struggles of urban renewal, as over half of the American renewal projects that had started in the early 1960s would remain unfinished in the next decade.[59]

Detroit was clearly losing direction in its battle against urban decay, prompting newcomers to enter the debate. The Detroit Edison Company, its director Walker Cisler long a supporter of urban renewal, commissioned Greek architect and urban designer Constantinos Doxiadis in 1965 to prepare a comprehensive study and design for Detroit and its region. His three-volume work reflected and amplified many of Blessing's modern urban design principles for downtown.[60] They can be seen as the last breath of modern urban planning and design in downtown Detroit, as its futurist visions had lost support, resources, and relevance. More importantly, the planners were in denial about the socioeconomic spiral that Detroit had entered and the racial and political structure of the city. As inner-city Detroit hollowed out, the last thing downtown needed was more bricks and mortar. Councilmembers and national lawmakers had come to realize that, without social improvements, Detroit was beyond redemption. At the local level, modernist renewal had reached a dead end; at the federal level, urban renewal funding was being reallocated to the new Model Cities Program that focused on social improvements rather than physical interventions. After displacing more than 700,000 families through urban renewal and highway construction, the federally funded modernization of America came to an end.[61]

Remove

Add

Remove and add on the same site

8.3
Downtown Detroit's blocks, buildings, parcels,
open spaces, parks, and river in 1967.
Total square footage: 52.9 million square feet
Added since 1961: 3.0 million square feet
Removed since 1961: 6.2 million square feet
Percent of downtown that is vacant or parking lot: 40%

IV WINTER

9 THE END OF URBAN RENEWAL: 1967–1977

The Cavanagh administration, more fearful than ever that civil unrest would soon alight in Detroit, had plenty of preparations in place. Yet no one seems to have expected the gravity of the events that unfolded in the summer of 1967. The spark was lit by a drawn-out police raid on an African American "blind pig" on Twelfth Street, the area that had solidified into Detroit's densest, most crime-ridden, and most socially deprived area, absorbing thousands of African Americans uprooted by the various urban renewal schemes throughout the city. After years of racially biased harassment under the guise of combating vice, locals decided that they had had enough and took to the streets.[1] Following a day of mostly peaceful demonstrations on the plight of poverty, poor housing conditions, police brutality, a lack of jobs, and continuing socioeconomic inequality, the situation descended into chaos on the second day.[2]

As the last flames were extinguished, the toll was shocking. After five days, the disorders had left 43 dead, 1,189 wounded, 7,231 arrested, 2,509 looted or burned stores, 412 other buildings burned, and hundreds of families homeless. From the air, the city looked as if it "had been bombed."[3] The damage made it all too clear that the racial and social tensions of Detroit could not be changed by physical interventions alone—if anything, urban planning had played a role in worsening the situation of Detroit's African Americans. As in many other cities, Detroit's urban renewal projects had uprooted African American residents more than anyone else, failing to replace more than 90 percent of the 8,000 low-income homes the renewal projects had demolished since the 1950s.[4] And as elsewhere, hopes and reality simply weren't aligned. As audacious blueprints had turned black communities into barren brownfields, dissent had only grown. No matter how many federal dollars or top designers came to the city, Detroit could not build its way out of trouble anymore. And despite all the federal programs that had been set up over the two preceding decades, from the physical determinism of 1950s urban renewal, highway construction, and public housing acts to the social conscience of the 1960s Model Cities and Neighborhood Services programs, Detroit was more divided and less prosperous than before.[5] From the local to the federal level, leaders awoke to the reality that progress required a different path—and that options were running out.

While Mayor Cavanagh convened a "New Detroit Committee" of business and community leaders immediately after the disorders, their conversations about racial reconciliation and progress could not keep up with events.[6] Those who could leave Detroit did so, in unprecedented numbers. Population loss accelerated sevenfold between 1966 and 1969; most emigrants were middle-class whites, and population loss was strongest in the districts near downtown.[7] More major employers such as Kresge and Chrysler left Detroit, further bolstering edge cities such as Troy and Dearborn. Even African American icon Motown Records left its birthplace for Los Angeles in 1972.[8] Only significant investments could turn the tide, but outside investors had grown scared of the city, and Detroit's own industry remained aloof from downtown.[9] Detroit's plight only worsened with the 1973 oil crisis, as the market for American fuel-thirsty cars all but dried up, cutting automobile production to 1950 levels and taking 110,000 jobs out of the city between 1967 and 1977.[10] Detroit's continued reliance on the automobile industry had turned from fortune to liability as the city's main job base collapsed.[11]

As remaining Detroiters faced an acute lack of opportunities, the crime rate in the city almost doubled between 1967 and 1970, and the downtown area certainly saw its share.[12] Robberies and assaults in broad daylight and murders at night became commonplace in downtown, prompting the *Detroit News* editorial board to proclaim that downtown was "fighting for its life" by the end of the 1960s—a far cry from the boosterism they professed during the previous decades.[13] The reputation of Detroit was tarnished nationally, as the widely televised disorders were the final proof to many Americans that the Motor City was a lost cause. After the 1967 civil disorders, in the minds of Americans Detroit had turned from a place of hope to an omen of social decline, crime, and abandonment, derided as "Problem town, USA."[14] National media coverage extensively focused on Detroit's unsafety, to the point where Mayor Cavanagh

9.1
The devastated corner of Grand River Avenue and Dumbarts Street after the
1967 civil disorders. Image courtesy of Walter P. Reuther Library, Archives of
Labor and Urban Affairs, Wayne State University. Image from *Detroit News*,
July 28, 1967.

complained, "People think there is a no-man's-land down here, that you get your head shot off or knifed on Woodward at noon."[15] As aptly described by historian Robert Conot, "twilight was settling upon the city; the twilight of an eclipse."[16]

While downtown had not featured in the 1967 disorders, it became a highly visible focal point in their aftermath. The Central Business District Association started the "I care about Detroit" campaign in 1968 to "fight against fear," but downtown retail sales fell away as suburban customers became afraid to enter Detroit entirely.[17] Hudson's became the scene of various assaults, and losses due to theft were mounting rapidly at many other downtown retailers. Footfall declined rapidly, and special sales and events did little to stem the decline for downtown's major department stores.[18] While downtown's retail giants were mostly able to hang on, many smaller businesses were forced to shut down. Any remaining businesses holding a significant amount of cash fortified themselves with walls, plywood, and bulletproof glass—a style cynically dubbed "Riot Renaissance."[19] While the barricaded shopfronts reflected a seemingly ephemeral distrust between tenants and passersby in a time of social stress, the disconnect between buildings and public space became more permanently engrained with new construction. Continuing a decades-long trend of increasing distance between offices and the street, new downtown office construction began to reflect a true sense of fortification for the first time. Following a set of massive concrete panels to fortify the 1971 Manufacturers Bank Operations Center in the financial district, the McNamara Federal Building that opened on the west side of downtown was such a fortress that even the usually benevolent local press called it a "terribly unfriendly place."[20]

The 1967 disorders prompted more than just social, economic, and physical transformation for Detroit and its downtown. They catalyzed a paradigm shift that had been over a decade in the making, finally halting the political, fiscal, and cultural machine that had fueled downtown Detroit's drastic modernization. The chaotic aftermath of the disorders coincided with the end of federal and state funding for wholesale urban renewal, and Detroit itself was fiscally unable to compensate.[21] Instead, federal funding for urban development began to refocus on community improvements and public participation, and funds were drastically cut in the 1970s. Seemingly untouched by the political and financial vacuum he was working in, Charles Blessing and his team continued to draft their visions for the inner city, one more grandiose and elusive than

9.2
The Manufacturers' Bank (now
Comerica Bank, top) and McNamara
Federal Building (bottom) materialize a
distrust of public space in their horizontal
and vertical separation from the street.
Both images by author, 2017.

another. While Blessing's "dreams" for downtown had always been somewhat separated from Detroit's more sobering on-the-ground reality, the persistent drawings of futuristic raised walkway systems connecting phantom office towers on the northwest side of downtown and the near-demolition of entire swaths of the inner city became almost laughable in the face of Detroit's fight for survival.[22] As Blessing's modernist machine continued to produce glossy plans for a new civic center, a community college, a sports stadium, and a subway system, citizens and jobs left Detroit in droves, downtown emptied out, and transit ridership dwindled to historic lows. Instead of the centralizing transit networks of many of its peers, a 1972 federal study concluded that Detroit had the worst transit system of America's top dozen cities.[23]

Three decades after prompting the start of urban renewal, Detroit's politicians would finally lay it to rest. At a keynote address at the 38th National Planning Conference at Cobo Hall in 1972, sociologist and Detroit councilmember Mel Ravitz argued that urban planners had been unable to change the course of the city, especially with regard to ameliorating its social, economic, and racial problems.[24] Ravitz's advocacy of the end of modernist planning in Detroit gained political momentum with the election of the city's first African American mayor, Coleman Young, in early 1974.[25] A former resident of the Black Bottom that was leveled under modernism, Young was deeply distrustful of the bureaucratic forces that had shaped the city during his youth. During his tenure, large-scale urban planning would be marginalized, profoundly shifting the powers that would transform downtown. Beyond Young's ideology, this shift was also prompted by the city's dire financial situation during the 1970s, as he could not count on the city's dwindling budget or significant federal funding for urban renewal. In short, he had to address more urban issues with far fewer resources. Young chose to focus on high-visibility projects to show Detroiters and the world at large that his city was still an entity to be reckoned with. Downtown remained the focal point of the city, at least for out-of-town visitors and media, ensuring that central projects remained a high priority.[26]

While Young strongly disavowed the physical determinism and technocratic masking of racial prejudice of previous planning regimes, aimed at protecting mostly white downtown interests, the paradigm for downtown renewal hence did not shift as much as one would expect. He continued to focus on downtown as a job generator, and he could get the most media bang for his limited budget by continuing to construct buzz-generating physical projects.[27] Physical downtown renovation remained a goal,

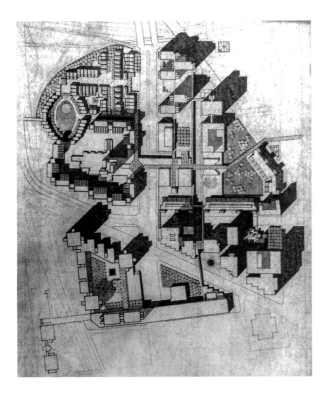

9.3
A rendering of western downtown by the City Plan Commission under Charles Blessing starkly contrasts with the area's relentless reality in the 1960s. Top image from 1969 rendering of Downtown West, found in the City Plan Commission oversize files at the Burton Historical Collection, Detroit Public Library. Bottom image courtesy of Walter P. Reuther Library, Archives of Labor and Urban Affairs, Wayne State University; image from *Detroit News*, April 24, 1963.

THE END OF URBAN RENEWAL: 1967–1977

although the means drastically shifted. The federal fuel supply for the modernist bull-dozer was cut off in 1974 with the replacement of the Housing Act budget by Community Development block grants, prioritizing social improvements over bricks and mortar.[28] That same year, Detroiters also approved a new city charter that dealt the final blow to the city's tradition of modern urban planning and design, restructuring the Planning Commission into three subdepartments, which lost a significant portion of their efficacy and funding over time.[29] Stripped of most of his powers, a bitter Charles Blessing left his position soon after. The forces shaping downtown after 1967 would become generally less grandiose in scale, and more often privately funded.

Instead of relying on an apparatus of planners and city bureaucrats, Young used his strong ties to the federal government and his talent as an "inventive and aggressive" instigator and negotiator to secure a series of high-profile projects that would transform Detroit's urban core in the late 1970s and 1980s.[30] In the 1970s, one of Young's most important sources for federal funding was the Urban Development Action Grant (UDAG), initiated by the Department of Housing and Urban Development during the Carter administration. The program was specifically intended to leverage private investments, and Young's close ties to President Jimmy Carter and the Democratic National Committee yielded over half a billion dollars of grants during his tenure, more than any other city would receive.[31] The first test for Young's new style of downtown redevelopment was the arduous but ultimately successful construction of the Joe Louis Arena on the riverfront next to Cobo Hall, retaining the Red Wings hockey team in Detroit. While previous administrations had fruitlessly proposed a riverfront stadium on the site of the new arena, Young's federal connections secured $5 million in federal funding, and his negotiating skills brought in a hard-fought agreement by the Red Wings to play in the arena and city approval for additional bonds to cover its costs.[32] While the stadium had originally been intended for the Detroit Lions football team and the building was smaller and far more sober than originally intended, Young's hardball negotiation had finally materialized downtown's first sports stadium—an early victory.[33]

The diminished role of Detroit's planning apparatus in the city as well as the city's inability to fund major public improvements started a trend of land privatization and consolidation that would profoundly transform downtown regardless of political cycles. Most notably, the Detroit Edison Company announced in 1970 that it planned to redevelop most of the northwestern part of downtown into a 66-acre mixed-use campus comprising its offices, dwellings, and shops around a plaza and pedestrian mall, reflecting the determination of "the business community to bear a share of the burdens of this city."[34] Other private initiatives started out more modestly, but eventually prompted similarly significant impacts on downtown. In the same year as Detroit Edison announced its plans, city business leaders including the Central Business District Association, the Chamber of Commerce, and the Ford Motor Company formed Detroit Renaissance, feeling Detroit's problems were so vast as to be practically "insoluble."[35] Detroit Renaissance initially rarely acted as a direct developer or financer of its proposals, instead sponsoring planning reports, marketing campaigns, and small improvements. Within a few years, the group began to actively support development projects such as the renovation of Music Hall and residential construction near downtown.[36]

The influence of Detroit Renaissance would become far more profound when Henry Ford II, one of its leaders, realized it was time to step up the group's efforts and determined to create a landmark project to show the world that Detroit was a vibrant city worth investing in.[37] The project needed "to be of such scale, of such critical mass, as to have an effect on the whole city." In 1971, he laid out plans for a massive riverfront mixed-use complex to City Council and began to gather support among his suppliers, creditors, and, interestingly, his competitors.[38] The complex would be located on several blocks of riverfront land east of the Civic Center, mostly occupied by vacant industrial buildings and a struggling railway station, the final remnants of Detroit's days as a riverfront city. After a long struggle for financing, Ford managed to gather 51 companies in the "largest investment group ever assembled for a redevelopment project," ultimately investing over $350 million dollars in a project that singlehandedly shifted the paradigm and the scale of downtown Detroit.[39] The proposal promised to revitalize the physical condition but also the image of downtown Detroit, marred by the negative press coverage from the previous decade. Ford commissioned John Portman to design a "city-within-a-city," complete with the world's tallest hotel structure at 70 stories, four 39-story office towers, a multistory shopping mall, and later phases which included residential towers and parking, all connected by an elaborate system of interior public spaces. In 1973, the complex would receive its name as a result of a contest: Renaissance Center.[40]

9.4

The Renaissance Center with downtown in the background, designed by John Portman. Only the middle complex was developed. Image from Americal Development Corporation, "Traugott Schmidt & Sons, a Melieu of Entertainment Experiences!" (Detroit, 1974).

Criticism of the project's introverted architecture began to flood the press even before the building was completed. The sheer size of the Renaissance Center, its introversion, and its poor orientation to its surroundings made it a building that removed rather than added street life and interactivity to downtown Detroit. Especially the decision to shield the complex from the street by a 25-foot berm containing HVAC systems became highly controversial and generated much criticism from citizens and architects alike.[41] The separation demonstrated to many opponents that the center was a blatantly private and exclusive building in a city hitherto used to large public renewal projects.[42] The project would soon earn national scorn for its disconnection from the surrounding city, exemplified by urban scholar William Whyte's criticism of the building's defensive architecture in his popular books and media presentations.[43] Urbanist Nan Ellin would later coin the term "postmodern urbanism" to describe the security-focused introversion of the Renaissance Center and its contemporaries.[44] Portman seemed immune to the criticism, defending his prioritization of the internal quality of the complex over its appearance to the city: "never mind just the façade, the street is not everything."[45] While much of the official language on the center concealed the design's focus on security, Portman later acknowledged that his view of Detroit's social downturn was key to his design: "the threat of crime was an important factor ... society required protection, that was a fact of life."[46] The Renaissance Center's poor connectivity to its surroundings was also caused by the fact that the complex was never fully finished as planned, especially suffering from the omission of a shopping bridge that would have connected the center to downtown.

Even before its opening the Renaissance Center already exerted a negative influence on its vicinity, as supporting parking garages, street-widening projects and land clearance for the center's potential growth eroded its surroundings. Perhaps more importantly, its purported benefits to downtown never materialized. In Detroit's struggling business climate, the Renaissance Center was forced to recruit tenants from many of the other struggling buildings in the downtown area in a hunger to fill its 2.4 million square feet of office space, hundreds of shops, and 1,400 hotel rooms. Partly because of this aggressive recruitment strategy, downtown office and hotel vacancy skyrocketed in the 1970s, especially hurting downtown's older and more remote building stock. Office buildings like the Broderick Tower were losing tenants, with owners struggling to maintain basic services like heat, water, and security.[47] Hotels like the Tuller, Statler, and Fort Shelby suffered from a high transience in both patrons and ownership, leading to failure and closure by the mid-1970s.[48] Similarly, the once venerable Book-Cadillac Hotel went through various owners and sat mostly empty toward the end of the decade.[49]

9.5
The interior environment of the Renaissance Center offers shelter and architectural awe. Image courtesy of Wayne State University "Building the Detroit Renaissance Center" collection. Image copyright Wayne State University.

The Renaissance Center's introversion reflected an architectural resignation to the struggling social and economic conditions of downtown and changed the debate on future interventions. As downtown Detroit died off at street level, some advocated a new system of raised pedestrian walks, and Detroit started its own downtown "skyway" system in the mid-1970s. Major office buildings would be linked on the second-floor level by air-conditioned walkways, taking pedestrians off the street. While officially praised for protecting pedestrians from weather and traffic, the system was undoubtedly influenced by the defensive concept of the Renaissance Center and the great increase in downtown crime.[50] Detroit's plans reflected a nationwide trend of shifting the public realm away from the street into an "analogous city" for the middle class (a term coined by urban observer Trevor Boddy).[51]

While many of the envisioned skyways were constructed over time, the city's real second-floor transportation system would become the raised People Mover, an automated transit system looping around downtown that would connect major buildings, parking facilities, and a potential web of rapid transit lines radiating from downtown.[52] The system was first proposed in 1973 by the regional transit authority, which argued that it "could pull the central business district together" and connect to a $2.4 billion regional rapid transit system the regional authority was developing.[53] Even in the project's earliest stages, criticism was fierce, especially focusing on the limited time benefit of the system and the fact that it took the few remaining people off downtown's sidewalks.[54] Federal and private interest in automated people movers was also waning as initial test tracks had yielded unconvincing financial and connectivity benefits.[55] Nevertheless, the state decided to fund a study that would determine a route, ridership estimates, and a fairly detailed design for the system by 1974, facing surprisingly little public opposition.[56] The project gained significantly more traction when Mayor Young became a fierce supporter, garnering and maintaining federal support for it under three administrations, starting with President Gerald Ford in 1975.[57] By the next year, the federal government chose the People Mover as one of four demonstration projects by the newly instated Urban Mass Transportation Administration.[58] The People Mover needed all the help it could get, as it would become one of Detroit's most controversial projects in the decade to come.

The plans for the People Mover and the skyway system did not necessarily mean that the city paid no attention to improving ground-level public spaces. Several proposals were drafted for some of downtown's main open spaces, meant to reinvigorate private investment. Washington Boulevard was slated for renovation, to include more pedestrian space, parks, plazas, and a trolley line to connect the struggling area to the convention crowd at Cobo Hall and later to the tenants of the Renaissance Center, making the struggling boulevard more friendly to business and "more people-oriented."[59] A similar but more extensive improvement was proposed for Woodward Avenue in 1974, closing Detroit's main retail street to all but public transit and widening its sidewalks.[60] In 1971, the riverfront Hart Plaza finally created a proper footing to Woodward Avenue, with a privately donated fountain designed by sculptor Isamu Noguchi—completing a dream of planners that ran back to the turn of the century.[61] Unfortunately, the plaza was rather undefined by surrounding buildings and only drew crowds during major events. In any case, the public space improvements never had a chance to succeed, as downtown was rapidly losing its economic and cultural vitality, and was on the verge of losing its critical mass as an urban and regional destination.[62]

Meanwhile, as Hudson's was increasingly losing customers and merchandise, rumors had started to spread that it was retreating from downtown and planned to rent a significant portion of its mammoth store to third parties, a move that the neighboring Crowley's store had successfully made a decade before.[63] After a series of failed modernization efforts, Hudson's indeed began to close off upper sales floors, dwindling to only three of its seventeen original floors by the early 1980s.[64] Most of the store's elaborate window displays were replaced by metal plates to cut cost and curb crime. The former cathedral of consumption had become a fortress, defending itself from—instead of presenting itself to—passersby. Hudson's director admitted that in Detroit's rapidly decaying urban core, "people weren't coming … to window shop any more."[65] Crowley's followed a similar path of downsizing and announced its eventual closure in 1976, noting that its downtown sales were even lower than during the worst Depression years.[66] Smaller retailers failed in the wake of the department store woes, halving the number of downtown establishments between 1961 and 1977. Detroit's entertainment scene followed a similar downward path, with many theaters resorting to live burlesque shows or porn to remain open.[67] Downtown's entertainment offerings simply couldn't keep up the image of a safe and carefree leisure environment that suburban consumers demanded. As the monopoly rights to first-run movies expired for downtown theaters in the mid-1970s, the remaining aboveboard theaters became increasingly threadbare and were frequently cited for health code violations.[68]

For the first time, even the already diminished "solid" retail and entertainment core of Detroit's downtown was starting to show gaps: vacant storefronts, parking lots, or even vacant lots. Suffering from a lack of money or an overall vision for downtown, most revitalization projects were incoherent, insufficient, and reactive to the Renaissance Center's dual promise of revitalization and threat of cannibalizing. The west end of downtown turned into a sea of isolated architecture, fences, and parking structures, with Detroit Edison's fledgling corporate campus, a new local Bell headquarters tower to the south, and an IRS office to the west. While the area was dubbed a "New Detroit," initial dreams of mixed-use or walkable urban districts had clearly faded.[69] To the north, the Plum Street retail experiment from the late 1960s had devolved into rampant drug trade, panhandling, and gang-related crime.[70] On the south end of Washington Boulevard, the newly constructed Pontchartrain Hotel focused on the same riverfront and convention-going clientele as the Renaissance Center, and was similarly aloof to public space.[71] While historic preservation suffered from a lack of political backing,[72] a proposal to repurpose a former Greektown warehouse as a "melieu [sic] of entertainment experiences" reflected the first signs of a reappreciation of downtown Detroit's history. The concept was inspired by the "festival marketplaces" that were being constructed in other cities such as San Francisco and Atlanta, in which existing historic buildings were used to create an exciting and secure environment for the suburban and downtown consumer, as well as for conference and tourist visitors.[73] In many ways, the project was ahead of its time, as difficulties in finding financing would delay its opening by almost a decade.

Despite the departure of Blessing, the disconnect between downtown development dreams and reality persisted—only the dreamers had changed from public agencies to private developers. The western riverfront saw no fewer than three failed proposals for apartments, stadiums, and hotels. A hotel on Michigan Avenue was shelved, as was the redevelopment of the Kern block as well as a housing project across the street from it. Twin towers with spectacular footbridges across Michigan Avenue never materialized, nor did Wayne State's proposal to move one of its colleges downtown. Almost all the plans were killed by investors' fear of crime and further deterioration. The *Detroit News*

9.6
Section of the Traugott Schmidt and Sons development, depicting an internalized consumption and entertainment center. Image from Americal Development Corporation, "Traugott Schmidt & Sons, a Melieu of Entertainment Experiences!" (Detroit, 1974).

estimated that over half a billion dollars in failed proposals had been launched between the mid-1950s and the early 1970s, concluding that in Detroit, "the dreaming has been bigger than the building."[74]

If the downtown core was having difficulties maintaining a critical mass, the downtown fringe fared even worse. By the mid-1970s, Cass Park had solidified as Detroit's place of last resort, hosting several substance abuse centers, a halfway house, and six homeless shelters, as well as several bars, dance halls, pawn shops, and pool halls. Its drug trade and prostitution attracted a regional clientele.[75] Almost half of the area comprised vacant land and vacant buildings, and arson was a regular occurrence. Along Park Avenue, Tuller's former hotels had turned into affordable residences for Detroit's "forgotten and lonely people"—mostly impoverished retirees. Seemingly, only Cass Tech saw the potential of the district as it began to purchase large tracts of land to expand its buildings into an educational campus.[76] In an effort to turn the tide in Cass Park, its local business association hired external consultants to draft plans for improvements, but with little effect.[77] To the east in Brush Park, the Woodward East project to revitalize the neighborhood was started in 1976 as part of Detroit's bicentennial celebration. Two residents of the district successfully petitioned to have it designated as historic, at least halting further planned demolitions but barely stemming the continuing deterioration.[78] The City Plan Commission resigned itself to the deterioration of downtown's peripheral business streets by allocating them to gas stations, car workshops, and even light manufacturing; the fringe further eroded into a muddle of asphalt, neon, warehouses, and ragweed.[79] By 1972, more than 50 percent of stores along Grand River Avenue near downtown were vacant; as a local business owner described it, "It's like giant termites had eaten their way along Grand River."[80]

As figure 9.7 shows, downtown Detroit continued to erode between 1967 and 1977. All public urban renewal projects had finished, of which the completed highway ring around downtown is most visible (1), ultimately cutting the urban core off from its troubled residential surroundings. The failure of many projects to materialize is illustrated by the many vacant blocks throughout downtown. Other large-scale projects were still ongoing, such as the construction of warehousing around Eastern Market (2), which had increasingly turned into a wholesale center.[81] The large footprint of the Renaissance Center (3) was completed as well, and the riverfront Hart Plaza had only partially opened (4). In much of the rest of downtown, vacancy and deterioration continued unchecked. The vacancy along the city's arterial avenues is especially apparent, with Woodward, Gratiot, Grand River, and Michigan avenues suffering from empty lots and empty storefronts as customers could now reach downtown via the new freeway system. The sunken freeways were now squarely blamed for the exodus that left "the core city as an empty shell."[82] In downtown itself, property ownership patterns had begun to consolidate, with companies like Detroit Edison, Hudson's department store, and Stroh's brewery owning whole blocks of downtown. Other landowners simply sat on their land, waiting for downtown's tide to turn. Most of their holdings were serving as parking lots, with almost 75 percent of downtown now devoted to cars.[83] Devoid of any historical structures or viable future, the place held only the ephemeral blandness of the present, "Parking Lot U.S.A."[84]

Remove
Add
Remove and add on the same site

9.7
Downtown Detroit's blocks, buildings, parcels, open
spaces, parks, and river in 1977.
Total square footage: 59.7 million square feet
Added since 1967: 12.8 million square feet
Removed since 1967: 6.0 million square feet
Percent of downtown that is vacant or parking lot: 44%

10 RENAISSANCE AMONG RUINS: 1977–1988

The dedication of the Renaissance Center in 1977 brought much-needed renewed spirit to the city. The complex was an initial success: upon opening, the hotel was fully booked, the offices were already 75 percent leased, convention business was at a record level, and retailers were swarmed by the suburban clientele they were looking for.[1] At the opening ceremony, Henry Ford II proudly proclaimed, "Detroit has reached the bottom and is on its way back up." He added, "If we all co-operate together and do things together, we can once again make this the great city it was during World War II."[2] Capitalizing on the positive energy from the opening of the Center, the Community and Economic Development Department—which had emerged as a powerful successor to the Planning Commission in downtown affairs—sponsored the publication of a *Detroit Free Press* special issue on all the projects that were "rebuilding" Detroit, as "the Detroit development picture is growing so fast and in so many different ways that describing it is an extraordinary task." The issue listed over seventy downtown projects that were either built, under construction, or planning to break ground soon; "Downtown Detroit's spectacular rebirth is happening right now."[3]

This would prove to be an overly rosy view on downtown development, however. Downtown's fate would only worsen over the next decade, and measures to counter its decline would prove not only insufficient but often counterproductive. The downtown retail market continued its decline into irrelevance, with sales plummeting to an insignificant 2.1 percent of the metropolitan area's total.[4] In the shadow of the Renaissance Center opening, Crowley's department store closed due to declining sales, taking many smaller retailers like jeweler Wright Kay & Co. in its wake.[5] The sparkle of the Metropolitan Building's jewelers had long worn off when the city of Detroit took over the aging skyscraper and closed it in 1979.[6] The closures reflected the continuing exodus of shoppers from downtown, as the number of people entering downtown had decreased by a third between 1960 and 1974.[7] Downtown retail was clearly losing the fight against its suburban competition, no matter how many new projects went up there.

Much of downtown's decline was due to continued fear, as citizens and suburbanites alike were afraid to go there, especially at night—even if actual safety numbers had improved since the 1967 disorders. High-profile assaults were widely covered in regional and national media, and by the mid-1970s Detroit had the highest per capita murder rate of any large American city. Both the direct effects and the reputation of Detroit's crime rate were haunting the city and its downtown.[8] The result was silence. An out-of-town journalist commented: "At 6.30pm downtown Detroit is a desolate wasteland. The Loop in Chicago has more activity at 4 a.m. than Woodward Avenue, Detroit's main drag, has at 4 p.m."[9]

The opening of the Renaissance Center didn't improve this situation. If anything, the Center continued to lure business tenants out of older buildings throughout downtown. Almost 40 percent of Center office tenants came from other downtown buildings, demonstrating downtown's dangerous zero-sum game.[10] As a result, office vacancy in downtown went from bad to worse, with owners sacrificing monumental buildings like the Michigan Theatre for parking in a desperate bid to retain office tenants, and many other older buildings fully vacant by the mid-1980s.[11] Every single downtown property lost value after the construction of the Renaissance Center, with the total assessed value of all downtown property shrinking by almost 10 percent just in the year after it opened. Some of Detroit's oldest skyscrapers were worth less even than the land they stood on.[12] Those offices that remained occupied sometimes leased at less than a third of the price of suburban counterparts, and realtors openly wondered whether some of the weakest (and oldest) buildings shouldn't just be torn down, their land serving for much-needed parking.[13] By 1984, the total square footage of offices located in Oakland County's edge cities like Southfield and Troy surpassed Detroit's, with no new significant office construction in the pipeline for downtown.[14] Hotels followed a similar path, with the Book-Cadillac Hotel hanging by a (city-funded) thread to survive through the 1980 Republican National Convention, then closing in 1984 to be renovated as a mixed-use tower but not opening again for over two decades. The convention

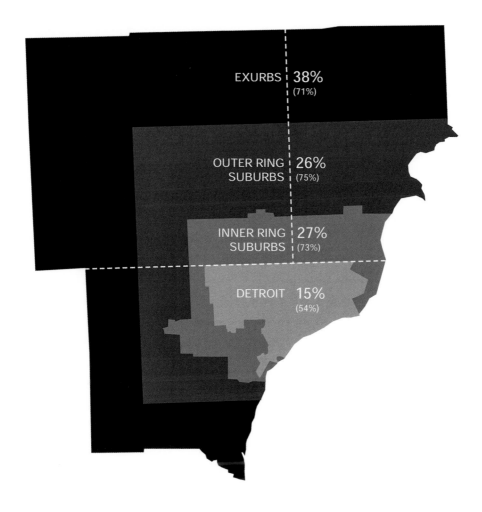

EXURBS 38%
(71%)

OUTER RING 26%
SUBURBS (75%)

INNER RING 27%
SUBURBS (73%)

DETROIT 15%
(54%)

10.1

Percentage of respondents fearful of being out alone during the day in downtown Detroit in 1979 (at night in parentheses). Redrawn by author after Citizens Research Council of Michigan, "Police Precinct One in Downtown Detroit: A Survey of Trends in Crime, Economic Activity, and Public Attitudes," Report No. 258 (Detroit, 1979).

and hotel markets were mutually depressing: convention business had dwindled due to a lack of hotel rooms, and hotel business had dwindled due to a lack of convention traffic. While the city tried to emerge from this stalemate, none of its proposals ultimately panned out due to its inability to fund them.[15]

Besides its mixed effect on Detroit's downtown, the Renaissance Center was hardly a successful venture by itself. The riverfront fortress's offices weren't universally valued, as office workers complained of their separation from the rest of the city, making them feel like "inmates."[16] Despite its novelty and relative safety, the Renaissance Center also soon lost its sheen as a retail refuge. Almost from the outset, its retail base was a failure.[17] Rather than feeling sheltered, visitors mostly felt lost in a "forbidding, even oppressive" maze of corridors, stairways, and doorways.[18] The economic recession of the late 1970s proved too much to bear, and the complex had to be sold at a significant loss in 1982 to avoid outright bankruptcy.[19] Subsequently the retail segment was drastically downsized and remodeled, and the Center finally received a proper front door to the city.[20] The Center's need for parking[21] continued to eat away at its surroundings, causing one Detroiter to comment: "It seems like the whole downtown area is becoming a parking lot for the Renaissance Center."[22] Downtown business interests exacerbated this pattern, pressuring the city to construct more public garages or provide subsidies to lower parking fees in a bid to compete with suburban office parks.[23] As they had for decades, downtown stakeholders continued to believe that in order to beat suburbia, downtown had to join it; the destructive cycle of automobile attrition went unacknowledged in their quest for a downtown rebirth.

Mayor Coleman Young had to try to revitalize downtown while his city was experiencing an accelerating socioeconomic collapse, and with little private interest in investing in the city—let alone in its crumbling core. With his agile management style and lacking other resources, Young built up a constellation of organizations to continue the transformation of downtown, propped up by various fiscal constructs.[24] The Downtown Development Authority (DDA), created in 1976 as one of the first such agencies in the nation, was mainly funded by tax increment financing (TIF), a system that leveraged anticipated increased tax revenues and special assessment taxes to obtain public investment money up front.[25] Certainly not all of the TIF revenues went to public projects—most of the money was used as "gap financing," necessary for many downtown

10.2

The grand hall of the Michigan Theatre has served as a parking garage since the 1970s.
Image courtesy of Gordon Shukwit via Flickr; Creative Commons license.

projects to proceed as private funding and federal Urban Development Action Grants became increasingly scarce.[26] As the overseer of this new funding source, the DDA became the new vehicle for "priming the pump" under Young's agenda of downtown revitalization-by-dealmaking. To facilitate economic development, Young set up a series of economic development agencies, of which the Detroit Economic Growth Corporation was the most visible and successful.[27] The Corporation has been able to incentivize businesses to return to or stay in downtown by providing them access to loans, land, and advice, while also working on public space renovations.[28] In the absence of major privately initiated projects, these agencies' proposals would become the major drivers reshaping downtown during the next decade—all within arm's reach of Mayor Young.

Among the first projects the DDA took on were the previously proposed public space improvements for downtown; the first to open, in 1977, was Woodward Avenue's reinvention as a transit-only mall. More than two decades after its initial conception in the minds of Charles Blessing, Victor Gruen, and prominent Detroit architects like Yamasaki and Rossetti, Detroit's main retail street was finally closed to cars (perhaps because traffic on Woodward Avenue had decreased so much that closure would no longer cause the congestion feared in the 1950s and 1960s).[29] Yet, as in similar projects in other U.S. cities, pedestrianization did little to spur business. The mall was also fraught with start-up problems, including an unfinished roof and poorly designed street furniture.[30] Within five years the mall was already considered a failure and the street reopened to cars.[31] Conservative *Detroit News* columnist Pete Waldmeir scalded the city for the failed plan and its botched execution, as "Woodward merchants were surrounded, isolated and systematically destroyed." City Council President Erma Henderson seemed to agree: "We know the Woodward Mall is a joke. We've sunk millions of dollars into the ground and all we've done is kill off business there."[32] Similarly, Washington Boulevard's transformation into a semi-pedestrian park designed by Rossetti Architects, soon after the closure of Woodward Avenue, aimed to turn the boulevard into Detroit's "other plaza" after Hart Plaza—complete with plenty of seating, "perhaps the world's most amazing light sculpture," and a vintage trolley line.[33] It soon became apparent that the renovated boulevard had failed to spur business, and its extravagant aesthetic was not universally popular with Detroiters. Ridership of its trolley dropped over 90 percent between its 1976 opening and the end of the century.[34]

While public space improvements at street level failed to deliver the promised revitalization, the most controversial downtown infrastructure investment would become the elevated People Mover, proposed in the mid-1970s to revitalize downtown by connecting its main destinations through a "faster, safer and more convenient" mode of transit.[35] Allied with Mayor Young on this proposal, the Central Business District Association vigorously lobbied the state and federal governments to implement the system, arguing that it might be the last way for downtown retailers to remain viable.[36] Management mismatches, path dependency, and sunk costs resulted in a system that was much

10.3

Despite its elaborate redesign and vintage trolley system,
Detroiters did not return to Washington Boulevard. Image
courtesy of David Wilson.

less useful to revitalization than proposed, at a public cost that became a source of
national ridicule. Even before construction had started, the project suffered from
almost constant conflicts between the various federal, state, and regional agencies that
were involved. Especially suburban pushback against a project they saw as only benefiting Detroit, serving downtown commuters who no longer existed, agitated federal
agencies, which killed off the regional transit portion of the system.[37]

Soon after construction started in 1983, costs had already skyrocketed due to poor
oversight and unforeseen structural issues.[38] To prevent the project from stalling

completely during construction, Mayor Young ultimately took over responsibility for it—shouldering further cost escalation and ignoring continued evidence that the system would never be utilized to its full capacity.[39] When the loop finally opened in 1987, it hardly had any destinations left to connect to, and it would mainly serve as a parking distributor for large events, with ridership falling far below the original expectations.[40] The long-drawn-out construction process had further imperiled the already fragile state of many downtown businesses—which were never big proponents of the system anyway.[41] While Young continued to chase his dream of the People Mover as a hub for a larger regional transit system, his proposals were consistently ignored by the federal government.[42]

Another significant DDA focus was boosting the middle-class population in downtown. The number of downtown residents had dropped by more than 75 percent from a peak in the 1940s, and the city argued that new residents could provide a customer base for commercial improvements.[43] As suburban customers, new corporations, retailers, and developers steered clear of downtown, City Council had few other options than to focus on attracting local residents as a downtown audience.[44] The local press largely agreed, holding that "it's only when people in great numbers live in and use a city by day and by night that a city functions fully."[45] The several projects that were implemented by the DDA for this purpose had mixed results, however.[46] The first project to open was Trolley Plaza, a downtown high-rise apartment building on top of a parking garage funded with federal Urban Development Action Grant money, with a small number of retail units on the ground floor fronting Washington Boulevard.[47] The city saw the Plaza complex as the catalyst to build thousands of new apartments along the boulevard, including converting older buildings.[48] These other projects never followed, however, and while Trolley Plaza was quite successful in attracting tenants, it mostly turned away from public space; besides the recessed lobby, "the building's main connection to the street is the black hole of automobile entrances and exits."[49] Right across the street from the Renaissance Center, a similarly introverted complex, the Millender Center, included a mixture of apartments, shops, and a hotel on top of a large federally funded parking garage; it even converted a block of downtown Larned Street into a car tunnel.[50] The project's raised connections to the Renaissance Center and the People Mover via skywalks ensured that its residents would not have to walk on the street.[51] Finally, developers Max Fisher and Alfred Taubman rather reluctantly developed a set of three riverfront apartment towers west of the new Joe Louis Arena, facing Jefferson Avenue with a hostile five-story parking garage.[52] These three residential projects brought a "new breed" of highly educated professionals back to live downtown, but had very limited effects on street vitality.[53]

The ineffective People Mover, futile public space improvements, and introverted apartment buildings demonstrated the inability of the DDA to reverse downtown's decline, but at least these projects were built. The agency's keystone project to boost downtown retail never was, and left a trail of destruction in its wake. Hudson's department store joined forces with retail developer Alfred Taubman to call in 1977 for a multistory downtown mall to replace its aging and oversized Woodward Avenue store. Inspired by other urban malls, the modern and self-contained Cadillac Center mall was to have covered multiple central retail blocks to spur "the renaissance of retailing of downtown Detroit."[54] Hudson's decision to demolish its historic home drew ire from locals, who joined forces as People for Downtown Hudson's to save the building, but Mayor Young, City Council, and ultimately the federal government agreed that the venerable department store building was standing in the way to progress.[55] Hudson's namesake president extolled the virtues of the replacement plan, connecting it to the perceived positive momentum of the Renaissance Center: "The Renaissance Center was Phase One, Phase Two should be the Cadillac Center."[56]

The big difference was that, while Ford's might stood behind the Renaissance Center, Hudson was not able to muster sufficient financial and commercial backing to start the project on his own. The project stalled when federal funding was not fully secured and loan interest rates soared,[57] and it died when private interest from other anchor retailers never truly materialized.[58] While Hudson's warned that it was running out of patience, Mayor Young quietly conceded that the plan was effectively dead by 1980 due to continuing economic and fiscal adversity. True to his assertive style, most of the land for the mall had already been cleared before the deal was finalized, and some of downtown's prime blocks would lie derelict for decades to come.[59] Other parts of the project were left to die on their own. Suffering from being in the path of the Cadillac Center, several proposals to renovate the run-down remains of Detroit's former entertainment hub along Monroe Avenue were rejected; the block was ultimately in such bad shape that it had to be mostly demolished—a classic case of planner's blight.[60]

10.4
Trolley Plaza (left) addresses the street with a parking garage; the Millender Center
(right) is buffered by asphalt, the overhead People Mover, and pedestrian walkways.
Images by author, 2017.

10.5

Decay on Monroe Avenue after the failure of the Cadillac Center. Image courtesy of Library of Congress, from Historic American Buildings Survey, HABS MICH, 82-DETRO, 58-1.

It would be unfair to blame the DDA's failure to spur downtown growth on political handwringing or mismanagement. The devastating economic recession of the early 1980s had killed the market for downtown development, after the 1970s oil crises and continued slump in Detroit car manufacturing had brought Detroit's economy to its knees.[61] Under the Reagan administration, Detroit could also no longer count on the federal government to step in—leaving it with only its own TIF funding.[62] Combined with several legal issues, City Hall faced another deep fiscal crisis in the early 1980s— hardly the climate for making significant downtown investments.[63] The recession brought another wave of downtown retail closures, most notably Hudson's department store after the 1982 Christmas season. Over the years, the once-grand "Matriarch of Woodward" had become a shadow of its former self, described by historian Jerry Herron as "a forlorn place that could have been the stage set for a period movie."[64] With its closure, a third of downtown's sales were immediately wiped out, causing an inevitable ripple of smaller store closures.[65] Despite this high-profile failure, Young refused to lay out a clear master plan for downtown revitalization, fueling investor uncertainty. He continued to oppose master plans for the damage they had done in the past, fueling land speculation and curbing the city's ability to make deals with private investors and the federal government on the high-visibility projects he sought.[66] Following developer and Council pressure, a draft downtown master plan was finally unveiled in 1985—by a skeleton Planning Department with only 25 staff members left. The overly vague plan was widely criticized and almost immediately abandoned by its drafters, followed by years of silence.[67] In frustration, downtown business leaders would start working on their own strategic plan for revitalization.[68]

As in previous decades, the periphery of downtown fared even worse than the core. When built at all, peripheral projects often focused on cars over people, and defensibility over transparency. The fringe suburbanized further with the growth of Detroit Edison's introverted corporate campus, two large prison facilities, and the conversion of Stroh's former brewery into a low-density office campus.[69] Outside the highway ring, beyond the reach or interest of Young and the DDA, only neglect remained in Detroit's oldest neighborhoods. Struggling Brush Park and Corktown were designated as historic districts by the city, but continued to decline.[70] Between these two neighborhoods, Cass Park remained one of the highest crime areas in the city.[71] Building deterioration,

10.6
The last days of Hudson's closed department store: a mostly vacant shadow
of its former glory, presenting itself to the virtually empty downtown with
shuttered windows. Image courtesy of Walter P. Reuther Library, Archives of
Labor and Urban Affairs, Wayne State University. Image from *Detroit News*,
November 2, 1985.

vacancy, and parking attrition continued unabated, especially along formerly grand radials like Woodward, which now read as "a long trail of steel gates—slammed shut across store windows by nervous merchants—and neglected, vacant store fronts."[72] City-funded beautification schemes couldn't mask the fact that these avenues had simply lost their relevance as access points to downtown, as aptly identified by *Detroit News* columnist George Cantor: "The freeway system has been in place for so long that most commuters are quite literally lost without it. The surface streets are just names on an overpass. There are thousands of people working downtown who haven't actually seen Detroit in years. All they know of it is what they can glimpse from the ditch. It's the automobile's final revenge on the city. It has made it invisible."[73]

However, the periphery of downtown was also the location of the first beginnings of a trend of privately financed preservation and entertainment-led revitalization. After two false starts by others,[74] former Ford dealership scout Chuck Forbes bought up the nearby Fox, State, and Gem theaters to renovate them into a similarly themed "Theater District," aimed at a younger audience that hadn't witnessed the frustrating decline of downtown. Forbes explains his focus: "Young people … don't know about this great downtown that existed in the '40s and the '30s, maybe even the '50s. All they know is that *this* is their downtown and this is where the big buildings are. And they can come down and take it for what it is."[75] Using personal savings, investment income, and connections to Detroit's elite, Forbes ultimately amassed over thirty surrounding properties.[76] While he arguably bit off more than he could chew, Forbes can be seen as Detroit's first pathbreaker for historic preservation, demonstrating that leveraging downtown's past could lead to a better future.

As in many other North American cities, young and highly educated Detroiters were indeed slowly finding their way back to downtown as an unexplored territory, prompting renewed interest in loft living and entertainment.[77] A few blocks south of Forbes's project, a group of DJs opened the Music Institute on Broadway, the world's first "techno" club. While techno culture was inspired by the New York and Chicago electronic music scene and had sprouted in suburban Belleville, Music Institute cofounder Alton Miller became fascinated with the sense of freedom that downtown's emptiness offered: "You had to be an urban warrior to make your way through [downtown]. …

We were on an island unto ourselves for the most part."[78] The techno music scene saw old Detroit as a key part of its underground identity, with prominent DJs like Jeff Mills and the Electrifying Mojo playing in downtown clubs. Slowly, concerts matured from rave parties in empty buildings to permanent clubs like The Works in Corktown and Saint Andrew's Hall in downtown. Though downtown's theaters continued to suffer from a lack of maintenance, they became centers for Detroit's growing dance scene, hosting weekly shows like Club Land at the State Theatre, and heavily advertised events like the 1984 Motor City Break Dance competition at the Fox Theatre.[79]

To the east of downtown, the Eastern Market reemerged as a place for consumption as well as encounter. A suburban visitor complimented the market's vibrancy amid Detroit's decay: "Eastern Market is the most citylike place in Detroit."[80] Nearby Greektown had grown into another success story, its eclectic cluster of shops and restaurants remaining one of central downtown's last vibrant commercial strips. The limits for downtown Detroit's entertainment market would soon show, as developments that tried to spin off from Greektown withered. After running out of money in 1982, the 1970s Greektown festival marketplace received a heavily subsidized 1983 reboot as Trappers Alley, opening two years later. The "upscale festival mall of shops" was initially successful, prompting several expansion plans, but within a few years it began to experience poor retail sales along with a significant turnover of tenants.[81] Grassroots projects to start a nightlife and entertainment cluster to Greektown's south in the newly named Bricktown district, spruce up storefronts on Broadway west of Greektown, or increase security in shops relieved merchants' short-term concerns but did little to stem the decline in the long run.[82] However, the various peripheral entertainment- and commerce-led enterprises laid the conceptual groundwork for future downtown transformation, proving that with enough investment and proper theming, suburban audiences could be lured back downtown.

More than twenty years after the civil disorders of 1967, downtown Detroit had never fully recovered. The 1988 map shows that the rot that had started decades ago in the periphery had fully made its way into the retail core, with a continuity of buildings—let alone occupied buildings—no longer present anywhere downtown. Even the former main retail strip on Woodward Avenue was now mostly deserted, and the venerable buildings along Washington Boulevard had given way to decay (1).

Undermaintained parking lots permeated downtown as "a symbol of defeat"; their own purpose was in question as visitor numbers plummeted.[83] The freeways that had been bulldozed through Detroit's fabric to save its downtown had become similarly quiet, as more than three-quarters of Detroit metropolitan residents no longer lived or worked in the city by the late 1980s.[84] Peripheral blocks that once reflected the modern hopes of rebooting downtown now faced the indefinite twilight of vacancy, as entire swaths of land on the west and east sides of downtown lay fallow (2). Devoid of any prospect, the neighborhoods circling downtown continued their long spiral of decline, the central retail strips along Detroit's main boulevards now nearing the point of extinction (3). The only new construction had been heavily subsidized with public money, such as the new downtown and riverfront apartments (4) and an expansion of Cobo Hall into Cobo Center (5).[85] Hardly any of these buildings added to the street-level vibrancy of downtown.[86]

The dire state of downtown toward the end of the 1980s reflected the ultimate failure of Young's strategy of attracting private investment with large, high-profile projects. While he had started his career with ties to the federal government and local business leaders that secured a continuing flow of money into the city and its downtown, one by one his connections had faltered.[87] The failure of Young's downtown plans was inevitable, as the city had to swim against a tide of overall socioeconomic decline and increasingly organized suburban competition.[88] A 1987 opinion poll revealed that three-quarters of Detroiters expected to move to the suburbs over the next five years, including two-thirds of the African American population.[89] The city suffered from the highest poverty rate and job loss rate of America's ten largest cities.[90] In a dystopian 1987 movie rendition of "Old Detroit," gangs and corporations rule the city's streets, to be saved by RoboCop. Above the first page of the script, screenwriter Ed Neumeier had ominously scribbled: "The Future left Detroit behind."[91] Seeing their dreams wither, Young's planning director Corrine Gilb, retail developer Alfred Taubman, and retailer Joseph Hudson commented resignedly that the collapse of downtown Detroit was its destiny from the outset. Flat land, high wages, and a decentralized industry had created a city that never lent itself to downtown density in the first place.[92] Such defeatist statements echoed throughout the region, and the local press started to lose hope for Young's agenda for downtown. The city's constellation of quasi-public agencies hadn't increased

Remove

Add

Remove and add on the same site

10.7
Downtown Detroit's blocks, buildings, parcels, open
spaces, parks, and river in 1988.
Total square footage: 62.2 million square feet
Added since 1977: 8.0 million square feet
Removed since 1977: 5.6 million square feet
Percent of downtown that is vacant or parking lot: 44%

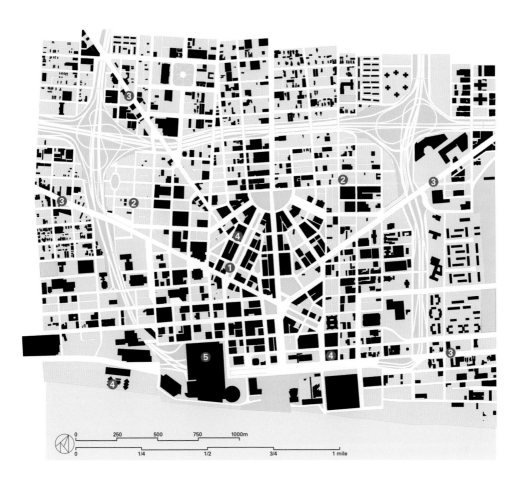

10.8

The Tuller Hotel's former grand ballroom sits empty and vandalized in 1989. Image courtesy of Library of Congress, from Historic American Building Survey, HABS MICH, 82-DETRO, 65-29, June 1989.

its efficacy, funded with TIF money that was increasingly viewed as "[robbing] the future to pay the present."[93] Circled by a practically empty People Mover, downtown Detroit's streets were lined with vacant storefronts and office lobbies; Young's grand visions without a grand plan had little spinoff beyond their own perimeter.[94]

11 THE LEISURE CITY: 1988–2001

In 1990, the *New York Times* visited Detroit again, and its observations of downtown were far more sobering than those it made four and six decades earlier. "Detroit today is a genuinely fearsome-looking place. ... Worst of all is the downtown. Several of the landmarks on Woodward Avenue remain, and in the last few years, there have been several grandiose building projects, but they can't obscure the fact that downtown Detroit is now pretty much empty. Entire skyscrapers—hotels, office buildings and apartment houses—are vacant and decaying; you can walk a downtown block during business hours without passing a living soul."[1] The *Times'* street-level observations matched more official counts, as almost 50 buildings with more than 7 million square feet of space lay vacant in Detroit that year. Detroit's busiest former streets were now mostly vacant, haunted by gangs and a refuge for the homeless.[2] Downtown had shed yet another 18,500 jobs in the 1980s, and the end was not in sight.[3] Heavily subsidized zero-sum developments, a seemingly arbitrary downtown development strategy, the loss of federal support for renovations, and Detroit's ongoing fiscal and economic downturn had created a stalemate. Renovating downtown buildings was too pricey, but so was demolition, leaving only neglect. Historic Hotel Fort Shelby's owner explained, "I pay my taxes and I sit and wait."[4] Visiting Detroit in 1992, Chilean-born photographer Camilo Vergara observed downtown's dereliction: "On the streets, wanderers and madmen sit on the sidewalks or push shopping carts. ... Late at night the People Mover, reduced to one brightly lit car, loops around completely empty, as if carrying a party of phantoms from station to station. ... This is a downtown mothballed, a stage set hoping for a replay of the 1930's, a place to wait for the millennium amid the homeless, ... the pigeons and bats."[5] Downtown had turned from a symbol of hope into a vacant monument to failure, an embarrassment for the city.

On his way out, Mayor Coleman Young finally presented a master plan for the city and its downtown in 1992. The plan remained as flexible as possible to enable his typical governance style of revitalization through piecemeal deals.[6] Yet this style had only resulted in disconnected nodes of activity, struggling and scattered in a downtown landscape of parking, blank walls, and deterioration. In a four-page special, the *Detroit News* lamented the combination of defensive architecture, car dependence, and laissez-faire planning that had resulted in an unexciting, unwalkable, and often downright unsafe downtown streetscape. Famed Philadelphia postwar urban designer Edmund Bacon stressed the importance of continuity of street-level activity that was sorely lacking in downtown: "Things just aren't tied in together in Detroit. The Renaissance Center is in isolation. Hart Plaza is in isolation. Trappers Alley and Greektown are great, but they don't relate synergistically with anything else. The rest of downtown is only a blur."[7] Up in the air, the People Mover that was supposed to tie Young's projects together mostly functioned as a leisure ride for suburbanites, and ran at such a deficit that he was only narrowly able to fend off a 1992 proposal to shut the system down.[8] While Young had spent or cajoled billions of dollars for downtown projects during his tenure, they had not crystallized into the renaissance he had hoped for, the sort that was lifting up so many of Detroit's North American peers.[9]

Yet the 1990s saw a slow turn in the tide for downtown, helped by four trends. The first was a political paradigm shift that followed the election of Dennis Archer as mayor of Detroit in 1993, which especially improved the planning, development, and economic climate of downtown Detroit. Archer reinstated a fully functional Planning and Development Department and drastically improved Detroit's ties with regional businesses, assuring them that he was able to provide a stable environment for downtown investments.[10] Archer understood the importance of more organized downtown development—although he remained focused on projects reflecting prestige and power. He was also able to benefit from an uptick in employment in the automobile industry in Detroit. Having reinvented themselves, the Big Three were back in full swing, investing in new factories and, in some cases, their first downtown offices.[11] Thirdly, downtown benefited from a national rediscovery of urban cores as places to live, play, and work. Primarily this was the result of a realization of the value and permanence of historical structures, although Detroit was late to catch up.

The reappreciation of downtown's past solidified during the 1990s and was joined by a fourth and national shift: a focus on downtowns as entertainment centers. While for some downtown was a gritty symbol of failure, a new generation increasingly saw it as a playground to be explored and exploited. Beyond the underground ravers and techno music enthusiasts, a larger cohort of suburbanites began to return downtown. It had lost its role as a place for business and struggled to become a place to live, but downtown could surely be a place to play. Detroit was part of a national trend to bring entertainment back to cities, spurring a multibillion-dollar entertainment and development industry by the 1990s.[12] While downtown's reboot was slow in the 1990s, strands of these four trends created a beneficial climate for its renaissance in the decades to follow.[13]

Besides these larger trends, Archer was also able to benefit from a few ongoing local development processes. Downtown's refocus as an entertainment destination had started under Mayor Young, albeit rather slowly. In 1987, the city had pressured over-burdened developer Chuck Forbes to sell the crown jewel Fox Theatre to Michael Ilitch, owner of the Little Caesars pizza chain. Reeling from the loss of major corporations to the suburbs, including competing pizza chain Domino's to Ann Arbor, Young was desperate for good corporate news and found Ilitch willing to move back to his hometown. With significant city support, Ilitch renovated the theater and moved his corporate headquarters into it.[14] Ilitch agreed to join forces with Forbes to transform the vicinity of the Fox Theatre into an entertainment district in which a mainly suburban target clientele could enjoy Detroit in security and comfort, "a sizable amount [of which] haven't ventured into the city since we had our problems in the late 1960s."[15] Keen to bring business back to downtown, the city continued to support Ilitch with direct subsidies and tax breaks—to the chagrin of locals who argued this funding took away from much-needed neighborhood improvements.[16] Furthermore, the city gave Ilitch and Forbes a surprising amount of leeway to transform "their" district as they wished, with relatively little need for public vetting. Ilitch brought what Detroit Edison had achieved on the west side of downtown and Forbes had started to the north to the next level—private entities effectively controlling entire downtown districts. Ilitch's holdings in the area grew to become Foxtown, a distinct restaurant, bar, and entertainment district in

11.1
After fifteen years of vacancy, the Tuller Hotel was demolished in 1991.
Image © Detroit Free Press/ZUMA.

the city. The bet had paid off: the Fox Theatre became the nation's top-grossing theater by 1989, helping Forbes's nearby theaters to blossom as well.[17]

Ilitch's real masterstroke was to expand his sports entertainment offerings. Speculation about stadium construction for three different teams would start a game of chess in the northern part of downtown for most of the 1990s, resulting in a rather disjointed urban landscape at the dawn of the new millennium. The first move came in 1992, when Ilitch purchased the Detroit Tigers from a rival pizza tycoon and openly contemplated a move from their aging Corktown ballpark to a location right across Woodward Avenue from his head offices—fulfilling the wish of City Hall to keep the team close to downtown.[18] Ilitch already had experience with sports and stadium dealings, as he had owned the downtown-based Detroit Red Wings since the 1980s.[19] In 1994, he presented a grand vision for an entertainment district encompassing almost all of downtown between Grand Circus Park and the Fisher Freeway, centered on a new Tigers Stadium to the east, connected to his Woodward Avenue holdings by a range of shops, a Motown Museum, a movie theater, and various restaurants, topped by condominiums. Due to rampant land speculation and opposition to the public subsidies that he asked to build the district, Ilitch presented a pared-down plan for a stadium west of Foxtown a year later, receiving public approval for city funding in a 1996 ballot and court approval for state funding soon after.[20]

The stadium plans changed again when Detroit Lions owner William Clay Ford proposed a downtown stadium for his team, opening the opportunity for the two stadiums to share parking facilities.[21] As a result, Ilitch shifted his planned stadium back to the east of Woodward Avenue. Despite protests from preservationists and antitax activists, the city, county, and state supported the proposals with significant amounts of tax revenue, bonds, and their power of eminent domain to purchase most of the downtown area between Grand Circus Park and the Fisher Freeway. A special authority was set up to quickly purchase the land to stave off further speculation, and to sell bonds to finance this process.[22] Dozens of buildings including the historic downtown YMCA were subsequently razed to make way for the stadiums; others were moved, such as the Gem Theatre and Elwood Grill owned by Chuck Forbes.[23]

Subsidizing the plans of a multimillionaire with tax money was sharply criticized by some as "corporate welfare," although the Tigers had a relatively high equity share compared to contemporary stadium deals.[24] But apart from fiscal spinoffs, the stadiums hardly generated downtown commerce or street life beyond their perimeters. While Ilitch and Ford spared no expense to build high-quality stadiums that resonated more than the bland Joe Louis Arena,[25] they were allowed to internalize all entertainment, bar, and restaurant concessions, creating a self-sufficient "entertainment destination."[26] Comerica Park built an atrium and Ford Field used a former Hudson's warehouse to integrate its full range of dining and entertainment facilities.[27] Vast amounts of parking pervaded the district, especially blighting the area west of Woodward Avenue.[28] This land, briefly considered for a stadium location and now on hold for a potential future project, was covered with gravel and merely used for overflow parking until well into the new millennium.[29] As a result, northern downtown Detroit turned into a "virtual fiefdom" of privatized, car-oriented entertainment, from which downtown Detroit would only serve as a backdrop during sports games.[30] On game nights, a wave of suburban cars and trucks would enter downtown Detroit for a few hours, leaving it as quiet as ever when they left.

Casinos were another large and controversial newcomer in downtown. Since Mayor Young's first attempts to permit them in the 1970s, citizens had staved off gambling in referenda, but the promise to use casino revenues to stem Detroit's tide of rising city taxes and poor public services, and to counter the competition of a Canadian casino across the river in Windsor, finally swayed them in 1994.[31] In 1996, City Hall proposed three downtown casinos, which it was promised would return vitality to downtown, bring 3,000–4,000 jobs, and contribute to a fund to renovate or demolish blighted homes and downtown buildings.[32] State legislation issues, intense land speculation, and political handwringing would delay the casino openings for years, leaving a trail of missed opportunities, vacant land, and litigation instead. Especially Mayor Archer's close involvement in the development process of the casinos proved counterproductive, as he frequently changed his plans, leaving investors confused, sites unused, and landowners furious. Initially, Archer was strongly opposed to opening casinos near the waterfront or any of the stadiums under construction, and he ultimately selected three inland downtown sites to allow for maximum spinoff effects.[33] After two years of land speculation based on this plan, Archer suddenly changed his mind and insisted on riverfront locations for the casinos, thrilling casino owners yearning for a glamorous

11.2

At Comerica Park, the downtown skyline all but frames the sports experience.

Image courtesy of Dan Gaken via Flickr.

location, shocking riverfront preservationists, killing a fledgling entertainment district, and stalling proposals for a mixed-use Rivertown district on the site.[34]

While riverfront negotiations were still ongoing, the casinos were allowed to construct temporary buildings, scattered around downtown.[35] The MGM casino would be the first to start out in a temporary facility in a former federal building on Michigan Avenue. Partly owned by Michael Ilitch's wife, the Motor City Casino opened soon after on the northwest side of downtown, ultimately transforming a former bread bakery into a self-contained complex covering more than four city blocks.[36] The Greektown casino was the last to open in place of the Trappers Alley complex, which had declared bankruptcy in the mid-1990s.[37]

The same rampant speculation that had obstructed Archer's aim for downtown casino locations, combined with fierce local resistance, killed his riverfront dreams in 2001.[38] The casinos were to stay in their respective locations, mostly on the periphery of downtown, while Rivertown was mostly left for dead. In the end, Archer's micromanagement of the casino site locations had only fueled political opposition, land speculation, and casino investor uncertainty.[39] Casino revenues turned out far lower than promised, and were mostly used to plug the increasing holes in Detroit's city budget. The haphazardly constructed "decorated sheds" also didn't generate much spinoff business for downtown, instead facing the street with parking lots, ramps, and blank walls.[40] Casinos retained patrons as long as possible in a completely controlled environment of sights, sounds, and smells, wrapped into buildings that served more as icons for passing motorists than as interactive parts of the city fabric, a Las Vegas Strip trait that fit poorly into the downtown Detroit context.

The corporatization of downtown development took place not only on the periphery but also in Detroit's core—albeit more quietly. In many ways, the issues plaguing the core were different from those on the periphery. Besides the fringe's parking lots, downtown's core contained sizeable office towers that had suffered from decades of vacancy, making their renovations ever more expensive—and less lucrative, as office vacancy continued to rise. As the Renaissance Center had done in the 1970s, new riverfront office buildings like One Detroit Center and 150 West Jefferson took tenants from older downtown buildings in the 1990s—especially turning the lights off in inland office corridors. Once-proud buildings like the Broderick, Stott, Penobscot, Whitney, and Book towers were either almost empty or padlocked by creditors, their smaller floorplates, aging elevators, and lack of technical amenities losing out to modern competitors. With the Tuller Hotel already torn down and the Statler empty, it seemed only a matter of time before the Fort-Shelby and Book-Cadillac underwent the same fate.[41] Some older skyscrapers changed hands with plans by the new owners to renovate, but their intentions were grounded on sentiment rather than business acumen and consistently fizzled. While some larger owners were able to invest millions, dozens more were needed, and investors steered clear as downtown rental rates simply couldn't cover

11.3
The MGM (top), Motor City (middle), and Greektown (bottom) casinos dominate the periphery of downtown Detroit. Photos by author, 2018.

renovation costs.[42] Those developers and owners who did find funding complained that the maze of semigovernmental organizations, two competing planning departments, and the inertia of the city's understaffed bureaucracy obstructed their plans.[43] Still a keen observer of downtown's stalemate, photographer Camilo Vergara made the "immodest proposal" to turn the former retail core of the city into a ruin park, a vertical "American Acropolis."[44]

Facing a lack of market interest and public resources for significant renovations, the city understood that it simply did not have the means to bring its hulking and vacant skyscrapers back to life without outside support. Young's public agencies like the DDA and DEGC had lost most of their federal, state and local TIF funding, and had proved that publicly subsidized injections of concrete simply couldn't revive a downtown without a pulse. Instead, Archer would increasingly defer downtown planning powers to the market itself, relying on a new network of public-private partnerships to augment the city departments. Archer convened a lean grouping of the Big Three automakers, other corporate leaders, and downtown stakeholders to start tackling downtown redevelopment on its own, under the leadership of Taubman Company executive Robert Larson.[45] Unlike the often grandiosely announced downtown revitalization efforts of the previous decades, the Greater Downtown Partnership mostly operated behind closed doors, starting its work six months before its existence was even made public. The secrecy had a purpose: the organization had decided that in order to make a difference in downtown, it had to enter the development game itself, purchasing buildings in the emptied retail core of the city. "We thought we'll never have an opportunity to do something with it unless we've got [the land]," an unnamed corporate member explained in an interview. "A lot of us said to ourselves, 'We've got to take a risk. We've got to take a gamble.'" The Partnership uniquely enjoyed both public power and deep private pockets, allowing it to acquire significant downtown properties without the burden of involving the public in its activities.[46]

While the Partnership initially had no overarching plan for its purchases, it hired Toronto-based Urban Strategies designer Ken Greenberg to draft a vision for the urban core to guide building acquisition and redevelopment. Understanding downtown's lack of coherence, Greenberg defined its remaining loose nodes of activity as "urban villages," and focused his efforts on their interconnection into a coherent yet diverse urban environment. Instead of perpetuating the pattern of large investments with little spinoff, downtown's growth was to consist of humanly scaled redevelopment of the areas between these nodes, likened by *Detroit Free Press* architectural critic John Gallagher to the "mortar between the bricks."[47] The Archer administration proudly presented the plan and its focus on connectivity as a strategy to create "a critical mass that is so important to the development of our core downtown district."[48]

Greenberg's vision for incremental development between downtown's hotspots reflected the beginning of a trend. With relatively little city funding and hardly reliant on a central plan, several small infill developments had begun to spin off from the on-the-ground success of Foxtown, the stadiums, and casino developments. Most of all, they benefited from a drastic shift in the public perception of downtown Detroit, from an area of missed opportunities and hollow shells to a blank canvas ripe for transformation. These developments had a common thread of entertainment and heritage, focusing on a growing cohort of middle- and upper-class suburban remigrants. Between the successful Greektown and Foxtown developments and close to the newly reopened Music Hall and the Detroit Opera House, Broadway and Harmonie Park experienced a modest rebirth.[49] Smaller vacant office buildings and retail stores began to be transformed into loft apartments for those who sought an urban lifestyle in an increasingly suburbanized region.[50] The relaxation of national and state building codes, a rise in local investor confidence, historic preservation tax credits, and the rising demand for unique downtown living spaces generated many renovation projects, early signs of a viable downtown loft market.[51] More organically than Young's major residential complexes of the 1980s, these smaller residential conversions spurred the growth of retail and entertainment options throughout downtown, although they remained scattered gems in a sea of blight. Benefiting from the success of Midtown's revitalization to the north, downtown loft renovation projects were slowly being picked up by investors. Perhaps more importantly, their success changed the regional conversation about downtown, setting an upward cycle in motion.[52]

Greenberg's plan encompassed the entire downtown, but the Greater Downtown Partnership continued to focus on its holdings in the retail core, in the understanding that a concentrated effort in the heart of the city could spawn larger improvements over time. The first priority was to address the largest scar left after downtown's postwar

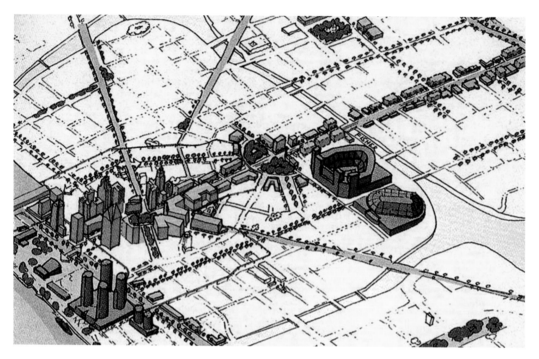

11.4

Urban designer Greenberg's vision of a reconnected downtown,
with the seeds of the Campus Martius development proposals in
orange. Image courtesy of Ken Greenberg / Urban Strategies.

demise: Hudson's department store.[53] The Partnership soon decided the building
should be demolished, and as they were joined by Mayor Archer, other business organizations, and the local press, Hudson's fate seemed sealed. The reasoning for demolition was surprisingly consistent among these powerful stakeholders: the hulking
building was deemed simply too expensive to renovate, and was holding up a prime
location for a downtown revitalization project.[54] The president of the Greater Downtown Partnership praised the demolition as enabling "one of the most significant development opportunities in urban America today."[55]

Even without elaborating what these opportunities would be, the Partnership overcame the obstacles of a skeptical City Council, other proposals for renovations, and concerted opposition from preservationists and journalists who questioned the transparency of the decision-making process. By 1997, the Council voted for Hudson's demolition—only three months after the Partnership had officially cleared its title.[56] The next year, Hudson's was imploded with "a deafening roar that will echo in the hearts of Detroiters for decades."[57] While three development teams later submitted proposals for the site, now renamed Campus Martius after Detroit's central square to the south, silence ensued.[58] All that came from the grand plans for Hudson's was an underground parking garage, with hopeful steel beams reaching for the roots of new development for two decades to follow.[59] The *Detroit News* strongly criticized this turn of events, warning that "cities are made up of equal parts of hope and memory. ... The danger is that hope can be mistaken for accomplishment."[60]

The momentum of the same Campus Martius plan that spawned the Hudson's demolition did enable a landmark development just to the south of the former department store. On the Kern block, software company Compuware announced plans to construct a million-square-foot fifteen-story headquarters as the centerpiece of the Campus Martius development, a "bold, fresh start" for the struggling downtown core, with the adjacent Crowley's block redeveloped as a massive parking garage with shops on the ground floor. Compuware expressly based its decision to locate downtown on its desire to obtain and retain a highly educated workforce, many of whom were starting to become drawn to downtown Detroit—as their HR vice president put it, "We want to be where the action is."[61] The Compuware move was accompanied by plans for an extensive renovation of Campus Martius itself as a vibrant urban park, to become an anchor in the improvement of the quality of downtown public space—an improvement first envisioned by Ken Greenberg.[62] Despite these announcements, Archer and the Greater Downtown Partnership had overplayed their hand; only a small part of their gleaming proposals for a mixed-use heart of the city actually came to fruition.[63]

The downtown riverfront received a boost with the renovation of the Renaissance Center, bailed out for the second time in its short existence, this time by General Motors, which purchased the building in 1996 for cents on the dollar. While many of the improvements were internal, the Center also finally received an improved front door onto Jefferson Avenue and a winter garden facing the Detroit River, coinciding with plans for a riverfront pathway and a mixed-use district east of the Center.[64] The state-subsidized riverfront improvements were the first step toward reconciling downtown with the Detroit River since the Civic Center of the 1950s, as most adjacent riverfront lots had been underutilized for decades following various failed proposals.[65] The Renaissance Center's seemingly ever-growing perimeter of parking garages began to respond to the rest of the city by constructing ground-floor retail, including an "Asian Village" collection of ethnic restaurants at the corner of Beaubien and Atwater streets, which unfortunately failed soon after opening.[66]

The residential districts on the periphery of downtown would also receive their first boost in decades, although results were highly mixed. Brush Park was able to benefit from federal Empowerment Zone funding that Mayor Archer's administration had secured for the city, funding the first significant planning and development in the district for over a century.[67] While Brush Park's historic mansions continued to crumble, a mixture of new townhomes, apartments, and condominiums did stabilize the neighborhood and saved it from Michael Ilitch's swelling sea of parking lots around his entertainment destinations to the south.[68] While Cass Park similarly received Empowerment Zone status, its renewal stalled as crime and transience persisted.[69] Despite heightened developer interest, the area only deteriorated further from land speculation, with former Tuller-built hotels like the Eddystone serving as homeless shelters suffering from rampant drug use, prostitution, and poverty. The decline of the district and their own temple prompted the Freemasons to move out in 1999.[70] West of downtown, Corktown benefited from a state tax break under the Neighborhood Enterprise Zone program, taking a more grassroots approach to its revitalization.[71]

As the twentieth century came to an end, downtown Detroit had reinvented itself once again. Having largely shed its role as a place of residence, industry, or commerce, the urban core had risen again, now mostly as a place of leisure. New developments such as Foxtown (1), Comerica Park (2), and casinos (3) were making their marks on the brittle urban fabric of downtown, continuing a trend of introverted megastructures in the downtown periphery. Like their predecessors, these buildings failed to prompt any significant revitalization of the existing shuttered businesses that surrounded them, with the vacant Hudson's block (4) reminding visitors of Detroit's long road ahead. As a result, downtown's sidewalks became lined by a curious medley of existing dereliction and new disaffection. The modernist echoes of Charles Blessing had ironically culminated in privatized and postmodern splendor on publicly condemned peripheral superblocks. Between the vacant remnants of Detroit past and the gaudy hulks of its future, Greenberg's grand vision of an interconnected and walkable downtown remained a pipe dream.

Dennis Archer's strategy of large-scale entertainment investments hardly created the consistently vibrant downtown that many had hoped for. In many ways, Archer was facing the same lack of downtown momentum that his predecessor Young had struggled with for two decades. While Archer's casinos, sports stadiums, and office renewals may have given more sheen and glamour to downtown, they were still heavily supported by public subsidies and failed to reach a critical mass to reboot downtown as an interconnected destination. Only a corner away from the bright lights, Detroit's most central blocks still looked like a "Canyon of Blight," its scores of vacant storefronts only interspersed with liquor, wig, and beauty supply stores.[72] The reinvention of downtown as a leisure destination may have improved its national reputation, but after the crowd returned home to the suburbs from the newly constructed entertainment palaces, silence ensued. And while downtown Detroit had successfully projected an image of safety and leisure suitable for its suburban clientele, suburbs soon copied the urban entertainment formula.[73] Perhaps by default, certainly by outcome, Archer's grand plans continued a long tradition of public ignorance on what makes a downtown tick—a layered, conflicting, but subconsciously self-reinforcing system of acts and actors, reflected and intertwined in a fine-grained physical setting. Upon visiting downtown Detroit, urban scholar Roberta Brandes Gratz warned the city administration: "A city is an intricate web of activities, businesses and people tied together. … A collection of visitor destinations a city does not make. By replacing [downtown's fabric] with suburban enclaves, Detroit risks losing the diminishing opportunity to rejuvenate a world class city. Replacement, not renewal, seems to be official policy. A rebuilt, not reborn city, will be the result."[74] While the 1990s had demonstrated that Detroit's past could pave a way to a brighter future, Gratz's recommendations would only be fully taken to heart in the following decade.

Remove
Add

11.5
Downtown Detroit's blocks, buildings, parcels, open
spaces, parks, and river in 2001.
Total square footage: 64.5 million square feet
Added since 1988: 7.5 million square feet
Removed since 1988: 5.2 million square feet
Percent of downtown that is vacant or parking lot: 50%

0   250   500   750   1000m

0   1/4   1/2   3/4   1 mile

12 A ROARING END: 2001–2011

At the dawn of the twenty-first century, Detroit celebrated its 300th birthday. While proud of its age, the city still seemed to have little regard for its past, as downtown was rapidly transforming into a generic conglomeration of suburban casinos, sports stadiums, and corporate campuses. Generations of downtown plans—from the bureaucratic bibles of the 1950s to the shotgun deals of the 1980s—had tried to compete with the suburbs on their terms, consistently envisioning downtown as a safe but sufficiently exciting place to work, shop, and later live and play. They never quite met their potential, as Detroiters had plenty of other places to choose from in the region that were closer, cleaner, safer—but most of all, newer. Masked by heavy public subsidies, planners persisted in their efforts to reshape downtown to an image of progress, ignoring the fact that true market demand for space and activity there had all but evaporated by the late twentieth century. Mere steps away from the ceremonial ribbon cuttings, most of downtown continued its hibernation.[1] Downtown's problem wasn't physical or organizational but existential. What was its purpose in the twenty-first century, especially in a region that has consistently looked beyond, favoring the new over the old? For the heart of Detroit to truly start beating, it had to search for its soul.

The new century did not signal any deviation from downtown's path of suburbanization and corporatization, with private companies and semipublic organizations like DEGC and the Greater Downtown Partnership taking an increased responsibility for planning downtown. In the downtown periphery, incoming mayor Kwame Kilpatrick inherited uncertainty about the permanent location of three casinos, swaths of city-owned vacant riverfront land, and a pile of litigation. In contrast to Archer's unsuccessful micromanagement of casino locations, Kilpatrick took a far more hands-off approach, allowing the casinos to select their ultimate locations.[2] Rather than cluster-ing in the downtown core, the casinos spread out, taking up massive amounts of down-town land and minimizing any spinoff among them or from them to the surrounding neighborhoods.[3] For example, the new design for the sprawling MGM Grand trans-formed no less than thirteen blocks in the struggling northwest portion of downtown into a massive gaming, entertainment, and hotel complex, wrapped in a mixture of lawns, driveways, neon, and blank walls. The casino would mark a new architectural milestone for Detroit, in which automobile accessibility and garish iconography trumped human scale and interaction. The periphery of downtown Detroit had finally succumbed to its suburban parasite, suburbanizing itself.

Detroit Edison's new corporate campus replicated MGM's urban paradigm across the street. Over the past decades, the energy company had forgone its initial dreams for a mixed-use "Electric City" in favor of a "grab bag of buildings" surrounded by an ephemeral sea of parking lots, utilities, and vacant spaces. In 2009, the company was able to pull together several blocks of downtown into a secured "dream campus," with several landscaped plazas and integrated parking surrounded by fences, hedgerows, and blank walls, with Edison employees passing to their parking garage through a secured overhead walkway.[4] In a more haphazard way, the federal building south of Edison's campus was similarly turned into a fortress, with makeshift roadblocks pre-venting car access to its heavily secured offices. As a result, the western end of down-town had effectively turned into two superblocks through the combined powers of private corporations and public agencies.

The peripheral suburbanization of downtown reflected the continuation of Detroit's traditional pioneering mindset that favored novelty over permanence and grandeur over incrementalism. Demolitions continued to eat into downtown's shrinking stock of historic properties, many of which had almost irreversibly deteriorated after decades of vacancy and vandalism. North of Detroit Edison's campus, Cass Tech constructed a new building in 2002, after which the old building was left to the elements until its almost inevitable demolition in 2011. After alumni were unable to save the old school building, one of them lamented: "it is a shame when a civilization destroys important parts of its heritage. *Sic transit gloria mundi*."[5] The growing need for downtown parking and the continuing deterioration of downtown buildings demonstrated that tarmac

12.1

The periphery of downtown Detroit has become a drivable corporate campus. Image by author, 2014.

still made the highest and best land use for many lots. As the historic Madison-Lenox Hotel was demolished for parking in 2005, the Ilitch family owners simply commented: "the numbers did not work for any [other] proposals."[6] Many other buildings met their end by neglect, with some malevolent owners cunningly deferring demolition costs to the city after buildings were deemed a public hazard. The city was often more than happy to oblige, keen to rid downtown of the image of failure that vacant buildings projected. For the nationally televised 2006 Super Bowl, held at the newly opened Ford Field downtown, the hosting committee created a "cleanup fund" to dress up strategic vacant buildings with paint, signs, and awnings. Many others were demolished for event parking, most notably the former Motown Music headquarters which made way for only 50 parking spots. Clearly, history hadn't changed Detroit's disregard for it.[7]

12.2

The announcement for Super Bowl XL on the Renaissance Center, viewed
through the rubble of the former Motown Music headquarters, 2006. Image
courtesy of Sean Doerr.

Amid the rubble, a countermovement grew to downtown's erosion into erasure. A slowly growing slate of smaller development and preservation projects began to benefit from their interconnection by renovated public spaces. Following the previous decade's plans for upgrading Campus Martius and leveraging the grand opening of the Compuware Building in 2003, a nonprofit corporation chaired by Ford Motors gathered funds from various businesses to redesign Detroit's central Campus Martius and Cadillac Square from a traffic junction into a high-quality public park. The grand opening of the new spaces in 2004 brought street life back to Detroit's heart for the first time in decades, acting as a "primary catalyst of downtown."[8] As the successful new public spaces soon found a place in the hearts of Detroiters, more people were starting to notice downtown's untapped potential, prompting a slow rise in nearby development activity, with some of the vacant retail palaces on Woodward Avenue redeveloped as lofts on "Merchant's Row."[9] Admitting defeat on its 1970s renovations of Washington Boulevard and Woodward Avenue, the city reverted to a more traditional street layout.[10] Along the boulevard, the Book-Cadillac Hotel was restored and reopened in 2008 with significant public funding, followed by the nearby Fort Shelby Hotel the same year.[11]

The outcomes from downtown's transformation at the dawn of the twenty-first century can be seen in figure 12.3. All three casinos have landed in the periphery of downtown (1), and the Ford Field stadium has been completed next to Comerica Park (2). On the riverfront, the start of the Renaissance Center's rapprochement with the Detroit River gathered steam with the formation of the Detroit Riverfront Conservancy by the city, GM, and the Kresge Foundation to provide Detroiters with public access to the river through a more than five-mile-long riverfront trail system (3).[12] While still in progress, this vision has created significant development momentum, with architects SOM designing the East Riverfront Masterplan that includes 480 acres of development, plans for an urban beach, and a "road diet" to make Jefferson Avenue more pedestrian- and bicycle-friendly.[13] The improvements to downtown public spaces have paired well with a revival of downtown events, augmenting Detroit's long-running Thanksgiving parade on Woodward Avenue with various ethnic and music festivals like the African World Festival, the Detroit Jazz Festival, and the Detroit Electronic Music Festival that draw millions to the city from across the world. The first editions of the Detroit Electronic Music Festival each brought more a million people to Hart Plaza, cementing the city's international reputation for techno music.[14]

Remove

Add

Remove and add on the same site

12.3
Downtown Detroit's blocks, buildings, parcels, open
spaces, parks, and river in 2011.
Total square footage: 73.0 million square feet
Added since 2001: 14.7 million square feet
Removed since 2001: 6.3 million square feet
Percent of downtown that is vacant or parking lot: 45%

A ROARING END: 2001–2011

13 A NEW BEGINNING: THE PAST AS FUTURE

The year 2011 was a turning point for downtown Detroit, as fledgling strands of historic preservation, public space improvements, and economic development intensified and coalesced. For the first time since the paradigm shifts of the 1920s skyscrapers, the 1950s dream city, and the post-1967 renaissance, the rebirth of downtown Detroit was driven not by reinvention but by repurposing. For the first time, downtown's past truly became an asset instead of a liability. After decades of demolition, the success of a single billionaire freed the conversation on historic preservation from sentimentalism and philanthropy. Quicken Loans founder and Cleveland Cavaliers owner Dan Gilbert understood that underneath downtown's crumbling brick and terracotta lay gold, and he was the first to have the power to mine it. One by one, Gilbert has been able to purchase and transform downtown buildings into his vision: a creative urban haven or a hipster theme park, depending on your point of view.

Downtown was ready for the taking. Its neglected building stock was cheaper than ever, and Detroit was starting to shift upward in the American imaginary, from a place of destitution and failure to one of freedom and opportunity. Detroit's RoboCop days were over, and the city made way for a new generation of urban pioneers. As cult icon Johnny Knoxville visited Detroit in 2010 in a highly popular online video series, he interviewed Larry D'Mongo of the namesake and recently reopened downtown bar: "If you could bring Cadillac, the early pioneers who founded this city … with the kids that come in this club, there's a lot of things y'all gonna have in common."[1] In search of this same audience of young, educated millennials, Gilbert brought thousands of his Quicken Loans employees to the Compuware building in downtown in 2010: "Kids coming out of college want that urban core excitement, more and more."[2] While precursors like Little Caesars and Compuware had similarly moved employees into downtown, Gilbert understood that his audience wasn't the suburban office worker, but a growing global elite of creative-class workers for whom urbanity had become a precondition to resettle.[3]

What set Gilbert further apart from his predecessors was his persistence and ability to build a critical mass of downtown destinations to attract this new audience. Gilbert's unprecedented level of investment echoed the formula that Tony Goldman had used to redevelop SoHo in New York and South Beach in Miami: if you control a sufficient number of urban properties, you control the fate of an area. This resemblance is not a coincidence, as Goldman had publicly expressed his interest in repeating his recipe in Detroit, giving it the potential to become "the artistic Berlin of the United States." Goldman passed away soon after expressing his faith in the city, but not before talking with local developers, including Dan Gilbert.[4] Goldman passed on the belief that a critical mass of historic preservation and urban development could create the spinoff effects that other downtown Detroit projects had failed to achieve. As long as projects brought the unique values of urban life to the market, they were sure to earn favor with America's growing cohort of young professionals yearning for excitement and authenticity—manufactured or not.

Beginning with his first conversion of a theater into a tech hub, Gilbert has paid heed to Goldman's hopeful message by purchasing around a hundred downtown properties at fire sale prices—a process he dubbed a "skyscraper sale."[5] Now amounting to triple the floor space of the Renaissance Center, his holdings are mainly comprised of the remaining cluster of historic buildings in the core district around Washington Boulevard, Woodward Avenue, and Broadway. Incrementally, Gilbert has gained control over Detroit's former retail core, transforming buildings into a mixture of dwellings, offices, and ground-floor amenities. Understanding that the majority of his target audience of young professionals would appreciate downtown only as a complete urban experience, he launched a network of companies and consultancies to simultaneously act as developer, broker, and tenant. After successfully testing the market with a pop-up retail cluster in 2011, Gilbert worked with retail consultants to revitalize the ground-floor economy of downtown with an eclectic mixture of bars, restaurants, and shops, almost exclusively aimed at an upmarket millennial audience. To assume further control over the ground-floor landscape of downtown, Gilbert has even taken over ground-floor leases of buildings he did not control to create a critical mass of walkable destinations. His ultimate aim was nothing short of a paradise.

What makes Gilbert's vision so unique is the latitude he has found to implement it. Not only has he been able to benefit from downtown's bargain basement building stock to gather millions of square feet in holdings; Detroit's unprecedented public power vacuum has enabled him to use these buildings in any way he desired. As the city struggled to keep itself fiscally afloat and ultimately succumbed to the largest municipal bankruptcy in American history in 2013, urban planning and development have taken a back seat to survival of city services and pensions.[6] As a result, philanthropic and private organizations have picked up public tasks that include a foundation-sponsored citywide master plan, as Gilbert joined forces with the Downtown Detroit Partnership and the Detroit Economic Growth Corporation to plan for downtown's future under the Opportunity Detroit moniker. This mostly privately led organization has commissioned various plans to transform downtown into a "great urban neighborhood that has a unique point of view, where people will choose to live, work, shop and play," a concept that positions downtown as a self-sufficient entity rather than a hub for the still-decaying city that surrounds it, clearly targeting a demographic of creative millennials and empty nesters.[7] The divide would soon be noticed by the local press, with *Detroit News* columnist Laura Berman warning that "Detroit is running on two parallel tracks at breakneck speed. One is fresh, vibrant, optimistic. This is the city that's drawing young people with college degrees and dreams of creating meaningful change. … Look out the window from the other track, though: you'll see much of Detroit's 138 square miles as industrial wasteland, tossed-out junk or people living in these places, praying for a better life."[8]

Nevertheless, City Hall has welcomed the private initiatives with open arms—it hardly had a choice. As Detroit's police and public works departments were treading water in the city's troubled neighborhoods, they gladly relinquished downtown safety and upkeep to a newly instated Business Improvement Zone in 2014, in which a supplementary tax on downtown businesses helps to pay for public improvements and privatized security, overseen by the Downtown Detroit Partnership.[9] Transportation was the next public service to be taken over when federal support for a new streetcar

13.1

A rendering for a remodeled Capitol Park depicts active public space with young professionals. Image from Opportunity Detroit, Project for Public Spaces, and D:hive Detroit, "A Placemaking Vision for Downtown Detroit" (Detroit, 2013), 43.

line to connect downtown to the rest of the city faltered in 2011. As two of the main downtown business interests, Dan Gilbert and Michael Ilitch joined forces with other major corporations and foundations to take control of the project and help fund the construction of its first phase.[10] The private support focused on the successful completion of a stretch from downtown to Midtown and New Center, which over the past decade has become Detroit's fastest-growing corridor of businesses, institutions, and highly educated professionals and has been rebranded as the "7.2 square miles."[11]

While the outcomes may look different, Gilbert's ability to consolidate and control a significant portion of downtown bears a remarkable resemblance to Detroit Edison's corporate campus, Ilitch's entertainment district, and the sports arenas and casinos scattered about downtown Detroit. Benefiting from significant local, state, and federal tax benefits for historic preservation and downtown redevelopment, Gilbert has been given virtually free rein to construct avant-garde parking garages with art-filled alleyways, purchase the Greektown Casino, build Michigan's tallest tower on the former Hudson's site, plan for a soccer stadium, reconstruct the Monroe block, and even branch out into Brush Park to construct housing for his employees and target audience.[12] As a result, Detroit's most central streets have transformed into a veritable playground for young, highly educated workers in the design language of a single owner.[13] Fitting Detroit's spirit of pioneerism, downtown has been rediscovered by the Antoine Cadillac of finance, proudly proclaiming his conquest of "Detroit 2.0."[14]

Gilbert's unprecedented grip on downtown has prompted critics to dub his holdings "Gilbertville," a comparison to Ilitch's Foxtown north of downtown.[15] Opponents of Gilbert's strategies specifically focus on his private surveillance of downtown's main public spaces and his displacement of longtime residents and business tenants. As downtown is running out of historic properties, pressure on long-standing business owners to sell their properties to Gilbert and move out their tenants has grown. His successful investments have caused rents to skyrocket throughout downtown, even displacing tenants from buildings he does not own or operate.[16] Similarly, downtown's homeless population has felt pressure to steer away from downtown, even though many of their facilities are located in or near the urban core.[17] On the other hand, Gilbert's influence has actually diminished as a result of his success, as a growing number of competing investors have entered the market.[18] After being stuck with the Broderick Tower since the 1970s, the owner of the 34-story skyscraper joined forces with other investors to start a $55 million residential renovation in 2011, opening at full occupancy the next year.[19] Similarly, the Whitney Building has been transformed into a hotel and upscale apartments for over $90 million.[20] The influx of investment into downtown also accelerated the 20-year-old Harmonie Park renovation project with $50 million of investment, rebranding the area as the Paradise Valley Cultural and Entertainment District after its former African American roots.[21] Meanwhile, home prices in Corktown and Lafayette Park have steadily risen due to the "Dan Gilbert effect" of their reinvigorating neighbor.[22]

Gilbert's success even inspired the late Michael Ilitch and his family to continue their land development on the northern side of downtown. Taking a far more guarded and

13.2

Downtown Detroit's rebirth contrasts past and present. More than a century after its construction, the Dime Building, outfitted by Dan Gilbert's Bedrock Detroit with cameras and loudspeakers for security and beautified with a planter, awaits a new ground-floor tenant. Image by author, 2018.

less bravura approach than Gilbert, and in contrast to Gilbert's incrementalism, the Ilitches have continued their pattern of gaining ownership of an entire district and clearing it for a fully controlled experience.[23] In 2014, the family announced they would move the Red Wings hockey team to a new stadium north of Foxtown, fulfilling a long-time dream of abandoning the cramped and rather underwhelming Joe Louis Arena. Paying homage to Gilbert's successful urban formula, the stadium was promised to become the center of a dense and mixed-use district of dwellings, shops, restaurants, offices, and event spaces, richly intermixed with parking garages.[24] Instead of a mere stadium, the Red Wings' arena would become the anchor of "The District Detroit," a six-neighborhood "home to the young and the young at heart … [connecting] Downtown and Midtown into one contiguous, walkable area, where families, sports fans, entrepreneurs, job seekers, entertainment lovers and others who crave a vibrant urban setting can connect with each other and the city they love."[25]

While this description sounded urban, the development of the District itself followed the same formula that Ilitch had used in the previous decades, locating this "catalyst development project" on a half-dozen blocks cleared from the last remains of struggling Cass Park. Buildings that were considered roadblocks to the realization of the District were cleared, with only the former Eddystone Hotel surviving the Ilitch bulldozers.[26] Rather than connect with the surrounding city, the District mostly aims to bridge Ilitch's Foxtown holdings with his family's Motor City Casino, and stay away from the competing MGM Grand on the western end of downtown—which is why the vacant land west of Foxtown wasn't considered for the stadium. Over time, the landholdings may urbanize into a coherent district, mostly connected with residential, retail, and entertainment development.[27] As with his previous stadium projects, Ilitch's District has relied on extensive public land clearance and subsidies, with some critics arguing that the high level of state and local tax money, stadium naming rights, and other fees he received for the new stadium were only possible due to the political vacuum left by the 2013 Detroit bankruptcy, recalling his upper hand in dealing with a desperate Detroit in the 1980s and 1990s.[28]

In the map of downtown Detroit today, the incredible transformation of downtown Detroit over the past centuries is clearly visible, especially as it has accelerated over the past decades. Armed with public powers of condemnation and tax breaks, and fueled

■ Remove
■ Add

13.3
Downtown Detroit's blocks, buildings, parcels, open
spaces, parks, and river in 2018.
Total square footage: 75.9 million square feet
Added since 2011: 4.1 million square feet
Removed since 2011: 1.2 million square feet
Percent of downtown that is vacant or parking lot: 44%

by fire sale prices for dilapidated downtown buildings, massively scaled renewal projects have transformed the periphery of downtown Detroit into a landscape geared to the automobile—at the highest annual rate of construction since the 1920s boom years. Like the tarmac ring of parking from the 1920s, the "suffocating" ring of blight from the 1940s, the concrete ring of freeways from the 1950s, a neon ring now surrounds downtown and cuts its increasingly bright lights off from the decaying city that surrounds it. Vast casino (1), sports (2), convention (3), and office (4) "groundscrapers" and their seemingly insatiable hunger for parking have surrounded downtown's core with vast swaths of blank walls, infrastructure, car parking, and suburban landscaping, aimed at convenience and security. Similarly fueled by landholdings, the former retail core of Detroit is undergoing a rebirth with the renovation or reopening of various buildings on newly renovated streets, especially in Dan Gilbert's extensive landholdings (5). The future bodes well for downtown, as DTE (formerly Detroit Edison) is reaching out to the rest of the city with the construction of a public park at the edge of its campus (6) and the Michigan Department of Transportation has agreed to replace the eastern branch of the downtown highway loop with a surface street (7).

After decades of neglect, it has taken a new generation of dreamers to reimagine the potential of their predecessors' materialized aspirations. Downtown Detroit's new shapers have found success by venturing beyond nostalgia for past dreams or the nightmares that followed, instead balancing past, present, and future. As they have been able to amass rapidly growing portfolios of buildings born of past dreams, downtown's rebirth runs the risk of reflecting the dreams of only a few powerful investors. Gilbert's creative-class hub and Ilitch's neon ring of entertainment may reflect only their visions of a vibrant urban area, ignoring the lived realities of those who don't fit into these visions. Will downtown remain the place where all of Detroit can dream?

14 CONCLUSION

As downtown Detroit is experiencing a rebirth, it may finally come to embrace the dreams that have shaped it—from the notebook of Judge Woodward, the empires of Hudson, Tuller, the Books, and Goldberg, the African American clubs of Paradise Valley, the blueprints of Blessing and Mackie, and the showmanship of Ford II and Young to the neon lights of Ilitch and the lattes of Gilbert. The acceptance of its past would be a new thing for a city that has persisted in looking to the future, leaving downtown in a near-constant limbo it is still emerging from. Where most of the city could easily shrug off any signs of trouble and move further into the Michigan prairies, the permanence of its downtown has forced it into a constant dialogue with the materialized dreams of previous generations.

That forced dialogue makes downtown a bit of an anomaly in the city. On the other hand, the resulting contrast has made it one of North America's most fascinatingly layered places. Downtown has been the host of Detroit's oldest buildings and its newest, its largest and its smallest, its gaudiest and its most destitute. Downtown has witnessed Detroit's creation, suffered from its destruction, and now epitomizes its reinvention. The series of figure-ground maps in this book illustrate the fever that has underlain Detroit's spirit of progress, and the repercussions it has had on the built landscape. Downtown Detroit never took the time to build a "stabilizing persistence of place," which philosopher Edward Casey links to the potential to build a collective memory of a city.[1] Instead, downtown's most central locations had already been fully rebuilt two or three times over in the nineteenth century alone, a pace that would only intensify in the century to follow. During downtown's heyday in the 1910s and 1920s, it grew by 75 percent while simultaneously losing 30 percent of its previous building stock—a turnover rate unheard of in any other district.

Many authors have framed downtown's transformation in a narrative of postwar decline,[2] but demolition has always been a part of downtown's story—even during its peak. The annual rate of downtown demolition was actually the highest not just during the urban renewal era of the 1950s and 1960s, but also during the rapid growth of downtown in the 1920s.[3] When downtown grew, demolition was simply followed by more construction. As a result, the only times that downtown shrank was between the Depression and the end of urban renewal. In lean times, Detroit's cranes and bulldozers alike ground to a halt. Downtown's square footage has actually grown every year since 1967, and is now bigger than at its 1929 peak.

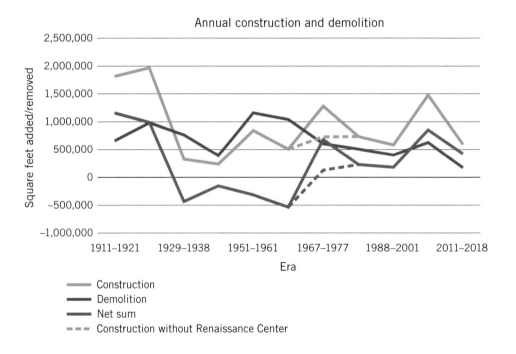

14.1

Annual square footage of construction and demolition, showing a decreasing rate of demolition and a relative stability of new construction, leading to a growth of downtown since 1967.

Total downtown size

14.2

Total square footage of all downtown buildings between 1911 and 2018.

A map of *where* demolition and construction took place can help explain these unexpected findings. Except for a few core downtown buildings, almost all of downtown has been demolished at some point during the twentieth century. Downtown clearly faced a pattern of attrition from the inside out, with the first significant demolitions taking place for parking lots in the 1920s, followed by a ring of demolition in the decades that followed as growth halted and urban renewal began. Furthermore, building demolitions display trends of acceleration and contagion, as they spread to adjacent properties. Especially parking lot demolitions snowballed in Detroit's downtown, as they often made adjacent lots less desirable for commercial and residential uses and more desirable for further parking. More than any other land use, retailers were vulnerable to the loss of continuity and critical mass that resulted from downtown's erosion, declining exponentially near building demolitions. The maps prove urbanist Jane Jacobs right in seeing cities as interwoven networks of social and economic contacts— once this ecosystem was disrupted, it rapidly withered.

Yet in all but three decades, new construction outstripped demolition, nearly tripling downtown's total floor space over the past century. Figure 14.4 shows the location

| 1911-1921 | 1921-1929 | 1929-1938 | 1938-1951 | 1951-1961 | 1961-1967 | 1967-1977 | 1977-1988 | 1988-2001 | 2001-2011 | 2011-2018 |

14.3
Building demolitions that were not directly followed by a replacement building, by era.

of new construction in downtown after it was fully built out in the nineteenth century. The map demonstrates that while growth has happened throughout downtown, it has focused on its periphery since the second half of the twentieth century—exactly in those areas where demolition was also the strongest. In other words, downtown's success and failure were closely interlinked. The result is a pattern of older buildings in the core surrounded by newer construction, with the older urban fabric only reappearing

| 1911-1921 | 1921-1929 | 1929-1938 | 1938-1951 | 1951-1961 | 1961-1967 | 1967-1977 | 1977-1988 | 1988-2001 | 2001-2011 | 2011-2018 |

14.4
New construction by era.

in the inner-city neighborhoods of Corktown and Brush Park—a temporal cross-section that can be seen in many other North American cities. The scale of new buildings has also drastically grown over the past century, reflecting an ongoing process of capital accumulation. From the early traders of the nineteenth century to today's downtown powerhouses, the downtown elite has consistently been able to consolidate land and resources for the construction of ever-larger complexes. While retailers like Hudson's and Crowley's ate their way through downtown's most central blocks in the 1910s, government-enabled land clearance, urban renewal, and entertainment construction has allowed the same process to take place more recently in the periphery, and at a much larger scale. These new developments have effectively transformed the ring around downtown into a car-oriented district that is hard to distinguish from the suburbs it was meant to compete with.

This unfortunate trend reflects downtown's slow dehumanization, with people replaced by parking. In many ways, the Motor City's core hardly stood a chance against its own offspring. The first Detroit car may have been born in a downtown Bagley Street barn; it would soon turn against its birthplace. The car not only hollowed out the wealth and population of Detroit and its downtown; it similarly hollowed out its paradigm for growth, as downtown has fruitlessly tried to beat the automobile and its suburban progeny at their own game for over a century. In a desperate bid to keep downtown accessible to Detroit's automobile class, City Hall has cast aside transit and walkability to make way for cars since the 1910s, replacing Black Bottom's dense tenements to make way for the modern suburban lifestyle of Lafayette Park in the 1950s, and clearing dozens of downtown blocks for sports stadiums and mega-casinos over recent decades. Meanwhile, downtown suburbanized itself more incrementally by turning its periphery into a sea of parking lots. From a few scattered lots in the 1910s, downtown parking soon spread into a ring of tarmac through a spiral of depreciating land values, decreased walkability and transit viability, and induced demand. Detroit's planners were complicit in this cycle, enabling downtown's automobilization through freeway and parking garage construction and subsidy. For more than half a century, the majority of downtown's land has been dedicated to cars, and parking has taken up the lion's share of downtown growth. In fact, apart from parking garages, downtown's square footage has *shrunk* every decade since the Depression, as shown in figure 14.6.

Automobile attrition and self-suburbanization may not be unique to downtown Detroit, but their extent is unprecedented among American cities. One explanation for this is Detroit's consistent spirit of hope and restlessness, the same forces that propelled it from a French outpost to an industrial powerhouse and subsequently fueled its retreat into the Michigan prairie. The inertia of downtown's fabric was repeatedly cast aside, either as an obstruction to progress in its boom years or as an embarrassing reminder

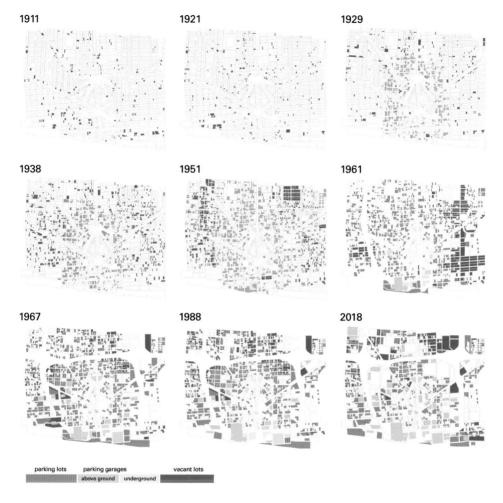

1911 1921 1929

1938 1951 1961

1967 1988 2018

parking lots parking garages vacant lots
above ground underground

14.5
The growth of parking lots and vacant lots over time reveals a
steady erosion of downtown, with a solid ring of parking
already in place by the 1920s.

of failure in the decline that followed. As with automobile attrition, most design and
planning professionals only amplified this tendency. Detroit's embrace of the national
discourse on blight in the 1940s paved the way for Blessing's disqualification of downtown as "almost raw land" in the decades to follow. And even as planners' dreams often

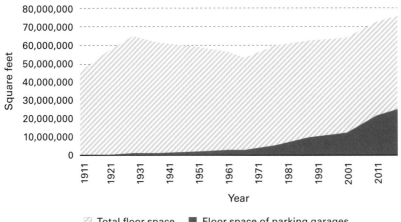

Downtown floor space with parking

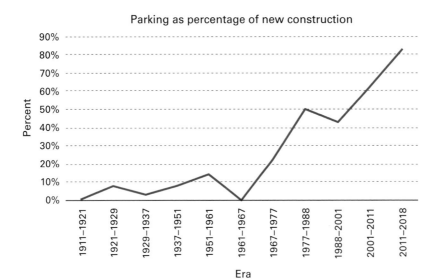

Parking as percentage of new construction

14.6

The built square footage of downtown is increasingly taken up by parking garages, which have made up over 80 percent of new construction in recent years. As a result, downtown's space for people has actually shrunk compared to its space for cars.

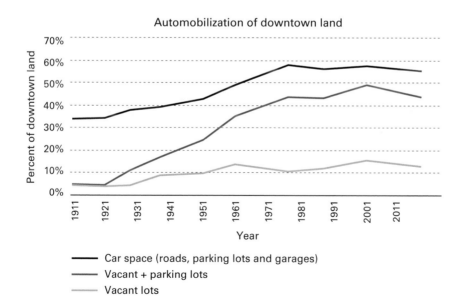

New construction minus parking garages and Renaissance Center

Square feet

Era

Automobilization of downtown land

Percent of downtown land

Year

— Car space (roads, parking lots and garages)
— Vacant + parking lots
— Vacant lots

sprouted only ragweed, blindly aspirational demolitions like that of Hudson's and the former Motown Music headquarters continued until well into the twenty-first century. Detroit's faith in progress not only ran roughshod over its physical past, but also disregarded the underprivileged who were forced to occupy it—an omission that came to a boil with the 1967 civil disorders. As the modernist bulldozer ran out of federal and local fuel, and downtown similarly ground to a halt, downtown's emptying buildings became stuck in a twilight between life and death, changing downtown from a monument to what could be to a warning of what had been. Then again, downtown's late twentieth-century nadir enabled its renaissance in the twenty-first century, as its failure has preserved a unique historic building stock that peer cities like Chicago and New York have long replaced with taller successors.

The result of downtown's unique path is a morphology of opposites, a checkerboard of success and failure in which glistening high-rises overlook crumbling tarmac. Yet this seeming contrast between solid and void masks a symbiosis between them. New construction has almost always accompanied a need for open space—especially with the growth of automobility over the past century. Without buildings, there wouldn't be a need for parking lots, and without parking lots, the buildings wouldn't be accessible to their automobile clientele. Detroit's downtown architecture reflects this symbiosis, as buildings offer blank walls to adjacent voids in anticipation of further growth, adorned with advertisements that leverage the value of emptiness. Even at its peak, downtown never completely filled up, and its unregulated jumble of buildings includes open spaces in a landscape that emanates aspiration as much as defeat. Figures 14.8 and 14.9 demonstrate that downtown's oldest buildings are directly adjacent to its oldest voids, a pattern that becomes more coarsely grained when moving outward into the larger lots of urban renewal and postrenewal downtown.

Downtown's landscape of disconnects also reflects a centuries-old lack of choreography between its private and public powers, in which the latter consistently led the wrong dance or stepped in too late. Though he left Detroit bitter and his baroque dreams remain mostly unfulfilled, Augustus Woodward has yet to cede to a more powerful successor in shaping downtown's urban form. Successive urban planners and designers have been able to wield surprisingly limited power in shaping downtown, and their results were often out of touch with the reality of the city. As downtown was

14.7
Built form and open space are not opposites, but reinforce one another. One of Detroit's oldest voids on Fort Street allowed an adjacent building to put up an advertisement. Image by author, 2018.

eroded by parking lots, urban planners and designers were preoccupied with water-front improvements. Their destructive street widenings of the 1920s didn't generate nearly the amount of business they anticipated, and were antiquated almost as soon as they opened. When zoning was implemented two decades later, the harm of industrial and parking creep into Detroit's oldest neighborhoods had already been done. The modern renewal of downtown replaced thousands of African American residents and hundreds of historic buildings with the weeds of market disinterest, some of which mature to this day. If anything, the postwar era marks the start of a near-permanent disconnect between lofty downtown planning goals and a citywide market collapse. Even during Young's staunch antiplanning reign, aspirational public demolition continued, raising unfulfilled dreams to a new level with the People Mover. Well into the twenty-first century, public dreams and private reality failed to align.

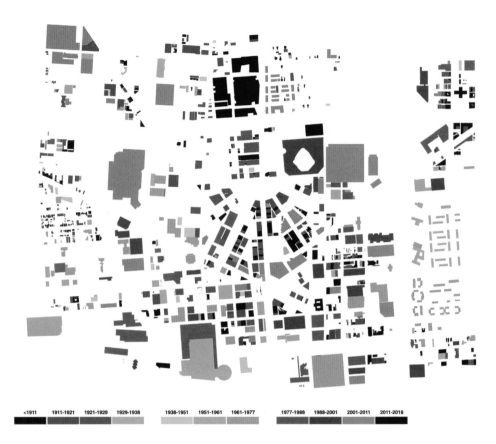

| <1911 | 1911-1921 | 1921-1929 | 1929-1938 | 1938-1951 | 1951-1961 | 1961-1977 | 1977-1988 | 1988-2001 | 2001-2011 | 2011-2018 |

14.8

Every building in present-day downtown Detroit, categorized by the era of its construction.

Planners and politicians simply did not understand that without proper land, funding, and political power, their dreams would never materialize. While Saarinen's civic vision for the riverfront withered in the 1920s, Max Goldberg's self-propelled parking empire flourished. While Blessing's modernist megastructures never saw the light of day, they were reincarnated as postmodern casinos and sports stadiums. And while Young's shotgun projects swam in a sea of downtown decline, corporate magnates like DTE, Ilitch, and Gilbert understood that with a critical mass of landownership and deep pockets, they controlled the fate of downtown. Often below the radar of high-profile public projects, these investors slowly bought up downtown's fallout at fire sale

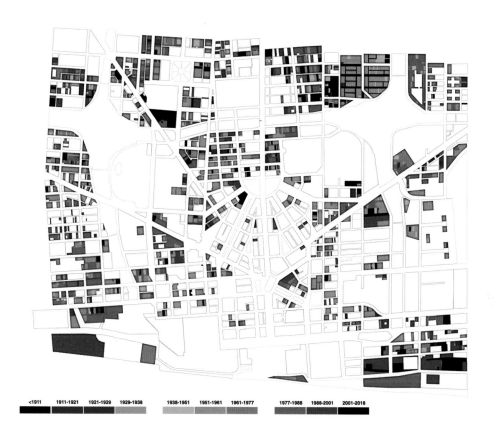

14.9

Every currently open parcel of land in Detroit, categorized by the era it first became vacant.

prices, amassing vast portions of the city's key land. The combination of their entrepreneurial insight, the public power vacuum, and downtown's unprecedented decline hence materialized into a unique pattern of consolidated landownership, in which a handful of powerful stakeholders have divided most of downtown into self-contained fiefdoms. Downtown has come full circle since the early nineteenth century, the French landholding elite replaced by a new power structure of large corporations and wealthy individuals. Downtown's current consolidated ownership and power ecosystem suffer from a lack of heterogeneity, running quite a risk if one of its major landholders fails or decides to divest.

14.10

Instead of a dreamed-of pedestrian civic mall, the west end of downtown turned into a haphazardly assembled and introverted corporate campus for DTE Energy. To the south, a planned International Village never materialized, leaving blocks of empty land until the federal, state, and local governments stepped in to build their own fortified settlement. Left image from "Planning Detroit 1953–1955"; right image courtesy of the Walter P. Reuther Library, Archives of Labor and Urban Affairs, Wayne State University, image from *Detroit News*, February 14, 1974.

Illtch   Gilbert   DTE   General Motors   MGM   Governments

14.11

Map of the private fiefdoms in and around downtown Detroit in 2018, demonstrating that a majority of downtown sites are controlled by only a few entities. Mapping by author, based on land records, news articles, press releases, and on-site observation.

Furthermore, downtown has become a disconnected fabric of introverted developments, each trying to contain its target audience while keeping trespassers at bay. Starting with the Renaissance Center's radical shift away from the street, much of downtown's periphery has replaced the front door with a parking bay, and the traditional public realm with a carefully filtered interior domain. Among these fiefdoms, Dan Gilbert's unprecedented ownership of downtown's key properties has resulted in an environment that blends control and serendipity. Not dependent on overly cautious outside financiers, the unpredictability of state and federal politicians, or the instability of the market, Gilbert has become his own downtown financier and power broker; he creates his own market. The resulting landscape may appear to have maintained the fine grain of the typical American downtown, but the homogenized aesthetic of cheerful building interiors, upscale ground-floor tenants, and piped music reveals that Gilbert's careful environmental orchestration for the creative class isn't too different from how the surrounding sports stadiums and casinos cater to the suburban middle class. For each of these audiences, downtown has been transformed into what sociologist John Hannigan terms the "Fantasy City," a place that takes Detroiters away from their daily cares—including the city itself.[4]

After centuries of broken dreams, downtown has become the dream itself. Mere decades after RoboCop's avant-garde vehicle ran down Old Detroit's crime-ridden streets, the Chrysler 200 emphasized New Detroit's embrace of its past for the American Super Bowl audience in 2011, proudly proclaiming: "It's the hottest fires that make the hardest steel." Detroit has leveraged its past failure for a new brand of grassroots power, appealing to a growing demographic yearning for authenticity. As scholars from Alison Isenberg to Sharon Zukin have argued, downtown is the place where authenticity can be found—or at least manufactured.[5] More than any other place in America, downtown Detroit's nadir has paved the way for another reinvention, in which its former diversity of ownership, history, and experiences has been transformed into a hyperreality where the real and the simulated are almost impossible to distinguish.[6] History is reinvented in the historic streetscape of Greektown and the artisanal retailers on Woodward Avenue; failure is repurposed in the commissioned street art in Gilbert's newly refurbished Belt alleyway, or carefully masked with Ilitch's peripheral parking structures. Downtown Detroit's roller coaster ride has been muted into a risk-free "urbanoid environment," a term coined by architectural critic Paul Goldberger.[7] Downtown certainly doesn't reflect Detroit's still-declining neighborhoods. Then again, downtown Detroit has never quite fallen in line with the city it served. Downtown has always been disconnected from its industrial job base, and aggressively disconnected itself from the rest of the city by annexing its mostly African American neighbors. The disconnect is now only more apparent due to the dichotomous fates of downtown and the rest of the city.[8]

In its fulfillment of new and select dreams, downtown Detroit is again serving as an amplification of the American urban core, a prototype of the preservation, privatization, and popularization that await many of its peers. Downtown is used to its role as a radical vanguard, predating the creation, destruction, and reinvention of downtown America. When American cities began to struggle with downtown traffic, downtown Detroit was already cutting through its urban fabric to make way for more cars. Downtown retail decline started in Detroit, as a branch of its main department store anchored North America's first major suburban shopping mall. When America's inner cities declined, Detroit had already cleared vast parts of its African American core for renewal and freeways; and Detroit was struck the hardest by the civil disorders that followed. While American downtowns struggled to stay relevant in subsequent decades, downtown Detroit's lights went out altogether. As downtown America looks to reinvent itself in an era of unprecedented austerity, downtown Detroit has already transformed itself into a privately owned and managed casino, sports, and craft cocktail destination. Coleman Young's prediction that "Detroit today has always been your town tomorrow"[9] may ring more true than ever.

NOTES

PREFACE

1. Jean-Paul Sartre, "American Cities," in *Literary and Philosophical Essays* (London: Hutchinson, 1955).

INTRODUCTION

1. On the quickening pace of development activity, see Kirk Pinho, "The Game Has Changed: Development Dollars Have Doubled in Downtown Detroit since Comerica Park Opened," *Crain's Detroit Business*, September 10, 2017.

2. Works include Dan Austin, Sean Doerr, and John Gallagher, *Lost Detroit: Stories behind the Motor City's Majestic Ruins* (Charleston, SC: History Press, 2010); Dan Austin, *Forgotten Landmarks of Detroit* (Charleston, SC: History Press, 2012); Jean Maddern Pitrone, *Hudson's: Hub of America's Heartland* (Franklin, MI: Altwerger and Mandel, 1991); Michael Hauser and Marianne Weldon, *Detroit's Downtown Movie Palaces* (Charleston, SC: Arcadia, 2006).

3. Works include C. Vergara, "Downtown Detroit: American Acropolis or Vacant Land?," *Metropolis* (1995); Yves Marchand, Romain Meffre, and Thomas J. Sugrue, *The Ruins of Detroit* (Göttingen: Steidl, 2010); Andrew Moore and Philip Levine, *Detroit Disassembled* (Bologna: Damiani Editore; Akron, OH: Akron Art Museum, 2010).

4. A first iteration of a series of figure-ground drawings depicting downtown Detroit's automobile erosion was drawn by architect Constantinos Doxiadis in the mid-1960s, appearing in *Emergence and Growth of an Urban Region: The Developing Urban Detroit Area* (Detroit: Detroit Edison Co., 1966). This series was augmented in Arthur Johnson, Camilo José Vergara,

Donald Moss, Dan Hoffman, Richard Plunz, and Patricia Phillips, "Detroit Is Everywhere" (StoreFront Art and Architecture, Columbia University Urban Design Studio, and Cranbrook Academy of Art Architecture Studio, New York, 1995). The figure-ground diagrams were later published in Richard A. Plunz, "Detroit Is Everywhere," *Architecture* 85, no. 4 (1996). These diagrams were augmented again by a team led by Douglas Kelbaugh, Roy Strickland, and Eric Dueweke and published in "Adding Three Dimensions to Downtown Detroit" (University of Michigan, Detroit Design Workshop, Ann Arbor, 2007)

5. The most prominent literature focuses on the social history behind Detroit's decline, such as Thomas J. Sugrue, *The Origins of the Urban Crisis: Race and Inequality in Postwar Detroit* (Princeton, NJ: Princeton University Press, 1996), and George C. Galster, *Driving Detroit: The Quest for Respect in Motown* (Philadelphia: University of Pennsylvania Press, 2012). Other authors have focused on the social and physical history of planning and design, such as June Manning Thomas, *Redevelopment and Race: Planning a Finer City in Postwar Detroit* (Baltimore: Johns Hopkins University Press, 1997); Brent D. Ryan, *Design after Decline: How America Rebuilds Shrinking Cities* (Philadelphia: University of Pennsylvania Press, 2012). More recent titles critique Detroit and its downtown as urban prototypes, such as Brian Doucet, *Why Detroit Matters* (Bristol: Policy Press, 2017); Andrew Herscher, *The Unreal Estate Guide to Detroit* (Ann Arbor: University of Michigan Press, 2012).

CHAPTER 1: FROM OUTPOST TO DOWNTOWN: 1805–1884

1. Cited in Clarence Monroe Burton, William Stocking, and Gordon K. Miller, *The City of Detroit, Michigan, 1701–1922* (Detroit: Clarke Pub. Co., 1922), 304.

2. Silas Farmer, The History of Detroit and Michigan or, the Metropolis Illustrated; a Chronological Cyclopedia of the Past and Present, Including a Full Record of Territorial Days in Michigan, and the Annals of Wayne County (Detroit: S. Farmer & Co., 1884), 490–491; Frank B. Woodford, Mr. Jefferson's Disciple: A Life of Justice Woodward (East Lansing: Michigan State University, 1953), 3–7. Some suspected the fire was started by the lumber industry: Burton, Stocking, and Miller, The City of Detroit, Michigan, 309. The Commons were deeded by the king of France during that country's rule over Detroit, and were a common pasture: ibid., 320. On Detroit's earlier history: Byron M. Cutcheon, "Fifty Years of Growth in

Michigan," Historical Collections 22 (Michigan Pioneer and Historical Society, 1894), 481; Almon Ernest Parkins, The Historical Geography of Detroit (Lansing: Michigan Historical Commission, 1918), 314; Farmer, The History of Detroit and Michigan or, the Metropolis Illustrated, 17, 21; Buford L. Pickens, "Early City Plans for Detroit, a Projected American Metropolis," Art Quarterly 6, no. 1 (1943): 36–37.

3. Woodford, Mr. Jefferson's Disciple, 6.

4. Melanie Grunow Sobocinski, ed., Detroit and Rome: Building on the Past (Dearborn, MI: Alfred Berkowitz Gallery, University of Michigan-Dearborn, 2005), 15, note 1; Henry Allen Chaney, "The Supreme Court of Michigan," Green Bag 2 (1890): 377; Woodford, Mr. Jefferson's Disciple, 30.

5. Letter from William Hull to Henry Dearborn, December 29, 1806; Thomas McIntyre Cooley, Michigan: A History of Governments (Boston: Houghton, Mifflin, 1885), 149.

6. Parkins, The Historical Geography of Detroit, 131; Woodford, Mr. Jefferson's Disciple, 1, 11–16.

7. His life and work in Washington brought him in close contact with the city's planner Charles L'Enfant, as Woodward not only held property there and admired L'Enfant's work but also had L'Enfant as one of the clients of his law practice. In Woodward Papers 1802–1804, entry for August 13, 1803, note 20, 37–38 (Burton Historical Collection, Detroit Public Library).

8. A remark by Woodward's surveyor Thomas Smith on October 10, 1816, in Brian Leigh Dunnigan, Frontier Metropolis: Picturing Early Detroit, 1701–1838 (Detroit: Wayne State University Press, 2001), 119.

9. Augustus Brevoort Woodward, "Letter to the Citizens of Detroit" (Burton Historic Collection, Detroit, 1806). Woodward not only planned the city's layout; he also drafted a system of laws and a banking charter, still at the base of Michigan's contemporary legal system, and started an education system: Sobocinski, Detroit and Rome, 127.

10. Dunnigan, Frontier Metropolis, 119.

11. In fact, Woodward had attached L'Enfant's map of Washington to his diary for 1802–1804, which he had taken to Detroit (Woodward Papers 1802–1804, Burton Historical Collection, Detroit Public Library). For a more detailed discussion of the predecessors to Woodward's

plans, see Pickens, "Early City Plans for Detroit," 45. The admiration for Roman architecture and society led Woodward to name the main square Campus Martius after the Roman piazza, and he even changed his own name from Elias to Augustus. Campus Martius was also the name of a main public space in Marietta, Ohio, a town that Woodward had passed through on his way to Detroit.

12. By the account of Detroiter John Gentle, Woodward's plans were even celestially inspired: "To his profound observations of the heavenly regions the world is indebted for the discovery of the streets, alleys, circles, angles and squares of this magnificent city—in theory equal in magnitude and splendor to any on the earth." In reality, Woodward strongly relied on Thomas Smith for surveying the land. The accuracy of Gentle's account should be taken with a grain of salt, as he wrote it as part of a letter of complaint about Woodward. John Gentle, "On the Evils Which Have Proved Fatal to the Republics No. II," *Pittsburgh Commonwealth*, June 3, 1807.

13. Woodford, Mr. Jefferson's Disciple, 40.

14. Clarence Monroe Burton, William Stocking, and Gordon K. Miller, *The City of Detroit, Michigan, 1701–1922*, vol. 2 (Detroit and Chicago: S. J. Clarke Pub. Co., 1922), 1447.

15. When the settlement expanded north of Jefferson Avenue, new construction was first located on the regularly gridded blocks along Woodward Avenue. As a result, settlement along radial streets only gained momentum well over two decades after the plan was drafted.

16. Woodford, Mr. Jefferson's Disciple, 74.

17. Woodward countered that the naming was in fact quite logical, as the street ran "woodward." The street ran perpendicular to Detroit's main riverside arterial, named after his friend Thomas Jefferson: ibid., 47; James Valentine Campbell, *Outlines of the Political History of Michigan* (Detroit: Schober & Company, 1876), 253.

18. Hull was later sentenced to death for cowardice for his prompt surrender, but was ultimately pardoned by President Madison: Woodford, *Mr. Jefferson's Disciple*, 107–123; Parkins, *The Historical Geography of Detroit*, 132, 281–284.

19. Upon his arrival, Cass settled on a farm just west of the city. Woodford, *Mr. Jefferson's Disciple*, 107–123.

20. The first regular freight service via wagon and boat between Detroit and New York was instated in 1817: Dunnigan, *Frontier Metropolis*, 150; David Lee Poremba, *Detroit in Its World Setting: A Three Hundred Year Chronology, 1701–2001* (Detroit: Wayne State University Press, 2001), 97; Burton, Stocking, and Miller, *The City of Detroit, Michigan*, 672–673; Elkanah Watson, *Men and Times of the Revolution* (New York: Dana & Company, 1856), 427–430; Parkins, *The Historical Geography of Detroit*, 244–245.

21. Robert E. Roberts, *Sketches and Reminiscences of the City of the Straits and Its Vicinity* (Detroit: Free Press Book and Job Printing House, 1884), 72; Burton, Stocking, and Miller, *The City of Detroit, Michigan*, 506. By 1818, Detroit counted 142 homes and no fewer than 131 commercial, industrial and public buildings. The city counted 24 dry goods and grocery stores by the next year: ibid., 505; Friend Palmer et al., *Early Days in Detroit* (Detroit: Hunt & June, 1906), 585; Silas Farmer, *History of Detroit and Wayne County and Early Michigan*, 3rd ed. (Detroit: S. Farmer & Co., for Munsell & Co., New York, 1890), 793. The market was financed by land sales in a nearby 10,000-acre tract, which also financed a university, a jail, and a church in the years to follow: Chaney, "The Supreme Court of Michigan," 377. The market was demolished in 1835.

22. The steamboat *Walk in the Water* drastically shortened the travel time to Buffalo. The decreased dependence on wind as a propellant made travel times more reliable as well: Dunnigan, *Frontier Metropolis*, 150. Although agricultural production grew, the area was still not able to fully support its own demand. Agricultural settlement was still mostly limited to waterfront properties: Parkins, *The Historical Geography of Detroit*, 143–146.

23. By a semantic trick, in fact, the entire Woodward Plan was declared void. Augustus Brevoort Woodward, "Protest by Judge Woodward against the Sale of Certain Lands in Detroit, June 1, 1818," *Michigan Historical Collections* (Michigan Pioneer and Historical Society) 12 (1908): 473–483; Woodford, *Mr. Jefferson's Disciple*, 50–52. Citizens gained more power to vote on local matters with the instatement of home rule in 1815: Poremba, *Detroit in Its World Setting*, 97.

24. Woodward was furious at the superseding of his plans. In a protest, he wrote: "cities are the work of time, of a generation, of a succession of generations. Their original ground-plan must remain, and cannot be changed without the height of inconvenience, trouble and expense.

A proper and prudent foresight can alone give to a great city its fair development" (quoted in Poremba, *Detroit in Its World Setting*, 97). See also C. M. Burton, "Augustus Brevoort Woodward," *Michigan Historical Collections* 29 (Michigan Pioneer and Historical Society) 29 (1901): 662–663.

25. Burton, Stocking, and Miller, *The City of Detroit, Michigan*, 673; Palmer et al., *Early Days in Detroit*, 565, 575, 832; William Lee Jenks, *St. Clair County Michigan, Its History and Its People*, 2 vols. (Chicago: Lewis Publishing Co, 1912), 384; Burton, Stocking, and Miller, *The City of Detroit, Michigan*, 673; Farmer, *History of Detroit and Wayne County and Early Michigan*, 887.

26. Palmer et al., *Early Days in Detroit*, 555, 582. Many of Cass's roads followed former Native American trails: Thomas James Ticknor, "Motor City: The Impact of the Automobile Industry upon Detroit, 1900–1975" (Ph.D. diss., University of Michigan, 1978), 53.

27. Roberts, Sketches and Reminiscences of the City of the Straits, 85–86; Parkins, The Historical Geography of Detroit, 261–262.

28. Farmer, History of Detroit and Wayne County and Early Michigan, 41; Burton, Stocking, and Miller, The City of Detroit, Michigan, vol. 2, 1450.

29. Democratic Free Press, December 23, 1835, cited in C. M. Burton, History of Detroit 1780 to 1850—Financial and Commercial (Detroit, 1917), 102.

30. An example is the slow accumulation of the block on Jefferson and Bates Street by Peter Desnoyers to eventually construct the Desnoyers Block of retail, dwellings, and offices: Palmer et al., *Early Days in Detroit*, 469–470. For other examples, see Farmer, *History of Detroit and Wayne County and Early Michigan*, 457, 458; Palmer et al., *Early Days in Detroit*, 488–489.

31. *Niles' Weekly Register* 29, p. 180, cited in Parkins, *The Historical Geography of Detroit*, 176, 246–247; Dunnigan, *Frontier Metropolis*, 177; Robert E. Conot, *American Odyssey* (New York: Morrow, 1974), 17.

32. Trade volume increased from 393 tons in 1820 to 6,700 tons in 1837: John C. Schneider, *Detroit and the Problem of Order, 1830–1880: A Geography of Crime, Riot, and Policing* (Lincoln: University of Nebraska Press, 1980), 10; Parkins, *The Historical Geography of Detroit*, 224–225. To enable this large volume of goods to enter Detroit, the city improved the embankments of the river in 1827: Dunnigan, *Frontier Metropolis*, 182; Parkins, *The Historical*

Geography of Detroit, 219; Farmer, *History of Detroit and Wayne County and Early Michigan*, 911–912.

33. Palmer et al., *Early Days in Detroit*, 688.

34. Gene Scott, Detroit Beginnings: Early Villages and Old Neighborhoods (Detroit: DRCEA, 2001), 68; Dunnigan, Frontier Metropolis, 176.

35. Parkins, The Historical Geography of Detroit, 181.

36. By 1846, the African American community had three churches in this area, often also serving as schools: David M. Katzman, *Before the Ghetto: Black Detroit in the Nineteenth Century* (Urbana: University of Illinois Press, 1973), 11–25.

37. Geo. C. Bates, "The By-Gone Merchants," *Historical Collections* 22 (1894): 386.

38. Farmer, The History of Detroit and Michigan or, the Metropolis Illustrated, 927.

39. Caroline M. Kirkland, *A New Home—Who'll Follow? Or, Glimpses of Western Life* (New York: C. S. Francis; Boston: J. H. Francis, 1839), quoted in Miroslav Base, "The Development of Detroit 1701–1920: A Planning History" (working paper, Center for Urban Studies, Wayne State University, 1970), 39.

40. Burton, *History of Detroit 1780 to 1850*, 122–123; Arthur Pound and E. H. Suydam, *Detroit, Dynamic City* (New York: D. Appleton-Century, 1940), 165–166; George Byron Catlin, *The Story of Detroit* (Detroit: Detroit News, 1923), 460–462. While initially criticized for its remoteness, the Capitol would soon spur significant new building activity in the Woodward plan: Burton, Stocking, and Miller, *The City of Detroit, Michigan*, 351.

41. Ten years later, the city operated five banks, most within a block of the Bank of Michigan: Catlin, *The Story of Detroit*, 456; Clarence M. Burton, "Detroit in 1849," *Detroit Free Press*, September 25, October 2, October 9, 1910.

42. *Democratic Free Press*, January 1836, cited in Burton, *History of Detroit 1780 to 1850*, 100–101; *Detroit Free Press*, March 24, 1836, cited in ibid., 125; Burton, Stocking, and Miller, *The City of Detroit, Michigan*, 684; Farmer, *History of Detroit and Wayne County and Early Michigan*, 893–894, 898; Frank Bury Woodford and Arthur M. Woodford, *All Our Yesterdays: A Brief History of Detroit* (Detroit: Wayne State University Press, 1969), 194–195; Schneider,

Detroit and the Problem of Order, 7, 34. After the Michigan Central opened its station on the riverfront, the Campus Martius depot remained in use by the state until it was sold in 1856. Burton, Stocking, and Miller, *The City of Detroit, Michigan*, 359. The new riverfront depot was bombed and burned in 1850, allegedly by a group of disgruntled farmers from the west of the state to retaliate for their loss of cattle struck by trains—known as "The Great Railroad Conspiracy": Catlin, *The Story of Detroit*, 466–468; Bill Loomis, "The Great Railroad Conspiracy," *Michigan History Magazine*, September/October 2013.

43. Parkins, The Historical Geography of Detroit, 315–316; Conot, American Odyssey, 28.

44. *Detroit Advertiser*, April 18, 1849, cited in Burton, *History of Detroit 1780 to 1850*, 161–162. The 1848 fire burnt several blocks between Bates and Randolph and Jefferson and Beaubien streets, leaving 200 buildings burnt and hundreds of families homeless: Farmer, *History of Detroit and Wayne County and Early Michigan*, 493; "Detroit in Ashes. The City Almost Wiped Off the Map—by the Awful Conflagration of '48 Which Swept over It," *Evening News*, January 27, 1889.

45. *Gazetteer of the State of Michigan 1840*, 273, cited in Melvin G. Holli, *Detroit* (New York: New Viewpoints, 1976), 34.

46. Farmer, The History of Detroit and Michigan or, the Metropolis Illustrated, 457–459; Catlin, The Story of Detroit.

47. Palmer et al., *Early Days in Detroit*, 467.

48. Early hotels were usually quite provisional, as they were often expanded, refurbished, demolished, or burnt and rebuilt in rapid succession. Many of them had central roles in Detroit's social life, serving as political meeting halls and entertainment venues.

49. George B. Catlin, *A Brief History of Detroit in the Golden Days of '49* (Detroit: Detroit Savings Bank, 1921).

50. Katzman, *Before the Ghetto*, 28.

51. Churches on Woodward Avenue included the First Methodist Episcopal Church, Episcopal Church, and First Presbyterian Church. Churches for other denominations were located close by. Farmer, *History of Detroit and Wayne County and Early Michigan*, 594.

52. Burton, Stocking, and Miller, The City of Detroit, Michigan, 506; Farmer, History of Detroit and Wayne County and Early Michigan, 374.

53. The system matured by the 1850s: Burton, Stocking, and Miller, *The City of Detroit, Michigan*, 674; Farmer, *History of Detroit and Wayne County and Early Michigan*, 888.

54. For comparison, Chicago's population had already surpassed Detroit's population at almost 30,000 by 1850, as had St. Louis's population at almost 80,000 and Buffalo's population at more than 40,000, with Cincinnati still dominating the region at around 115,000. These numbers are provided by the United States Decennial Census.

55. Conot, *American Odyssey*, 42, 49; Catlin, *The Story of Detroit*, 489. For an impression of Detroit in the late 1850s, see "Twenty Years Ago: A Pen Picture of Detroit in Eighteen Hundred and Fifty-Eight," *Evening News*, August 17, 1878. An early plan to dig a railway tunnel under the Detroit River in the current location of Belle Isle never came to fruition: Burton, Stocking, and Miller, *The City of Detroit, Michigan*, 456; Farmer, *History of Detroit and Wayne County and Early Michigan*, 890–891, 901–903, 904, 914; Parkins, *The Historical Geography of Detroit*, 316–317.

56. Woodford and Woodford, *All Our Yesterdays*, 200–207; Conot, *American Odyssey*, 66; Schneider, *Detroit and the Problem of Order*, 15; Parkins, *The Historical Geography of Detroit*, 274, 294–295, 300–301; Holli, *Detroit*, 422–434; Tenth United States Census, cited in Olivier Zunz, *The Changing Face of Inequality: Urbanization, Industrial Development, and Immigrants in Detroit, 1880–1920* (Chicago: University of Chicago Press, 2000), 16–18. The opening of the St. Mary's Canal prompted most copper smelters to leave Detroit to locate closer to their ore mines in northern Michigan by the 1870s: Parkins, *The Historical Geography of Detroit*, 294–295. Detroit did become the world leader in stove manufacturing in the nineteenth century, forming the city's main industry and producing the majority of stoves in America between 1860 and 1880. During the 1920s, the city's stove industry consisted of five major manufacturers, producing 600,000 articles and employing 5,000 Detroiters: Catlin, *The Story of Detroit*, 475–478. By the mid-twentieth century, other forms of heating supplanted stoves, and the industry faltered. Woodford and Woodford, *All Our Yesterdays*, 207–208; Parkins, *The Historical Geography of Detroit*, 307.

57. Palmer et al., Early Days in Detroit, 826–828; Farmer, The History of Detroit and Michigan or, the Metropolis Illustrated, 516.

58. The area's further commercial growth was bolstered by the doubling of the market behind City Hall in 1861 with an eastern shed, to house a growing range and quantity of merchandise on offer: Cheri Y. Gay, *Lost Detroit* (London: Pavilion Books, 2013), 8; Farmer, *History of Detroit and Wayne County and Early Michigan*, 794.

59. Farmer, History of Detroit and Wayne County and Early Michigan, 41.

60. Catlin, *The Story of Detroit*, 444–448. The Opera House on Campus Martius marked the start of an entertainment district that would grow eastward: W. Hawkins Ferry, *The Buildings of Detroit; a History* (Detroit: Wayne State University Press, 1968), 323; Farmer, *History of Detroit and Wayne County and Early Michigan*, 355, 479.

61. Ferry's building eventually extended back toward Farmer Street to accommodate business growth. The opening ceremony was covered in "Opening Day at Newcomb, Endicott & Co's— the Formal Dedication of a Magnificent New Business Structure," *Detroit Free Press*, April 7, 1881. The move date is wrongly stated as 1879 in Woodford and Woodford, *All Our Yesterdays*, 221. Ferry's seed emporium eventually grew to 50 million shipments by 1883, prompting him to construct an elaborate four-story multiblock warehouse on Brush Street just east of his headquarters: Farmer, *History of Detroit and Wayne County and Early Michigan*, 773–776.

62. As Mabley occupied several buildings, each was dedicated to a certain type of merchandise, ranging from fashion and shoes to home goods: Farmer, *History of Detroit and Wayne County and Early Michigan*, 770–773.

63. An example of retail construction on Campus Martius was the three-story Coyl Building opened in 1860: Farmer, *History of Detroit and Wayne County and Early Michigan*, 471. Many business pioneers north of this invisible frontier still failed in the 1870s. For example, Henry Weber's furniture store constructed only a block north of Campus Martius ultimately went bankrupt, as did two businesses housed in the same building: Burton, Stocking, and Miller, *The City of Detroit, Michigan*, 510.

64. The value of imports is measured by the custom duties paid at the port of Detroit: ibid., 773.

65. Richard Edwards, Industries of Michigan, City of Detroit: Historical and Descriptive Review—Industries, Institutions, Commercial and Manufacturing Advantages (New York: Historical Publishing Co., 1880), 58; Schneider, Detroit and the Problem of Order, 91; "City Sketches—the Streets of Detroit—Their Changes and Characteristics," Detroit Free Press, November 21, 1869; Burton, Stocking, and Miller, The City of Detroit, Michigan, 510; "Detroit Forty Years Ago—the Houses, Stores and Business Men of That Period," Sunday News-Tribune, October 2, 1898. By the 1850s, Jefferson Avenue already suffered from commercial decline: Ferry, The Buildings of Detroit, 35, 89. On wholesale growth along the avenue: Farmer, History of Detroit and Wayne County and Early Michigan, 779–783. Wholesalers benefited from permission by the Detroit custom house to have "bonded" spaces where foreign goods could be stored exempt from American taxes until sold to a third party: ibid.

66. Besides the post office, the federal building would house various federal legal and inspection agencies: Farmer, *The History of Detroit and Michigan or, the Metropolis Illustrated*, 883; Farmer, *History of Detroit and Wayne County and Early Michigan*, 459; Woodford and Woodford, *All Our Yesterdays*, 219; Palmer et al., *Early Days in Detroit*, 460–461; "The Postoffice Question: How the Present Building Was Erected, and What It Cost," *Evening News*, May 29, 1882.

67. Farmer, History of Detroit and Wayne County and Early Michigan, 459–463.

68. Burton, Stocking, and Miller, *The City of Detroit, Michigan*, 390–391.

69. Reflecting Detroit's building fever, real estate values could double in three years. "City Real Estate—Its Importance and Increasing Value to Detroit—Improvements and Reforms in Progress," *Detroit Free Press*, March 17, 1868; Ferry, *The Buildings of Detroit*, 35.

70. Catlin, *The Story of Detroit*, 556–558.

71. Edwards, Industries of Michigan, City of Detroit, 58; Schneider, Detroit and the Problem of Order, 91.

72. By 1841, the city had already demolished a "house of evil resort" on the near east side: Farmer, *History of Detroit and Wayne County and Early Michigan*, 201. City Council was requested to address prostitution several times, with little result: Schneider, *Detroit and the Problem of Order*, 15–31.

73. Schneider, *Detroit and the Problem of Order*, 37–45. The name Potomac was a reference to the sarcastic Civil War song "All quiet along the Potomac": Conot, *American Odyssey*, 78. Downtown had other slum districts such as Swill Point, located around Larned and Second streets. "Old Auntie" and "Old Saunders": "Detroit at Night—the Dark Side of Metropolitan Life as Seen in a Midnight Ramble," *Evening News*, August 3, 1875. On crime: *Detroit Free Press*, March 26, 1865, and August 23, 1865, cited in Schneider, *Detroit and the Problem of Order*, 67–69. On living conditions: Katzman, *Before the Ghetto*, 27–31; Conot, *American Odyssey*, 78. The strong concentration of African Americans in the district did create a base for thriving business on St. Antoine Street: Katzman, *Before the Ghetto*, 53–80, 104–134.

74. An early racially inspired disorder occurred in 1863 when white immigrants raided an African American district after the false accusation of rape of a white woman by African American William Faulkner: Katzman, *Before the Ghetto*, 44–47; Woodford and Woodford, *All Our Yesterdays*, 184; Farmer, *History of Detroit and Wayne County and Early Michigan*, 478. On ethnic enclaves: ibid., 669–693, 928.

75. Farmer, *History of Detroit and Wayne County and Early Michigan*, 478. The Germans also started a range of newspapers and periodicals: ibid., 669–693.

76. Farmer, *The History of Detroit and Michigan or, the Metropolis Illustrated*, 928. Dutchtown refers not to the Dutch but to Germans—the Deutsch. At a certain point, Gratiot Avenue in the center of this district was even referred to as Little Berlin: Katzman, *Before the Ghetto*, 57.

77. "City Sketches—the Streets of Detroit—Their Changes and Characteristics," cited in Schneider, *Detroit and the Problem of Order*, 46.

78. Farmer, *History of Detroit and Wayne County and Early Michigan*, 202–204.

79. Ibid.

80. While Detroit had no police force, a modicum of social peace was kept by a local sheriff and nearby army troops. After using several locations in the city, the sheriff's operations were consolidated into a residence and jail on Clinton and Beaubien streets in 1847, the

location that still houses the Wayne County courthouse and jail: Burton, Stocking, and Miller, *The City of Detroit, Michigan*, 412–413.

81. Schneider, Detroit and the Problem of Order, 58–60, 70–86, 98, 121–125; Burton, Stocking, and Miller, The City of Detroit, Michigan, 406; Farmer, History of Detroit and Wayne County and Early Michigan, 203–204.

82. Ferry, The Buildings of Detroit, 94–95.

83. Two initial lines ran along Jefferson and Woodward avenues but were unreliable and slow, resulting in a near bankruptcy of the company. An 1867 reorganization resulted in significant service improvements and expansion: Burton, Stocking, and Miller, *The City of Detroit, Michigan*, 391–392.

84. The wealthiest Detroiters liked to live large, resulting in the nation's largest land area and dwelling size per inhabitant by 1880: Farmer, *The History of Detroit and Michigan or, the Metropolis Illustrated*, 376.

85. Roberts, *Sketches and Reminiscences of the City of the Straits*, 120. The horizontal expansion of the city benefited from the drainage of surrounding wetlands in Wayne County, enabled by state legislation approved in 1861: Burton, Stocking, and Miller, *The City of Detroit, Michigan*, 490–491.

86. East of Brush Park, more affordable homes were constructed on smaller lots, interspersed with commercial buildings to serve the district: Scott, *Detroit Beginnings*, 48–49; Historic Designation Advisory Board, "Proposed Brush Park Historic District—Final Report" (City of Detroit, 2010).

87. Cass Park was one of Detroit's first proper parks, as the open lands in the Woodward plan were in very poor shape: Catlin, *The Story of Detroit*, 405–406; "Detroit Forty Years Ago—a Dull Town on a Hot Day, and Still Something of a Sawdust Town," *Sunday News-Tribune*, October 9, 1898. Cass's land donation was controversial as councilmembers and some citizens were hesitant to take on responsibility for its maintenance, seemingly benefiting only the General's bottom line: David W. Hartman, *The Development of Detroit's Cass Corridor: 1850–1975*, vol. 3 (Detroit: Wayne State University Press, 1975), 2–3; Palmer et al., *Early Days in Detroit*,

412–413; "Annual Freemen's Meeting—Lengthy and Interesting Discussion on the Acceptance of the Cass Park," *Detroit Free Press*, June 5, 1860.

88. Historic Designation Advisory Board, "Proposed Cass Park Local Historic District—Final Report" (City of Detroit, 2014).

89. Farmer, *History of Detroit and Wayne County and Early Michigan*, 928; Gretchen Griner, "Historic and Architectural Resources of the Cass Farm Survey Area, Detroit, Wayne County, Michigan" (National Park Service, Department of the Interior, 1997), 6. The increased traffic from both districts prompted the widening of Woodward Avenue in 1878: Farmer, *History of Detroit and Wayne County and Early Michigan*, 927; "Widening Woodward Avenue," *Evening News*, April 5, 1882.

90. By 1892, the *Evening News* boasted of rapid sales of hundreds of lots in mere days and described the "building restrictions" like minimum home values: "Detroit—Michigan's Magnificent Metropolis. A Glance at Its Early History and Present Commercial Importance," *Evening News*, May 5, 1892.

91. Schneider, Detroit and the Problem of Order, 92–95.

92. Zunz, The Changing Face of Inequality, 162–176.

93. Ferry, *The Buildings of Detroit*, 74; Schneider, *Detroit and the Problem of Order*, 88–91; Woodford and Woodford, *All Our Yesterdays*. Suburbanization also eased social tensions and crime: Schneider, *Detroit and the Problem of Order*, 125, 136.

94. Farmer, *The History of Detroit and Michigan or, the Metropolis Illustrated*, 475–476; Daniel M. Bluestone, "Detroit's City Beautiful and the Problem of Commerce," *Journal of the Society of Architectural Historians* 47 (1988): 245–262. While impressive, the building was built remarkably pragmatically—an extra French-inspired mansard roof was added while construction was already under way to reflect the fashion of the time: Dan Austin, *Forgotten Landmarks of Detroit* (Charleston, SC: History Press, 2012), 15; Roberts, *Sketches and Reminiscences of the City of the Straits*, 116.

95. Sidney Glazer, *Detroit: A Study in Urban Development* (New York: Bookman Associates, 1965).

96. Conot, *American Odyssey*, 91; Ferry, *The Buildings of Detroit*, 86; Burton, Stocking, and Miller, *The City of Detroit, Michigan*, 355. The building only survived a decade, from 1879 to 1889.

97. Farmer, *History of Detroit and Wayne County and Early Michigan*, 798–799; Randall Fogelman and Lisa E. Rush, *Detroit's Eastern Market* (Charleston, SC: Arcadia, 2013).

98. Willard W. Glazier, *Peculiarities of American Cities* (Philadelphia: Hubbard Brothers, 1884), 192–193; Burton, Stocking, and Miller, *The City of Detroit, Michigan*, 764–767.

99. Information from the introductory of Jacob W. Weeks and Ralph L. Polk, *Detroit City Directory for 1884* (Detroit: J. W. Weeks & Co., 1884). The number of metropolitan citizens include directly attached settlements such as Springwells, Hamtramck, and other nearby places.

100. Between 1880 and 1890 manufacturing investment and jobs tripled, but Detroit ranked only seventeenth in the nation for its industrial output in 1890: Woodford and Woodford, *All Our Yesterdays*, 200–207; Holli, *Detroit*, 59–60.

CHAPTER 2: GOING UP AND OUT: 1884–1911

1. The decline of other branches of industry is described in various sources, such as Almon Ernest Parkins, *The Historical Geography of Detroit* (Lansing, MI: Michigan Historical Commission, 1918), 304; Robert E. Conot, *American Odyssey* (New York: Morrow, 1974), 90, 130–131; Thomas James Ticknor, "Motor City: The Impact of the Automobile Industry upon Detroit, 1900–1975" (Ph.D. diss., University of Michigan, 1978), 81–82. Detroit became famous for manufacturing the Pullman sleeping cars, but their operation moved to the Chicago area in 1893. By that decade, Detroit's steel industry had also faltered under competition from larger plants fueled by cokes in other parts of the Midwest: Parkins, *The Historical Geography of Detroit*, 300–301. For the first three years of car manufacturing, almost all car bodies could be manufactured in existing Detroit factories without the need to build new plants. Combined with the experience and skillset of existing car body plants, this efficiency allowed a Detroit body to be manufactured at a 40 percent lower cost than in rival cities on the East Coast: Clarence Monroe Burton, William Stocking, and Gordon K. Miller, *The City of Detroit, Michigan, 1701–1922* (Detroit: Clarke Pub. Co., 1922), 569.

2. Frank Bury Woodford and Arthur M. Woodford, *All Our Yesterdays: A Brief History of Detroit* (Detroit: Wayne State University Press, 1969), 265–266; W. Hawkins Ferry, *The Buildings of Detroit; a History* (Detroit: Wayne State University Press, 1968), 178.

3. Arthur Pound and E. H. Suydam, *Detroit, Dynamic City* (New York: D. Appleton-Century, 1940), 278–279. A case in point is the story of Ransom Olds's search for East Coast investors for his car manufacturing venture. After a fruitless voyage to New York and New Jersey, a Detroit copper baron assured him of start-up funds and Olds chose to remain in Detroit: Burton, Stocking, and Miller, *The City of Detroit, Michigan*, 563–564.

4. Conot, *American Odyssey*, 117–126; Burton, Stocking, and Miller, *The City of Detroit, Michigan*, 562.

5. George S. May, *R. E. Olds, Auto Industry Pioneer* (Grand Rapids, MI: Eerdmans, 1977), quoated in G. T. Bloomfield, "Shaping the Character of a City: The Automobile Industry and Detroit, 1900–1920," *Michigan Quarterly Review* 25, no. 2 (1986): 170.

6. Pound and Suydam, *Detroit, Dynamic City*, 278. While Olds soon moved to Lansing, Michigan, his company's production methods and profitability left a legacy of skills and capital in Detroit: Ticknor, "Motor City," 100–101. Car manufacturing was very decentralized in the early days: Burton, Stocking, and Miller, *The City of Detroit, Michigan*, 564–565; Conot, *American Odyssey*, 126.

7. A significant element in the early growth of Ford came from efficiency improvements such as standardization of production, the popularization of the conveyor belt, and the financial buffer afforded by a large network of dealerships—all while suppressing organized labor: Conot, *American Odyssey*, 144–155.

8. Ibid., 131.

9. Bloomfield, "Shaping the Character of a City," 173; Conot, *American Odyssey*, 129; Parkins, *The Historical Geography of Detroit*, 303–308; Ticknor, "Motor City," 103–105.

10. Chicago Association of Commerce and Industry, "Things about Detroit," *Chicago Commerce* 8 (1904).

11. Olivier Zunz, *The Changing Face of Inequality: Urbanization, Industrial Development, and Immigrants in Detroit, 1880–1920* (Chicago: University of Chicago Press, 2000), 16–18.

12. Burton, Stocking, and Miller, *The City of Detroit, Michigan*, 535.

13. John C. Schneider, *Detroit and the Problem of Order, 1830–1880: A Geography of Crime, Riot, and Policing* (Lincoln: University of Nebraska Press, 1980), 92.

14. Leonard Seltzer Wilson, "Functional Areas of Detroit, 1890–1933," *Papers of the Michigan Academy of Science, Arts and Letters* 22 (1936): 398–401.

15. Studying the locations of major land uses in Detroit over a half century, geographer Leonard Wilson noted that industrial growth between 1890 and 1900 almost solely concentrated around the railway nodes outside the downtown area (ibid.). See also Conot, *American Odyssey*, 161–165.

16. Wilson, "Functional Areas of Detroit," 401–406; Conot, *American Odyssey*, 138. Detroit's first east-west streetcar route opened in 1895 as part of Mayor Pingree's Detroit Railway Company, a competitor to the existing private streetcar operators. "Pingree at the Lever—He Started the First Car on the Detroit Railway," *Detroit Free Press*, July 9, 1895.

17. The comment was made in the context of an old Detroit mansion that was being demolished in the financial district. "Old Landmark Gone—the Picturesque Thompson House Has Just Been Pulled Down," *Evening News*, June 12, 1898.

18. For more information on the role of the city's street configuration in its centralization, see Sophia Psarra, Conrad Kickert, and Amanda Pluviano, "Paradigm Lost: Industrial and Post-Industrial Detroit—an Analysis of the Street Network and Its Social and Economic Dimensions from 1796 to the Present," *Urban Design International* 18, no. 4 (2013).

19. Judge Robert E. Frazer quoted in Dan Austin, *Forgotten Landmarks of Detroit* (Charleston, SC: History Press, 2012), 170–171.

20. David Lee Poremba, *Detroit in Its World Setting: A Three Hundred Year Chronology, 1701–2001* (Detroit: Wayne State University Press, 2001), 138. Savvy developers had forecast the northward growth trend of the city: Ferry, *The Buildings of Detroit*, 90; Burton, Stocking, and Miller, *The City of Detroit, Michigan*, 513.

21. *The Detroit Journal 13th Anniversary Edition* (Detroit: Detroit Journal, 1896); Silas Farmer, *History of Detroit and Wayne County and Early Michigan*, 3rd ed. (Detroit: S. Farmer & Co., for Munsell & Co., New York, 1890), 363.

22. "Lower Woodward Avenue Historic District Final Report" (City of Detroit, 1999).

23. The church struggled due to the decreasing number of nearby residents: Thomas J. Holleman, James P. Gallagher, and Smith Hinchman and Grylls Associates, *Smith, Hinchman & Grylls: 125 Years of Architecture and Engineering, 1853–1978* (Detroit: Wayne State University Press for Smith, Hinchman & Grylls Associates, 1978), 52.

24. Jean Maddern Pitrone, *Hudson's: Hub of America's Heartland* (Franklin, MI: Altwerger and Mandel, 1991), 32–33; *The Detroit Journal 13th Anniversary Edition*. Hudson's success prompted conversations about other viable retail locations in the city, such as Washington Boulevard and Grand Circus Park: "Grand Circus Park Locality the Focus of Many Eyes. Messrs. Fyfe and Warren Predicting Great Things for It," *Detroit Free Press*, January 12, 1896.

25. "Great Business Event—Ernst Kern's Magnificent New Store, Corner Woodward and Gratiot Avenues, to Be Opened Next Thursday Noon," *Detroit Free Press*, October 24, 1897.

26. "New Firm Assumes Entire Control and Ownership of Big Pardridge and Blackwell Department Store," *Detroit Free Press*, May 13, 1909.

27. For example, Benjamin Siegel grew from a small clothier to the world's largest cloak store on Woodward Avenue: Cheri Y. Gay, *Lost Detroit* (London: Pavilion Books, 2013), 108.

28. Instead, Edison, Detroit Gas, and Michigan State Telephone located their headquarters on the street by the end of the 1900s, earning it the nickname of "public utility row": Jacob Nathan, "Recollections of a Veteran Newspaper Reporter—Washington Boulevard," *Detroit News*, August 5, 1928; "The Washington Arcade a Credit to Detroit. This Edifice, Which Has Just Been Completed, Is a Model of Modern Shop Construction in All of Its Details," *Detroit News-Tribune*, September 21, 1902. The expansion of business on Washington Boulevard as "an avenue of escape from the enormous demand" came at the cost of the remaining dwellings on this street: "The Making Over of Washington Blvd. Big Undertaking Proposed in Changing All the Conditions of a Prominent Street," *Detroit News Tribune*, March 31, 1907. The *Detroit News-Tribune* worried that due to retailers being priced out, Woodward Avenue would undergo the same fate of retail decline which "on Jefferson Avenue some years ago brought that street to its present second-class condition": "Is Woodward Avenue Doomed to Retrogress?," *Evening News-Tribune*, March 24, 1907. The news articles may have been part of a

campaign by Washington Boulevard landowners and developers to narrow the street, which they considered too wide for business: "To Make a New Business Street—Washington Boulevard Property Owners Want That Thoroughfare Changed. Would Take It out of Park System, Remove Plot from Center and Reduce Its Width," *Detroit News-Tribune*, March 25, 1907.

29. Attempts by a department store to locate further north and start "the new shopping district of Detroit" in Brush Park failed: Woodford and Woodford, *All Our Yesterdays*, 226–229. Elliot-Taylor-Woolfenden business brochure in Gay, *Lost Detroit*, 43.

30. Hammond purchased the land under his building for $350,000. The fact that it had been worth only a few hundred dollars when first purchased in 1809 is an apt reflection of the new centrality of the Campus and the accelerating growth of Detroit: Burton, Stocking, and Miller, *The City of Detroit, Michigan*, 513–514.

31. Austin, *Forgotten Landmarks of Detroit*, 69–79. Upon its announcement, the local press described the building rather neutrally as "Detroit's most conspicuous building": "Here's the Building—Which Will Be a Sky Scraper Opposite the City Hall," *Sunday News*, February 24, 1889.

32. The new Majestic Building spared no expense in its construction, ultimately overstretching the owner's financial capacity. When the building opened in 1896, Mabley's department store was but a ground-floor tenant of its own conception, as Christopher Mabley had been forced to sell the building to stay afloat. His business soon failed: Austin, *Forgotten Landmarks of Detroit*, 101–115.

33. The buildings were among the first applications of steel frame construction in the Midwest outside of Chicago. The surrounding area had fully established itself over the previous decades as Detroit's financial center, containing most of the city's main banks, offices, wholesale trade houses, and rookeries: Woodford and Woodford, *All Our Yesterdays*, 228–230; Conot, *American Odyssey*, 101; Poremba, *Detroit in Its World Setting*, 177; "The Union Trust Co.—Here's the Way Its New House Will Look," *Evening News*, August 13, 1894.

34. Woodford and Woodford, *All Our Yesterdays*, 219; "To Be Detroit's Tallest Skyscraper," *Detroit News-Tribune*, June 25, 1906.

35. Albert Kahn opened his office in 1895 and competed with the office of Sheldon and Mortimer Smith. The latter grew into Smith, Hinchman and Grylls by 1906, and the two offices were responsible for most new downtown construction until well into the twentieth century: Conot, *American Odyssey*, 128. One of Detroit's top real estate developers was William W. Hannan, whose career had grown on apartment buildings, hotels, offices, and subdivisions: Lewis Publishing Company, *Michigan* (Chicago: Lewis Publishing Company, 1915), 257–258.

36. Woodford and Woodford, *All Our Yesterdays*, 223; Austin, *Forgotten Landmarks of Detroit*, 180–182; Ticknor, "Motor City," 106. The *Detroit News* reminisced about the bar's heyday as the forum of Detroit's auto industry: "men gathered there from the four corners of the earth. It was a new quest. Excitement charged the air. A new prosperity was in the making. Fortunes were being gambled. Men played hard, but they also worked desperately." The article cites Henry Ford's publicist E. LeRoy Pelletier, who approached the owner of the hotel to suggest he replace the lobby's rug; "get some red paint [and] have a great circle drawn on the lobby floor with this red paint and within that circle [inscribe] this legend: THE HEART OF THE AUTO INDUSTRY": "The Pontchartrain—the Heart of the Auto Industry—Its Bar Was a Gay Spot, but a Workroom Too Where the Latest Was Exhibited," *Detroit News*, May 29, 1946.

37. Austin, *Forgotten Landmarks of Detroit*, 149–153.

38. Gay, *Lost Detroit*, 130.

39. "Wonderland Opening," *Detroit Free Press*, September 23, 1900; "Theater Is Magnificent," *Detroit Free Press*, December 20, 1901; Andrew Craig Morrison, *Theaters* (New York: W. W. Norton; Washington: Library of Congress, 2006), 151–152.

40. The Opera House fire also took down several adjoining buildings, including six businesses, nearly missing Hudson's new department store: "Mass of Ruins—All That Now Remains of the District Last Night Swept by Fire. The Detroit Opera House Building Completely Wiped Out," *Evening News*, October 9, 1897. The Wonderland Theatre had moved from a smaller building closer to the riverfront on lower Woodward Avenue, which subsequently underwent renovation into a burlesque theater: Michael Hauser and Marianne Weldon, *Detroit's Downtown Movie Palaces* (Charleston, SC: Arcadia, 2006), 9.

41. Lisa Maria DiChiera, "The Theater Designs of C. Howard Crane" (master's thesis, University of Pennsylvania, 1992), 13; Andrew Craig Morrison, *Opera House, Nickel Show, and Palace: An Illustrated Inventory of Theater Buildings in the Detroit Area* (Dearborn, MI: Greenfield Village & Henry Ford Museum, 1974).

42. Woodford and Woodford, *All Our Yesterdays*, 233–238; George Byron Catlin, *The Story of Detroit* (Detroit: Detroit News, 1923), 700–704; Charles K. Hyde, "100–102 Monroe Avenue (Commercial Building)—Written Historical and Descriptive Data" (Historic American Buildings Survey, National Park Service, Department of the Interior, 1989).

43. Hauser and Weldon, *Detroit's Downtown Movie Palaces*, 7. On the Lafayette Boulevard entertainment district, see Ferry, *The Buildings of Detroit*, 323.

44. Ferry, *The Buildings of Detroit*, 323.

45. Sidney Glazer, *Detroit: A Study in Urban Development* (New York: Bookman Associates, 1965), 77; Austin, *Forgotten Landmarks of Detroit*, 85–100; "It's a Go. The New Union Depot, Assured by Incorporation Today—Three Great Railroads to Build It," *Evening News*, August 24, 1889. A subsequent plan to construct a third terminal between the Michigan Central and Union Depot by the Pennsylvania Central Railroad never came to fruition: "Penn—a New Road's Coming to Town," *Evening News*, December 27, 1895. To counter the competition from the Union Depot, the Michigan Central Depot unsuccessfully tried to purchase land to move up to the corner of First Street and Jefferson Avenue by 1891: "To Buy Four Blocks," *Evening News*, April 26, 1891.

46. The 1915 opening of the Wayne Hotel spa was a reaction to the loss of patronage due to the Michigan Central Railway station opening in Corktown in 1913. The hotel went bankrupt in the late 1910s and was demolished by the early 1930s: Gay, *Lost Detroit*, 52.

47. Conot, *American Odyssey*, 92. With the announcement of the depot's construction in 1889, the *Evening News* already warned of the transformation of the station area: "Fort Street residences will have much of their desirability as homes swept away by the proximity of the new depot. The section about is already begun to go into business": "It's a Go. The New Union Depot." A day later, the newspaper commented that "a general exodus of wealthy residents of

the new depot's neighborhood is bound to follow its establishment on Fort Street": "To Come at Last. Detroit to Have a Grand Union Depot," *Evening News*, August 25, 1889.

48. Zunz, *The Changing Face of Inequality*, 61, 65–66.

49. Real estate advertisement in the *Detroit Free Press* in 1887, reproduced in David W. Hartman, *The Development of Detroit's Cass Corridor: 1850–1975*, vol. 3 (Detroit: Wayne State University Press, 1975), 3.

50. The art museum's location on Jefferson Avenue was the result of an arduous multiyear effort to locate the civic building in a dignified setting at reasonable expense. Finally, a streetcar company and a group of surrounding landowners donated the land for the building. Daniel M. Bluestone, "Detroit's City Beautiful and the Problem of Commerce," *Journal of the Society of Architectural Historians* 47 (1988): 249–251.

51. Zunz, *The Changing Face of Inequality*, 62–63.

52. *Detroit Free Press*, 18 May 1891, cited in Bluestone, "Detroit's City Beautiful and the Problem of Commerce," 251. The replacement of religion by commerce was not new to the city. Almost two decades before, the smaller First Baptist Church at the corner of Fort and Griswold was purchased and rather haphazardly renovated into a commercial block, which was torn down for the Dime Savings Bank in the early twentieth century. Gay, *Lost Detroit*, 22.

53. Bluestone, "Detroit's City Beautiful and the Problem of Commerce," 252.

54. Russell Jaehne McLauchlin, *Alfred Street* (Detroit: Conjure House, 1946), 13–14.

55. Gretchen Griner, "Historic and Architectural Resources of the Cass Farm Survey Area, Detroit, Wayne County, Michigan" (National Park Service, Department of the Interior, 1997), 5. By 1890, seven streetcar companies operated eighteen lines on seventy miles of tracks, "running out like arteries in every direction from the throbbing heart in the Campus Martius." Yet not all lines ran through downtown, as the Michigan Central Belt Line ran around the city on railroad tracks, stopping at New Center and Belle Isle, catering to an increasingly decentralizing clientele. While the tangential line was "placed in operation before the city was ready for it," Detroit's suburbanization would soon catch up: "Intramural Traffic—the Extensive Municipal Transit System of Detroit," *Evening News*, August 3, 1890. By 1898, Detroit's three streetcar companies ran all-electric cars on more than 150 miles of track throughout the city. The length

of the streetcar lines was little less than the 235 miles of paved roads in the city (not taking double lines into account). Suburban rail lines reached even further into the Michigan hinterland: Clarence Monroe Burton, *Burton's Condensed Statistics of Detroit, Mich. 1898* (Detroit: Wolverine Printing Co., 1898), 13–15.

56. Historic Designation Advisory Board, "Proposed Brush Park Historic District—Final Report" (City of Detroit, 2010); Palmer "Beneath Electric Stars," scrapbook, vol. 13 from Burton Historical Collection, cited in Hartman, *The Development of Detroit's Cass Corridor*, vol. 3, 3.

57. Historic Designation Advisory Board, "Proposed Cass Park Local Historic District Final Report" (City of Detroit, 2014), 6–7.

58. By the turn of the century, only 13.3 percent of Detroiters lived in multifamily homes—far lower than in any similarly sized city on the East Coast: Zunz, *The Changing Face of Inequality*, 156–160.

59. Griner, "Historic and Architectural Resources of the Cass Farm Survey Area," 6–7.

60. Detroit Association of Charities, *Fourth Annual Report of the Central Committee* (Detroit: Chas. M. Rousseau's Printing House, 1883), 13–14, cited in Zunz, *The Changing Face of Inequality*, 62.

61. David M. Katzman, *Before the Ghetto: Black Detroit in the Nineteenth Century* (Urbana: University of Illinois Press, 1975), 131–174.

62. Zunz, *The Changing Face of Inequality*, 57–59; Wilson, "Functional Areas of Detroit."

63. For example, residents of Champlain Street were ultimately successful in renaming their street as Lafayette Street, reflecting its more dignified western counterpart: "Want Champlain Street Purged," *Detroit News*, September 23, 1909.

64. Charles Mulford Robinson, *Modern Civic Art; or, the City Made Beautiful* (New York: Arno Press, 1903), 82.

65. *Detroit Free Press*, 4 September 1895, cited in Bluestone, "Detroit's City Beautiful and the Problem of Commerce," 253.

66. Randall Fogelman and Lisa E. Rush, *Detroit's Eastern Market* (Charleston, SC: Arcadia, 2013), 7–8; Gay, *Lost Detroit*, 8; "A Black Eye—the Central Market Is Probably Doomed, an Overwhelming Majority against It," *Evening News*, April 20, 1892; "Regenerated—Marvelous Change in Cadillac Square," *Sunday News-Tribune*, August 21, 1896.

67. "There Was Much Talk—No Action Taken in Regard to Washington Avenue," *Detroit Free Press*, September 5, 1894; "May Have to Pay for It—Abutters Stuck for Washington Avenue Improvement," *Detroit Free Press*, November 12, 1895; George B. Catlin, "Washington Boulevard of Altered in 108 Years," *Detroit News*, November 24, 1915.

68. "Proposed Fire Limits—There's Considerable Objecting to Them," *Evening News*, February 16, 1894.

69. For a more detailed account of Pingree's administration, see Catlin, *The Story of Detroit*, 592–632; and Burton, Stocking, and Miller, *The City of Detroit, Michigan*, 387–388.

70. Besides Mayor Pingree, many Detroiters were keen to improve the waterfront, such as newspaper magnate George G. Booth: "Diagram Showing Convention Hall and Other Features Suggested by George G. Booth for the Bi-Centennial Celebration," *Evening News*, December 29, 1898; Poremba, *Detroit in Its World Setting*, 215.

71. Austin, *Forgotten Landmarks of Detroit*, 22; "The Mayor's Latest—He Will Spring an Eye-Opener on the Council. His Great Scheme for a $6,000,000 Park," *Evening News*, January 13, 1891; "Detroit's Fine River Front—the Part the River Has Played in History—Palmy Days of Early Steamboating and Evolution of the Modern Freight-Carrier," *Detroit News-Tribune*, July 27, 1902; Miroslav Base, "The Development of Detroit 1701–1920: A Planning History" (working paper, Center for Urban Studies, Wayne State University, 1970), 70; Conot, *American Odyssey*, 101–103; Catlin, *The Story of Detroit*, 590–596.

72. Bluestone, "Detroit's City Beautiful and the Problem of Commerce," 255. Olmsted was brought into the planning process after Robinson's initial plans had turned out rather vague and hastily put together: Donald E. Simpson, "Civic Center and Cultural Center: The Grouping of Public Buildings in Pittsburgh, Cleveland, and Detroit and the Emergence of the City Monumental in the Modern Metropolis" (Ph.D. diss., University of Pittsburgh, 2013), 198–204.

73. Griner, "Historic and Architectural Resources of the Cass Farm Survey Area," 8.

74. Pound and Suydam, *Detroit, Dynamic City*, 355; Catlin, *The Story of Detroit*, 568–570, 586; Burton, Stocking, and Miller, *The City of Detroit, Michigan*, 433.

75. Historian Burton states that "before the auto came into general use, not more than one-fourth of the lots on the boulevard were occupied. Now [in 1922] there are very few vacant." The tangential nature of the boulevard meant that it never had a streetcar line running along its length: Burton, Stocking, and Miller, *The City of Detroit, Michigan*, 434.

76. "120-Foot Woodward, Dream of a Century, Now Comes True," *Detroit News*, September 15, 1935; National Register of Historic Places, "New Center Commercial Historic District Registration" (National Park Service, Department of the Interior, 2016), 19–20.

77. The location of a gas station on Fort Street illustrates how this elite district had transformed into a commercial fringe: Woodford and Woodford, *All Our Yesterdays*, 267; Russell Harris, "First Gasoline Station in Detroit Still Going Strong," *Detroit News*, September 10, 1961; Chris Meister, "Albert Kahn's Partners in Industrial Architecture," *Journal of the Society of Architectural Historians* 72, no. 1 (2013); "Complete in All Appointments," *Detroit Free Press*, August 17, 1902.

78. Gay, *Lost Detroit*, 52; Poremba, *Detroit in Its World Setting*, 222.

79. "Improving Grand River Ave.," *Evening News*, April 5, 1891. The subway plan was a platform for Mayor Codd's reelection, and part of an anti-streetcar rhetoric that prevailed in the city: Conot, *American Odyssey*, 138; "Half Revealed—Subway Plan Said to Be Only Small Portion of Big Scheme," *Detroit Free Press*, March 1, 1906; "Hen Still on—Mayor Codd's Subway Project Said to Be More Tangible Than Generally Supposed," *Detroit Free Press*, March 14, 1906; "Subway Project Now—Codd Has Gigantic Plan to Help Him to Second Term," *Detroit Free Press*, February 27, 1906; "Will Spring It—Subway-Rapid Transit Deal Goes to Common Council Tuesday, April 10," *Detroit Free Press*, March 31, 1906.

80. "Green Lanterns to Light Campus," *Detroit News*, August 18, 1909, 222; Poremba, *Detroit in Its World Setting*.

81. "Beautification of Detroit—the Commission to Be Appointed by Mayor Breitmeyer Has an Important Work before It," *Detroit Free Press*, May 16, 1909.

82. "Donaldson Leads New Commission," *Detroit Free Press*, June 2, 1909. Burnham only agreed to serve as Bennet's advisor in this project as he planned to retire from city planning, dying two years later: "Talk Methods of City Betterment—Commissioners Hear Plans of Famous Municipal Engineers Discussed at Luncheon," *Detroit Free Press*, February 20, 1910.

83. Simpson, "Civic Center and Cultural Center," 209–214. The early commission's focus on beautification and its merely advisory role prompted later derision as a "picture plan stage" of Detroit urban planning, leading to aesthetically pleasing plans with little practical value: City Plan Commission, "Annual Report" (Detroit, 1927), 3; Ferry, *The Buildings of Detroit*, 217; Bluestone, "Detroit's City Beautiful and the Problem of Commerce," 246.

84. The April 1900 U.S. Census sets the Detroit population at 285,704.

85. R. L. Polk & Company, *Detroit City Directory* (Detroit: R. L. Polk & Company, 1911), 6–10.

86. C. M. Burton and Detroit Convention and Tourist Bureau, *Detroit, a City of Today* (Detroit: Richmond & Backus Co., 1912), 6. Many of the newcomers were immigrants, as almost half of the 1900 population was born outside the United States: Glazer, *Detroit: A Study in Urban Development*, 52–53.

87. An article on the growth of the central business district specifically applauds the replacement of "old shacks of unsavory reputation" by a "fine business block": "Business Is Reaching Out," *Detroit Free Press*, December 23, 1906. Similarly, the replacement of rooming houses by new commercial buildings is praised in "Old Residence and Rooming House Section of the City Where Wonderful Transformation Has Been Worked," *Detroit Free Press*, October 28, 1906.

88. "Brushaber's New Store to Be Forerunner of Business Extension of Michigan Avenue," *Detroit Free Press*, May 13, 1910.

89. Fogelman and Rush, *Detroit's Eastern Market*, 9.

90. Poremba, *Detroit in Its World Setting*, 225; "What the Michigan Central Has Done for Detroit," *Michigan Manufacturer and Financial Record*, October 23, 1915.

1. C. M. Burton and Detroit Convention and Tourist Bureau, *Detroit, a City of Today* (Detroit: Richmond & Backus Co., 1912), 7–8; Melvin G. Holli, *Detroit* (New York: New Viewpoints, 1976), 118–119; G. T. Bloomfield, "Shaping the Character of a City: The Automobile Industry and Detroit, 1900–1920," *Michigan Quarterly Review* 25, no. 2 (1986): 174; Clarence Monroe Burton, William Stocking, and Gordon K. Miller, *The City of Detroit, Michigan, 1701–1922* (Detroit: Clarke Pub. Co., 1922), 566, 570; Olivier Zunz, *The Changing Face of Inequality: Urbanization, Industrial Development, and Immigrants in Detroit, 1880–1920* (Chicago: University of Chicago Press, 2000), 292; David Allan Levine, *Internal Combustion: The Races in Detroit, 1915–1926* (Westport, CT: Greenwood Press, 1976), 99; Frank Bury Woodford and Arthur M. Woodford, *All Our Yesterdays: A Brief History of Detroit* (Detroit: Wayne State University Press, 1969), 256–261.

2. Burton, Stocking, and Miller, *The City of Detroit, Michigan*, 588–592. The need for factory workers became even more intense as around 65,000 Detroiters had been drafted to fight in the war, among other things prompting a significant growth of the female labor force: Sidney Glazer, *Detroit: A Study in Urban Development* (New York: Bookman Associates, 1965), 86–88.

3. A local news editor's opinion of Detroit in 1918, cited in Thomas James Ticknor, "Motor City: The Impact of the Automobile Industry upon Detroit, 1900–1975" (Ph.D. diss., University of Michigan, 1978), 135.

4. An actual comment on the benefits of decentralized industry in terms of congestion and pollution: Almon Ernest Parkins, *The Historical Geography of Detroit* (Lansing, MI: Michigan Historical Commission, 1918), 200.

5. Heather B. Barrow, *Henry Ford's Plan for the American Suburb: Dearborn and Detroit* (DeKalb: Northern Illinois University Press, 2015), 3–13, 31.

6. Henry Ford, *Ford Ideals; Being a Selection from "Mr. Ford's Page" in the Dearborn Independent* (Dearborn, MI: Dearborn Publishing Co., 1922), 154–158.

7. The Outer Belt was constructed by the Detroit Terminal Railway, six miles north of downtown. More information on the creation of the Outer Belt rail line can be found in "The

Tremendous Additions to Facilities," *Michigan Manufacturer and Financial Record*, October 23, 1915.

8. Zunz, *The Changing Face of Inequality*, 292; Barrow, *Henry Ford's Plan for the American Suburb*; Donald F. Davis, "The City Remodelled: The Limits of Automotive Industry Leadership in Detroit, 1910–1929," *Histoire Sociale/Social History* 13, no. 26 (1980): 456; Burton, Stocking, and Miller, *The City of Detroit, Michigan*, 573, 698–699.

9. Leonard Seltzer Wilson, "Functional Areas of Detroit, 1890–1933," *Papers of the Michigan Academy of Science, Arts and Letters* 22 (1936): 406–407.

10. News articles at the end of the nineteenth century already demonstrated the high turnover in the city's elite. For example the *Sunday News-Tribune* proclaimed in 1898 that "of the men who were prominent in 1858 less than 30 per cent remain": "Detroit Forty Years Ago—the Houses, Stores and Business Men of That Period," *Sunday News-Tribune*, October 2, 1898.

11. Julian Street and Wallace Morgan, *Abroad at Home; American Ramblings, Observations, and Adventures of Julian Street; with Pictorial Sidelights* (New York: Century Co., 1914), 80–82.

12. A citation of Packard Motor president Henry B. Joy in W. Hawkins Ferry, *The Buildings of Detroit; a History* (Detroit: Wayne State University Press, 1968), 214. The effort was successful. The move of the auto barons to a separate club, combined with the outdated room facilities at the Pontchartrain hotel, were the Pontchartrain's death knell, and the building closed in 1920—less than 14 years after opening: Dan Austin, *Forgotten Landmarks of Detroit* (Charleston, SC: History Press, 2012), 185–186; Don Lochbiler, *Detroit's Coming of Age, 1873 to 1973* (Detroit: Wayne State University Press, 1973), 215–220; Ferry, *The Buildings of Detroit*, 211–212.

13. The wage increase was a tremendous success. The number of employees increased from 12,880 in 1914 to 32,702 in 1916: Levine, *Internal Combustion*, 99; Woodford and Woodford, *All Our Yesterdays*, 256–261; Ticknor, "Motor City," 182.

14. Holli, *Detroit*, 118–119. Ford's wage hike caused a near doubling of the average wages in Detroit between 1914 and 1919. Over the same time period, the number of jobs increased by more than 100,000. Burton, Stocking, and Miller, *The City of Detroit, Michigan*, 533–534.

15. Barrow, *Henry Ford's Plan for the American Suburb*, 112.

16. Myron E. Adams, "Detroit—a City Awake," *The Survey—a Journal of Constructive Philanthropy*, August 5, 1911, cited in Wilma Wood Henrickson, *Detroit Perspectives: Crossroads and Turning Points* (Detroit: Wayne State University Press, 1991); Barrow, *Henry Ford's Plan for the American Suburb*, 112.

17. Pushed by the deterioration of their formerly prominent neighborhoods, the gradual suburbanization of Detroit's downtown elite accelerated, as the percentage of prominent families living within Grand Boulevard declined from more than 50 percent to slightly over 20 percent during the 1910s alone. The center of gravity for the Blue Book upper class shifted further northwestward to the New Center area as well as northeast to Grosse Pointe: Roderick Duncan McKenzie, *The Metropolitan Community* (New York: McGraw-Hill, 1933), 123, 182–185; Zunz, *The Changing Face of Inequality*, 343–398.

18. Ford's policies were a success: his employees' homeownership increased 99 percent in the first eighteen months of the program: Levine, *Internal Combustion*, 99; Woodford and Woodford, *All Our Yesterdays*, 256–261; Ticknor, "Motor City," 182.

19. "Detroit Growing at a Rate of over Eighty Thousand Yearly," *The Detroiter*, November 29, 1915. *The Detroiter* was a rather boosterist magazine, naming itself as "the spokesman of optimism." In 1911 alone, more than $19 million was spent in Detroit on new construction, exceeded in that year only by San Francisco and Boston: see table 79 in McKenzie, *The Metropolitan Community*, 230.

20. Parkins, *The Historical Geography of Detroit*, 199–200.

21. Communities welcomed annexation as it brought city services like running water and sewer, increasing property values as a result: Zunz, *The Changing Face of Inequality*, 287–292.

22. For example, Oakman Boulevard ran between the Ford Highland Park and River Rouge plants, named after real estate developer Robert Oakman. Benefiting from the boulevard's boost to land values, Oakman ultimately "gifted" the boulevard to the city, which would be responsible for its maintenance from then on. The Department of Parks and Boulevards paid for boulevard paving and maintenance: Arthur Pound and E. H. Suydam, *Detroit, Dynamic City* (New York: D. Appleton-Century, 1940), 354–355; "Gift of Boulevard Is Held Up a While," *Detroit Free Press*, September 16, 1921.

23. Woodford and Woodford, *All Our Yesterdays*, 277.

24. In the same article, real estate dealer John I. Turnbull proposes another iteration of riverfront improvements. "Suggests New River Front Plan," *Detroit News*, March 17, 1912.

25. Parkins, *The Historical Geography of Detroit*, 201; William Barclay Parsons and Eugene Klapp, "Report on Detroit Street Railway Traffic and Proposed Subway" (Board of Street Railway Commissioners, Detroit, 1915), 10–11.

26. Parkins, *The Historical Geography of Detroit*, 276–277.

27. Parsons and Klapp, "Report on Detroit Street Railway Traffic and Proposed Subway," 52–53.

28. The First National Building housed the First National Bank, one of the first banks to open after the adoption of the National Bank Act of 1862, commencing "the history of modern banking": Burton, Stocking, and Miller, *The City of Detroit, Michigan*, 650–651. In 1819, lots near Campus Martius had sold for a few dollars each, and the purchaser was subsequently mocked: "A fool and his money are soon parted." Farmer, *History of Detroit and Wayne County and Early Michigan*, 41.

29. "Is Detroit Prosperous?," *Detroit Free Press*, October 12, 1913.

30. "L.W. Tuller Started Business Movement to Grand Circus Park," *Detroit Tribune*, November 1, 1914.

31. For more information on the hoteliers Statler and Tuller, see "Meet Mine Hosts of the Grand Circus," *Detroit Tribune*, November 1, 1914. In the same section, Tuller advertised his hotel as being in the center of Detroit's business district.

32. The *Detroit Tribune* had dedicated an entire section to the new buildings rising along Grand Circus Park, totaling a $10 million investment: Dan Austin, Sean Doerr, and John Gallagher, *Lost Detroit: Stories behind the Motor City's Majestic Ruins* (Charleston, SC: History Press, 2010); "The Transfiguration of Grand Circus Park," *Detroit Tribune*, November 1, 1914.

33. Austin, *Forgotten Landmarks of Detroit*, 153. The Statler hotel was the third in a chain of hotels constructed by Ellsworth Statler, famed for his similarly named hotel in New York built in 1919: Cheri Y. Gay, *Lost Detroit* (London: Pavilion Books, 2013), 136.

34. "Boulevard's Growth Is the Result of a Farsighted Program," *Detroit Saturday Night*, April 21, 1923.

35. Milton R. Palmer, "Washington Boulevard Will Become Detroit's Fashionable Shopping Center," *Detroit Saturday Night*, December 30, 1916.

36. A special section of the *Detroit Saturday Night* weekly was dedicated to the Book family and their vision for Washington Boulevard. "Book Building," *Detroit Saturday Night*, December 30, 1916. Most of the visions did not materialize, although the Book Cadillac Hotel was constructed in 1924 and the Book Tower in 1926.

37. Robert E. Conot, *American Odyssey* (New York: Morrow, 1974), 214.

38. "Book Estate Takes in Hotel Cadillac," *Detroit News*, April 27, 1918.

39. Ferry, *The Buildings of Detroit*, 212.

40. National Convention of Building Managers, "Detroit Achieves New Building," *Buildings* 18, no. 10 (1918).

41. The commercial growth of downtown Detroit mirrored the economics of retail construction in most other US metropolises. For new skyscraper construction, the retail ground floor was often the most profitable floor. Carol Willis, *Form Follows Finance: Skyscrapers and Skylines in New York and Chicago* (New York: Princeton Architectural Press, 1995).

42. After visiting counterparts on the Pacific Coast, the director of the new Broadway Market boasted that "nothing in the west will in any way compare with Detroit's new Broadway Market": "Detroit's New Market Structure to Excel Any Other in the West," *Detroit Free Press*, May 19, 1922.

43. By the 1910s, the Hudson family had grown into one of the city's most prominent families, living side by side with industrialists like the Fords and Dodges in the Boston-Edison district of the city. Joseph Hudson invested in his own line of automobiles, and his niece married Henry Ford's son Edsel—forming an interesting personal mix between downtown and automobile interests. Conot, *American Odyssey*, 185.

44. "Hudson's Annex Will Open Today—New Ten-Story Building on Woodward Contains Latest in Goods and Fixtures," *Detroit Free Press*, October 17, 1911.

45. Especially the store's cooperation in the Retail Research Association in 1916 helped stream-line operations: Jean Maddern Pitrone, *Hudson's: Hub of America's Heartland* (Franklin, MI: Altwerger and Mandel, 1991), 62.

46. "Kern's Business Forces Extension," *Detroit Free Press*, July 27, 1913; "Kern's Remodeled Store Has Opening," *Detroit Free Press*, September 30, 1915; Michael Hauser and Marianne Weldon, *20th Century Retailing in Downtown Detroit* (Charleston, SC: Arcadia, 2008).

47. "Lower Woodward Avenue Historic District Final Report" (City of Detroit, 1999).

48. Lisa Maria DiChiera, "The Theater Designs of C. Howard Crane" (master's thesis, University of Pennsylvania, 1992), 15–16.

49. "Stott Leases Theater He Is Soon to Build," *Detroit News*, February 2, 1912.

50. Michael Hauser and Marianne Weldon, *Detroit's Downtown Movie Palaces* (Charleston, SC: Arcadia, 2006), 10.

51. Ibid., 17; "'Clean Up or Close Up,' Says Mayor to Theaters," *Detroit News*, November 24, 1915.

52. Lars Björn and Jim Gallert, *Before Motown: A History of Jazz in Detroit, 1920–60* (Ann Arbor: University of Michigan Press, 2001), 7–8.

53. "Fourteen-Story Office Building Adjoining B. of C.," *Detroit News*, November 10, 1913.

54. Ticknor, "Motor City," 138.

55. A damning article by Commissioner Fenkell revealed that some City Hall tenants had resorted to using squirt guns against cockroaches, and the basement resembled an "ancient ruin": George H. Fenkell, "City Hall Is Filthy; New One Needed," *Detroit News*, December 4, 1914.

56. Kevin Boyle, *Arc of Justice: A Saga of Race, Civil Rights, and Murder in the Jazz Age* (New York: Macmillan, 2007), 105–115.

57. This description comes from an account of the transformation of Fort Street, conveniently located between a major railway station and downtown: "Passing of Fort Street West," *Detroit Free Press*, November 9, 1913. A similar decline was documented for Jefferson Avenue: "Jefferson Avenue Has Lost Its Glory," *Detroit Saturday Night*, April 27, 1918.

58. Reports of prostitution note that rooming houses themselves were clear of any issues, as prostitutes would not want to draw attention to them; instead they worked a few blocks in downtown: "Heart of City Swarms with Street Women," *Detroit Free Press*, September 7, 1913. Prostitution was a very visible part of American downtowns during the 1910s, including Detroit. Part of this was attributable to the relative imbalance between single men and women in the city: Conot, *American Odyssey*, 187–188.

59. Conot, *American Odyssey*, 189–190.

60. Zunz, *The Changing Face of Inequality*, 287–292.

61. Those who could leave the districts had already left. The original Irish immigrants had all but disappeared from Corktown by 1920, as had the Germans concentrated on Detroit's east side. Only the poorest immigrants and African Americans were still confined to the inner districts of the city. The immigration of southern blacks had greatly accelerated during World War I, and most of the newcomers were forced to settle in the existing slum on the near east side. They made up more than 4 percent of the population by 1920—a nearly tenfold increase over the past two decades. Although black migration was not uncommon in northern industrial cities, Detroit saw a more rapid influx than any other major city due to high demand for manufacturing labor during World War I: Levine, *Internal Combustion*, 1–5, 124–125.

62. Ibid., 27.

63. Björn and Gallert, *Before Motown*.

64. Jeremy Williams, *Detroit: The Black Bottom Community* (Charleston, SC: Arcadia, 2009), 17.

65. Alison Isenberg, *Downtown America: A History of the Place and the People Who Made It* (Chicago: University of Chicago Press, 2004), 110–121.

66. Starting with the Vaudette Theatre on Gratiot, three African American-managed theaters were already counted in 1917, along with more than thirty saloons and poolrooms: Björn and Gallert, *Before Motown*, 5–6, 20.

67. Rather than using zoning, the city tried to stem commercial and industrial intrusion on a case-by-case basis. Ultimately this approach proved largely fruitless, as commercial and

small industrial land uses continued to creep into the relatively cheap parcels of the near east and west side: "Residential Oases," *Detroit Free Press*, June 29, 1919; Levine, *Internal Combustion*, 124–125.

68. Davis, "The City Remodelled," 479.

69. Gretchen Griner, "Historic and Architectural Resources of the Cass Farm Survey Area, Detroit, Wayne County, Michigan" (National Park Service, Department of the Interior, 1997), 15–17. A land sale at the southwest corner of Ledyard Street and Second Avenue facing the park was heralded as "one of the most desirable in the city for a high-class apartment hotel," but the site remained unchanged during the 1910s: "Corner Overlooking Cass Park Is Sold—H. E. Beecher and Others Buy Property Held Nearly 40 Years in Benham Family," *Detroit Free Press*, October 10, 1915. The decline of the neighborhood accelerated as its central park became a hotspot for youth crime by the end of the 1910s: "Cass Park 'Clean-up' Due; Officer 288 on the Job," *Detroit Free Press*, August 22, 1917.

70. Helen E. Keep and M. Agnes Burton, *Guide to Detroit* (Detroit: Detroit News Company, 1916), cited in David W. Hartman, *The Development of Detroit's Cass Corridor: 1850–1975*, vol. 3 (Detroit: Wayne State University Press, 1975), 4.

71. By the mid-1910s, an estimated 40,000 cars drove Detroit's streets. The National Petroleum Association estimated there were between 25 and 30 drive-in gas stations in Detroit by 1915, and even more curbside gas pumps: "No Bitter Garage Competition in Detroit," *National Petroleum News*, August 1915. The city proudly built the first 24-mile stretch of concrete highway from Ford's Highland Park plant outward to Pontiac by 1916, a precursor to the first national highway act passed the same year: Conot, *American Odyssey*, 148, 192–193.

72. Street and Morgan, *Abroad at Home*, 74–79.

73. "The Parked Automobile—Detroit's Latest Problem Arising from Her Unparalleled Prosperity," *Detroit Tribune*, October 12, 1913.

74. Conot, *American Odyssey*, 194. Couzens, a former associate of Henry Ford, subsequently became the city's first mayor under the new 1918 city charter, which adopted a strong mayor system: Glazer, *Detroit: A Study in Urban Development*, 90; Burton, Stocking, and Miller, *The City of Detroit, Michigan*, 333.

75. Many of Goldberg's contemporaries similarly did not depend on parking as a main source of income. Nevertheless, his gamble paid off, and he expanded his holdings to 36 downtown lots by the mid-1930s. By that time, several other companies had also entered the market: John A. Jakle and Keith A. Sculle, *Lots of Parking: Land Use in a Car Culture* (Charlottesville: University of Virginia Press, 2004), 48–50.

76. The article made Detroit's first recommendations for road widenings: "Relieve the Central Congestion," *Detroit Free Press*, October 28, 1911; "Has Plans for Relief of Traffic," *Detroit Free Press*, June 6, 1912.

77. "Try Skip Stop Plan for Another Month," *Detroit News*, June 27, 1916; Richard W. Longstreth, *City Center to Regional Mall: Architecture, the Automobile, and Retailing in Los Angeles, 1920–1950* (Cambridge, MA: MIT Press, 1997).

78. "'Crow's Nest' Bosses Six Streets," *Detroit News*, October 9, 1917.

79. "Proposed Plan to Transform Washington Boulevard," *Detroit News Tribune*, March 10, 1912; Conot, *American Odyssey*, 193.

80. Over a ten-hour period, 18,424 cars passed the corner of Woodward and Michigan avenues: cited in "Lower Woodward Avenue Historic District Final Report."

81. Parsons and Klapp, "Report on Detroit Street Railway Traffic and Proposed Subway," 46. Between 1904 and 1913, the length of streetcar lines had increased by 14.8 percent, while the number passengers had increased by 180 percent: ibid., 11. Cross-town lines also received support as they could connect Detroit's decentralized homes and factories: "Cross-Town Line Needed," *Detroit Free Press*, October 29, 1911; "Railway Favors Changing to New Crosstown Line," *Detroit Free Press*, November 15, 1912. The opening of a Grand Belt streetcar line in the early 1910s led to "initial traffic … so heavy as to indicate that it will develop into a useful connecting link." At its busiest point just south of Campus Martius, almost 400 streetcars an hour passed Woodward Avenue by 1913. By 1915, 14 out of Detroit's 20 streetcar lines still ran through downtown: Parsons and Klapp, "Report," 40.

82. Interestingly, the plan predicted that without the subway investments, further growth would "congest the population in the present city area in apartment and other compact forms

of residences, changing completely the independent home characteristic of the city": Parsons and Klapp, "Report," 22.

83. Charles K. Hyde, "Planning a Transportation System for Metropolitan Detroit in the Age of the Automobile: The Triumph of the Expressway," *Michigan Historical Review* 32, no. 1 (2006): 60–61.

84. John Frost, the proposer of a monorail, went on to start his own company, the Michigan Elevated Railway Company. An effort to build a test track in Oakland County in the early 1920s also did not materialize: Burton, Stocking, and Miller, *The City of Detroit, Michigan*, 663–664; "Will Build One Mile of Elevated Tracks," *Michigan Manufacturer and Financial Record*, July 15, 1922.

85. Robert M. Fogelson, *Downtown: Its Rise and Fall, 1880–1950* (New Haven: Yale University Press, 2001), 265–271, 294–296.

86. Most of the successful implementations were located outside of the city's built-up area, principal exceptions being the construction of the Detroit Institute of Arts and the central Public Library in Midtown: Edward H. Bennett and Cass Gilbert, "Preliminary Plan of Detroit" (City Plan and Improvement Commission, Detroit, 1915). See also Gay, *Lost Detroit*, 121.

87. Walter H. Blucher, "City Planning in Detroit," *City Planning* 3, no. 2 (1927); June Manning Thomas, *Redevelopment and Race: Planning a Finer City in Postwar Detroit* (Baltimore: Johns Hopkins University Press, 1997), 37. The charter also reduced the political influence of ward aldermen in the city, increased mayoral power, and generally reduced "machine politics" and corruption in the city: Glazer, *Detroit: A Study in Urban Development*, 88–91.

88. "Commission Plans Zoning of Detroit," *Detroit Free Press*, June 29, 1919; "City to Mark Business Zone," *Detroit Free Press*, June 24, 1919.

89. The argument for zoning was one of stability: "Detroit's growth … has *occurred* as the immediate occasion dictated and individual development has always been paramount to the general public good. A valuable piece of real estate today might be utterly worthless tomorrow." Harvey Whipple, "City Plan Commission Begins Its Great Task of Bringing Order out of Detroit's Chaos," *Detroit Saturday Night*, May 3, 1919, cited in Barrow, *Henry Ford's Plan for the American Suburb*, 69. Five zoning districts were distinguished: First Residence, Second

Residence (allowing multifamily dwellings), Commercial, Industrial, and Unrestricted districts. Zoning regulations of Los Angeles in 1909 and New York in 1916 were specifically cited: City Plan Commission, "A Building Zone Plan for Detroit" (Detroit, 1919).

90. For more information on Detroit's zoning history, see a series of six articles by Martin S. Hayden in the *Detroit News* titled "Detroit's Master Plan," published between July 7 and 12, 1947.

91. "Cross-Town Thorofares for Auto Traffic Pressing Need, Head of D.P.W. Points Out," *Detroit News*, August 28, 1918.

92. "Commission Plans East, West Street—New Thoroughfare 12 Miles Long Recommended to Relieve Congestion," *Detroit Free Press*, September 28, 1919; City Plan Commission and Rapid Transit Commission, "Vernor Highway—Report Presented to the Common Council of the City of Detroit" (Detroit, 1925). Previous smaller widening projects had been implemented, like the widening of the corner of Gratiot and Randolph streets. Many others were stillborn. The proposed extension of Washington Boulevard by George Booth of 1898 is an example, as are proposals to extend East Fort Street into Cadillac, to which "various suggestions have been made in a promiscuous way" in the late nineteenth century: "The New Cadillac Square," *Evening News*, January 31, 1900.

93. "Cross-City Avenue Opposed by Nagel—Councilman Urges Delay in Dix-High-Waterloo Highway Construction," *Detroit Free Press*, November 4, 1919.

94. The arguments in favor of the new road were summarized in an advertisement by the Detroit Real Estate Board, citing a *Detroit Journal* editorial in favor and the official opinion of the board itself: Detroit Real Estate Board, "The Truth about the Dix-High-Waterloo Plan," *Detroit Journal*, November 8, 1921; E. A. Baumgarth, "How the Motor Car's Impact Has Transformed a Great City," *Detroit News*, May 29, 1946.

95. "Dix-Waterloo Road Approved—Twelve-Mile Crosstown Highway Receives Final O.K. of City Council," *Detroit Free Press*, September 30, 1920; "Dix-Waterloo Project Running 1,637 Votes Ahead," *Detroit Free Press*, November 9, 1921. The highway was named in honor of prominent citizen James Vernor. The plan was already obsolete before it was even finished: when all properties were acquired, the City Plan Commission voted to increase the width of the new street by another 50 percent: Blucher, "City Planning in Detroit." More information in

Marilyn Florek, "West Vernor Highway Historic District" (National Register of Historic Places multiple property documentation form, 2002); "Commission Plans East, West Street," *Detroit Free Press*, September 28, 1919; "Couzens Again Flays Council on Veto Action," *Detroit Free Press*, July 24, 1921. Vernor Highway mirrored the successful completion and partial widening of Warren Avenue as a downtown bypass in the late nineteenth century: "Great Street Opening. The Warren Avenue Case Ended Last Night," *Evening News*, January 13, 1891.

96. From the 1910s onward, voters and political leader consistently deemed the several transit proposals and reports, drafted by a range of external consultants and the Board of Street Railway Commissioners, as too costly, cumbersome, or unnecessary. Street widening was seen as a cheaper alternative which could also be more easily phased. As a result, no fewer than thirteen studies for mass transit were left on the shelf between 1914 and 1939: Hyde, "Planning a Transportation System for Metropolitan Detroit in the Age of the Automobile."

97. "New Building Vast Project—Durant Structure Plans Call for 30 Acres of Floor Space," *Detroit News*, May 2, 1919.

98. National Register of Historic Places, "New Center Commercial Historic District Registration|" (National Park Service, Department of the Interior, 2016), 20.

99. Another reason for GM's locational decision was that its president Durant was unable to assemble a large enough parcel of land for his envisioned head office downtown. Due to the relative ease of finding a large parcel of land for a low price away from downtown, the new office building sprawled into four wings of fifteen stories each rather than expanding vertically: "Durant Tells Gigantic Aims of Expansion," *Detroit Free Press*, April 4, 1919, 215; "G.M.C. Occupies New Building," *Detroit Free Press*, November 25, 1920; Randall Fogelman, *Detroit's New Center* (Charleston, SC: Arcadia, 2004); Conot, *American Odyssey*, 242; Ferry, *The Buildings of Detroit*. Originally Durant envisioned locating all of General Motors' office staff in the Detroit building and naming it after himself, but ultimately the office was named after the company and an existing office in Midtown New York remained in use: Burton, Stocking, and Miller, *The City of Detroit, Michigan*, 596.

100. Joel Garreau describes edge cities as commercial districts that mirror or even supersede downtown functions. For a more detailed definition, see Joel Garreau, *Edge City: Life on the New Frontier* (New York: Doubleday, 1991).

101. The city had been instrumental in assembling the land for the railway station through condemnations, and the 1915 Bennett Plan proposed to construct a diagonal street between it and the new cultural center—of which only Roosevelt Park was actually completed. The depot and distribution for downtown's federal building and post office were slated to follow westward, as their late nineteenth-century building proved "uncomfortably crowded" before it had even opened, despite an addition. Burton, Stocking, and Miller, *The City of Detroit, Michigan*, 370; "What the Michigan Central Has Done for Detroit," *Michigan Manufacturer and Financial Record*, October 23, 1915.

102. Burton, Stocking, and Miller, *The City of Detroit, Michigan*, 850–854.

103. Ibid., 767–768.

CHAPTER 4: GROWING PAINS: 1921–1929

1. R. L. Polk & Company, *Detroit City Directory* (Detroit: R. L. Polk & Company, 1921).

2. Miroslav Base, "The Development of Detroit 1701–1920: A Planning History" (working paper, Center for Urban Studies, Wayne State University, 1970), 88. For example, Walter P. Chrysler restructured an ailing car manufacturer into the Chrysler Corporation in 1925, growing further with the acquisition of the Dodge Motor Company in 1928. Sidney Glazer, *Detroit: A Study in Urban Development* (New York: Bookman Associates, 1965), 93.

3. Cyril Arthur Player, "Detroit: Essence of America," *New Republic*, August 3, 1927.

4. The article was part of a series of articles on the transformation of American cities. R. L. Duffus, "Our Changing Cities: Dynamic Detroit," *New York Times*, April 10, 1927.

5. Foreign immigration had severely declined with the passing of the 1924 Immigration Act.

6. Player, "Detroit: Essence of America," 272–274.

7. Duffus, "Our Changing Cities." A similar description of the city's growth was given in the *Detroit News*: "The wide streets have become trim; the business district has continued to rebuild itself, more and more in the character of the newborn civic spirit; the residential districts, aided by swift transportation, have spread and acquired more breathing space. The city,

so to speak, 'fills in.'" "The City—What Lies Behind Veil That Conceals Its Future?," *Detroit News*, March 20, 1927.

8. While half of Detroit's notables lived within three miles of downtown in 1910, less than eight percent were left there in 1930—far fewer than in comparable larger US cities: Melvin G. Holli, *Detroit* (New York: New Viewpoints, 1976), 120–122; Roderick Duncan McKenzie, *The Metropolitan Community* (New York: McGraw-Hill, 1933), 123.

9. Donald F. Davis, "The City Remodelled: The Limits of Automotive Industry Leadership in Detroit, 1910–1929," *Histoire Sociale/Social History* 13, no. 26 (1980): 457.

10. Glazer, *Detroit: A Study in Urban Development*, 94–95.

11. The development of subdivisions during the 1920s far exceeded population growth, leading to significant vacancy, especially in their commercial plots, which were estimated to offer five times more square footage than there was current demand for. Michigan Planning Commission, "A Study of Subdivision Development in the Detroit Metropolitan Area" (Lansing, 1939). With the speed offered by the automobile, residents were able to locate as far as fifteen miles from downtown. Davis, "The City Remodelled," 457.

12. Ironically, city planners initially ascribed the decline to displacement of residents by downtown businesses, envisioning that all residentially declining areas would eventually become part of the downtown business district. The population decline was measured between 1923 and 1927. The director of Detroit's bureau of statistics estimated that downtown Detroit would eventually encompass almost a third of the city: H. J. Kaufmann, "City Moving to Outskirts— Expansion of Business and Industry Kills Off Old Neighborhoods," *Detroit News*, March 18, 1928.

13. City Plan Commission, "Annual Report" (Detroit, 1929), 11. The quotation from Keyserling came from his pamphlet on African American rights in the United States: Hermann Keyserling, "What the Negro Means to America," *Atlantic Monthly*, October 1929, 444.

14. Most modern manufacturing plants were over a million square feet, occupying lots measuring dozens of acres—a far cry from the nineteenth-century inner-city factories that fit within one or a few city blocks: Thomas James Ticknor, "Motor City: The Impact of the Automobile Industry upon Detroit, 1900–1975" (Ph.D. diss., University of Michigan, 1978), 187–189.

15. The growth of Dearborn brought Ford back to his roots west of the city, and followed his vision of suburban living to promote the moral and physical health of workers. An interesting pattern of reverse commuting resulted for many of the River Rouge workers, as they preferred to stay in Detroit so they could switch employers in time of need: Heather B. Barrow, *Henry Ford's Plan for the American Suburb: Dearborn and Detroit* (DeKalb: Northern Illinois University Press, 2015), 14–33, 75; Frank Bury Woodford and Arthur M. Woodford, *All Our Yesterdays: A Brief History of Detroit* (Detroit: Wayne State University Press, 1969), 285–287. Ford production moved to the River Rouge plant from Highland Park, another Detroit suburb. Nevertheless, the move was a deliberate attempt to further suburbanize the working environment and locate within a municipality where he could effectively reign without local opposition: Robert E. Conot, *American Odyssey* (New York: Morrow, 1974), 235; Barrow, *Henry Ford's Plan for the American Suburb*. Decentralization was not just a matter of control. The automotive industry's notorious instability of employment due to the annual manufacturing cycle prompted General Motors to decentralize its plants to spread the burden of layoffs to multiple communities: Ticknor, "Motor City," 118–119.

16. G. T. Bloomfield, "Shaping the Character of a City: The Automobile Industry and Detroit, 1900–1920," *Michigan Quarterly Review* 25, no. 2 (1986): 178–180.

17. Ticknor, "Motor City," 89–90, 205–209. The annual changes required frequent plant alterations and retooling, which proved too burdensome for smaller manufacturers. As a result, the market consolidated from 230 active manufacturers in 1908 to 44 in 1927. By 1929, the Big Three had a market share of 73.5 percent: ibid., 111–112. One manufacturers' association reported a decline in employment of more than 80 percent between July 1, 1920 and the end of the year: Clarence Monroe Burton, William Stocking, and Gordon K. Miller, *The City of Detroit, Michigan, 1701–1922* (Detroit: Clarke Pub. Co., 1922), 534.

18. David Allan Levine, *Internal Combustion: The Races in Detroit, 1915–1926* (Westport, CT: Greenwood Press, 1976), 27.

19. Citing statistical research, the article states that "Detroit will follow Chicago, New York, Boston and Philadelphia in that for the first time in its history, there will be a remarkable development of its suburbs": "New Development Era Looms for Woodward," *Detroit Free Press*, March 23, 1924.

20. "From Battleground to Shopping Center, Boulevard's History," *Detroit Saturday Night,* April 21, 1923.

21. Duffus, "Our Changing Cities."

22. Jean Maddern Pitrone, *Hudson's: Hub of America's Heartland* (Franklin, MI: Altwerger and Mandel, 1991), 51–84; Michael Hauser and Marianne Weldon, *Remembering Hudson's: The Grande Dame of Detroit Retailing* (Charleston, SC: Arcadia, 2010), 9–15; "Fitted to Do Largest Retail Trade in Nation," *Detroit Free Press,* November 4, 1928. The floor area of Hudson's was larger than any of the shopping malls in the Detroit region today.

23. John Thomas Mahoney and Leonard Sloane, "Inside Hudson's 49 Acres—a New Book Reveals a Detroit Phenomenon," *Detroit Free Press,* January 15, 1967, 18.

24. Paul Vachon, *Forgotten Detroit* (Charleston, SC: Arcadia, 2009), 38.

25. Michael Hauser and Marianne Weldon, *20th Century Retailing in Downtown Detroit* (Charleston, SC: Arcadia, 2008), 74.

26. Dan Austin, Sean Doerr, and John Gallagher, *Lost Detroit: Stories behind the Motor City's Majestic Ruins* (Charleston, SC: History Press, 2010), 89–92.

27. The *Detroit Free Press* dedicated an entire newspaper section to the opening, adding that city officials welcomed the new stores. "Sears, Roebuck Stores Open Tomorrow," *Detroit Free Press,* June 13, 1928.

28. "16 Stores Open in Two Decades," *Detroit Free Press,* April 26, 1951.

29. Counts from Polk's *Detroit City Directory* of 1929.

30. On the Association's agenda during the first years: lowering taxes, a proposal for rapid transit, and plans for a collective parking garage. Central Business District Association, "Annual Development Report" (Detroit, 1992).

31. Cheri Y. Gay, *Lost Detroit* (London: Pavilion Books, 2013), 40.

32. "Plans to Build 6 More Skyscrapers on Boulevard," *Detroit News,* June 15, 1924. The Books continued their vision by proposing an eighty-one-story tower along the boulevard, which never materialized.

33. This statement refers to the new lighting system installed on the street, initiated by one of the Book brothers: an early example of building owners taking ownership of public space (albeit in this case through general city funds): "Turning Night into Day on Washington Boulevard," *Detroit Free Press*, June 8, 1928; "Washington Boulevard's New Lights, Now Ready, Interesting Other Streets," *Detroit News*, July 8, 1928; Rex G. White, "Heart of City a Silver Blaze," *Detroit News*, July 11, 1928.

34. This tower is now known as the Broderick Tower after its purchase by David Broderick in 1944: Austin, Doerr, and Gallagher, *Lost Detroit*, 15.

35. Harold Heffernan, "Gay Dedicatory Program Marks Fox Opening," *Detroit News*, September 22, 1928; *Detroit Free Press*, cited in W. Hawkins Ferry, *The Buildings of Detroit; a History* (Detroit: Wayne State University Press, 1968), 325. The Fox was actually almost a carbon copy of a similar theater under construction by Fox in St. Louis. The theater was to be the second largest in the nation, after the Paramount Theatre in New York: "Movie House to Be Unique," *Detroit News*, May 29, 1927. Soon after the Fox Theatre opening, the Crane-designed Fisher Theatre opened in Detroit's New Center, arguably the "last of the great movie palaces to be built in Detroit": Ferry, *The Buildings of Detroit*, 326.

36. "Magnificent New United Artists Building Thrown Open—Third Unit in Bagley Improvement Drive," *Detroit Free Press*, January 29, 1928; "18-Story Building for New Theater—United Artists and Detroit Properties to Spend 6 Million," *Detroit News*, January 14, 1927, both cited in Austin, Doerr, and Gallagher, *Lost Detroit*, 119. The growing number of movie theaters prompted the construction of a Film Exchange in Cass Park to store films and house local film distribution agencies: "Film Exchange Building Is Formally Opened," *Detroit News*, January 30, 1927.

37. Michael Hauser and Marianne Weldon, *Detroit's Downtown Movie Palaces* (Charleston, SC: Arcadia, 2006), 10.

38. Ticknor, "Motor City," 148; Writers' Program of the Works Projects Administration, *Michigan: A Guide to the Wolverine State* (New York: Oxford University Press, 1941).

39. "Black and tan" establishments referred to those that catered to a mixed-race audience. The term does not necessarily refer to ownership or management. Lars Björn and Jim Gallert,

Before Motown: A History of Jazz in Detroit, 1920–60 (Ann Arbor: University of Michigan Press, 2001), 8–35. The black and tan entertainment scene existed in many other African American neighborhoods in large American cities such as New York's Harlem and Chicago's South Side: John Hannigan, *Fantasy City: Pleasure and Profit in the Postmodern Metropolis* (London: Routledge, 2010), 21.

40. The 1921 Polk directory reflects an interesting increase in downtown establishments selling soft drinks: Details in David Lee Poremba, *Detroit in Its World Setting: A Three Hundred Year Chronology, 1701–2001* (Detroit: Wayne State University Press, 2001). Mayor Coleman Young admitted to his role in smuggling and distributing illicit alcohol during Prohibition in his autobiography: Coleman Young and Lonnie Wheeler, *Hard Stuff: The Autobiography of Coleman Young* (New York: Viking, 1994), 21–22.

41. Ernest W. Mandeville, "Detroit Sets a Bad Example," *The Outlook*, 22 April 1925; Holli, *Detroit*, 125, 151; Glazer, *Detroit: A Study in Urban Development*, 95.

42. By 1926, the American Social Hygiene Association counted more brothels in Detroit than in New York City—a city five times its size: Ticknor, "Motor City," 180.

43. To facilitate the continued growth of automobile production, manufacturers like Ford began to offer installment plans for the purchase of newer models—many of which were administered in Detroit: Conot, *American Odyssey*, 255.

44. The resulting cruciform floorplates were a positive contrast to the Chicago-style light wells in Detroit's older skyscrapers, as they also allowed for the building to look less massive and for light and air to enter the street. The Buhl's recessed aesthetic was not a response to a zoning mandate such as in New York after 1916, as Detroit still had no building restrictions: Ferry, *The Buildings of Detroit*, 329.

45. The buildings were the result of the Cadillac Square Improvement Association, formed by the brothers Barlum and mayor William Thompson. "Barlum Tower Third Skyscraper in District," *Detroit News*, November 13, 1927; "New 6-Million Skyscraper to Tower on Cadillac Sq.," *Detroit Free Press*, February 6, 1927.

46. Ferry, *The Buildings of Detroit*, 330.

47. James W. Tottis, *The Guardian Building: Cathedral of Finance* (Detroit: Wayne State University Press, 2008), 23; Ferry, *The Buildings of Detroit*, 330–331. This image of solidity proved rather untrue, as the Union Trust's bankruptcy played a major role in the Depression, with the building now known as the Guardian Building named after the Guardian Detroit Union Group which would emerge from the Union Trust's ashes: Darwyn H. Lumley, *Breaking the Banks in Motor City: The Auto Industry, the 1933 Detroit Banking Crisis and the Start of the New Deal* (Jefferson, NC: McFarland, 2009).

48. Ferry, *The Buildings of Detroit*, 331.

49. "Building Detroit's Grand Canyon," *Detroit News*, March 6, 1927.

50. Ferriss drew 22 of Detroit's buildings on a visit to the city. His remarks on Detroit future prospects were based on the new connections over water and through the air to Europe that would enable Detroit so serve as a gateway between the continents: "Builder of Dream Cities Pictures Detroit of Tomorrow," *Detroit News*, August 28, 1927.

51. Emil Rosenger, "$100,000,000 Gives Detroit a New Skyline—Giant Buildings Rising in Last 18 Months Show Faith in City's Future," *Detroit News*, May 13, 1928.

52. E. G. Pipp, "This Spells Faith of Detroit Men in Detroit's Future," *Pipp's Magazine*, 1927. Pipp was a realtor in the city and a great booster of its potential, asking in his 1927 promotional leaflet *Opportunities in Detroit*: "Do Detroit's men of wealth expect Detroit to grow, to double in ten years? If not, why are they putting up so many tall office buildings this very year?"

53. "Big $30,000,000 Fisher Bldg. Is Announced," *Detroit Free Press*, January 16, 1927; Ticknor, "Motor City," 186–187. A page-sized ad promised that the Fisher Building was "in the very heart of the Detroit which has developed and which is developing today. Tenants of the new Fisher Building will save an hour every workday in traveling to and from their homes, as compared with occupants of office buildings south of Grand Circus Park": "In the Heart of Detroit," *Detroit News*, August 28, 1927. The Albert Kahn-designed Art Deco Fisher Building opened in 1928 as a massive yet elaborate complex housing an innovative 1,100-bay parking garage as well as an arcade of shops, restaurants, and a theater in its eleven-story base, crowned by a twenty-eight-story office tower: Ferry, *The Buildings of Detroit*, 333–335.

54. Calculations by author; Austin, Doerr, and Gallagher, *Lost Detroit*, 78.

55. The financing of General Motors cars through their Acceptance Corporation had started in 1919, but was conducted from their New Center headquarters, per records of the Federal Financial Institutions Examination Council. Henry Ford's strained relationships with American banks first surfaced during a 1921 business downturn. Rather than ask the banks for a loan, Ford forced his dealers to buy up more cars in cash, in a sense forcing them to loan the company money. Subsequently, the company's cash reserves were deposited in banks across the country and abroad to spread risks. In the mid-1920s, his son Edsel Ford started the Guardian Detroit Company, later becoming the Guardian Detroit Union Group. The bank gained significant traction by merging with the car-financing branch of Ford into the Guardian Detroit Union Group. The Fords ultimately lost a significant sum of money with the closing of the Guardian Detroit Union Group in 1933: Lumley, *Breaking the Banks in Motor City*; Associated Press, "Ford Is Dead at 83 in Dearborn," *New York Times*, April 7, 1947.

56. In the year ending September 1929, right before the market crashed, Detroit had $7,512 of clearings per capita, compared to $65,931 in New York. Detroit's per capita clearings were also lower than Cleveland's, Cincinnati's, and St Louis's, but higher than Buffalo's. Detroit's total bank clearings were $11,784,509,000, Chicago's were $37,125,374,000, and New York's were $456,937,947,000. In total amount of clearings, Detroit ranked below Boston and Philadelphia as well: see table 97 in Comptroller of the Currency, *Report of the Comptroller of the Currency* (Washington, DC: Government Printing Office, 1929), 714. Detroit's clearings had actually increased relative to Chicago's and New York's: in 1920, Detroit had cleared less than 20 percent of Chicago's annual money, and less than 3 percent of New York's: Homer Hoyt, *One Hundred Years of Land Values in Chicago* (Chicago: University of Chicago Press, 1933); "Week's Bank Clearings," *Detroit Free Press*, October 16, 1921.

57. Ferry, *The Buildings of Detroit*, 365.

58. John R. Fugard, "What Is Happening to Our Central Business Districts?," *American Planning and Civic Annual* (1940). Detroit had constructed 16 million square feet of office space, ranking fifth among American cities. Ticknor, "Motor City," 186.

59. E. B. Burgess, "Concentric Zone Model of Urban Structure and Land Use," *Landmark Publication* 125 (1925). The concept of distinct urban zones was further popularized by economist Homer Hoyt.

60. E. J. Beck, "Runs 23 Parking Lots in Downtown Detroit and Watches over Them with a Spy Glass," *Detroit News*, September 20, 1928.

61. The "Cass Tech" high school catered to a wide variety of scholarly fields, including chemistry and physics laboratories, workshops and learning kitchens, as well as hosting modern amenities such as an indoor swimming pool, running track, and 3,000-seat auditorium: Austin, Doerr, and Gallagher, *Lost Detroit*, 29–33.

62. Gretchen Griner, "Historic and Architectural Resources of the Cass Farm Survey Area, Detroit, Wayne County, Michigan" (National Park Service, Department of the Interior, 1997), 9. Historic Designation Advisory Board, "Proposed Cass Park Local Historic District Final Report" (City of Detroit, 2014), 7–9. Commercial expansion also occurred in the western periphery of downtown, as the Bell Company added twelve stories to its exchange building to accommodate the rapid growth of telephone traffic, "looking down loftily on Park Place": "Bell Telephone Company to Make Its Home a Skyscraper—Bell Telephone Building Will Be Made 19 Stories," *Detroit News*, March 27, 1927.

63. "New Restrictions for Old Cass Farm Area—Business Wins a Partial Victory in Long Fight against Majority of Property Owners in District," *Detroit News*, November 6, 1927.

64. Dan Austin, *Forgotten Landmarks of Detroit* (Charleston, SC: History Press, 2012), 157–159; "To Develop Park Avenue—New Assocation of Property Owners Proposes Extensive Building Improvements," *Detroit Free Press*, June 10, 1923.

65. David W. Hartman, *The Development of Detroit's Cass Corridor: 1850–1975*, vol. 3 (Detroit: Wayne State University Press, 1975), 4–5.

66. Conot, *American Odyssey*, 293; Richard W. Longstreth, *City Center to Regional Mall: Architecture, the Automobile, and Retailing in Los Angeles, 1920–1950* (Cambridge, MA: MIT Press, 1997); Richard W. Longstreth, *The Drive-in, the Supermarket, and the Transformation of Commercial Space in Los Angeles, 1914–1941* (Cambridge, MA: MIT Press, 2000).

67. City Plan Commission, "Annual Report" (Detroit, 1928), 14.

68. Martin S. Hayden, "Detroit's Master Plan" (series of six articles), *Detroit News*, July 7–12, 1947); City Plan Commission, "Annual Report" (1928 and 1929); "An Outsider's View of Zoning in Detroit," *Detroit Saturday Night*, July 23, 1927.

69. For a more detailed description of the background and layout of the proposal, see Donald E. Simpson, "Civic Center and Cultural Center: The Grouping of Public Buildings in Pittsburgh, Cleveland, and Detroit and the Emergence of the City Monumental in the Modern Metropolis" (Ph.D. diss., University of Pittsburgh, 2013), 222–226.

70. An earlier and similarly unbuilt Memorial Hall plan would have cost an estimated $5.5 million; Saarinen's proposal would have cost twenty times as much. Furthermore, a new convention hall was completed in Midtown in 1924, which diminished the need for the convention facilities Saarinen's buildings would have offered. New mayor John Smith took the condemnation for the site off the ballot in 1925: ibid., 227–228. Since Hazen S. Pingree's proposal to improve the riverfront in 1890, five proposals had already come and gone, leading the *Detroit Free Press* to lament the "talk-much, do-nothing" attitude of Detroit's leadership on the riverfront: Charles Weber, "Talk Much—Do Nothing. City's Planning Gathers Dust in Files Dating Back to 1890," *Detroit Free Press*, January 15, 1947. Mayor Lodge in particular wanted to see the riverfront cleaned up as a matter of civic pride, and Eliel Saarinen planted the seeds for his son Eero's later combination of government, memorial, and convention buildings, successfully constructed in the 1950s by focusing on civic pride: "How Father, Son Changed Detroit Dream," *Detroit Times*, July 17, 1959; Robert J. Mowitz and Deil S. Wright, *Profile of a Metropolis; a Case Book* (Detroit: Wayne State University Press, 1962), 141–142; Ferry, *The Buildings of Detroit*, 363. Saarinen's proposal was part of a longer lineage of plans for the riverfront: "The City—What Lies Behind Veil That Conceals Its Future?," 142; "Detroit's 1928 Riverfront Dream," *Detroit News*, May 22, 1973; Gay, *Lost Detroit*; "Brown Urges Civic Center," *Detroit News*, February 20, 1927; "Asks City Hall on River Front—Prominent Lawyer Says It Should Be First Unit of Detroit Civic Center," *Detroit News*, January 30, 1927; "Urges City Buy on River Front," *Detroit News*, February 20, 1927. Lodge's support prefaced larger plans he had for the transformation of the entire riverfront of the city for industry, transportation, and recreation: "Proposed Development of Waterfront," *Detroit News*, December 19, 1928.

71. Some proponents of the riverfront revitalization lamented that Detroit lacked civic pride, as citizens "have been too much absorbed by their personal concerns to give enough thought to the vital concerns of the city as a whole." Others lamented the loss of "common necessity [over] private ambition or greed." Yet the local press rightfully asserted that most citizens had not seen any civic improvements to their direct neighborhoods, and "to a citizen whose

immediate physical surroundings are neglected the abstract idea of large civic improvements loses much of its attractiveness": George B. Catlin, "How Detroit Lost Its Beautiful Waterfront and Wouldn't Take It Back," *Detroit News*, June 12, 1927; "Civic Pride and Civic Center," *Detroit News*, March 7, 1927; "Building of a Great City," *Detroit News*, September 25, 1927.

72. Between 1914 and 1927, car traffic on Grand River Avenue had increased 3,400 percent, and by 1924 almost 75,000 cars entered downtown every morning. Detroit's main arterials carried almost 20 percent more traffic than their Manhattan counterparts: City Plan Commission and Rapid Transit Commission, "Vernor Highway: Report Presented to the Common Council of the City of Detroit" (Detroit, 1925), 5.

73. Charles K. Hyde, "Planning a Transportation System for Metropolitan Detroit in the Age of the Automobile: The Triumph of the Expressway," *Michigan Historical Review* 32, no. 1 (2006): 63.

74. Ibid.

75. Between 1899 and 1913, the per capita mileage of streetcar tracks halved, although the transition to municipal ownership did result in new investments: Barrow, *Henry Ford's Plan for the American Suburb*, 78–81.

76. Rapid Transit Commission, "Vehicular Traffic in the Business District of Detroit" (Detroit, 1924), 10, 15; Sidney D. Waldon, "The Superhighway Plan of the Detroit Metropolitan Area" (paper presented at the Proceedings of the Thirteenth Annual Conference on Highway Engineering, Ann Arbor, MI, 1927), 165. The last interurban commuter line closed in 1934: Conot, *American Odyssey*, 237; Department of Street Railways, "How Are We Going to Thread the Traffic Needle?" (Detroit, 1924). Streetcar and bus trips had already started to decrease by 1916: Sidney D. Waldon, "Superhighways and Regional Planning," in *Planning Problems of Town, City and Region* (Washington, DC: William F. Fell, 1927).

77. "The City—All Dressed Up and Plenty of Places to Go," *Detroit News*, February 20, 1927; Player, "Detroit: Essence of America"; Base, "The Development of Detroit 1701–1920," 93; Conot, *American Odyssey*, 186; Woodford and Woodford, *All Our Yesterdays*, 280–281; Davis, "The City Remodelled," 467.

78. Rapid Transit Commission, "Rapid Transit System for the City of Detroit" (Detroit, 1926), 22–23.

79. Hudson's department store even went so far as to publish a statement by the Rapid Transit Commission's president in one of their advertisements as part of "a series written by men and women of national reputation": Sidney D. Waldon, "The Master Plan Meets Traffic Growth," in "Report of the Greater and Better Detroit Committee," 1927.

80. In fact, Ford had participated in the construction of various suburban streetcar lines in the past to ease the commute to and between his plants: Barrow, *Henry Ford's Plan for the American Suburb*, 76–78. The last effort of the Rapid Transit Commission's predecessor in 1923 was the proposal of a series of streetcar tunnels under downtown streets. The report acknowledged that Detroit wasn't growing inland as much as it was growing along the factory belts east and west of the city: Board of Street Railway Commissioners, "Plan for Initial Underground Transit" (Detroit, 1923).

81. The streetcar tunnels were meant to appease the Department of Street Railways: Robert M. Fogelson, *Downtown: Its Rise and Fall, 1880–1950* (New Haven: Yale University Press, 2001), 86–88.The landslide defeat of the referendum was caused by the sentiment that the subway line favored profiteering out-of-town industrialists, central business interests, and inner-city slum dwellers, making it a nonstarter in a city whose electorate increasingly consisted of blue-collar homeowners who lived well away from downtown and its subway access. The special assessments that were to be levied to finance the subways were another hurdle. For a more detailed analysis of the voting process, see Davis, "The City Remodelled," 467–486; Barrow, *Henry Ford's Plan for the American Suburb*, 81–91; Fogelson, *Downtown*, 86–88, 94. Meanwhile, a proposal by the Grand Trunk Railroad to double their tracks and stack them with a freeway for a "rapid transit" connection to Pontiac was foiled by the stock market crash of 1929: Howard Warren, "An Unfulfilled Dream—Rapid Transit to Pontiac," *Detroit News*, January 9, 1974.

82. Detroit's total streetcar ridership had decreased over 25 percent between 1916 and the end of the 1920s, remarkable in light of the city's simultaneous rapid growth. Transit ridership in cities that had implemented rapid transit had actually increased between 1916 and 1928: Street Railway Commission and Rapid Transit Commission, "Report of the Street Railway

Commission and the Rapid Transit Commission to Hon. John C. Lodge, Mayor, and the Honorable the Common Council on a Rapid Transit System for the City of Detroit" (Detroit, 1929), 4–5. Most rapid transit investments in other cities had been completed in the late nineteenth century, starting in New York in 1870, Chicago in 1893, and Boston in 1897: J. Rowland Bibbins, "Rapid Transit Development and the Modern City Plan," *Annals of the American Academy of Political and Social Science* 133 (1927). Historian Hyde describes how Rapid Transit Commission president Sidney Waldon—a retired former vice president at Packard Motor—was "swimming against the current of professional and popular opinion about urban transportation, for reasons that he never clearly stated": Hyde, "Planning a Transportation System for Metropolitan Detroit," 65.

83. Sidney D. Waldon, "How Wider Streets Here Will Mean Better Rapid Transit Facilities," *Detroit Motor News* 6 (March 1926).

84. Rapid Transit Commission, "Proposed Super-Highway Plan for Greater Detroit" (Detroit, 1924). Rights-of-way were indeed acquired, with significant help from Wayne, Oakland, and Macomb counties.

85. Davis, "The City Remodelled," 468.

86. The suburban refusal to chip in led to one of the first proposals for the "creation of a metropolitan transportation district including all political subdivisions inside the 15-mile circle" which could also fund parks and sewer and water systems. Board of Street Railway Commissioners and Rapid Transit Commission, "Report to Hon. John C. Lodge, Mayor by Board of Street Railway Commissioners and Rapid Transit Commission on Financing a Subway Plan" (Detroit, 1929).

87. The difference between the 240- and 120-foot widths meant that mass transit would be routed in underground tunnels below the urban roads, as against in suburban ground-level medians: Rapid Transit Commission, "Proposed Super-Highway Plan for Greater Detroit," 22.

88. Waldon, "The Superhighway Plan of the Detroit Metropolitan Area," 165; Fogelson, *Downtown*, 86.

89. Road widening outside of the Detroit city limits was cheaper and could be covered by state gasoline taxes, while widening inside city limits had to be paid for without state support and was far more expensive: Barrow, *Henry Ford's Plan for the American Suburb*, 82–84.

90. Bibbins, "Rapid Transit Development and the Modern City Plan," 5. On the various means of funding rapid transit throughout the United States, see American Electric Railway Association Committee on Rapid Transit, "Report of the Committee on Rapid Transit—106," in *Convention of the American Electric Railway Association* (Cleveland, 1926).

91. City Plan Commission and Rapid Transit Commission, "Vernor Highway," 9. A report mentioned that the downtown ring road could be widened to more than 120 feet, as land acquisition costs in Black Bottom were lower than average: Rapid Transit Commission, "Vehicular Traffic in 1928" (Detroit, 1929), 64, footnote 2.

92. The report on Chicago's road widening is part of the Rapid Transit Committee's archive at the Burton Historical Collection—a clear signal that the Committee was paying close attention to their western counterpart. The widenings had resulted in significant property value increases, even when they weren't constructed yet: John J. Sloan, "Street Widening in Chicago—a Record of Accomplishment," *Concrete Highway Magazine* 10, no. 12 (1926).

93. Levine, *Internal Combustion*; Thomas J. Sugrue, *The Origins of the Urban Crisis: Race and Inequality in Postwar Detroit* (Princeton, NJ: Princeton University Press, 1996).

94. Waldon, "How Wider Streets Here Will Mean Better Rapid Transit Facilities."

95. Rapid Transit Commission, "Proposed Super-Highway Plan for Greater Detroit," 22.

96. The citation comes from a summary made by the Erie County Highway Committee of Sidney Waldon's presentation of the Detroit plan. Waldon developed his plan to bolster downtown through infrastructure investments: "Defensive Planning." Erie County Highway Committee, "What Should Buffalo Do for Increased Motor Travel? What Are Other Cities Doing? Detroit Is Providing Now for Future Highway Needs," in Erie County Highway Department *Bulletin* (Buffalo, 1927).

97. Waldon, "The Superhighway Plan of the Detroit Metropolitan Area," 163.

98. Ibid., 169–170.

99. "Urge Widening of Woodward," *Detroit News*, November 16, 1924.

100. Griner, "Historic and Architectural Resources of the Cass Farm Survey Area," 10.

101. "Edsel Ford as a Witness," *Detroit News*, April 30, 1929.

102. Bernard E. Meyers, "That Superhighway Vision of 1923 Is Coming True!," *Detroit Realtor* 9, no. 9 (1927).

103. While the Michigan and Gratiot Avenue widenings were approved by more than a two-thirds margin, Woodward Avenue's widening only narrowly passed with 53.4 percent of the votes. Detroit Common Council, Advisory Committee, "Carrying out the Master Plan" (Detroit, 1925), 2.

104. A 1927 traffic strategy deprioritized the widening of Woodward Avenue to settle a rift between the mayor and city council. Curiously, cost estimates were strongly adjusted downward for most widening projects in the document. Nevertheless, a wish list of 22 widenings still cost over $100 million dollars, the city's portion of which would exhaust almost all property taxes over the next decade: "New Widening Plan Revealed—Transit Board Recommends $102,825,000 Be Spent on 22 Streets," Detroit News, September 16, 1927.

105. "One More Widening Complication," *Detroit Saturday Night*, July 23, 1927.

106. "'Benefited' Owners Protest Widenings—Wider Vernor Highway Brings Higher Taxes, Special Assessments, but No Trade Compensation, They Say," *Detroit News*, September 27, 1929. All but one respondent of a survey by the *Detroit News* complained that their property values had dropped due to road widenings, and urged other sources for funding such as gasoline taxes: "Street Widenings Cut Values, Say Owners—Few Believe Broadening of Thoroughfares Add Worth of Holdings; Suggestions Made for Financing," *Detroit News*, November 17, 1929.

107. By the mid-1920s, the city had begun to realize that widenings didn't benefit abutting properties as much as anticipated, and had proposed spreading out the assessments over a larger area: City Plan Commission and Rapid Transit Commission, "Vernor Highway—Report Presented to the Common Council of the City of Detroit" (Detroit, 1925), 11–13; "Wider Highways Help Traffic, Hurt Business," *Detroit News*, April 9, 1928; Hayden, "Detroit's Master Plan," 17.

108. A comment made by Gratiot Avenue Realty Owners Association's W. B. Wreford in an attempt to set a clear schedule for widenings and avoid local assessments on the projects: "Wants Bonds for Widenings—W. B. Wreford Proposes City Abolish Assessments on Abutting Property," *Detroit News*, September 18, 1929.

109. Lee C. Richardson, "Parking Lots Provide New Use for Land," *Detroit Realtor*, April 1929.

110. Matthew Stephenson, "Detroit: City of Tomorrow," *Outlook*, February 13, 1929. The private parking lots were supplemented by over a dozen parking garages: "Auto Parking a Big Industry," *Detroit News*, April 28, 1929.

CHAPTER 5: EARLY EROSION: 1929–1937

1. Andrew Bernhard, "Dedication Welds International Area as Tunnel Is Opened," *Detroit News*, November 9, 1930.

2. Robert E. Conot, *American Odyssey* (New York: Morrow, 1974), 275. Those that remained had to accept far lower salaries than the famed $5 a day Ford offered in 1914—fueling the growing and ultimately successful clamor for labor unions: ibid., 284–286.

3. Sidney Glazer, *Detroit: A Study in Urban Development* (New York: Bookman Associates, 1965), 104. The city and federal governments were among the only organizations that still commissioned new buildings, such as the revamped downtown public library in 1931 and a new federal building on the site of its predecessor in 1934: Dan Austin, *Forgotten Landmarks of Detroit* (Charleston, SC: History Press, 2012), 58, 137–139.

4. Helen Hall, "When Detroit's out of Gear," *The Survey*, April 1, 1930; Melvin G. Holli, *Detroit* (New York: New Viewpoints, 1976), 124–127, 203.

5. By 1932, the city spent 40 percent of its budget on debt service. The next year, Detroit had begun to default on its debt, forced to write "scrip" to promise payment to its employees: Glazer, *Detroit: A Study in Urban Development*, 99; Conot, *American Odyssey*, 273–275.

6. "Without Vision No City Can Become Really Great," *Detroit News*, July 27, 1933; Martin S. Hayden, "Why Did City Dream and Get Little Done? Answer Is That There Was No Concerted Planning for Future before 1940," *Detroit News*, July 11, 1947. During the Depression, the city was unable to successfully apply for a new subway proposal. The City Plan

Commission's greatest achievement was its application for three swimming pools: June Manning Thomas, "Josephine Gomon Plans for Detroit's Rehabilitation," *Journal of Planning History* 1, no. 21 (2017).

7. Per capita spending dropped by almost two-thirds between 1929 and 1932; even spending on food dropped by about a third: Conot, *American Odyssey*, 287.

8. Tina Grant, *International Directory of Company Histories*, vol. 19 (Detroit: St. James Press, 1998), 106–111; Jean Maddern Pitrone, *Hudson's: Hub of America's Heartland* (Franklin, MI: Altwerger and Mandel, 1991), 85. Despite the drop in sales, the Thanksgiving parade continued through the Depression: Pitrone, *Hudson's*, 86–96.

9. Sam's had quickly become another growing empire in central Detroit, founded by Russian immigrant Sam Osnos in 1917: William W. Lutz, "Cigar and $350 Started Success Saga of Sams," *Detroit News*, January 26, 1961; Michael Hauser and Marianne Weldon, *20th Century Retailing in Downtown Detroit* (Charleston, SC: Arcadia, 2008), 120–121. The Opera House narrowly escaped demolition in 1934, when it was slated for replacement by a city office building: George W. Stark, "Wreckers' Hammers Beat Ancient Glories into Dust," *Detroit News*, October 28, 1934; "Lease Ends Plan for City Building," *Detroit News*, September 6, 1935.

10. Robert M. Fogelson, *Downtown: Its Rise and Fall, 1880–1950* (New Haven: Yale University Press, 2001), 218. The Temple Theatre was demolished for an office building that never materialized—a fate the next-door Opera House was able to escape: George W. Stark, "The Temple Joins March to Theater's Hall of Dead," *Detroit News*, November 18, 1934.

11. Author's measurements based on business directories, covering the greater downtown area. *Architectural Record* illustrated how a Woodward Avenue fashion store was renovated in this style: Frederic Arden Pawley, "The Retail Store," *Architectural Record* 80 (1935): 52; Gabrielle M. Esperdy, *Modernizing Main Street Architecture and Consumer Culture in the New Deal* (Chicago: University of Chicago Press, 2008).

12. In 1925, an estimated 1,233,025 people traversed the corner of State Street and Woodward Avenue in an 18-hour day, which was considered Detroit's busiest corner. In 1936, only 41,883 people walked on the west side of Woodward Avenue between Grand River and State Street in seven hours. Due to data incompatibilities, a direct comparison between 1936 and 1925 is not

possible, but the difference remains stark. Sources: Michigan State Highway Department, "Street Traffic, City of Detroit 1936–1937" (Lansing, 1937), 138; "Lower Woodward Avenue Historic District Final Report" (City of Detroit, 1999), 7.

13. Business was down citywide: along main outlying arterials, business vacancy had reached the point that the City Plan Commission suggested rezoning these areas to residential uses: "Use Suggested for Idle Plots—'Garden Homesteads' and Terraces on 'Business Frontage' Urged," *Detroit News*, June 4, 1935.

14. As the crowning piece of his real estate empire on Washington Boulevard, Book had planned to erect a building of no less than eighty-one stories, a "symptom of overconfidence of the times": W. Hawkins Ferry, *The Buildings of Detroit; a History* (Detroit: Wayne State University Press, 1968), 214; David Lee Poremba, *Detroit in Its World Setting: A Three Hundred Year Chronology, 1701–2001* (Detroit: Wayne State University Press, 2001), 255.

15. Ultimately, Detroit's banking crisis prompted a federal freeze on banking as one of the first measures taken by new President Franklin D. Roosevelt: Conot, *American Odyssey*, 287–306.

16. Cheri Y. Gay, *Lost Detroit* (London: Pavilion Books, 2013), 107.

17. Orin F. Nolting and Paul Opperman, "The Parking Problem in Central Business Districts," ed. Public Administration Service (Chicago: R. R. Donneley & Sons, 1939), 3.

18. Austin, *Forgotten Landmarks of Detroit*, 22–25.

19. Conot, *American Odyssey*, 271.

20. Frontage foot values in the downtown fringe would decline by more than two-thirds between 1929 and 1938, while values on the main corner of Woodward Avenue and State Street declined at about half that rate. Board of Assessors, "Land Valuation Maps" (Detroit, 1929); "Land Valuation Maps" (Detroit, 1938).

21. Commuter decline is derived from outbound cordon count between 5 pm and 6 pm, a good measure of commuter traffic. From Detroit Department of Transportation, "Detroit Central Business District Cordon Count 1966–1974" (Detroit, 1974).

22. Fogelson, *Downtown*, 218.

23. "Traffic Jams Business Out," *Architectural Forum* 72 (1940). The number of parking lots in downtown shot up from 110 in 1927 to 265 in 1933, holding more than 17,000 cars. The estimate was made by city planner Walter Blucher: "Parking Lots Prosper," *Detroit News*, December 30, 1933.

24. Goldberg was the largest operator in downtown, with triple the number of lots of the next largest competitor. Many lots were owned by small operators, who were from surprisingly diverse ethnic backgrounds: John A. Jakle and Keith A. Sculle, *Lots of Parking: Land Use in a Car Culture* (Charlottesville: University of Virginia Press, 2004), 50–51.

25. The city proposed that lot owners should prevent dust from gathering: "Keep Down the Dust," *Detroit News*, June 4, 1936. The editors of the *News* complained that "these dust storms downtown are at best an ugly nuisance and at worst a menace to health and eyesight": "Downtown Dust Storms," *Detroit News*, June 2, 1938.

26. A comment by visiting journalist Fred C. Kelly in "Writer Finds Beauty Here—'Cancerous Buildings' Vanish, and Detroit Again Becomes Attractive, Says Article," *Detroit News*, July 18, 1934.

27. The proposal was made by then city treasurer Albert Cobo, predating his bolder plans for downtown renewal in the following decade. Interestingly, Cobo argued that removing downtown buildings for parking would not only improve adjacent land values by aesthetics alone; he also argued that reducing competition would bring more tenants to the remaining buildings: "Condemnation Move for More Parking Areas Urged by Cobo," *Detroit News*, November 18, 1935. The city ultimately did become involved in the parking business through its Department for Street Railways, providing an early park-and-ride system to downtown. The parking lots tied in with existing bus lines, allowing patrons to park and ride for a single fee—"providing a new type of service": "DSR Studies Parking Plan—Would Buy Lots Outside Loop, Furnish Buses," *Detroit News*, January 18, 1939. Parking lot owners protested, saying the city unfairly competed with their investments: "Meeting Called on D.S.R. Lots—60 Owners of Parking Places Plan Protest," *Detroit Free Press*, June 15, 1939; "Appeal Denied Foes of D.S.R.—Court Unable to Find Violation of Order," *Detroit Free Press*, June 2, 1939.

28. "Detroit: It Changed the World's Pattern of Life and Is Now the Fourth City in the Land" (New York, 1939), 62. A state document stated that this pattern was only temporary, and that

the post-Depression upswing would quickly fill vacant lots (causing a renewed parking shortage): Michigan State Highway Department, "Street Traffic, City of Detroit 1936–1937," 164.

29. "Detroit: It Changed the World's Pattern of Life," 56.

30. Walter R. Kuehnle, "Central Business District Paradox," *Journal of the American Institute of Real Estate Appraisers* 4 (1935): 139.

31. James B. Steep, "Traffic Troubles Pare Property Values, Expert Declares," *Detroit News*, October 8, 1939, 18. Steep's words were taken very seriously, and he became a member of the City Plan Commission in 1949.

32. Having finished the superhighway network outside Detroit's city limits, the Wayne County Road Commission offered to take over inner-city road widening projects—an offer initially met with resistance as agencies competed for relevance during the Depression: "County Board under Attack—Seeks Widenings in City Only to Provide Jobs, Charges Lee," *Detroit News*, January 19, 1933. Much of the funding for road widening came from the Horton Act of 1932, which allocated the majority of Michigan's gasoline tax revenue to counties and cities based on the number of registered vehicles, greatly benefiting car-rich Detroit. The viability of rapid transit further declined in 1938 when a state amendment allocated gasoline tax funding solely to road and highway projects: Charles K. Hyde, "Planning a Transportation System for Metropolitan Detroit in the Age of the Automobile: The Triumph of the Expressway," *Michigan Historical Review* 32, no. 1 (2006): 87; "State to Pay Half Widening—Green Puts Proposal up to Mayor and Council for Decision," *Detroit News*, April 9, 1935.

33. "120 Feet Fixed for Michigan—Council Finally Determines Width: Cut to Be on South Side," *Detroit News*, October 15, 1930.

34. "Court Upholds Widening Tax—Holds City Has Right to Assess Even Where No Immediate Benefit Is Shown," *Detroit News*, March 14, 1930; interview with Walter Blucher, April 17, 1985, in Perry L. Norton, "Woodward's Vision for Detroit," *Michigan Quarterly Review* 25, no. 2 (1986): 165.

35. "Woodward Owners Urged to Take Pay—Head of Protective Association Seeks to Speed Widening," *Detroit News*, April 17, 1934.

36. "Woodward Widens," *Detroit Free Press*, August 14, 1934; Henry George Hoch, "Old Faces Fade on Church Row," *Detroit News*, February 9, 1935; "100,000 Detroiters Cheer City's Salute to Progress," *Detroit News*, September 21, 1935; "Woodward Memories," *Detroit News*, September 23, 1935.

37. "120-Foot Woodward, Dream of a Century, Now Comes True," *Detroit News*, September 15, 1935; "The New Woodward," *Detroit News*, September 19, 1935; "New Building Fronts Scored," *Detroit News*, May 3, 1935. Architects fruitlessly aimed to regulate new construction and renovations along Woodward Avenue to ensure "uniformity of design," preventing the avenue from becoming "another Gratiot Avenue," which had filled during the 1920s with haphazard construction—if any at all: "New Woodward to Be Uniform—Civic Groups Unite in Move to Assure Care in Renovation of Buildings," *Detroit News*, March 5, 1933; Carl B. Rudow, "Wider Avenue Beauty Sought—a Symmetrical Architectural Background Planned for Woodward," *Detroit News*, April 1, 1934; "Proposal for Beautifying Wider Woodward Given—Architect Offers Suggestions for Block between Columbia and Montcalm; Other Areas Being Studied," *Detroit News*, March 12, 1933. Local realtors, the City Plan Commission, and the *Detroit News* supported the effort: "Architecture on Woodward," *Detroit News*, April 28, 1934.

38. Other factors that had ruined the viability of businesses along Woodward Avenue were the decline of nearby population and the relaxation of deed restrictions in the nearby Cass Park district, prompting businesses to move there instead: "Future of Widened Woodward Still a Matter of Speculation—Opinions Divergent," *Detroit News*, October 18, 1936.

39. Even after new proposals were halted, and though the blocks closest to downtown were never touched, construction would take years more to complete. Plans to widen Grand River Avenue, Detroit's final original radial, never materialized: "Michigan Widening Plan Is Outlined—Work between 6th and 29th Included in Scheme," *Detroit News*, June 18, 1935; "The Michigan Avenue Widening," *Detroit News*, July 5, 1935.

40. Sidney D. Waldon, "Metropolitan Highways," in *Sixteenth Annual Convention of the American Association of State Highway Officials* (Pittsburgh, 1930), 12. The report made its first allusion to the cutting of expressways through the city.

41. It was proposed to implement the plan simultaneously with the 1925 master plan: Board of Wayne County Road Commissioners, "Proposed County Superhighways," *ATS Review* 9, no. 9

(1930); "Huge Highway Plan Broached—70 Miles of Super Routes in Detroit Proposed to Supervisors," *Detroit News*, June 23, 1930.

42. "'Blighted Area' Cure Advance—Writer in Realtor Magazine Suggests New Highways to Aid Districts," *Detroit News*, October 5, 1930.

43. Fogelson, *Downtown*, 315.

44. The near east had a crime rate 750 percent higher than Detroit's average and a tuberculosis rate 650 percent higher: Arthur Pound and E. H. Suydam, *Detroit, Dynamic City* (New York: D. Appleton-Century, 1940), 249.

45. Conot, *American Odyssey*, 311.

46. Works Progress Administration, "Real Property Survey" (Bureau of Governmental Research, Detroit, 1939). These surveys were conducted in many other American cities as well. A strong correlation existed between unfit housing conditions and non-white population on the near east side, but was absent on the near west side.

47. City Plan Commission, "Annual Report" (Detroit, 1932, 1933, 1934); Ferry, *The Buildings of Detroit*, 370; Thomas, "Josephine Gomon Plans for Detroit's Rehabilitation"; Karen R. Miller, *Managing Inequality: Northern Racial Liberalism in Interwar Detroit* (New York: NYU Press, 2016), 251–252. The federal government had also picked up the opportunity to couple infrastructure improvements and slum clearance; the Federal Emergency Housing Corporation called for clearing Hastings Street for a superhighway in 1934, even though the street had grown to become the main business street for Detroit's African American population. The city fortunately ignored this initial request: "Fehc Demands Wide Hastings," *Detroit News*, September 14, 1934. On Hastings Street's role as an African American main street, see Kevin Boyle, *Arc of Justice: A Saga of Race, Civil Rights, and Murder in the Jazz Age* (New York: Macmillan, 2007); "Remedy Plans under Debate—Necessity of Improving All Properties in Particular Zone Is Stressed," *Detroit News*, April 23, 1933.

48. June Manning Thomas, *Redevelopment and Race: Planning a Finer City in Postwar Detroit* (Baltimore: Johns Hopkins University Press, 1997), 24; Conot, *American Odyssey*, 362–363.

49. Mentioned as one of Detroit's ills by ULI special representative Carl S. Wells in "Downtown Detroit Plan Published," *Detroit Free Press*, June 28, 1942. Second quote by James Steep in Steep, "Traffic Troubles Pare Property Values."

CHAPTER 6: BATTLING BLIGHT: 1937–1951

1. Detroit's population had only grown 3.5 percent between 1930 and 1940 due to the Depression and the crisis in the automotive industry.

2. Carl S. Wells, "Proposals for Downtown Detroit" (Urban Land Institute, Washington, DC, 1942), 14. A positive side effect of this thinning population was that the overheated housing market in central Detroit and the resulting high rents significantly eased: Thomas James Ticknor, "Motor City: The Impact of the Automobile Industry upon Detroit, 1900–1975" (Ph.D. diss., University of Michigan, 1978), 193.

3. Ticknor, "Motor City," 126.

4. Furthermore, Detroit was clearly a one-industry town, with car manufacturing forty times larger than the second industry, meatpacking: Melvin G. Holli, *Detroit* (New York: New Viewpoints, 1976), 278–279; US Bureau of the Census, *Sixteenth Census of the United States* (Washington, DC: US Government Printing Office, 1942).

5. Only St. Louis suburbanized faster between 1910 and 1940. Seventy percent of auto workers still lived within Detroit, allowing manufacturers to evade property taxes while workers' amenities were paid by the city: Ticknor, "Motor City," 201–203.

6. Thomas J. Sugrue, *The Origins of the Urban Crisis: Race and Inequality in Postwar Detroit* (Princeton, NJ: Princeton University Press, 1996), 19.

7. Robert Fishman, "Detroit: Linear City," in June Manning Thomas and Henco Bekkering, eds., *Mapping Detroit: Land, Community, and Shaping a City* (Detroit: Wayne State University Press, 2015).

8. W. Hawkins Ferry, *The Buildings of Detroit; a History* (Detroit: Wayne State University Press, 1968), 357.

9. Robert E. Conot, *American Odyssey* (New York: Morrow, 1974), 377.

10. The urban population of Detroit would grow 14 percent between 1940 and 1950, and the suburban population would grow almost 20 percent.

11. Arthur Pound and E. H. Suydam, *Detroit, Dynamic City* (New York: D. Appleton-Century, 1940), 354.

12. Albert Kahn associate George Miehls in Ferry, *The Buildings of Detroit*, 340.

13. E. A. Baumgarth, "How the Motor Car's Impact Has Transformed a Great City," *Detroit News*, May 29, 1946."

14. "'1500 Block' of Woodward Avenue Reveals the 'New Look,'" *Detroit News*, November 5, 1948.

15. Cheri Y. Gay, *Lost Detroit* (London: Pavilion Books, 2013), 136. While the Tuller's renovation was touted as "an ultra-modern look," it encompassed removing most of the building's original interior marble and wood details: Dan Austin, *Forgotten Landmarks of Detroit* (Charleston, SC: History Press, 2012), 160.

16. Jean Maddern Pitrone, *Hudson's: Hub of America's Heartland* (Franklin, MI: Altwerger and Mandel, 1991), 97–109.

17. The slow replacement of streetcars by buses was highly contentious, with a public referendum narrowly avoided in 1939: "Avoids Vote on DSR Issue—Council Hears Proposed Ballot Assailed," *Detroit Free Press*, July 31, 1939. Buses were not always seen as a service downgrade. A former streetcar line on Lafayette Avenue saw a 50 percent increase in passengers when buses replaced the old cars, even when the fee to ride almost doubled: "Revenues Attest to Bus Popularity," *Detroit Free Press*, July 11, 1939; "Car-Bus Vote Still in Doubt after Hearing," *Detroit Free Press*, August 1, 1939.

18. Pound and Suydam, *Detroit, Dynamic City*, 359–360.

19. The number of people leaving downtown between 5 pm and 6 pm (a good indicator of daytime commuter population) decreased from 80,867 in 1925 to an estimated 67,000 in 1940: Wells, "Proposals for Downtown Detroit," 10.

20. Ticknor, "Motor City," 186.

21. Writers' Program of the Works Projects Administration, *Michigan: A Guide to the Wolverine State* (New York: Oxford University Press, 1941), 232. The guide went on to describe the lack of culture in downtown Detroit, while "the world of fashion is [also] not of prime importance." In other words: Detroit had neither the quantity nor quality of citizens to support a wholesome downtown cultural life.

22. Gay, *Lost Detroit*, 117.

23. Saks's arrival was announced in an advertisement by the President of Fisher & Company, boasting that the area was predicted to "develop into one of the most important shopping centers in America": Charles T. Fisher, "Fisher & Company Announce That Saks Fifth Avenue Will Open a Store in the New Center Building," news release, March 26, 1940; "Saks Fifth Ave. to Open in City," *Detroit Free Press*, March 26, 1940.

24. Ticknor, "Motor City," 200.

25. Centers in the suburbs were not yet counted: Wells, "Proposals for Downtown Detroit," 25.

26. "Ban Is Asked on Burlesque," *Detroit News*, March 13, 1947.

27. Efforts to counter decentralization were covered in a series of articles in the *Detroit News* by its real estate editor: E. A. Baumgarth, "Decentralization Trend Discounted by Los Angeles Realtor," *Detroit News*, November 12, 1939; "Decentralization Problem Is Tackled by Real Estate Boards," *Detroit News*, February 11, 1940; "Stable Future for Central Business Areas Predicted," *Detroit News*, September 1, 1940; "Hopes Brighten for Solving Decentralization Problem," *Detroit News*, July 21, 1940.

28. Sugrue, *The Origins of the Urban Crisis*, 25–28.

29. According to the *Detroit News*, "Paradise Valley" received its name in 1936: "Detroit Harlem Named—It's Paradise Valley Now," *Detroit News*, October 20, 1936. As Ken Coleman describes, the name may have been picked by "mayor" Lightfoot, or it may have been the result of a contest held by a local booking agent. The names Paradise Valley and Black Bottom are sometimes used interchangeably, and the exact demarcations of the districts are as contested as the Valley's naming: Ken Coleman, *Million Dollars Worth of Nerve: Twenty-One People Who Helped to Power Black Bottom, Paradise Valley and Detroit's East Side* (Detroit: Detroit Coleman Communications, 2015).

30. Lars Björn and Jim Gallert, *Before Motown: A History of Jazz in Detroit, 1920–60* (Ann Arbor: University of Michigan Press, 2001), 39–44. Despite the growth of black-owned businesses in the near east side, many businesses were still owned by former Jewish residents, often leading to tensions over territory and perceived price gouging: Conot, *American Odyssey*, 378. African Americans joined a growing cohort of Greek immigrants that had settled around Monroe Avenue in the previous century: Rex G. White, "Where Greek Meets Greek," *Detroit News*, September 24, 1939.

31. "Detroit Harlem Named—It's Paradise Valley Now"; Coleman, *Million Dollars Worth of Nerve*; Kirk Pinho, "Hastings Street Blues: The Economic Roots That Contributed to Detroit's Worst Summer," *Crain's Detroit Business*, June 18, 2017.

32. Blues singer and guitarist John Lee Hooker arrived in Detroit in the 1940s and produced over 200 songs, most of which he played in Paradise Valley clubs and subsequently recorded in Detroit. "Hastings Street Opera" and "Hastings Street Woogie Man" were played by Detroit Count, a contemporary of Hooker: Björn and Gallert, *Before Motown*, 173–177.

33. The urban-renewal demolition of Black Bottom and Paradise Valley later fed Young's animosity toward planning, and the quoted description was part of his argument against renewal by demolition. Young describes how Black Bottom was "red-tagged by the government as a sort of Yankee Doodle sacrifice, a trespasser upon somebody's sacred bureaucratic vision of America": Coleman Young and Lonnie Wheeler, *Hard Stuff: The Autobiography of Coleman Young* (New York: Viking, 1994), 143–144.

34. Paradise Valley arguably served as a bridge between the mainly white downtown and the exclusively African American Black Bottom district. Its rich array of jazz and blues venues provided popular entertainment to all audiences: Björn and Gallert, *Before Motown*.

35. Sugrue, *The Origins of the Urban Crisis*, 44–47.

36. The number of African Americans in Paradise Valley and Black Bottom almost doubled between 1940 and 1950 from 87,000 to 140,000, with almost no new construction or renovation taking place: Conot, *American Odyssey*, 402.

37. "City-Owned Shack Falls; 12 Shaken Up (Thunder Causes House to Collapse)," *Michigan Chronicle*, August 30, 1947; "Death Comes for a Victim of Bad Housing," *Michigan Chronicle*, March 22, 1947; in Coleman, *Million Dollars Worth of Nerve*.

38. David W. Hartman, *The Development of Detroit's Cass Corridor: 1850–1975*, vol. 3 (Detroit: Wayne State University Press, 1975), 5–6.

39. Russell Jaehne McLauchlin, *Alfred Street* (Detroit: Conjure House, 1946), 13; Historic Designation Advisory Board, "Proposed Brush Park Historic District—Final Report" (City of Detroit, 2010). A 1947 proposal to cut the neighborhood's namesake central park in half to allow traffic to pass through more efficiently marked how far the formerly noble area had fallen. The proposal did not pass, like those that preceded and followed: "Cass Park Cut Urged," *Detroit News*, February 21, 1947.

40. Shockingly, the police first responded by arresting the African American newcomers to the district, as they were being assaulted: Sugrue, *The Origins of the Urban Crisis*, 44–47; Richard W. Thomas, *Life for Us Is What We Make It: Building Black Community in Detroit, 1915–1945* (Bloomington: Indiana University Press, 1992), 143–145.

41. While the Home Owners Loan Corporation was short-lived, the federal tendency to refuse mortgage insurance to integrated neighborhoods or African American homebuyers persisted via the Federal Housing Administration and Veterans Administration: George C. Galster, *Driving Detroit: The Quest for Respect in Motown* (Philadelphia: University of Pennsylvania Press, 2013), 136–158.

42. *Life* magazine described factory worker morale as among the lowest in the nation due to the social unrest spreading throughout the city, as workers refused to cooperate with African Americans, let alone live near them: "Detroit Is Dynamite," *Life*, August 17, 1942. The issues outlined were so dire that the article was censored from foreign editions of the magazine.

43. Frank Bury Woodford and Arthur M. Woodford, *All Our Yesterdays: A Brief History of Detroit* (Detroit: Wayne State University Press, 1969), 347.

44. During the 1940s, hate groups like the Ku Klux Klan and Nazi-sympathizing National Workers League spoke freely and had central roles in Detroit's social debate, inciting further

intolerance between races and classes: Galster, *Driving Detroit*, 183–184; Conot, *American Odyssey*, 378–379.

45. Björn and Gallert, *Before Motown*, 123–167. The NAACP only concluded that all downtown establishments were open to African Americans by 1950, but the situation was unstable until further into the decade: ibid. The decline of Paradise Valley was described by the *Michigan Chronicle* as an aging process, prompting a drastic decrease of patronage: Martin S. Hayden, "City's Growing Days Over, Planners Find," *Detroit News*, July 18, 1946; Larry Chism, "Many Changes Seen in Night Life During Past 10 Years," *Michigan Chronicle*, April 13, 1948.

46. Detroit City Plan Commission, "Funds Needed for Postwar Program," *The Planner* (July 1943): 5–6, quoting an observation of British planner Sir Ernest Simon. In response, the City Plan Commission was "reluctant to claim for Detroit a distinction which may well belong to some other city."

47. Besides the poor state of the structure, City Hall's single interior stairway wasn't up to city code: Austin, *Forgotten Landmarks of Detroit*, 27.

48. The program amounted to a more than fifteenfold increase of capital investment compared to the era between 1932 and 1944: Conot, *American Odyssey*, 393.

49. The budget for the City Plan Commission rose from $26,595 in 1940 to $214,744 in 1951.

50. Martin S. Hayden, "How Decay's Spread Has Hit Wide Areas," *Detroit News*, July 8, 1947.

51. Martin S. Hayden, "Detroit's Master Plan," *Detroit News*, July 7–12, 1947, 6. To emphasize the importance of the new ordinance, the document stated that "there was no Detroit planning prior to 1940": ibid., 19. Zoning had been forced by City Council onto the ballot in 1939, the first time an actual plan had been put on the ballot. At the time, Jeffries was president of the Council. The zoning ordinance had strong ties to the 1938 Real Property Survey, as the survey gave the city a first look at what land uses were present: "Council Cuts Delay on Zone Ordinance—City Planner and Head of Property Survey to Tell When Plan Can Be Placed on Ballot," *Detroit News*, January 16, 1939.

52. National Urban Land Institute director Charles T. Stewart admitted, "There is nothing to lead us to believe that we shall need [the blighted ring around downtown] for commercial or industrial purposes": Charles T. Stewart, "Our Disease—Disintegration: For Healthy Land

Values the Remedy Is Reintegration," *Real Estate* (1941); Robert M. Fogelson, *Downtown: Its Rise and Fall, 1880–1950* (New Haven: Yale University Press, 2001), 344.

53. June Manning Thomas, *Redevelopment and Race: Planning a Finer City in Postwar Detroit* (Baltimore: Johns Hopkins University Press, 1997), 37.

54. Almost 85 percent of all requests for zoning variances were honored by the Board of Appeals: Conot, *American Odyssey*, 392.

55. "Toward a Greater Detroit" (City Plan Commission, Detroit, 1945), 5.

56. Pound and Suydam, *Detroit, Dynamic City*, 356.

57. "Toward a Greater Detroit."

58. The definition of blight was ambivalent, sometimes drawing on the early twentieth-century definition of an area with falling land values, sometimes on the later view of it as including slums which contained dilapidated or otherwise obsolete buildings, often combined with socioeconomic ills. For a more detailed definition of blight, see Fogelson, *Downtown*, chapter 7.

59. "Master City Plan Sought—Called Vital to Future Development," *Detroit News*, January 11, 1940. All recommendations were brought forward into the official document: Thomas, *Redevelopment and Race*, 38.

60. E. A. Baumgarth, "Master Plan Study Starts—Advisory Committee Holds First Meeting," *Detroit News*, July 16, 1943.

61. "City's Street System Must Be Modernized, City Planner Says," *Detroit News*, November 29, 1942.

62. "Master Plan Needed to Aid in Solution of Detroit's Problems—Planner Discusses Post-War Detroit," *Detroit News*, December 20, 1942. Art historian Donald E. Simpson states that the plan was strongly influenced by Eliel Saarinen's ongoing work on a regional plan, developed at Cranbrook, that envisioned a future Detroit of 1990 strongly focused on "organic decentralization." Saarinen regarded the "disorderly compactness" of central cities as the root of slum formation, suggesting that "when large areas of the present centers have become vacated, these might prove to be suitable residential districts for those having their work in the cities' hearts"—a prelude to Detroit's slum clearance for Lafayette Park's middle-class

dwellings: "Architects Plan Metropolitan Area of 5,000,000—Saarinen Explains Decentralizing Idea," *Detroit News*, October 10, 1943; Donald E. Simpson, "Civic Center and Cultural Center: The Grouping of Public Buildings in Pittsburgh, Cleveland, and Detroit and the Emergence of the City Monumental in the Modern Metropolis" (Ph.D. diss., University of Pittsburgh, 2013). Several other architects made more detailed plans for areas outside Detroit following Saarinen's decentralization concept: "City Planning Should Start with the Home, Saarinen Holds—Architects' Group Reports Progress," *Detroit News*, June 9, 1946.

63. Detroit City Plan Commission, "An Urban Redevelopment Project in Detroit: Rebuilding Deteriorated Areas of the City" (Detroit, 1942), 3.

64. The city had spent a considerable amount of money on the road widening projects of the 1920s and was still paying off bonds from this era. Outside subsidies were hard to come by: the 1937 Housing Act provided some subsidy for the redevelopment of slums, but its focus was on providing low-income housing, not on bringing back higher-income residents to downtown as city planners wanted.

65. Galster, *Driving Detroit*, 176; Conot, *American Odyssey*, 403–405; Coleman, *Million Dollars Worth of Nerve*.

66. In 1942, an area bound by Myrtle, Trumbull, Henry, and 14th streets was chosen as a pilot site for redevelopment. However, the site remains untouched today: Detroit City Plan Commission, "An Urban Redevelopment Project in Detroit." In 1944, the City Plan Commission selected a site just east as "typical of the 13,000 acres of badly blighted land in this city" and proposed a survey—again to no avail: E. A. Baumgarth, "Blighted Area Chosen for Housing Survey—35-Block Tract at Downtown Edge Is Selected as Typical," *Detroit News*, July 30, 1944. That same year, a group of contractors under the Communities Redevelopment Corporation of New York proposed to purchase and raze parts of Corktown and Black Bottom, to be ultimately paid for by city bonds. The plan was seriously considered by the City Plan Commission, but City Treasurer Cobo snubbed the plan, stating "financially it is the worst thing that has come to my attention since I've been in city government": "Cobo Defeats City Planners—Challenges Financial Project of Board," *Detroit News*, March 20, 1945; "$50,000,000 Plan Studied—Redevelopment Urged in 2 Blighted Areas," *Detroit News*, November 10, 1944; "Planning Detroit 1944" (City Plan Commission, Detroit, 1944).

67. The plan was drafted by the newly created Housing Commission: Detroit Housing Commission, "The Detroit Plan—a Program for Blight Elimination" (Detroit, 1946). The choice for Black Bottom was justified by "visual evidence of blight" and the invisible overcrowding, delinquency, and welfare rates. Social scientists Robert Mowitz and Deil Wright commented in their 1962 book on Detroit's urban renewal that "there was no question about Gratiot. It was a classic slum": Robert J. Mowitz and Deil S. Wright, *Profile of a Metropolis: A Case Book* (Detroit: Wayne State University Press, 1962), 17. For more information on civic planning in the 1940s, see Bernard J. Frieden and Lynne B. Sagalyn, *Downtown, Inc.: How America Rebuilds Cities* (Cambridge, MA: MIT Press, 1989), 18–19.

68. Thomas, *Redevelopment and Race*, 46–51.

69. Detroit Housing Commission, "The Detroit Plan."

70. The debate over which audience to build for was split along lines of racial integration or segregation, as well as economic concerns: Mowitz and Wright, *Profile of a Metropolis*, 46–55. Cobo sought to reduce public housing expenditure and concentrate housing sites near downtown, even removing African American advocates from the city's Housing Commission to silence dissent: Coleman, *Million Dollars Worth of Nerve*.

71. Coleman, *Million Dollars Worth of Nerve*.

72. Björn and Gallert, *Before Motown*; Fogelson, *Downtown*, 373–377. The condemnations progressed slowly due to legal challenges. Detroit was a national pioneer in trying to renew its inner city through slum clearance, and laws and jurisprudence were not yet in place to facilitate this contentious process. The Housing Act of 1949 offered a vast new source of funding for urban renewal, as long as the land use remained residential. In contrast to its 1937 predecessor, the 1949 act did not require new construction to be focused on providing public housing for low-income groups, allowing cities like Detroit to use federal funding to bring middle-income residents back downtown—at the cost of existing low-income slum residents. This change in focus was a clear result of lobbying by central business interests to use federal money to curb decentralization of the middle class: ibid., 377–379; Conot, *American Odyssey*, 402; Mowitz and Wright, *Profile of a Metropolis*, 20–27; Sugrue, *The Origins of the Urban Crisis*.

73. E. A. Baumgarth, "More Parking Need Stressed—Engineer Urges Double-Deckers Downtown," *Detroit News*, January 11, 1940; "Parking Issue More Acute," *Detroit News*, August 17, 1947. Examples of parking alleviation plans include parking management, proposing a ban on stopping along Detroit's busiest streets in 1938: John McManis, "First Changes in Traffic Regulations Made at City Hall—Parking to Be Ruled on 'Selective Basis,'" *Detroit News*, December 25, 1938.

74. E. A. Baumgarth, "New Type of Zoning Suggested by Emery," *Detroit News*, March 22, 1942; Lloyd B. Reid, "Detroit's Parking Needs—Central Business District" (Traffic Engineering Bureau, Detroit, 1946).

75. The three-level, 270-bay "Shopper's Parking Deck" was one of the first of its kind: "Parking Deck: Shopper's Parking Deck, Detroit, Mich. Smith, Hinchman & Grylls, Inc., Architects," *Architectural Record* 90 (1941).

76. In 1948, a city traffic engineer proposed municipal action to construct multilevel parking garages near the retail heart of the city, with an initial plan for an underground garage under Washington Boulevard stalled by its prohibitive costs—even when downtown property owners offered to tax themselves to subsidize the public investment: "Parking Issue More Acute"; John A. Jakle and Keith A. Sculle, *Lots of Parking: Land Use in a Car Culture* (Charlottesville: University of Virginia Press, 2004).

77. The efforts of the Department of Street Railways in the late 1930s were fought on the ground that "many owners of real estate have invested large sums of money in the parking lot business in the expectancy that is has a good future" and that municipal competition was unfair. The protest ultimately failed: "Meeting Called on D.S.R. Lots—60 Owners of Parking Places Plan Protest," *Detroit Free Press*, June 15, 1939; "Appeal Denied Foes of D.S.R.—Court Unable to Find Violation of Order," *Detroit Free Press*, June 2, 1939; "City Fights for Garages," *Detroit News*, December 19, 1948; "The Shortage Continues," *Detroit News*, February 14, 1950.

78. "3-Mile Parade Opens Street—Van Wagoner Principal Speaker at Ceremony," *Detroit News*, September 17, 1938. Small widenings were still being completed as late as 1941, but by then state highway commissioner Kennedy stated, "we are now turning from a policy of widening surface streets to a program of building high-speed elevated and depressed highways":

"Wider Street Goal in Sight—Woodward and Michigan near Final Stage," *Detroit News*, February 23, 1941.

79. Charles K. Hyde, "Planning a Transportation System for Metropolitan Detroit in the Age of the Automobile: The Triumph of the Expressway," *Michigan Historical Review* 32, no. 1 (2006): 59–65; Conot, *American Odyssey*, 400. In 1938, Detroit retained engineer Charles De Leuw to draft a proposal for a $40 million single-line subway underneath Woodward Avenue from the riverfront to the State Fairgrounds to the federal Public Works Administration, with an optional east-west cross route that roughly followed the route of the 1929 plan: Sidney D. Waldon and George R. Thompson, "Memorandum Re Rapid Transit Line in Woodward Avenue" (Rapid Transit Commission, Detroit, 1938); Charles E. de Leuw, "Report on the Proposed Woodward Avenue Subway to the Rapid Transit Commission" (Detroit, 1938). A final remnant of the many plans to provide underground transportation in downtown was a 1945 proposal for underground bus terminals, which was killed three years later: "DSR Scuttles Tunnel Plan—Bus Project Would Have Cost 18 Million," *Detroit News*, December 7, 1948.

80. Former Detroit planner and American Society of Planning Officials director Walter Blucher warned Detroiters that the dismantling of the city's streetcar system, coupled with increased automobility, had entered Detroit into a spiral of congestion and blight in which it was "disintegrating faster than almost any other major American city." Walter Blucher was active in the City Plan Commission from the time of the first master plan until the mid-1930s: Martin S. Hayden, "Planners Finds Buses Only Temporary Solution," *Detroit News*, January 9, 1947.

81. The *Detroit News* agreed and even argued for a refund of all local assessments, which would place a burden of several million dollars on the city: "Talk Refund on Widening—Property Owners May Get Money Back," *Detroit News*, October 19, 1939; "Unfair Assessments," *Detroit News*, October 21, 1939.

82. "Many of City's Woes Are Linked to Traffic," *Detroit News*, July 10, 1947.

83. "State Extends Highway Plan—Harper-Mcgraw Is First Link in Chicago Road," *Detroit News*, November 19, 1939.

84. While the Real Estate Board supported Cobo's plan, the City Committee on Transportation did not include it in their vision for Detroit's transportation needs: "Urges 2 Giant Roads in City—Cobo Proposes Mid-Town Highways Block Wide," *Detroit News*, April 21, 1939; "Cobo's Plan Wins Support—Van Deusen Says Detroit Must Improve Roads," *Detroit News*, April 23, 1939; "City Highway Plans Mapped," *Detroit News*, May 11, 1939.

85. Advertising the potential freeways, the downtown-sponsored *Detroit Shopping News* boasted that "the trip from home to the downtown shopping district will be made more quickly and pleasantly when Detroit's expressway system is completed," with a promised average time savings of 40 to 50 percent. The issue of *Shopping News* featured a plan of the expressway system, demarcating Detroit into sixteen numbered communities: "Expressways to Link Homes and Downtown—Six Lane Highways Will Speed Traffic Throughout City," *Detroit Shopping News*, September 24, 1945.

86. By the late 1930s, the federal government was considering its first multibillion-dollar bills to finance expressway construction. Wayne County Road Commission engineer Leroy C. Smith argued that "officials of Detroit, the County and the State will be woefully negligent if they are not standing outside of the Federal Road Commission door the day the bill is signed by the President." While acknowledging that county and city plans were often opposed, Smith pleaded to unite efforts between highway construction and slum clearance: "City Urged to Draft Super-Highway Plans—Delay May Cost Many Millions in Federal Grants, County Engineer Warns," *Detroit News*, December 31, 1939.

87. "Super-Route Plans Bared—State and City Confer on Express Highways," *Detroit News*, January 25, 1940.

88. "48-Million Highway Proposed—Super Route to Serve North Side," *Detroit News*, January 26, 1944.

89. W. Earle Andrews, "Detroit Expressway and Transit System" (Detroit Transportation Board, 1945).

90. City Plan Commission, "Detroit Master Plan" (Detroit, 1951), 85.

91. Young, *Million Dollars Worth of Nerve*.

92. A 1947 map of proposed rapid transit routes shows four lines radiating from downtown along each of the main expressways, going underground close to downtown. The subway under the Lodge Expressway was an exception in that it was to run under Woodward Avenue as far as New Center before entering the median of the expressway further north.

93. Hyde, "Planning a Transportation System for Metropolitan Detroit"; John M. Carlisle, "City Gets 240 Million Rapid Transit Plan—Increase in Present DSR Fares Urged before Any Improvements Are Made," *Detroit News*, February 27, 1945.

94. An ironic detail is that Mayor Lodge never owned a car or had a driver's license in his 87 years: Don Lochbiler, *Detroit's Coming of Age, 1873 to 1973* (Detroit: Wayne State University Press, 1973), 309–312.

95. The history of the two highways was discussed in a pamphlet celebrating their dedication in October 1955: "Dedication—Detroit Expressways Interchange" (Michigan State Highway Department et al., Detroit, 1955).

96. "Traffic Must Go over or Under," *Detroit News*, January 5, 1952; "Cobo Seeks Creation of Traffic Department," *Detroit Free Press*, July 10, 1951.

97. At least Jeffries thought that constructing the freeway system would be a good way to employ the thousands of wartime workers after World War II ended: "Federal Aid for Post-War Highway Construction" (U.S. House Committee on Roads, 1944), 764–768.

98. Conot, *American Odyssey*, 400.

99. "A New Detroit by 1990 Visioned by Planners—Architects Propose to Harmonize Citizen's Family Life and His Work," *Detroit News*, March 5, 1944. *Time* magazine praised Cranbrook as "the world's most active laboratory of city planning" during the 1940s, owing to the work of Saarinen. The architect and urbanist had been hired to teach at Cranbrook after his 1924 design for Detroit's riverfront. During his tenure at Cranbrook, Saarinen guided several thesis projects on Detroit city planning, including a regional plan for the city named "Detroit 1990" around the same time as the City Planning Commission started its master plan process. "Detroit 1990" proposed a decentralized pattern of more or less self-sufficient neighborhoods with housing, jobs, and community amenities. In 1943, Saarinen became a consultant to the Architects' Civic Design Group, chaired by the president of the City Plan Commission, to

inform this agency's planning process; one of its studies focused on the "Detroit 1990" plan. See Simpson, "Civic Center and Cultural Center," 239–245; Eliel Saarinen, *The City, Its Growth, Its Decay, Its Future* (New York: Reinhold, 1943).

100. "Planning Detroit 1944." The number of neighborhood units varied between 15 and 17, suggesting the uncertainty that planners were dealing with in this process: Martin S. Hayden, "How to Remake City That Already Is Built—Clean Sweep in Worst Areas Favored with Gradual Changes in Others," *Detroit News*, July 9, 1947. The balance between neighborhoods and downtown was precarious. For example, each of the neighborhoods revolved around high schools and planned shopping facilities, as "Detroit's newest and best home districts have no handy shopping centers"—furthering a trend of retail decentralization. Despite the decentralization of retail facilities, City Plan Commission director George Emery reassured that the "downtown business section would continue to serve the needs of the entire metropolitan area": "Detroit Studies Plan for 17 Cities in One—City of Tomorrow May Be Group of Self-Contained Units, Planners Say," *Detroit News*, October 15, 1944.

101. Another major impetus for development was the closure of the Detroit and Windsor Ferry dock on the riverfront due to competition from the bridge and tunnel between both cities: "Suggests Hall Site on Dock," *Detroit News*, May 20, 1937; "Look Ahead," *Detroit News*, May 21, 1937; "Build It on the River," *Detroit News*, July 8, 1937. A special committee was instated to study plans for a civic center on the riverfront by the late 1930s: "Civic Center Board Gets $2,500 Purse," *Detroit News*, April 29, 1938.

102. In its 1939 Annual Report, the Commission admitted its previous mistakes, but insisted that urban planning could not just be measured in financial terms, as it also offered "civic incentive" and "better citizenship effects": Simpson, "Civic Center and Cultural Center," 237–238.

103. "Planning Detroit 1944."

104. The main difference between Pilafian's and the Saarinens' designs for the Civic Center was an elongated and raised east-west building spanning several blocks north of Jefferson Avenue, which was never built: Simpson, "Civic Center and Cultural Center," 250–252; City Plan Commission, "Detroit Master Plan." Civic pride was in high demand: Detroiters were accused by the *Free Press* of having no "community pride," obstructing civic efforts such as urban

planning: Charles Weber, "City Motto Is Hope, but Officials Mope," *Detroit Free Press*, January 18, 1947; "Planners Stymied in 'No-Man's Land,'" *Detroit Free Press*, January 19, 1947.

105. A six-article series on the new master plan concluded that the new efforts had to be sold to citizens, but that the plan allowed citizens to rediscover "a Detroit that is beautiful and dynamic"—mixing two descriptions that the city had garnered in the late nineteenth and early twentieth century: Martin S. Hayden, "Taxpayers' Support Is Vital for Success—Quieting of Pressure Groups and End of Inferiority Complex Also Stressed," *Detroit News*, July 12, 1947.

106. After an initial ballot defeat to finance this administrative building, a joint building authority was set up under city treasurer Albert Cobo to circumvent this public refusal, and construction on the white marble-clad building commenced in 1951. Cobo came to regard the Civic Center as a personal priority as it reinvigorated downtown business investment, and its progress greatly helped his election as mayor in 1950. The City-County building had been proposed as early as 1944, although the two governmental bodies had already shared spaces in various other buildings: Mowitz and Wright, *Profile of a Metropolis*, 141–168; Conot, *American Odyssey*, 404; "Joint City-County Building Proposed," *Detroit News*, March 17, 1944.

107. Rex G. White, "City-County Project to End Saga of Famed Merrill Block," *Detroit News*, April 30, 1950.

108. Sugrue, *The Origins of the Urban Crisis*, 47.

CHAPTER 7: THE CITY OF TOMORROW: 1951–1961

1. The 1950 census establishes Detroit at 1,849,569 residents.

2. Sam Boal, "Detroit at 250: Lusty and Young," *New York Times*, July 29, 1951; Robert E. Lubeck, "We're Outward Bound—Growth of Suburbs Almost Overshadows Detroit, the Builder," *Detroit News*, January 6, 1952. Between 1947 and 1955, the Big Three built all their new plants outside Detroit's city limits: Heather B. Barrow, *Henry Ford's Plan for the American Suburb: Dearborn and Detroit* (DeKalb: Northern Illinois University Press, 2015), 149.

3. Barrow, *Henry Ford's Plan for the American Suburb*, 149.

4. Robert E. Lubeck, "Cities That Detroit Built," *Detroit News*, January 6, 1952; Sidney Glazer, *Detroit: A Study in Urban Development* (New York: Bookman Associates, 1965), 113–114.

5. Robert L. Wells, "Action Demanded on Expanded Loop," *Detroit News*, April 13, 1954.

6. William Harlan Hale, "Detroit: How to Save a Great City from Itself," *The Reporter*, October 31, 1957, 29.

7. "Transit Key of Expanded City to Come," *Detroit News*, April 11, 1954.

8. Most theater closures occurred in Detroit's neighborhoods, but at least one downtown theater was forced to shut its doors: John Finlayson, "City's 50 Closed Movie Theaters Dragging Down Many Neighboring Small Business Places," *Detroit News*, April 26, 1953.

9. George W. Stark, "What You Missed before TV—Blaze Sent Theater on Downgrade Here," *Detroit News*, February 25, 1954.

10. The term alluded to the fact that stores in these rings intercepted sales from suburbanites on their way to downtown: R. L. Nelson, *The Selection of Retail Locations* (New York: F. W. Dodge, 1958), 27.

11. Sales decline from comparisons between the 1948 and 1954 Census of Business by author.

12. "Commercialism Takes—and Wears—a New Look," *Ladies' Homes Journal* 71 (1954): 11, cited in Richard Longstreth, *The American Department Store Transformed, 1920–1960* (New Haven: Yale University Press, 2010).

13. Frank Beckman, "Caution Asked in Rebuilding City's 'Heart,'" *Detroit Free Press*, September 13, 1953.

14. These were traits that would later come to haunt Blessing as political opposition and social decline shaped urban renewal policy from the late 1960s onward: Robert E. Conot, *American Odyssey* (New York: Morrow, 1974), 480.

15. Hale, "Detroit: How to Save a Great City from Itself," 29.

16. "Blessing Urges Civic Design for Auto City," *Detroit News*, April 17, 1953.

17. John M. Carlisle, "Billion Dollar Boom Downtown," *Detroit News*, April 1, 1957.

18. Robert L. Wells, "Dream City on Horizon," *Detroit News*, June 6, 1956. In his quest to model urban design on automotive design, Blessing was also looking for sponsorship from automobile manufacturers to set up a design laboratory, to no avail: June Manning Thomas,

"Seeking a Finer Detroit," in Mary Corbin Sies and Christopher Silver, eds., *Planning the Twentieth-Century American City* (Baltimore: Johns Hopkins University Press, 1996).

19. Citation of economist Fred Kramer in May-June monthly report of the Detroit Housing Commission, in Rob Goodspeed, "Urban Renewal in Postwar Detroit" (honors thesis, University of Michigan, 2004), 21.

20. Robert L. Wells, "Cobo Seeks Top Brains to Plan Loop," *Detroit News*, April 12, 1954.

21. "Downtown Shopping Center on Suburban Lines Advised," *Detroit News*, July 29, 1956. The proportion of downtown sales in the metropolitan area dropped from 15.5 percent to 9.9 percent between 1948 and 1955, one of the lowest shares for any American city surveyed by the US Census of Business. Blessing greatly respected and envied the Northland Center, calling it "the finest prototype of a shopping center in the world" in a 1956 *Detroit News* interview: Wells, "Dream City on Horizon."

22. Robert Cantwell, "Detroit Is Taming Its Traffic," *Architectural Forum* 108 (1958).

23. Interestingly, the editorial also presaged a need for an income tax to offset Detroit's eroding tax base: "New Directions," *Detroit News*, August 15, 1955.

24. A 1953 article summed up Detroit's plans to redevelop 4,000 acres of urban land over the following 18 years: William C. Tremblay, "City Not Alone in Fight to Get Rid of Blight," *Detroit News*, May 11, 1953.

25. Central Business District Association executive secretary C. Bradford Hitt, quoted in "Transit Key of Expanded City to Come," *Detroit News*, April 11, 1954.

26. Albert Cobo, quoted in "Cobo Seeks Top Brains to Plan Loop," *Detroit News*, April 12, 1954.

27. Bernard J. Frieden and Lynne B. Sagalyn, *Downtown, Inc.: How America Rebuilds Cities* (Cambridge, MA: MIT Press, 1989), 17. Cobo's focus on fiscal arguments for radically altering the city was likely inspired by his background as an accountant: Wells, "Cobo Seeks Top Brains to Plan Loop"; "Oakman Predicts U.S. Will Help in Skid Row Job," *Detroit News*, April 25, 1954. Central businesses like Hudson's department store unsurprisingly backed Cobo's claim that it was better to invest in downtown's vast infrastructure and building stock than let it perish: Wells, "Action Demanded on Expanded Loop." The Central Business District

Association, which emerged from the earlier Downtown Property Association, included several committees to focus on a seven-point plan for downtown renewal, hinging on new construction of the Civic Center, transit, offices, downtown housing, parking, and parks: "Transit Key of Expanded City to Come." One of their first efforts was the instatement of Downtown Detroit Days, a twice-annual festival meant to "point up the glamour and the economy of visiting and shopping downtown": Harold Schachern, "Parking Is Called Key to Downtown Comeback," *Detroit News*, May 29, 1955.

28. John M. Carlisle, "Downtown Hub of Future—Cobo," *Detroit News*, September 12, 1954.

29. The *Detroit News* initiated the Detroit Tomorrow Committee, a growing group of "leaders in business, labor, government, religious and civic groups" to think about what the city and its downtown should be in 1975. Chaired by leadership from Hudson's, DTE, and the Detroit Trust, the committee echoed Cobo and Blessing's focus on downtown renewal as the key to a more vibrant and prosperous city: Detroit Tomorrow Committee, "Detroit Tomorrow Committee Report and Review" (Detroit, 1958); Conot, *American Odyssey*, 490; Wallace Hushen, "Detroit News Dynamic City Plan Started," *Detroit News*, July 2, 1954. A *Detroit News* reporter would describe the Committee's efforts as "team work" between the city and the elite: Paul Veblen, "Writer Sees Your City as Beautiful, Dynamic," *Detroit Free Press*, January 13, 1957. The *News* also sought professional advice by inviting an Urban Land Institute panel for a weeklong visit to suggest downtown improvements, most notably yielding the recommendation to attract the headquarters of major regional manufacturers—something the city hadn't even achieved in the 1920s, and would only manage to achieve in the 1990s: John M. Carlisle, "Experts Survey Downtown Blight," *Detroit News*, February 14, 1955; E. A. Baumgarth, "City's Central Area under Expert Study—Problem Is Stated by Group Hired by the Detroit News," *Detroit News*, January 28, 1955; "Uli Report," *Detroit News*, February 24.

30. Detroit Tomorrow Committee, "Detroit Tomorrow Committee Report and Review"; Conot, *American Odyssey*, 490; Wallace Hushen; "Planners Bare City of Future—Exhibit Goes on Display Showing Plan in 3 Stages," *Detroit News*, July 18, 1956. The Hudson's model incorporated Blessing's thoughts, but was actually significantly influenced and ultimately constructed by Norbert Gorwic, Blessing's senior planner in charge of design and partner at the planning and architecture office of Crane and Gorwic, Inc.: Crane and Gorwic Associates,

Planning, Urban Design, Architecture (Detroit, 1961); "Detroit's Rosy Future Depicted for 200 Notables at Hudson's," *Detroit News*, July 20, 1956; "The Detroit of Tomorrow on Display," *Detroit News*, July 21, 1956.

31. "Dramatic Rise for Big Construction: A Strong Sign of Recovery," *Life*, August 25, 1958.

32. City Plan Commission, "Central Business District Study: Land Use, Trafficways and Transit," Master Plan Technical Report (Detroit, 1956); Wells, "Dream City on Horizon."

33. "Planners Seek Woodward Mall," *Detroit News*, September 9, 1956.

34. "Shoppers' Paradise: Lights, Music, No Traffic—Woodward of Future," *Detroit News*, August 6, 1957.

35. "A Garden in the Street," *Detroit News*, July 22, 1956. The debate was especially inspired by a presentation from architect Minoru Yamasaki, who would take Blessing's original mall concept a step further by proposing a fully enclosed and air-conditioned four-block mall between Campus Martius and Grand Circus Park, inspired by the Milanese Galleria Vittorio Emanuele II: "Shoppers' Fairyland Designed for Detroit," *Detroit News*, August 30, 1959. When a commissioned report on the traffic impact of the closure was negative, the plan was tabled: William C. Tremblay, "Traffic Study Snarls Woodward Mall Plan," *Detroit News*, February 24, 1960.

36. E. A. Baumgarth, "Improved Central Area Envisioned by Planner," *Detroit News*, May 21, 1954; "City Completes Its Plans to Beautify Capitol Park," *Detroit News*, July 18.

37. Dan Austin, *Forgotten Landmarks of Detroit* (Charleston, SC: History Press, 2012), 81–84; W. Hawkins Ferry, *The Buildings of Detroit; a History* (Detroit: Wayne State University Press, 1968), 366–367.

38. John M. Carlisle, "City Plans Street Widening to Speed New Bank Building," *Detroit News*, March 10, 1955.

39. Ferry, *The Buildings of Detroit*, 368; Anthony Ripley, "Tower Set for 1963—Fall Start Due on Detroit Bank & Trust Building," *Detroit News*, July 23, 1961.

40. While the private parking industry continued trying to block public lots and garages, its popular support began to wane: "Certainly We Need Parking Lots," *Detroit News*, July 18, 1952. By 1953, Mayor Cobo had had enough; with an extensive plan for more municipal lots and

garages already in hand, he told parking lot owners to "do something about the parking prob-lem or the city will": "City Ultimatum to Park Lots—Operators Must Act, Cobo Says," *Detroit News*, February 27, 1953; John M. Carlisle, "Parking Program Rushed by Cobo," *Detroit News*, December 1, 1954.

41. Robert L. Wells, "Downtown Business Battles for Parking," *Detroit News*, April 4; "Our Future Overtakes Us," *Detroit News*, April 6; Schachern, "Parking Is Called Key to Downtown Comeback."

42. Joseph N. Hartmann, "City Finds Gold Underground in Grand Circus Park Garage," *Detroit News*, December 5, 1960; Robert L. Wells, "Offer $26 Million Plan for Loop Parking Spaces," *Detroit News*, April 18, 1954.

43. Benjamin J. Tobin, "Data on Parking Facilities of the Central Business District" (Office of the Auditor General, Detroit, 1954); Robert L. Wells, "20,527 Parking Spaces—More to Come!," *Detroit News*, May 6, 1957.

44. The Distributor Loop plan was never realized: City Plan Commission, "Central Business District Study: Land Use, Trafficways and Transit."

45. City Plan Commission, "Economic Analysis of the Central Business District Fringe" (Detroit, 1957); Thomas J. Sugrue, *The Origins of the Urban Crisis: Race and Inequality in Post-war Detroit* (Princeton, NJ: Princeton University Press, 1996), 37.

46. The study of downtown land use patterns in the late 1950s by economists Horwood and Boyce were highly influential in this thought process: E. M. Horwood and R. R. Boyce, *Studies of the Central Business District and Urban Freeway Development* (Seattle: University of Wash-ington Press, 1959). The core-frame model was propagated nationally to redevelop retail dis-tricts: Nelson, *The Selection of Retail Locations*.

47. The quadrangle described was bounded to the north by the Edsel Ford Expressway, as the Fisher Freeway was still in its early stages: E. A. Baumgarth, "New Inner Quadrangle-City Is Being Formed in Detroit," *Detroit News*, January 4, 1952.

48. The statement was made by Donald C. Hyde, general manager of Cleveland's transit system, corroborated by two leaders at the Toronto Transportation Commission: Robert S. Ball, "Mayor, Experts Row over Expressways—Planners Call Setup Unrealistic," *Detroit News*,

October 15, 1953. Mayor Cobo countered that transit would not be funded by Michigan's gasoline taxes, and retrofitting the existing Lodge and Ford expressways to accommodate transit would be prohibitively expensive. Instead, he proposed express buses, "a kind of rubber-tired rapid transit." Several lines were indeed implemented as such, but quickly faltered: "Cobo and Richards Back City Program," *Detroit News*, October 15, 1953.

49. "We Cast Our Lot with Cars," *Detroit News*, May 17, 1955.

50. This was in response to a comment by Toronto's highway baron, Frederick G. Gardiner, that the convenience of new highways defeated other mass transit, ultimately compounding the problem of congestion: Glenn Engle, "Detroit Experts Deny X-Ways Defeat Their Own Purpose," *Detroit News*, May 7, 1956.

51. John M. Carlisle, "7 Freeways in Ike Plan, Cobo Says," *Detroit News*, May 18, 1955.

52. June Manning Thomas, *Redevelopment and Race: Planning a Finer City in Postwar Detroit* (Baltimore: Johns Hopkins University Press, 1997), 70.

53. Robert J. Mowitz and Deil S. Wright, *Profile of a Metropolis; a Case Book* (Detroit: Wayne State University Press, 1962), 27–46.

54. The bid was made by an out-of-town bidder who had simply taken a plan originally designated for the West Coast and applied it to Detroit—including outside wooden stairways. The bid was canceled when the developer said that the city's quality requirements for the project simply weren't feasible: ibid., 55–59. Municipal plans to construct middle-class housing in former slum districts often met a lack of market enthusiasm. Developers looked for a sweet spot between subsidized clearance and market potential, "the blight that's right": Frieden and Sagalyn, *Downtown, Inc.*

55. The desperation behind setting up the committee was clear, as Mayor Cobo appointed Reuther to this influential committee though he deeply distrusted him for his alleged "communist" viewpoints: Conot, *American Odyssey*, 444.

56. Citizens' Redevelopment Committee report to City Council, December 20, 1954; in Mowitz and Wright, *Profile of a Metropolis*, 68. The plans extended significantly from the original Gratiot site to include housing to the east and south.

57. Lilian Jackson Braun, "Living Could Be Beautiful," *Detroit Free Press*, October 27, 1957.

58. Conot, *American Odyssey*, 444; Hale, "Detroit: How to Save a Great City from Itself." That same year, Detroit received another $10 million from Washington to expand the urban renewal project southward to Jefferson Avenue: "City Gets 10 Million to Add New Housing—22-Block Area to Be Improved," *Detroit News*, July 10, 1957.

59. Mowitz and Wright, *Profile of a Metropolis*, 75–79.

60. Ibid.; Coleman Young and Lonnie Wheeler, *Hard Stuff: The Autobiography of Coleman Young* (New York: Viking, 1994), 147–148. The Urban Land Institute recommended the replacement of low-income housing with middle class housing: "Improve the close-in areas for living by stepping them upward, not downward." Conot, *American Odyssey*, 435.

61. Ferry, *The Buildings of Detroit*, 371.

62. Thomas, *Redevelopment and Race*, 26. The designs for the towers in the Frederick Douglass and Jeffries projects were densified by about 25 percent at the last minute to alleviate public housing pressures: June Manning Thomas, "Reconsidering Relocation and Displacement: Lessons from Detroit's Public Housing Era," paper delivered at Society for American City and Regional Planning History, 17th National Conference on Planning History (Cleveland, 2017).

63. Only the 1954 Housing Act allowed for the redevelopment of Skid Row, even though it had many residences. This was due to the fact that most residents were single, and the 1949 Act was focused on improving housing for families only: Conot, *American Odyssey*, 421.

64. "Evidence of Blight Mich R-3 + Mich R4" (Detroit, ca. 1955). The author of this report is unknown, and the date is estimated from the contents. From Labadie Special Collection, University of Michigan.

65. Conot, *American Odyssey*, 435.

66. Harold Schachern, "Calls Skid Row Waste of Valuable City Land," *Detroit News*, September 24, 1953. Planners also cited the successful redevelopment of Skid Row districts in Kansas City and Sacramento as examples: Robert L. Wells, "Skid Row No. 1 on Project List for City Center," *Detroit News*, April 14, 1954. The northern portion of Skid Row disappeared from the plans in the late 1950s and was not redeveloped.

67. Citizens' Committee on Skid Row, "Tentative Draft of Findings and Recommendations of the Citizens' Committee on Skid Row" (Detroit, 1958). Research estimated that 50 percent of

Skid Row residents had an income, either from welfare, pensions, or day labor: William C. Tremblay, "Skid Row Roots Grow Deep," *Detroit News*, April 6, 1959.

68. "Raps Miriani on Skid Row," *Detroit News*, May 10, 1953.

69. John Gill, "Chinatown Fears 'Heart' Will Go with Buildings," *Detroit News*, May 28, 1961.

70. "Police Find No Answer to Skid Row," *Detroit News*, April 24, 1953.

71. Robert E. Lubeck, "The Deserted Village—Skid Row Has New Look; Bums and Bottles Gone," *Detroit News*, August 24, 1953; Jerome Aumente, "A New Blueprint for Change," *Detroit News*, August 14, 1966; Harry Golden Jr., "Skid Row Hasn't Gone," *Detroit Free Press Sunday Magazine*, August 11, 1963; Anthony Ripley, "Skid Row Crisis Defies Wreckers, Moves Elsewhere," *Detroit News*, December 18, 1961; "Nobody Wants a Mission Next Door," *Detroit News*, September 19, 1961. Even areas further north near New Center complained of an influx of "the worst possible kind of prospective tenants" from Skid Row: Earl B. Dowdy, "Tax Cuts Asked as Tenants Flee Skid Row Influx," *Detroit News*, March 6, 1963. While the city had instated a ban on "blight producing business" such as pawnshops, bars, and thrift stores in several areas near Skid Row, other areas were exempt, including downtown itself. Furthermore, the ban grandfathered in businesses that were already established in the many near-Skid Rows such as Cass Park: Jo Ann Hardee, "Birth of a Skid Row," *Detroit News*, May 13, 1963.

72. Historic Designation Advisory Board, "Proposed Cass Park Local Historic District Final Report" (City of Detroit, 2014), 9–10. Vice and alcoholism intensified in other vulnerable areas, such as Jefferson Avenue east of downtown, and ironically also in the blocks directly to the north of the new City-County Building: Conot, *American Odyssey*, 544.

73. David W. Hartman, *The Development of Detroit's Cass Corridor: 1850–1975*, vol. 3 (Detroit: Wayne State University Press, 1975), 7–8.

74. This vision fitted with a national trend for older industrial cities to retain manufacturing jobs by industrial renewal: Sugrue, *The Origins of the Urban Crisis*, 164–165. Especially smaller manufacturers clamored for more space and pressured the city to create space for them to stay: "Small Firms Find Squeeze in City Plan," *Detroit News*, October 26, 1952.

75. City Plan Commission, "Industrial Development; West Side Industrial District" (Detroit, 1958).

76. That effort was stopped by Mayor Jeffries himself, a Corktown native. The public housing project was constructed north of Corktown and named after the mayor: Mowitz and Wright, *Profile of a Metropolis*, 86.

77. "Corktown Takes Petition to City to Ban Rezoning," *Detroit News*, July 19, 1954; "Corktown Wins Stay in Plan to Tear Down Area," *Detroit News*, July 23, 1954.

78. "Progress Dooms Old Corktown," *Detroit Free Press*, July 11, 1957; Mowitz and Wright, *Profile of a Metropolis*, 81–139; "Council Approves Razing of Corktown," *Detroit News*, July 10, 1957. Planners had a strong hand in reducing investment in Corktown by leaving the district in limbo for decades after their earlier failed attempt to level it for public housing, and subsequently zoning it for light industrial use. The slum conditions were further exacerbated by the decision of the city to cut off road and sewer maintenance services during the Depression due to the high rate of tax delinquencies in the area: Conot, *American Odyssey*, 416–418.

79. "So Passes Old Corktown," *Detroit News*, July 11, 1957.

80. The report was one of the first accomplishments of newly elected highway commissioner John Mackie, who ran on a platform of reprioritizing state highway investments toward urban rather than rural areas: Mowitz and Wright, *Profile of a Metropolis*, 403–404, 407–408. Interestingly, Mackie also argued for constructing a rapid transit system, "or otherwise [Detroit will] suffer further the consequences": Don Hoenshell, "250 Miles of Expressways Envisioned by Mackie," *Detroit News*, July 16, 1957.

81. These statements were made by councilmembers William G. Rogell and Edward D. Connor. Another protesting councilmember was Louis C. Miriani, who would change his opinion when he became mayor of Detroit the next year: Sheldon L. Hochman, "Rap X-Way 'Ditches' as Boon to Suburbs," *Detroit News*, October 12, 1956.

82. Hale, "Detroit: How to Save a Great City from Itself," 28.

83. Mowitz and Wright, *Profile of a Metropolis*, 408–412. The director of Detroit's Department of Streets and Traffic wavered on the decision for the city's expressways, as he wondered whether "expressways will generate little new traffic for downtown. ... If that should be the case, we must decide whether future expressways should skirt the downtown section": Harold

Schachern, "New Expressway Routes up for Study by Planners," *Detroit News*, November 16, 1954; Mowitz and Wright, *Profile of a Metropolis*, 456–463.

84. Lars Björn and Jim Gallert, *Before Motown: A History of Jazz in Detroit, 1920–60* (Ann Arbor: University of Michigan Press, 2001), 105–108.

85. John Frederick Cohassey, "Down on Hastings Street: A Study of Social and Cultural Changes in a Detroit Community 1941–1955" (M.A. thesis, Wayne State University, 1993). As Black Bottom residents and businesses had moved west to the Twelfth Street corridor, so did the overcrowding, vice, and crime. As on the near east side, conflicts regularly arose between earlier Jewish tenants and African American newcomers: Conot, *American Odyssey*, 436. In a bout of either irony or pragmatism, Blessing proposed to use the excavated soil and demolition rubble from the freeway construction to form hill-shaped parks around downtown, breaking up "the monotony of our plains": Robert L. Wells, "Here's Cure for City's 'Flat Look,'" *Detroit News*, June 10, 1959. The fill was ultimately used to expand Detroit's river shore.

86. "X-Ways to Evict Thousands—Rehousing Help for Families Is Requested," *Detroit News*, December 1, 1956. Numerous historical landmarks, Detroit's first art museum, and the former elite Yondotega social club building also faced the axe: George W. Stark, "Hastings Expressway Will Doom Landmarks," *Detroit News*, February 14, 1957.

87. Glenn Engle, "X-Ways Fail to Save Time in Rush Hour," *Detroit News*, January 5, 1958.

88. Detroit Department of Transportation, "Detroit Central Business District Cordon Count 1966–1974" (Detroit, 1974).

89. Carlisle, "Billion Dollar Boom Downtown."

90. More information on the difference between the local transactions that retailers pursue and the global transactions of offices can be found in R. MacCormac, "Fitting in Offices," *Architectural Review* 181, no. 1083 (1987).

91. Report and Information Committee, "Detroit, the Newest Convention City" (Detroit, ca. 1959).

92. Before the Convention Center opened, the *Detroit News* editors complained: "every year … Detroit auto dealers talk of holding a major show right here, where it belongs. Every year their

careful search of the city finds no hall of adequate size and the project is dropped": "One of Our No. 1 Needs," *Detroit News*, February 23, 1951.

93. "Arena for the Auto Age," *Architectural Forum* 113 (1960).

94. City Plan Commission, "Commercial Renewal" (Detroit, 1958); "Redevelopment" (Detroit, 1954).

95. The federal government was not eager to step in, leading to further delays. Thomas, *Redevelopment and Race*, 75–78.

96. The benefits of the International Village were outlined in a brochure by the Friends of International Village, "International Village … What It Will Do for Detroit" (Detroit, n.d.).

97. "Vast Project in Their Hands," *Detroit News*, July 28, 1959.

98. For more information on the lack of private interest in urban renewal, see Robert M. Fogelson, *Downtown: Its Rise and Fall, 1880–1950* (New Haven: Yale University Press, 2001); Alison Isenberg, *Downtown America: A History of the Place and the People Who Made It* (Chicago: University of Chicago Press, 2004).

99. Thomas, "Seeking a Finer Detroit."

100. Sugrue, *The Origins of the Urban Crisis*, 47–55.

101. Conot, *American Odyssey*, 436–437.

102. Sugrue, *The Origins of the Urban Crisis*, 126–127. While metropolitan Detroit had 257,000 car manufacturing jobs in 1947, it had only 130,000 in 1958, increasing slightly during the 1960s: Thomas James Ticknor, "Motor City: The Impact of the Automobile Industry upon Detroit, 1900–1975" (Ph.D. diss., University of Michigan, 1978), 251. The market began to demand smaller cars that Detroit couldn't provide. Foreign manufacturers like Volkswagen made inroads as car imports increased more than tenfold between 1955 and 1960. Smaller manufacturers like Packard and Hudson were the first victims, and Chrysler was forced to downsize production: Conot, *American Odyssey*, 427–430. The 1959 opening of the St. Lawrence Seaway, better connecting Detroit to the Atlantic Ocean, ironically only made foreign imports easier: Frank Bury Woodford and Arthur M. Woodford, *All Our Yesterdays: A Brief*

History of Detroit (Detroit: Wayne State University Press, 1969), 361; Ticknor, "Motor City," 254.

103. In a 1956 survey by the City Plan Commission, car manufacturers had written off 44 percent of their urban plans due to the high tax burden, cramped quarters, obsolescence of vertical manufacturing, and urban congestion: Ticknor, "Motor City," 288; City Plan Commission, "Industrial Study: A Survey of Existing Conditions and Attitudes of Detroit's Industry" (Detroit, 1956). Government policy to decentralize manufacturing during the Cold War added to the migration of manufacturing to other cities and states: Young and Wheeler, *Hard Stuff*, 149.

104. By 1957, almost ten million square feet of factories lay vacant within Detroit's city limits: Sugrue, *The Origins of the Urban Crisis*, 148; Conot, *American Odyssey*, 453–455, 469. African Americans had few backup options for work, as other industries were highly reluctant to hire them. The steel and chemical industries opposed integration, and the downtown retailers rarely hired non-whites for fear of losing their dwindling white clientele. If retailers hired any African Americans, they were mostly put to work behind the scenes as janitors, porters, and other lower-level jobs. The level of integration was congruent with the desired clientele of the store. Some high-end downtown stores didn't even welcome African Americans as customers, while more affordable stores already had a significant number of African American employees to match the racial makeup of their customers: Sugrue, *The Origins of the Urban Crisis*, 112–114.

105. Sugrue, *The Origins of the Urban Crisis*, 144.

106. Conot, *American Odyssey*, 448.

107. Detroit Department of Transportation, "Detroit Central Business District Cordon Count 1966–1974."

108. William C. Tremblay, "Downtown Shopping to Stay No. 1, Hudson Official Says," *Detroit News*, September 11, 1957.

109. Michael Hauser and Marianne Weldon, *20th Century Retailing in Downtown Detroit* (Charleston, SC: Arcadia, 2008). The store was sold to a Buffalo department store in 1957, as director Otto Kern "didn't want the added responsibility of outlying stores": Cheri Y. Gay, *Lost Detroit* (London: Pavilion Books, 2013), 95.

110. Woodford and Woodford, *All Our Yesterdays*, 361; Conot, *American Odyssey*, 446–447, 451.

111. Conot, *American Odyssey*, 459–479.

CHAPTER 8: BOILING POINT: 1961–1967

1. Robert L. Wells, "How Long since You Really Looked at Detroit?," *Detroit News*, May 20, 1962.

2. "Detroit in Decline," *Time*, October 27, 1961.

3. This early skyscraper had seen steady occupancy, but had started to show signs of deterioration by the early 1950s. Its replacement by the bank was "another giant step forward in the multi-million-dollar rehabilitation of the whole Downtown district": Tom Kleene, "$10 Million Project Hailed as a Boon to Downtown," *Detroit Free Press*, November 27, 1960; Dan Austin, *Forgotten Landmarks of Detroit* (Charleston, SC: History Press, 2012), 116–118. Declared obsolete only decades after it was built, City Hall was increasingly deemed a hindrance to progress by the 1950s. Arguably, its true death sentence had been signed with the administration's move toward the newly constructed City-County Building a few years before. A mayoral committee tasked with deciding what should happen to City Hall had also recommended demolition in 1960: Joseph N. Hartmann, "City Hall Site Garage and Plaza Urged," *Detroit News*, April 4, 1960.

4. The *Free Press* column didn't necessarily reflect the popular opinion about City Hall, as more than half of Detroiters wanted to preserve the building: Judd Arnett, "City Hall? Rip It Down!," *Detroit Free Press*, January 17, 1960; Austin, *Forgotten Landmarks of Detroit*, 31. The *Detroit News* went so far as to call out opposing councilmember Mary V. Beck as having a "defeatist-obstructionist mentality": "Mary versus Progress," *Detroit News*, November 30, 1960.

5. W. Hawkins Ferry, *The Buildings of Detroit; a History* (Detroit: Wayne State University Press, 1968), 368; "Downtown Outlook—Can the People of the Motor City Learn to Walk Again?," *Detroit News*, July 26, 1990; Carl Konzelman, "Detroit Deeply Committed to Meeting the Challenge of Decay," *Detroit News*, October 12, 1962; "No Building at City Hall—Blessing,"

Detroit News, December 2, 1957; John M. Carlisle, "Merchants Urge Razing of City Hall for Garage," *Detroit News*, August 14, 1959.

6. The discussion specifically focused on City Hall, which Yamasaki had proposed to replace with a garage and park: Russell Lynes and Minoru Yamasaki, "Are Detroit's Landmarks Worth Saving?," *Detroit News*, January 17, 1960.

7. Charles Blessing, 1965 letter of recommendation, cited in June Manning Thomas, *Redevelopment and Race: Planning a Finer City in Postwar Detroit* (Baltimore: Johns Hopkins University Press, 1997).

8. Ford Motor Company, "Portrait of a City: Detroit" (Detroit, 1961).

9. Jerome Cavanagh, "Mayor Sends City New Year Greetings," *Detroit Free Press*, January 1, 1963, in David Maraniss, *Once in a Great City: A Detroit Story* (New York: Simon and Schuster, 2015).

10. Housing Commission, "Urban Renewal and Tax Revenue: Detroit's Success Story" (Detroit, 1960).

11. While mostly positive about the achievements of Lafayette Park by the late 1960s, architectural historian W. Hawkins Ferry did note that Mies van der Rohe was not able to complete his vision due to the death of one of his associates. The result was mixed: "although uniformity and in many cases quality were sacrificed, something was gained in variety": Ferry, *The Buildings of Detroit*, 371–373; Jerry Sullivan, "It's a Little Bit of Suburbia in the City," *Detroit News*, May 20, 1962.

12. Frank Beckman, "Detroit—Biggest Boom since '20s," *Detroit Free Press Sunday Magazine*, February 17, 1963; "The Shifting Skyline of the Soaring 60s," *Detroit News*, May 2, 1965.

13. Maraniss, *Once in a Great City*, 95–96; Ferry, *The Buildings of Detroit*, 369.

14. Cheri Y. Gay, *Lost Detroit* (London: Pavilion Books, 2013), 137–138.

15. Thomas, *Redevelopment and Race*, 103–104.

16. In the first of a series of articles on Detroit's urban renewal, Charles Blessing repeated his aim for a wholesale renewal of downtown Detroit: "Just grasp the sweep of it … we have an opportunity to build a virtually new city as surely as though holocaust or war had battered

much of the old one to rubble": Konzelman, "Detroit Deeply Committed to Meeting the Challenge of Decay."

17. Robert E. Conot, *American Odyssey* (New York: Morrow, 1974), 490. The boost in manufacturing signaled a slowing of customers' preferences for compact cars, which were mostly manufactured abroad. New models like the Ford Mustang proved a runaway success: Maraniss, *Once in a Great City*, 31.

18. Conot, *American Odyssey*, 490–493. The city's optimistic view of its modern future was pronounced in a 1963 promotional video supporting its bid for the 1968 Olympics: City of Detroit, "Detroit: City on the Move" (Detroit, 1963).

19. "Downtown Vital, Mayor Tells CBDA," *Detroit News*, January 24, 1963.

20. Thomas, *Redevelopment and Race*, 122–124.

21. Bernard J. Frieden and Lynne B. Sagalyn, *Downtown, Inc.: How America Rebuilds Cities* (Cambridge, MA: MIT Press, 1989), 43–44.

22. Carl Konzelman, "Downtown Updating Yields Offices," *Detroit News*, October 28, 1962; "Fresh Faces Downtown—Remodelings Add to Revitalized Appearance," *Detroit News*, August 6, 1965. When Detroit's First National Bank moved west to its new offices, the old building's co-owner Jason Honigan boasted that he was able to fill up all the vacated space, but acknowledged that new tenants were mostly lured from other downtown buildings by the First National building's drastic renovation: Anthony Ripley, "One Man's Optimism Fills a Whole Building," *Detroit News*, December 15, 1960.

23. By the mid-1960s, over half of new metropolitan office space and 70 percent of industrial space was being constructed outside the city: Conot, *American Odyssey*, 493.

24. John M. Carlisle, "Miriani's Mad at Merchants," *Detroit News*, January 21, 1960. A significant part of Miriani's anger was aimed at merchants who complained about their high taxes, despite several recent tax cuts: William C. Tremblay, "Downtown to Boom—Miriani: Mayor Attacks Tax Complaints by Merchants," *Detroit News*, January 20, 1960; Robert L. Wells, "Tax Assessments Slashed by $7 Million Downtown," *Detroit News*, March 19, 1961; "Cuts Tax to Spur Downtown—Council Aims to Stimulate New Building," *Detroit News*, March 16, 1961. The assessment protest actually calmed down when downtown redevelopment sped up in the

mid-1960s, but the Board of Commerce still complained that many downtown buildings were significantly overassessed. The issue was resolved in a statewide reassessment in 1966: Don Hoenshell, "Business Boom Quiets Downtown Tax Protests," *Detroit News*, December 24, 1964.

25. John Gill, "Wild 'Shrubs' Landscape Empty Lots," *Detroit News*, August 22, 1963.

26. "60-Story Towers Planned on River—Triple Skyscraper Apartments, Motel to Rise near Cobo Hall," *Detroit News*, July 6, 1962; Don Tschirhart, "Detroit's Unfinished Building Dream," *Detroit News*, August 26, 1971.

27. David P. Welsh, "U.S. Selects Downtown Office Site," *Detroit News*, February 19, 1964; "Tower Nears Go-Ahead," *Detroit News*, March 31, 1967; Michael Sorkin, *Variations on a Theme Park: The New American City and the End of Public Space* (New York: Hill and Wang, 1992).

28. A quote from Robert Roselle, head of Detroit's Community Redevelopment Commission, in Michael Maidenberg, "Downtown-West Comes Alive," *Detroit Free Press*, December 31, 1972. The outcome was a far cry from Charles Blessing's original vision of a pedestrianized precinct of corporate and federal headquarters: Carl Konzelman, "Downtown Detroit Rebuilding Slowly but Surely," *Detroit News*, July 25, 1969; "Downtown Outlook—Can the People of the Motor City Learn to Walk Again?," *Detroit News*, July 26, 1990; Harry Golden Jr., "Charley Blessing's Detroit—a Monumental Mall, New 'Cities,' a Grand Core," *Detroit Free Press*, August 14, 1966.

29. Jane Jacobs, *The Death and Life of Great American Cities* (New York: Random House, 1961).

30. Jerome Aumente, "A New Blueprint for Change," *Detroit News*, August 14, 1966. Still facing the threat of being razed for industrial buildings, a neighborhood priest in Corktown complained that "our neighborhood is rotting on the inside, and nobody is doing anything about it." The statement was made as Corktown set up a local committee to plan to turn its tide: Max E. Simon, "Launch Fight to Rekindle Ebbing Spirit of Corktown," *Detroit News*, March 11, 1962.

31. Jean Maddern Pitrone, *Hudson's: Hub of America's Heartland* (Franklin, MI: Altwerger and Mandel, 1991); City Plan Commission, "An Analysis of the Development Potential of Downtown Detroit," Detroit Central Business District Study (Detroit, 1969); "Hudson Confident, Cites Sales Volume—Big Business Is Downtown," *Detroit News*, March 11, 1961.

32. Conot, *American Odyssey*, 493. Only 16 percent of retail sales in metropolitan Detroit were made downtown in 1963. However, downtown remained the largest single retailing area with the best selection of goods during the 1960s: Larry Smith & Company, "Development Opportunities in Downtown Detroit—CBD #5" (Central Business District Association, Detroit, 1965), III-2–III-3; John Thomas Mahoney and Leonard Sloane, "Inside Hudson's 49 Acres—a New Book Reveals a Detroit Phenomenon," *Detroit Free Press*, January 15, 1967, 16.

33. By the 1960s, the movie theater had been purchased by two former employees: Arnold S. Hirsch, "Back from the Brink of Doom: The Fox," *Detroit News*, May 8, 1966; John Finlayson, "Shopping Center Theaters Pace Box Office Boom," *Detroit News*, February 7, 1965. Grinnell's was essential to Berry Gordy's establishment of Motown Records, putting Detroit on a map as an exporter of music. The main music venues for Motown were outside of downtown, mostly in Midtown: Maraniss, *Once in a Great City*, 47–49, 281.

34. Thomas James Ticknor, "Motor City: The Impact of the Automobile Industry upon Detroit, 1900–1975" (Ph.D. diss., University of Michigan, 1978), 267–272.

35. A strong national voice against freeway construction was urban historian Lewis Mumford, who in 1958 predicted that freeways would ultimately defeat themselves as they gutted cities: Frieden and Sagalyn, *Downtown, Inc.*, 48.

36. Carl Konzelman, "Detroit's Freeways: Cradle for Greatness," *Detroit News*, October 19, 1962.

37. Jo Ann Hardee, "Order City Review of Freeways—Cavanagh Acts as Council Balks at New Projects," *Detroit News*, July 12, 1963.

38. Deterioration was also caused by the long limbo of many freeway-adjacent buildings before and during construction: "Tells Plight of Freeway Landowner," *Detroit News*, September 10, 1965; Wayne County Road Commission, "Fisher Freeway—Route Location Study" (Detroit, 1961).

39. John A. Woerpel, "Detroit Wasting Space Downtown, Says Gruen," *Detroit Free Press*, October 19, 1963; Tom Delisle, "City Parking a Headache—and Costly," *Detroit Free Press*, December 20, 1970.

40. "Cavanagh Resurrects Mall Idea," *Detroit News*, January 19, 1962; "Mall Plan Shifted to Broadway," *Detroit News*, August 9, 1962; John F. Nehman, "Elevated Woodward Mall Eyed," *Detroit News*, March 25, 1965.

41. The mayor and the Central Business District Association welcomed the project, proposed by Sam's Cut-Rate owner Sam Osmos: Joseph N. Hartmann, "7-Story Shopping Center Set for Downtown Site—New Development Praised," *Detroit News*, January 26, 1961; "Center on Kern, Sams Sites," *Detroit News*, January 25, 1961; City Plan Commission, "Urban Design Study—Central Business District Project Number 5" (Detroit, 1964); "Who Said 'Dead' Downtown Detroit?," *Detroit News*, January 27, 1961.

42. The process for application for urban renewal funding started in 1962: Larry Smith & Company, "Development Opportunities in Downtown Detroit," III-8–III-13; Jo Ann Hardee, "Downtown Mall Project Spurred," *Detroit News*, July 19, 1962; "Kern Block Loses to Wreckers," *Detroit News*, May 3, 1966.

43. Ladd Neuman, "Kern Block Plans Jolted," *Detroit Free Press*, May 22, 1969.

44. Central Business District Association, "Annual Development Report" (Detroit, 1997); "Greektown's Buildings Kept Up in Fine Shape," *Detroit News*, February 11, 1960; "Greektown Face-Lift," *Detroit News*, May 15, 1966.

45. Jo Ann Hardee, "Tourist Lure Envisioned—Hope to Bring Back Bygone Era's Charm," *Detroit News*, January 30, 1966.

46. "Eye Agency to Save Landmarks," *Detroit News*, September 18, 1966. The organization had a rough start—mere days after its founding conference announcement, the historic Broadway Market was razed for a parking lot: John Gill, "Broadway Market to Be Sold, Razed," *Detroit News*, September 28, 1966.

47. With African Americans desperate for housing options, realtors made large sums of money by transforming the racial makeup of blocks from white to black, a process that often happened very quickly due to racial prejudice among whites. The separation of African Americans

by class follows a similar pattern of white immigrants in the previous century, revolving around narratives of status and exclusivity: Thomas J. Sugrue, *The Origins of the Urban Crisis: Race and Inequality in Postwar Detroit* (Princeton, NJ: Princeton University Press, 1996), 181–207; Coleman Young and Lonnie Wheeler, *Hard Stuff: The Autobiography of Coleman Young* (New York: Viking, 1994), 151–152.

48. Conot, *American Odyssey*, 481–483.

49. Don Ball, "5,000 Ghost Buildings Haunt Detroit Streets," *Detroit News*, April 1, 1970.

50. William C. Tremblay, "Grand River—Route of Many Moods," *Detroit News*, October 24, 1965. Store owners expressed "doubt, bitterness and, perhaps worst of all, fatalism" over the plight of their streets, citing crime and the changing demographics of the inner city as the major factors behind their decline: Berl Falbaum, "Blight Rides Arteries of a Great City," *Detroit News*, June 25, 1967.

51. David W. Hartman, *The Development of Detroit's Cass Corridor: 1850–1975*, vol. 3 (Detroit: Wayne State University Press, 1975), 8–15; Aumente, "A New Blueprint for Change." A survey of the conditions of Skid Row residents at the dawn of 1964 by the *Michigan Chronicle* illustrated the sobering reality of unemployment, homelessness, and survival: Ofield Dukes in Maraniss, *Once in a Great City*, 309–310; Michael Maidenberg, "10 Painful Years of 'Urban Renewal': What It Means When You Live There," *Detroit Free Press*, March 1, 1970.

52. Arthur Johnson in Maraniss, *Once in a Great City*, 174. Interestingly, the NAACP did not officially endorse the march due to disagreements with other local African American leaders.

53. Frank Bury Woodford and Arthur M. Woodford, *All Our Yesterdays: A Brief History of Detroit* (Detroit: Wayne State University Press, 1969), 349; Conot, *American Odyssey*, 471; Maraniss, *Once in a Great City*, 161–188.

54. As historian Thomas Sugrue put it, "A visitor walking or driving through Detroit in the 1960s—like his or her counterpart in the 1940s—would have passed through two Detroits, one black and one white." Sugrue, *The Origins of the Urban Crisis*, 179–258.

55. Especially in the areas around downtown Detroit crime was spiking, leading to an increasing divide between the mostly white police force and mostly African American

residents—despite Cavanagh's widely praised efforts to bridge the racial gap: Maraniss, *Once in a Great City*, 189–203.

56. The concession was made to a reporter from the *Los Angeles Times*, who remarked that "the city that gets blamed for the nation's traffic and smog is caught in its own trap." It was republished in the *Detroit News*: Ray Hebert, "Cars Strangle Detroit, Visitor Says," *Detroit News*, November 30, 1966.

57. About 20 percent of Detroit's neighborhoods were eligible for a conservation approach: Mayor's Committee for Community Renewal, "Method of Selecting Priorities for Urban Renewal," Technical Report (Detroit, 1966).

58. Jo Ann Hardee, "Malls, Plazas in Plan for Downtown," *Detroit News*, May 29, 1966; "Autos to Go Underground—Redevelopment May 'Sink' City's Sea of Parking Lots," *Detroit News*, June 6, 1966.

59. Similarly, a third of the American land cleared for urban renewal in the 1950s hadn't been sold by 1971: Frieden and Sagalyn, *Downtown, Inc.*, 44.

60. Constantinos A. Doxiadis, *Emergence and Growth of an Urban Region: The Developing Urban Detroit Area*, Developing Urban Detroit Area Research Project (Detroit: Detroit Edison Co., 1966). The work was planned to comprise ten volumes, but only three were ultimately published.

61. Christo Genkov, "Revitalization of the Detroit Central Business District" (Center for Urban Studies, Wayne State University, 1971); Frieden and Sagalyn, *Downtown, Inc.*, 29. Detroit councilmember and former planner Mel Ravitz expressed very similar sentiments as cited in Thomas, *Redevelopment and Race*, 143. On the federal funding allocation of the Model Cities Program and its implementation in Detroit, see Conot, *American Odyssey*, 497.

CHAPTER 9: THE END OF URBAN RENEWAL: 1967–1977

1. Robert E. Conot, *American Odyssey* (New York: Morrow, 1974), 522–525.

2. For more information on the socioeconomic background of this situation, see Thomas J. Sugrue, *The Origins of the Urban Crisis: Race and Inequality in Postwar Detroit* (Princeton, NJ: Princeton University Press, 1996). More information on the conditions of the disorders can be

found in Sidney Fine, *Violence in the Model City: The Cavanagh Administration, Race Relations, and the Detroit Riot of 1967* (Ann Arbor: University of Michigan Press, 1989); Hubert G. Locke, *The Detroit Riot of 1967* (Detroit: Wayne State University Press, 1969); and Thomas James Ticknor, "Motor City: The Impact of the Automobile Industry upon Detroit, 1900–1975" (Ph.D. diss., University of Michigan, 1978), 281–283. The timing of the disorders was not only related to the summer heat but to the seasonal unemployment cycle that spiked during summers: Conot, *American Odyssey*, 530.

3. A comment by Governor George Romney as he flew over Detroit to assess the damage on July 24, 1967; quoted in Conot, *American Odyssey*, 535.

4. Bernard J. Frieden and Lynne B. Sagalyn, *Downtown, Inc.: How America Rebuilds Cities* (Cambridge, MA: MIT Press, 1989), 52.

5. Conot, *American Odyssey*, 559.

6. A prominent member of the committee was Coleman Young, who would later comment that the committee's "preoccupation with the abstract turned off both the pragmatists and the militants and divided the effort." By militants, Young referred to the group of radical African American activists who emerged during and after the disorders of 1967: Coleman Young and Lonnie Wheeler, *Hard Stuff: The Autobiography of Coleman Young* (New York: Viking, 1994), 180. Though it spent millions on projects to elevate Detroit's African Americans, the committee's results were unclear and leadership changed within two years. The committee did set up the Economic Development Corporation, representing major business interests: Conot, *American Odyssey*, 602–603.

7. The oldest part of the city within Grand Boulevard saw its population drop by almost 60 percent between 1940 and 1970: Ticknor, "Motor City," 293–294.

8. Motown's move out of Detroit followed a short stay at an office building on Woodward Avenue between 1967 and 1972. The building has subsequently been leveled for a parking lot: David Maraniss, *Once in a Great City: A Detroit Story* (New York: Simon and Schuster, 2015), 373.

9. Jack Woerpel and Don Tschirhart, "What Detroit Needs," *Detroit News*, January 25, 1970; "The Stadium—Domed Facility Would Serve as a Catalyst for Downtown," *Detroit News*,

January 27. Interestingly, downtown office occupancy rates were actually higher than ever at 95 percent in 1970, according to a city study: "Offices 95 Pct. Leased," *Detroit News*, September 25, 1970.

10. Young and Wheeler, *Hard Stuff*, 216. Industrial jobs had already mostly located outside of Detroit since the 1950s rise of horizontal manufacturing; by the 1970s, 70 percent of new factories constructed in the region were outside of Detroit's city limits: Conot, *American Odyssey*, 604–608.

11. In 1970, no other city but Washington, D.C. was so reliant on one industry in its local economy: Ticknor, "Motor City," 262–263.

12. Conot, *American Odyssey*, 623–626. Murders increased at an even more rapid pace: ibid., 667.

13. "Downtown Detroit Fighting for Its Life," *Detroit News*, January 1, 1969.

14. Melvin G. Holli, *Detroit* (New York: New Viewpoints, 1976), 202; Susan McBee, "Detroit, Problem Town U.S.A., Grows Older, Poorer, Tougher," *Boston Globe*, March 4, 1973.

15. Jerry M. Flint, "Detroit's Pledge of Change after Riot Is Left Unfulfilled after Three Years," *New York Times*, July 23, 1970.

16. Conot, *American Odyssey*, 616.

17. Jerome Aumente, "Who Really Cares about Detroit?," *Detroit News*, October 4, 1968.

18. Hudson's profits declined almost 25 percent between 1965 and 1968: Jean Maddern Pitrone, *Hudson's: Hub of America's Heartland* (Franklin, MI: Altwerger and Mandel, 1991), 153; Michael Hauser and Marianne Weldon, *20th Century Retailing in Downtown Detroit* (Charleston, SC: Arcadia, 2008), 71–72. Continuing tough market conditions would prompt Hudson's to merge with the Minneapolis-based Dayton Corporation in 1969, arguably taking the locational decision-making process away from downtown Detroit.

19. Shop windows were replaced with indestructible materials or even bricked up as insurance rates for plate glass had skyrocketed since the 1967 disorders: Conot, *American Odyssey*, 609–610; Alison Isenberg, *Downtown America: A History of the Place and the People Who Made It* (Chicago: University of Chicago Press, 2004), 245.

20. Susan Slobojan, "Built-in Beauty—Presenting an Architectural Walking Tour of Downtown Detroit," *Detroit News*, August 18, 1978.

21. An income tax rate hike provided temporary relief, but ultimately convinced even more people to depart the city: Conot, *American Odyssey*, 613.

22. Excessive plans were not solely the domain of the City Plan Commission, as a Grosse Pointe architectural firm submitted a proposal to transform most of northern Corktown while only preserving some of its most historic properties, instigated by a local neighborhood non-profit corporation: David L. Good, "$100 Million Revitalization of Stadium Area Projected," *Detroit News*, December 20, 1970.

23. Civic Center West was to have been a spectacular mixture of commercial and residential towers, a community college, and a sports stadium: City Plan Commission, Design Division, "Civic Center West" (Detroit, n.d.). The idea for a subway was revived by an offer by Montreal to sell their rolling stock after Expo 67: "The Subway Plan," *Detroit News*, January 2, 1970; Clark Hallas, "Expo Car Offer Spurs Detroit Subway Plan," *Detroit News*, August 20, 1969. The Department of Street Railways was forced to cut service by 1970: "DSR Service Will Be Cut, Manager Says," *Detroit News*, September 26, 1970; Ted Douglas, "Detroit Area Worst in Transit Study," *Detroit News*, September 3, 1972.

24. Former city planner Walter Blucher vehemently disagreed in a letter to the *Detroit News*, providing a list of only physical improvements to the city, most of which were new roads: Walter H. Blucher, "Planning Aid Claimed for Detroit's Growth," *Detroit News*, May 20, 1972.

25. Young's election was mostly the result of Detroit's growing African American voter base, to whom "homegrown" Young had a strong appeal: Young and Wheeler, *Hard Stuff*, 200, 228.

26. June Manning Thomas, *Redevelopment and Race: Planning a Finer City in Postwar Detroit* (Baltimore: Johns Hopkins University Press, 1997), 150–151.

27. Young later argued: "if you have a billion dollars to spend in the city and spend every penny of it rebuilding the neighborhoods—giving people brand-new or refurbished houses—and *they don't have jobs,* within five years the goddamn place will be a slum again": Young and Wheeler, *Hard Stuff*, 200, 228; italics in the original.

28. Frieden and Sagalyn, *Downtown, Inc.*, 53–54.

29. Thomas, *Redevelopment and Race*, 145–147. The council-controlled Planning Commission and the mayor-controlled Planning Department would often work in parallel, or even at odds with one another. An example is the frequent refusal of the Planning Department to share information with the Commission or the Council on their budget or specific plans: Robert E. Roach and Monroe Walker, "Planning Unit Keeps Its 'Secrets'," *Detroit News*, April 27, 1982. The third planning body, the Community and Economic Development Department, was mostly tasked with neighborhood development projects, but would soon take on downtown planning.

30. Biographer Wilbur Rich argued that Young had no other choice than this assertive and creative style of getting projects off the ground, as sentiments among state and regional agencies were overwhelmingly negative on the city and Detroit was hardly able to fund projects on its own. Wilbur C. Rich, *Coleman Young and Detroit Politics: From Social Activist to Power Broker* (Detroit: Wayne State University Press, 1989), 168–169.

31. His ability to draw on his federal connections certainly helped to ease his reelections. Young boasted of his successful efforts in bringing in "pump-priming" UDAG grants in his campaign slogan "Bring Home the Bacon": Young and Wheeler, *Hard Stuff*, 225–227.

32. Young's typical daring style was reflected in the fact that he started construction for the arena even before he had secured full funding, acquired all the land, or even reached an agreement that the Red Wings would occupy it: ibid., 231; Thomas, *Redevelopment and Race*, 157–158; Cyndi Meagher and Theasa Tuohy, "Detroit May Buy Tiger Stadium," *Detroit News*, October 20, 1976; Rich, *Coleman Young and Detroit Politics*, 171–180. Mayor Cavanagh had actually promoted this proposal for a new stadium for the Detroit Tigers and Lions in the late 1960s: Berl Falbaum, "Mayor Urges a Downtown Dome Stadium," *Detroit News*, October 12, 1968; "Stadium Is Crucial to Downtown, Cavanagh Says," *Detroit News*, March 19, 1969. Cavanagh set up a committee which specifically praised the positive impact a stadium would have on downtown shops and restaurants and on the city's image. Coleman Young was one of the committee's members. In the face of Detroit's decline, the committee strongly recommended the stadium's construction, as it "may be the most important thing we have ever done for the future of our city"—inaugurating a worrying trend of overconfidence in singular projects as

saviors for Detroit: Don Tschirhart, "Study Urges Stadium on Riverfront," *Detroit News*, March 20, 1970; "New Stadium—$2 Billion Boon to Detroit," *Detroit News*, September 4, 1970.

33. Detroit Lions owner William Ford moved his team to Pontiac, stating, "I don't think any of us will live long enough to see a stadium in downtown Detroit": Pete Waldmeir, "Lions' Ford Scoffs at Riverfront Site," *Detroit News*, February 1, 1971; George Puscas, "How the Pontiac Stadium Came to Be," *Detroit Free Press*, August 24, 1975. Similarly, the Pistons basketball team moved from Cobo Arena to the suburbs in 1978.

34. The campus was designed by Constantinos Doxiadis, who had completed his regional vision for the city only years before: Berl Falbaum, "Edison Tells Plan for 66-Acre Complex on Downtown Site," *Detroit News*, May 7, 1970.

35. Detroit Renaissance, *Take Another Look at Detroit* (Detroit, 1972). A similar but smaller organization was founded by Joseph Hudson, called New Detroit: Thomas, *Redevelopment and Race*, 154.

36. Ticknor, "Motor City," 304–305.

37. At the time, Ford was under fire for being on the Detroit Renaissance committee while investing most of his money elsewhere: "How's Downtown? Looking Up, Thanks," *Signature*, June 1976.

38. "Ford Motor Plans 'Save Detroit' Project, $400 Million Housing-Hotel-Office Complex," *Wall Street Journal*, November 26, 1971. One of Charles Blessing's last actions in office was to oppose Ford's plans, stating that the envisioned riverfront complex did not fit into an aesthetically pleasing ensemble with the Civic Center: Thomas, *Redevelopment and Race*, 145–147.

39. "How's Downtown? Looking up, Thanks," 25; Robert W. Irvin, "Henry Ford Admits It's a Struggle to Get Renaissance Center Funds," *Detroit News*, January 17, 1975.

40. Michael Maidenberg, "Riverfront Project—Now It's Renaissance Center," *Detroit Free Press*, March 23, 1973.

41. Maryanne Conheim, "Riverfront Center to Be Shielded by 25-Foot Wall," *Detroit Free Press*, October 23, 1973; June Hicks, "Grim Wall Is a Challenge," *Detroit News*, December 10, 1976.

42. "'An Unashamed Capitalist'," *Detroit Monitor* 1972.

43. W. H. Whyte, *City: Rediscovering the Center* (New York: Doubleday, 1988); William Hollingsworth Whyte et al., *The Social Life of Small Urban Spaces* (Los Angeles: Direct Cinema Limited, 1990), videorecording, 1 videocassette (60 min.): sd., col.; 1/2 in.

44. Nan Ellin, *Postmodern Urbanism* (Cambridge, MA: Blackwell, 1996).

45. John Portman, interview by Paul Goldberger, 1988, transcript in Paolo Riani, *John Portman* (Milan: L'Arca Edizioni, 1990).

46. Portman specifically referred to the fear of social unrest as seen in the 1967 "insurrection": ibid., 36–40.

47. The Broderick was sold in 1969, modernized, and sold again to investor Michael Higgins in 1976 after vacancy soared. Many office buildings were bought up by Higgins in the 1970s. His company filed for bankruptcy in 1991: Dan Austin, Sean Doerr, and John Gallagher, *Lost Detroit: Stories behind the Motor City's Majestic Ruins* (Charleston, SC: History Press, 2010), 16.

48. Peter Gavrilovich, "Marketing a Renaissance—Problem: Take 39 Floors X 4 and Fill …," *Detroit Free Press*, August 22, 1976, 163–165; Dan Austin, *Forgotten Landmarks of Detroit* (Charleston, SC: History Press, 2012); E. A. Batchelor Jr., "Fort Shelby Hotel Closes—Victim of Changing Times," *Detroit News*, December 1, 1973.

49. Many of Detroit's downtown hotels stayed afloat with convention business, and the city's oldest hotels were often also too far removed from Cobo Hall for patrons to safely walk to the riverfront property: Bob Luke, "A Lady in Waiting—Radisson Cadillac Worries about Its Future as It Gets Ready for the City's Big 'Party'," *Detroit News*, January 6, 1980.

50. In official language, crime was concealed as "indignities heaped on pedestrians in big cities": Gerald Storch, "What's Up for Detroit? It Could Be Pedestrians," *Detroit News*, December 28, 1975. Earlier proposals included Blessing's vision for the separation of pedestrians and traffic, as outlined in John F. Nehman, "Elevated Woodward Mall Eyed," *Detroit News*, March 25, 1965.

51. Trevor Boddy, "Underground and Overhead: Building the Analogous City," in Michael Sorkin, *Variations on a Theme Park: The New American City and the End of Public Space* (New York: Hill and Wang, 1992), 124–134.

52. Southeastern Michigan Transportation Authority, "Proposal: Downtown People Mover Detroit, Michigan" (Detroit, 1976). The regional rapid transit component never materialized: Southeastern Michigan Transportation Authority, "Rapid Transit along Woodward" (Detroit, 1971).

53. The People Mover was inspired by the construction of a similar system by a Ford subsidiary between its headquarters and a nearby shopping mall in Dearborn, and by growing federal interest in these systems. The planned regional transit system depended on an 80/20 match from the federal government, and was to consist of several subway lines radiating from downtown, bus rapid transit for tangential connections, and upgraded bus service: Howard Warren, "254-Mile Mass Transit Plan Unveiled," *Detroit News*, March 21, 1974. The state governor and suburban-dominated Southeastern Michigan Transportation Authority dragged their feet on the proposals, much to Young's chagrin. He went so far as to state that the regional transit agency was intent on sabotaging Detroit's proposal—a curious accusation, since that agency had originally proposed it: Young and Wheeler, *Hard Stuff*, 290; Don Ball, "Young Wants Subway System Started," *Detroit News*, March 13, 1975. Ford Motors had actually presented a citywide people mover system to City Council the year before: Stephen Cain, "'People Mover' Plan Presented," *Detroit News*, May 1, 1973.

54. Journalist Jay Carr stated: "The best people movers are attractive sidewalks": Jay Carr, "Rencen, Don't Turn Your Back on Old Detroit," *Detroit News*, March 20, 1977.

55. By 1975, Ford Motors had already decided to shut down its people mover subsidiary, and the federal government had become far "less interested in developing exotic new technology": Gregory Skwira, "Ford Finds That People Movers Just Aren't Moving," *Detroit Free Press*, November 9, 1975.

56. Howard Warren, "'People Mover' Transit Plan Sails through Public Hearing," *Detroit News*, March 20, 1974; United States Urban Mass Transportation Administration and Southeastern Michigan Transportation Authority, "Downtown People Mover, Detroit, Michigan: Final Environmental Impact Statement" (U.S. Dept. of Transportation, Urban Mass Transportation Administration, 1980), II-1.

57. President Ford's agreement to fund $600 million for the People Mover was prompted by a visit from the bipartisan Move Detroit Forward Committee, comprising Mayor Young and several business leaders: Young and Wheeler, *Hard Stuff*, 221.

58. The agency would also fund larger subway systems such as those implemented in San Francisco and Washington, D.C.: Urban Mass Transportation Administration and Southeastern Michigan Transportation Authority, "Downtown People Mover," II-1–II-2.

59. Washington Boulevard struggled with the departure of retail tenants, and its hotels were losing the competition with the Pontchartrain for hotel patrons: Betty Frankel, "City's Digging to Get More People," *Detroit Free Press*, August 20, 1976; Lucille DeView, "Washington Boulevard Dream Changing, Not Dying, Boosters Insist," *Detroit News*, January 17, 1975; Mattie Greene, "Washington Blvd Facelift—Merchants Optimistic over Street's Future," *Detroit News*, September 23, 1975. The idea of pedestrianization had been introduced four years before by students at the University of Michigan in a class project suggested by the CBDA: Jack Woerpel, "A New Washington Boulevard—How U of M Design Team Would Reshape Downtown," *Detroit News*, August 18, 1972.

60. The transit mall on Woodward Avenue had been proposed by City Council in 1974 as a more workable version of the pedestrian malls proposed in previous decades: "Downtown Mall Plan Pressed," *Detroit News*, May 2, 1974. The mall was touted as going "a long way to putting new life downtown": "Facility Planned for Grand Circus Park—Transit Mall Contract Signed," *Detroit News*, March 1, 1975; Rossetti/Sims Joint Venture, "Woodward Avenue Improvement Program Report" (Community and Economic Development Department, Detroit, 1976).

61. Detroit Renaissance, *Take Another Look at Detroit*, 11.

62. The local press also frequently reported on robberies and murders occurring downtown, seemingly at random. A local store owner was resigned to the crime wave: "when your number is up, it is up": Robert S. Wisler, "Wary Is Word on Stretch of Griswold Where 2 Died," *Detroit News*, April 4, 1973.

63. In 1972 alone, $12 million of inventory was lost due to in-store theft: Pitrone, *Hudson's*, 155–169; Susan Watson, "Hudson's … Where Memories Fill the Aisles," *Detroit Free Press*, September 23, 1972.

64. Citation of director Joe Hudson in Pitrone, *Hudson's*, 166.

65. Howard Warren, "Downtown Hudson's Closes Off Half of Its 65 Display Windows," *Detroit News*, April 13, 1977.

66. Conversely to Hudson's, efforts to modernize Crowley's department store were obstructed by the building's complicated ownership structure: James Kenyon, "Crowley's Closing Ends a Detroit Era," *Detroit News*, July 3, 1977; Walter B. Smith, "Continuing Losses Cited—Crowley's to Vacate Downtown Store in '76," *Detroit News*, May 18, 1973.

67. Charles Manos, "Woodward Block Waits 3 Years for City Action," *Detroit News*, March 30, 1969. Downtown movie theaters had little choice but to resort to porn. The owner of a number of downtown theaters argued, "it's a choice of showing skin flicks or going out of business": James A. Treloar, "Skin Flicks in Livid Color (Green)," *Detroit News*, October 19, 1970. Even large theaters like United Artists were forced to close: "United Artists Movie Palace Closes Doors," *Detroit News*, September 15, 1971. The demise of downtown's movie theaters also meant the closure of the Film Exchange offices on Cass Avenue: John Finlayson, "Old Movie Mart Just Fades Away," *Detroit News*, March 19, 1972.

68. Theater owners responded that their downtown patrons "just aren't tidy people": Sue Hoover, "Downtown Theaters a Messy Sight," *Detroit News*, July 20, 1972; John Hannigan, *Fantasy City: Pleasure and Profit in the Postmodern Metropolis* (London: Routledge, 2010), 45.

69. Don Tschirhart, "Detroit's Unfinished Building Dream," *Detroit News*, August 26, 1971; "The 'New' Detroit," *Detroit News*, September 7, 1972. In the end, Detroit Edison's plans for a 66-acre mixed-use campus were abandoned under pressure from financial issues at the company. At the same time, construction on the Federal Building was still on hold due to funding problems: "Government Renewal Still Lags," *Detroit News*, September 11, 1972.

70. Plum Street resident David Valler described the rise and fall of this district: David J. Valler, "For Plum Street, One-Way to a Dead-End," *Detroit News*, September 21, 1969.

71. The Pontchartrain hotel was actually a pared-down version of an original proposal by Conrad Hilton: Tschirhart, "Detroit's Unfinished Building Dream."

72. While the Historic Preservation Committee found over 50 significant structures, most of which were in downtown, City Council was reluctant to enforce official policies to protect them. The Committee designated two historic districts but none in downtown: Beverly Eckman, "58 City Structures Singled Out for Historic Value," *Detroit News*, October 18, 1971. When the idea of a Downtown Development Authority with stronger condemnation powers was floated, the Detroit Historic Preservation Committee accelerated its efforts to catalog any buildings worth saving: Diane R. Pawlowski, "Fight Begun to Save Historic Downtown Buildings," *Detroit News*, May 22, 1974. To counter City Council disaffection, the Historic Preservation Committee presented a petition that demonstrated citizens' support for preservation: Diane Pawlowski, "Landmarks May Be Saved—Historic Restoration Draws Wide Support," *Detroit News*, May 9, 1975. Corktown was added to the National Register of Historic Places in 1978: Associated Press, "2 Auto Plants, Corktown Put on List of Michigan National Historic Sites," *Detroit News*, September 6, 1978.

73. The inner-city consumer seems conspicuously absent from the Greektown business proposal: Americal Development Corporation, "Traugott Schmidt & Sons, a Melieu of Entertainment Experiences!" (Detroit, 1974); Diane R. Pawlowski, "Greektown on Sunday Keeps Downtown Alive," *Detroit News*, March 19, 1974. The project was underwritten by the nearby Blue Cross Blue Shield in 1979 as a "sound investment": Jeff Gaydos, "Blues Back Renewal," *Detroit News*, April 27, 1979. For a critique of this style of entertainment-led redevelopment, see Hannigan, *Fantasy City*, 51–63.

74. Tschirhart, "Detroit's Unfinished Building Dream"; "Developers Unveil Twin Tower Plan," *Detroit News*, October 30; Clark Hallas, "Downtown to Get Apartments, Shops," *Detroit News*, March 5, 1972; Don Tschirhart, "Downtown WSU College Advocated by Gullen," *Detroit News*, March 31, 1974. The development of the Kern block was strung along for years by a New York investor who was ultimately unable to find financing, despite repeated concessions by the city: "The Kern Block—a Valuable Asset," *Detroit News*, June 6, 1973. After the deal fell apart, the city wanted to lure developers by including in the site the blocks south along Monroe

Avenue, Detroit's former entertainment district, and promising to clear them: "Add Monroe Area, Says Planner—Kern Site Called Too Small," *Detroit News*, February 26, 1975.

75. A survey of license plates of cars in Cass Park in the early 1970s revealed that 90 percent were from outside the city: James Tobin, "Blighted Area Shows Signs of Promise: Planners, Developers Believe Most Successes Hinge on Cass Corridor," *Detroit News*, April 13, 1997.

76. David W. Hartman, *The Development of Detroit's Cass Corridor: 1850–1975*, vol. 3 (Detroit: Wayne State University Press, 1975), 8–15. By the early 1970s, Cass Park residents called their neighborhood Detroit's "dumping ground": Don Tschirhart, "Cass Corridor Could Be Saved— a Blighted Area Still Hopes," *Detroit News*, September 6, 1972. A four-article series "Inside the Cass Corridor" in the *Detroit News* between November 7 and 10 revealed the contrasts between intellectuals, prostitutes, homeless, and seniors in the "toughest area in a tough town": Bill Gray, "Inside the Cass Corridor—Where Life Teaches Fear, Despair," *Detroit News*, November 7, 1976; "Inside the Cass Corridor—Hooker, Junkie, Mother, Dreamer," *Detroit News*, November 8, 1976; "Inside the Cass Corridor—a Lonely Life for Friendless Seniors on Tiny Pensions," *Detroit News*, November 9, 1976; "Inside the Cass Corridor—Drugs, Booze Dull the Pain," *Detroit News*, November 10, 1976; see also Don Tschirhart, "Street of No Hope—Park Ave.: Home of Old, Poor," *Detroit News*, July 8, 1974.

77. "Park Avenue Planners Seek to Return Dignity to Old Street," *Detroit News*, April 12, 1972. Cass Park wasn't Detroit's only Skid Row, as many former residents had moved east toward Brush Street, which had become "a street of broken bottles and derelict men who stake out an existence": John J. Green, "Skid Row Gone?—It's Only Moved to the East Side," *Detroit News*, August 25, 1968.

78. Gene Scott, *Detroit Beginnings: Early Villages and Old Neighborhoods* (Detroit: DRCEA, 2001), 48–49.

79. Don Ball, "Big Victory against Detroit Blight," *Detroit News*, May 12, 1970.

80. Don Tschirhart, "Downtown Detroit—Saga of Growth, Decay," *Detroit News*, December 3, 1972.

81. Paul Gainor, "The Eastern Market Getting a New Look," *Detroit News*, September 12, 1976.

82. A remark by Wayne State University professor Louis Friedland, quoted in David Blomquist, "Freeways Spurred Exodus," *Detroit News*, August 29, 1976.

83. Don Tschirhart, "The People Who Own Property in Downtown Detroit," *Detroit News*, July 15, 1974.

84. "New Title for City of Detroit?," *Detroit News*, May 30, 1974.

CHAPTER 10: RENAISSANCE AMONG RUINS: 1977–1988

1. Renaissance Center Partnership, "Renaissance Center Dedication Signals Cities' Revitalization," news release, 1977; Alex Taylor, "World of ($) Success at Rencen Shops," *Detroit Free Press*, October 22, 1978.

2. Susan Watson and Peter C. Gavrilovich, "Detroit Hails City Renaissance," *Detroit Free Press*, April 16, 1977; Christopher Willcox and Barbara Young, "It's a Gala Affair at Dedication for Rencen," *Detroit News*, April 16, 1977.

3. Community and Economic Development Department, "Detroit: Rebuilding a Great City," *Detroit Free Press*, December 18, 1977.

4. Downtown sales almost halved between 1963 and 1977 (figures from US Census of Business, 1963 and 1977). Hudson's sales fell 65 percent between 1953 and 1977: Jean Maddern Pitrone, *Hudson's: Hub of America's Heartland* (Franklin, MI: Altwerger and Mandel, 1991).

5. James Kenyon, "Crowley's Closing Ends a Detroit Era," *Detroit News*, July 3, 1977. Facing rising crime rates, jeweler Wright Kay & Co.'s downtown owner stated he'd rather "deploy our resources to where we can do the best job": Jim Neubacher, "Downtown Jeweler Will Close," *Detroit Free Press*, January 21, 1977.

6. Dan Austin, Sean Doerr, and John Gallagher, *Lost Detroit: Stories behind the Motor City's Majestic Ruins* (Charleston, SC: History Press, 2010), 94.

7. Furthermore, 73 percent of 1974 visitors arrived by car. Detroit Department of Transportation, "Detroit Central Business District Cordon Count 1966–1974" (Detroit, 1974).

8. Ze'ev Chafets, "The Tragedy of Detroit," *New York Times*, July 29, 1990; Citizens Research Council of Michigan, "Police Precinct One in Downtown Detroit: A Survey of Trends in Crime,

Economic Activity, and Public Attitudes," Report No. 258 (Detroit, 1979); Barbara Young, "Young Asks Grosse Pointers to Enjoy Downtown Detroit," *Detroit News*, May 2, 1977. Overall, the Citizens Research Council report was positive on downtown's outlook, noticing that there was significant interest among the 2,000 respondents in downtown housing and that 72 percent of young respondents were optimistic about Detroit's future. The Council concluded that perceptions of crime were simply "ingrained by time." James Tittsworth, "Downtown Called Safe," *Detroit News*, September 25, 1979; "The Perception of Crime," *Detroit News*, October 2, 1979.

9. Lou Gordon, "The Beautiful and the Ugly," *Detroit News*, March 20, 1977.

10. Jeffrey Hadden and Christopher Willcox, "Older Buildings Feel Effect of Tenant Shift to Ren Cen," *Detroit News*, June 22, 1977.

11. Like many downtown theaters, the Michigan Theatre entered a cycle of decline, briefly serving as a supper club before its final stint as a rock venue. The trashed remains were slated for demolition to become a parking lot for the adjoining office building, but the theater was deemed structurally inseparable from that building. Instead it was gutted and turned into a parking garage itself. It was spared by necessity—but certainly not treated with any respect. The nearby United Artists Theatre served for a while as a porn cinema and recording studio but has been vacant since 1983: Austin, Doerr, and Gallagher, *Lost Detroit*, 119–134, 141–144; Don Tschirhart, "Michigan Theatre Breathes Its Last; Cars to Park There," *Detroit News*, August 30, 1977. The Michigan Theatre was praised as "the only Italian Renaissance garage in Michigan, its golden cherubs frolicking over the old stage, its graceful arches casting exotic shadows, its marble pillars holding up an era that has ended": Michelle Andonian, "Historic Movie Palace Gets an Odd Curtain Call," *Detroit News*, February 23, 1984.

12. The 10 percent loss of value is calculated without the added assessed value of the Renaissance Center. Some older office structures that competed with the Renaissance Center lost more than 20 percent of their value, like the Cadillac Tower and the David Stott Building: Christopher Willcox, "Downtown's Tax Base Dips Despite Rencen," *Detroit News*, October 24, 1977.

13. Jack Woerpel, "16 Office Buildings Rising to Meet Demands of Area," *Detroit News*, May 6, 1979.

14. Robert E. Roach, "Southfield Paces Oakland Surge as Business Center," *Detroit News*, May 24, 1984.

15. Bruce Alpert, "Book Cadillac, Trappers Alley—Downtown Projects Get Lift," *Detroit News*, October 10, 1984; Robert E. Roach, "Hotel Plan Clears Financing Hurdle," *Detroit News*, April 17, 1980; "Socializing the 'Pontch,'" *Detroit News*, April 26, 1987; Bruce Alpert, "Detroit Wants to Buy Pontch—Downtown Hotel Tied to Cobo Plan," *Detroit News*, March 24, 1987. TIF financing still hinged on issuing bonds, which the market refused to provide the DDA at reduced interest rates to facilitate the hotel deals: "Collapse of the Pontch Deal," *Detroit News*, June 17, 1987.

16. "View from the Top," *Detroit Free Press*, April 20, 1978.

17. A year after opening, only 20 of the 100 envisioned shops were occupied, and four years later a third of the Center's retail space was still vacant, more than the already high downtown average: Betsey Hansell, "Retail Scene Looking Up in Other Major Cities," *Detroit Free Press*, December 14, 1983.

18. George Bullard, "An a-Maze-Ing Place to Get Lost," *Detroit News*, April 12, 1981; Jay Carr, "Rencen, Don't Turn Your Back on Old Detroit," *Detroit News*, March 20, 1977.

19. Ken Fireman, Luther Jackson, and Dorothy Weddell, "Rencen Sold at Loss to Investor Group," *Detroit Free Press*, April 29, 1982; Bernard J. Frieden and Lynne B. Sagalyn, *Downtown, Inc.: How America Rebuilds Cities* (Cambridge, MA: MIT Press, 1989), 221–222. The Center received a renovation by local architecture firm Smith, Hinchman and Grylls to improve legibility and achieve a more accessible retail mix, as well as providing a front entrance on Jefferson Avenue: Marcia Ming, "Rencen Revival," *Detroit News*, February 7, 1988; Suzanne Stephens, "Project Diary—SOM's Radical Renovation in Detroit, the G.M. Renaissance Center, Raises Hopes for John Portman's Famous Icon of the 1970s," *Architectural Record* 194, no. 2 (2006).

20. Beverly Hall Lawrence, "Retailing Has Shed Its Glitz," April 12, 1987; Patricia Montemurri, "Rencen at 10—All over Downtown, It Has Made Its Mark," *Detroit Free Press*, April 12, 1987.

21. Thomas C. Fox, "Parking Woes Grow Along with Rencen," *Detroit Free Press*, September 25, 1978.

22. "Need for Parking Gobbling Dozens of City's Buildings," *Detroit Free Press*, January 29, 1978.

23. Christopher Willcox and Jeffrey Hadden, "Lack of Parking Bars 'Rebirth' of Detroit," *Detroit News*, May 8, 1977; "Municipal Parking Vital in Struggle for Survival," *Detroit News*, May 14, 1977. The city could not respond to all demands, bound by its decades-old parking ordinance in several ways: Christopher Willcox, "Sell Parking System to Fund Other Projects, Young Asks," *Detroit News*, March 23, 1978.

24. Frieden and Sagalyn, *Downtown, Inc.*, 260–261.

25. The Downtown Development Authority was enabled by a state bill that was strongly supported by the Central Business District Association: Anne Getz, "State Bill Could Pave Way for Downtown Detroit Renewal," *Detroit News*, February 4, 1974; David A. Markiewicz, "$80 Million Ok'd for City Projects," *Detroit News*, August 13, 1986; Downtown Development Authority, "Tax Increment Financing Plan and Development Plan for Development Area Number 1" (Detroit, 1978).

26. TIF financing was not uncontroversial, as opponents (including the cash-strapped Detroit public school system) complained that it provided scarce public funds (or anticipated funds) to wealthy private developers: David A. Markiewicz, "Detroit Pushes Downtown Projects with Public Funds—Controversial TIFs Offer 'Gap Financing,'" *Detroit News*, April 13, 1987.

27. An initial Detroit Economic Growth Council was far less successful, as it duplicated other departmental efforts: William Dunn, "Detroit Effort to Woo New Business Snagged," *Detroit News*, February 27, 1977. Another organization, called the Detroit Economic Development Corporation, was set up in 1977 to attract new businesses with tax abatements and low-interest loans. The corporation played a key role in completing the General Motors' Poletown plant deal: Don Tschirhart, "Agency Promotes Detroit Worldwide," *Detroit News*, August 25, 1983.

28. The DEGC's annual budget of one and a half million dollars and a five-million-dollar line of credit hardly allowed them to become active developers themselves. Jamer A. Schaffer, the organization's director, referred to the Detroit Economic Growth Corporation as "trouble shooters, maybe trouble makers who get into the really tough projects that won't go. We've got our noses in everybody's business": David McNaughton, "In Search of Renaissance Risk

Takers," *Detroit News*, June 23, 1981; Don Tschirhart, "Agency Promotes Detroit Worldwide," *Detroit News*, August 25, 1983.

29. "Woodward Mall Work Start on Monday Will Ban Cars," *Detroit News*, May 6, 1977; Louis Cook, "Downtown Woodward Gets Malled," *Detroit Free Press*, May 11, 1977.

30. The mall was slated to have a roof covering it to emulate a suburban mall; this did not materialize because of the uncertain fate of some of the most prominent buildings lining the avenue that the roof was supposed to attach to. The canopy roof concept was ultimately abandoned in 1979: Joan Walter, "Detroit Pays $1 Million on Dead Project," *Detroit News*, December 19, 1979.

31. David McKeehan, director of the Chamber of Commerce, warned that reopening the avenue is "not a panacea for the problems of downtown and anyone who thinks that is fooling himself": Monroe Walker, "Traffic Back on Woodward Strip?," *Detroit News*, November 18, 1982. The Council still voted for the reopening: "Council Votes 7-1 to Scrap Mall Idea," *Detroit News*, November 19, 1982; "The Woodward Mall," *Detroit News*, November 23, 1982.

32. Pete Waldmeir, "Woodward Renewal Project Turns into a Design for Disaster," *Detroit News*, November 24, 1982.

33. David Kryszak (photographer), "Detroit's 'Other' Plaza," *Detroit News*, July 24, 1980.

34. The former Washington Arcade, later taken up by Himelhoch's department store, was remodeled into low-income senior housing: Bob Luke, "Boulevard Merchants Hope to Remain Viable," *Detroit News*, December 4, 1982; Jack Woerpel, "Himelhoch's Now a New Apartment Home for Elderly," *Detroit News*, June 5, 1983. Together, the renovations of Woodward Avenue and Washington Boulevard cost over $42 million, mostly paid for by federal grants but with DDA support: Waldmeir, "Woodward Renewal Project Turns into a Design for Disaster."

35. Downtown Development Authority, "Tax Increment Financing Plan and Development Plan for Development Area Number 1—Updated to 1992" (Detroit, 1992), 56.

36. Central Business District Association, "Annual Development Report" (Detroit, 1997), 32–33.

37. A 1978 survey indicated that fewer than 10 percent of Oakland County residents commuted into Detroit, and fewer than 3 percent to its downtown: "Survey Sharpens Subway Plan

'War,'" *Detroit News*, May 11, 1978. Another survey corroborates the likelihood of low ridership. In 1980, the number of workers commuting to the city (and mostly its downtown) to work had almost halved since the previous decade. Telephone surveys demonstrated that less than 20 percent of metropolitan residents planned to ride the People Mover: Wilbur C. Rich, *Coleman Young and Detroit Politics: From Social Activist to Power Broker* (Detroit: Wayne State University Press, 1989), 192–201; Louis Mleczko, "Mover Work Set to Start," *Detroit News*, October 30, 1983.

38. The People Mover had become such a headache at the federal level that its name was altered to pass any legislation connected to it: Luther Jackson, "People Mover Is 'a Bad Word' in D.C.," *Detroit News*, July 27, 1981; Louis Mleczko, "Firms Told to Help Pay Mover Tab," *Detroit News*, December 7, 1984; "Chronology—a Summary of Problems That Have Plagued the People Mover," *Detroit News*, July 21, 1994. The federal government briefly left open the possibility of extending the People Mover somewhat to make up for the lost regional subway: Howard Warren, "Reagan Releases Transit Aid—Detroit's People Mover Gets a Lift," *Detroit News*, August 6, 1981; "Panel Turns Down SEMTA Funds," *Detroit News*, May 18, 1984; Louis Mleczko, "Rail Plans Doomed by Mover Cost," *Detroit News*, November 14, 1984.

39. The Reagan administration had lost any hope of a positive outcome, and only with significant lobbying by Detroit Republican aristocrats like Max Fisher was the project even saved: Louis Mieczko, "People Mover Packs 'Em In," *Detroit News*, August 1, 1987. In his autobiography, Young argued that he was able to salvage $120 million for the People Mover from the original $600 million earmarked for a regional transit system in Detroit, and that he'd "save the subway battle for another day": Coleman Young and Lonnie Wheeler, *Hard Stuff: The Autobiography of Coleman Young* (New York: Viking, 1994), 290.

40. R. R. Tadi and U. Dutta, "Detroit Downtown People Mover: Ten Years After," paper delivered at 6th International Conference on Automated People Movers (Las Vegas, 1997).

41. Louis Mieczko, "The People Mover—Downtown Merchants Say It's Nice, but Not Crucial for Them," *Detroit News*, May 27, 1984; Arlena Sawyers, "Business Squeeze—People Mover Site Work Obstructs Retail Traffic," *Detroit News*, January 12, 1984.

42. Don Tschirhart, "Light Rail Asked for Woodward Area," *Detroit News*, April 5, 1984.

43. The downtown population was above 20,000 in 1948, but had dropped to little more than 4,000 in 1979. Source: US Census records.

44. The *Detroit News* editorial board stated that "the single most important element in the rebirth of downtown Detroit is new housing construction in and around the central business district": "Quality Downtown Housing," *Detroit News*, October 28, 1979.

45. This is the closing statement of a *Detroit News* editorial on bringing residents back to downtown Detroit: "The Key to Renaissance," *Detroit News*, September 22, 1978.

46. Christopher Willcox, "Detroit Gets a Downtown Revival Plan," *Detroit News*, February 23, 1978.

47. Thomas C. Fox, "The Hope: 2500 Midtown Apartments—the Reality: A Small, Costly Block," *Detroit Free Press*, October 30, 1977.

48. The grant for the garage covered $5 million of the $28 million project: Joan Walter and Don Tschirhart, "$28-Million High-Rise to Spur Detroit Boom," *Detroit News*, October 5, 1978.

49. "Downtown Outlook—Can the People of the Motor City Learn to Walk Again?," *Detroit News*, July 26, 1990.

50. John Spelich, "Detroit's Leading Citizens Sow Seeds of Redevelopment," *Detroit Free Press*, August 17, 1986; "Downtown 'Sky Mall' Passes Its First Test," *Detroit News*, April 13, 1978.

51. "Downtown Outlook—Can the People of the Motor City Learn to Walk Again?"; Robert E. Roach, "Elevated Walkway Plan Unveiled," *Detroit News*, May 20, 1980; Bruce Alpert, "New Skywalks Are Either Too Hot or Too Cold," *Detroit News*, May 13, 1987.

52. Coleman Young had pressured Taubman to participate in the development, as downtown needed rooftops for commercial success: Young and Wheeler, *Hard Stuff*, 227; Spelich, "Detroit's Leading Citizens Sow Seeds of Redevelopment"; Robert Brenson, "Riverfront: Detroit's Stuck with Mediocrity Once Again," *Detroit News*, November 29, 1983.

53. Dinah Eng, "New Breed of Detroiter Works, Lives Downtown," *Detroit News*, June 2, 1985. At the same time, seeing the first signs of gentrification and racial displacement, Mayor Young attempted to buy up apartments to keep African American Detroiters in desirable downtown

locations. Specifically, he wanted to buy up 1300 Lafayette East to prevent it from turning "lily white": Charlie Cain, "Young Tells Why City Wants 1300 Lafayette," *Detroit News*, May 7, 1980.

54. Charles W. Theisen and Clark Hallas, "Hudson's Plan for Detroit: Mammoth Downtown Mall," *Detroit News*, December 9, 1977; Cook, "Downtown Woodward Gets Malled." The historic Monroe retail block was unfortunately considered a roadblock to progress: Thomas C. Fox, "Old Buildings Imperil City Plans," *Detroit News*, August 15, 1977.

55. In 1979, the Council unanimously adopted a resolution that allowed for the clearing of Hudson's, though People for Downtown Hudson's had petitioned the U.S. Department of the Interior to designate it a historic site. The one caveat: the existing buildings could only be replaced by the Cadillac Center: John Nehman, "Council Puts an 'If' to Hudson Plan," *Detroit News*, December 13, 1979. The lack of an economic perspective led Mayor Young "reluctantly to conclude the numbers just didn't work out" to keep the building: Robert Roach, "Demolish Downtown Hudson's: Mayor," *Detroit News*, December 19, 1979. A historian and President of Wayne State University called the building "of very little [historic] value" in the subsequent federal hearing on the demolition. In return for creating a plan for preserving other downtown buildings, the federal government agreed on the demolition: Robert E. Roach, "U.S. Clears Way to Raze Hudson's," *Detroit News*, December 20, 1979.

56. Charles W. Theisen, "Hudson Drops a Hint on Mall for Downtown," *Detroit News*, December 8, 1977.

57. Martha Hindes, "Downtown 'Dream' Is Not Shared by All Merchants," *Detroit News*, May 11, 1980. The DDA had actually set up a loan fund to help small retailers who would be adversely affected by the mall: Stephen Cain, "Loan Fund Aims to Aid Merchants," *Detroit News*, October 16, 1979.

58. Although several retail chains initially mentioned that they were in negotiations, they ultimately didn't warm to the idea of opening a business in an area with declining income density and high crime rates: Alex Taylor, "Downtown Project Lacks Commitment of Store Chains," *Detroit Free Press*, March 10, 1979; Stephen Cain, "Penney, Sears Join Hudson in Downtown Mall," *Detroit News*, September 23, 1978; Thomas C. Fox, "City Could Purchase Hudson's Downtown," *Detroit Free Press*, January 18, 1978.

59. "Hudson's Gives City Ultimatum," *Detroit News*, July 11, 1978; "Hudson to Stay If Mall Is Built," *Detroit News*, July 12, 1978. The project suffered from a bureaucratic stalemate—millions of Urban Development Action Grant dollars were contingent on finding anchor stores to make the project viable, whereas anchor stores waited until federal money was forthcoming. Hudson's couldn't offer much of its own money as its first mall projects were also starting to lose money: Robert E. Roach, "Kern Block Project Shelved," *Detroit News*, September 14, 1982; Ken Fireman, "Kern Block Mall Plan Dead," *Detroit Free Press*, May 7, 1980; Robert E. Roach, "Pinch Puts Mall Plans under Cloud," *Detroit News*, October 2, 1980.

60. Betsey Hansell and Rick Ratliff, "Detroit's Downtown Dilemma—Who Is in Charge? Where Is It Going?," *Detroit Free Press*, December 11, 1983; Robert E. Roach, "Monroe Block 'Blight' Assailed," *Detroit News*, July 14, 1981; "The Monroe Block," *Detroit News*, May 29, 1983; Bruce Alpert, "7 Plans for Monroe Block Rejected—1 Gets Reprieve," *Detroit News*, December 12, 1984; Chauncey Bailey, "Razing of Monroe Block Opposed," *Detroit News*, September 13, 1988; "Preserving Old Detroit," *Detroit News*, September 14, 1988; "Requiem for a Landmark," *Detroit News*, May 26, 1988.

61. Young and Wheeler, *Hard Stuff*, 233; "The Recession in Detroit," *Detroit News*, April 20, 1980.

62. Federal funding for urban revitalization dropped from $50 million in 1980–1981 to $33 million in 1991–1992: John McCarthy, "Entertainment-Led Regeneration: The Case of Detroit," *Cities* 19, no. 2 (2002).

63. Though the Joe Louis Arena hosted the 1980 Republican National Convention at which Ronald Reagan was nominated, his subsequent election prompted significant cuts in federal aid for the city, causing a slowdown in downtown development. Under the Reagan administration, Urban Development Action Grant funding and Historic Preservation Tax Credits were cut significantly: John E. Peterson, "Tax Credit Loss May Doom Detroit Restoration Projects," *Detroit News*, June 22, 1985. Mayor Young commented: "To this day, it sticks in my craw that Ronald Reagan was nominated in the damn building that I put myself on the line for": Young and Wheeler, *Hard Stuff*, 255–257.

64. Jerry Herron, "The Forgetting Machine: Notes toward a History of Detroit," *Places* (2012); Pitrone, *Hudson's*, 178–179. Downtown sales had dropped 85 percent between 1953 and 1982:

Bob Luke, "Hudson Gives up Downtown," *Detroit News*, July 14, 1982. The building kept five floors as staff offices for a few years, and kept four window displays open as a promise to Mayor Young: Pitrone, *Hudson's*, 186.

65. August Gribbin, Chester Bulgier, and Rebecca Powers, "Hudson's Downtown Store Closes," *Detroit News*, January 18, 1983; Don Tschirhart, "More Stores Follow Hudson's Closing," *Detroit News*, May 1, 1983.

66. June Manning Thomas, *Redevelopment and Race: Planning a Finer City in Postwar Detroit* (Baltimore: Johns Hopkins University Press, 1997), 187.

67. The master plan was supposed to be finished a year after the 1974 charter change. Don Tschirhart, "Downtown 'Blueprint' Unveiled," *Detroit News*, December 15, 1983; Rick Ratliff, "Without Wide Support, Plan Only Blueprint of a Dream," *Detroit Free Press*, June 22, 1985; Monroe Walker, "Council Threatens 'Master Plan' Funds," *Detroit News*, October 1, 1982; Thomas J. Bray, "Coleman's Orphan: 'The 'Master Plan,'" *Detroit News*, July 28, 1985. The staff of the Planning Department was cut in half in 1984 due to Detroit's ongoing fiscal crisis, but also as a result of criticism that the department duplicated and interfered with the work of the Community and Economic Development Department: Arlena Sawyers, "City Will Drop 25 Planners—Half the Staff," *Detroit News*, June 19, 1984.

68. Thomas, *Redevelopment and Race*, 189–193.

69. Christopher Willcox, "Millions to Save Downtown OK'd," *Detroit News*, May 18, 1978; "Compromise Site for New County Jail," *Detroit Monitor*, February 15, 1978; Raymond Curtis Miller, *The Force of Energy: A Business History of the Detroit Edison Company* ([East Lansing]: Michigan State University Press, 1971); Joel J. Smith, "Stroh Project Work to Start Next Spring," *Detroit News*, November 2, 1985.

70. Chauncey Bailey, "Preserving History," *Detroit News*, February 10, 1983; Don Tschirhart, "Corktown's Historical District Plan Is Approved," *Detroit News*, December 13, 1984. When one of the grandest mansions of Brush Park, the Ransom Gillis house, was offered for sale by the city for only $1,000 in 1983, no one bought it. This may have also been due to the arduous process of obtaining the proper title for the house: Chauncey Bailey, "John R. Street Offers a Long View of 'Progress,'" *Detroit News*, September 2, 1984.

71. Ric Bohy, "Survivors—Cass Corridor Residents Eke Out a Life," *Detroit News*, December 23, 1984. Cass Park suffered from the presence of the nearby Brewster-Douglass projects, where over 1,000 arrests had been made in 1980 alone—more than the number of residents of the district: David Grant, "Drug Pushers Rule a Street of Fear—Tough Section Frustrates Police, Terrifies Residents," *Detroit News*, September 18, 1980. A proposal by a local nonprofit to redevelop the area just north of Cass Park for medical staff and students went unheeded due to concerns about gentrification and a lack of funding—the restoration of Midtown Detroit was still a distant dream: Arlena Sawyers, "Cass Corridor Renewal Plan Offered," *Detroit News*, June 9, 1984.

72. James Tittsworth, "Seedy Woodward Fighting for Comeback," *Detroit News*, January 30, 1978; Fox, "Parking Woes Grow Along with Rencen"; "Need for Parking Gobbling Dozens of City's Buildings."

73. George Cantor, "Grand River Makes It Hard to Praise Detroit," *Detroit News*, December 9, 1984; "Council Approves Beautification Plan," *Detroit News*, May 11, 1985.

74. The first attempt to renovate the area north of downtown came from the Grand Circus Park Development Association, with a self-funded master plan and a concrete proposal for townhouses: Denise Crittendon, "The 'Downtown' Detroit Forgot," *Detroit News*, August 29, 1980. Subsequently, Robert K. Werbe invested $2 million in the Fox to return it to its first-run movie glory days. This wasn't nearly enough to spruce up the massive building: "Grand Circus Park Area Revitalization Plan Announced," *Detroit Monitor*, November 8, 1979; Rick Ratliff, "An Old Area, a New Dream," *Detroit Free Press*, April 12, 1984; "Reviving the Fox," *Detroit News*, June 30, 1981.

75. Ric Bohy, "Downtown Detroit Life a Big Lure," *Detroit News*, December 23, 1984. Forbes knew that while he had invested $5 million of his own money, he needed far more to finalize his vision and that success wasn't guaranteed, calling his District proposal "a gamble." Forbes hired renovation expert Ray Shepardson, who had helped renovate Cleveland's theater district and the Fox's counterpart in St. Louis; he noticed the opportunity of attracting an African American middle-class audience to the venues. Ultimately, Forbes and Shepardson's plans failed to find significant funding, including a failed bid for an Urban Development Action

Grant: David A. Markiewicz, "Rebirth Hoped for Detroit's Theater District," *Detroit News*, June 16, 1985.

76. The president of Detroit Renaissance praised Forbes for his "one-man urban development program": Bernie Shellum, "Out-Foxed—Theater Is Sold, but Developer Still Has Big Plans," *Detroit News*, August 24, 1987.

77. David A. Markiewicz, "Detroit Pushes Downtown Projects with Public Funds—Controversial TIFs Offer 'Gap Financing,'" *Detroit News*, April 13, 1987. Interestingly, Forbes's theater renovation expert Shepardson stayed on the team with Ilitch: Bill McGraw, "Fox Captures Little Caesars—Pizza Chain Owner to Renovate Theater for Live Entertainment," *Detroit Free Press*, July 8, 1987. The view of downtown as virgin territory was aptly put by Saint Andrew's Hall owner Vince Bannon: "It's almost a pioneer kind of thing, like this is the new frontier": Jim McFarlin, "Downtown Rebound," *Detroit News*, February 14, 1986.

78. Uniquely for its time, the club and its contemporaries focused on mixing African American and white and straight and gay audiences. While only short-lived, the Institute set the bar for future downtown clubs: Ray Philp, "Nightclubbing: The Music Institute," http://daily. redbullmusicacademy.com/2017/05/music-institute-nightclubbing; Bill Brewster and Frank Broughton, *The Record Players: DJ Revolutionaries* (London: Virgin, 2012), 315–316.

79. Carleton S. Gholz, "'Where the Mix Is Perfect'—Voices from the Post-Motown Soundscape" (PhD diss., University of Pittsburgh, 2011); personal interview with Keith Harder Cavazos, March 17, 2018.

80. Barbara Hoover, "To Market, to Market—on Tuesday?," *Detroit News*, August 23, 1982. The market's success prompted the construction of the Eastern Market Plaza, a two-story indoor retail building, which unfortunately is mostly closed off toward the street: Molly Brauer, "Eastern Market Plaza—Detroiters to Build Retail Center," *Detroit News*, January 29, 1984.

81. "Trappers Alley Investors Sign," *Detroit News*, December 15, 1983. The mall was five stories tall, with 145,000 square feet of space for 70 upscale stores, constructed in five renovated buildings that date from 1853 to 1910. Ultimately, $7 million of the $20 million project cost came from state and federal funding sources: Trappers Alley, "History of Trappers Alley" (Detroit, 1994); George Bullard, "Trappers Alley Bowing in—Friday Opening Set for 'Festival'

Mall," *Detroit News*, May 5, 1985. Expansions included renovated buildings south and west of the original mall: David A. Markiewicz, "Expansion Planned for Trappers," *Detroit News*, October 30, 1985. As with other downtown developments, tensions often arose with inner-city youth, leading to frequent arrests while still scaring away suburbanites: "Youths Kept in Check in Greektown," *Detroit News*, May 4, 1986.

82. *Detroit News* columnist George Cantor praised the one-block stretch of Monroe Avenue in Greektown as "the most vibrant area of downtown," demonstrating that "once there are people on the street, anything can happen": George Cantor, "Let's Take a Lesson from Greektown to Help Rejuvenate City," *Detroit News*, February 17, 1983; Arlena Sawyers, "Trappers Tax Tied to Book Hotel," *Detroit News*, November 16, 1984. Bricktown was started by a local merchant and revolved around ten bistros in a three-block area between Greektown and the Renaissance Center. In the Broadway area, initiatives and ownership were more scattered, as landlords sat on their properties waiting for their value to appreciate with minimal investment: John Spelich, "Downtown's Future Bright, Merchant Feels," *Detroit News*, February 8, 1985; Molly Abraham, "A Vintage Area Blooms with Bistros," *Detroit News*, August 15, 1980; "Historic District Lives On," *Detroit News*, February 1, 1983; David A. Markiewicz, "Developers Renew Broadway-Randolph District," *Detroit News*, February 6, 1986. "Funds Asked for Complex," *Detroit News*, June 7, 1985.

83. The statement was made in the context of a *Detroit News* editorial, complaining that the city ordinance mandated minimum parking maintenance standards but they weren't enforced: "City Sores," *Detroit News*, September 11, 1978.

84. The Lodge Freeway even saw a decline of more than two-thirds of its traffic since the early 1970s. The drop can partially be accounted for by the opening of other freeways, but the local traffic authorities expected daily traffic on the Lodge to drop even further over the next decades: Louis Mieczko, "Lodge Reflects Metro Shift," *Detroit News*, April 19, 1987.

85. Constance Prater, "Some Big Moments; Some Bad Moments," *Detroit News*, January 5, 1989.

86. A column in the *Detroit News* by George Cantor argued that Detroit's downtown projects paled in comparison with Chicago's, arguing that Chicagoans would have never accepted buildings like the Millender Center and calling the Joe Louis Arena "the single ugliest structure

to go into any downtown in the last decade" and the nearby Riverfront Apartments "unforgivably bland": George Cantor, "New Downtown Buildings Are Not a Sight to Behold," *Detroit News*, October 31, 1985.

87. In an interview after his retirement, Young argues that Detroit's continuing economic headwinds, changing business leadership, and—in his opinion unjustified—attacks on his dealings had broken the alliances he had built his popularity on. The numerous federal investigations into the dealings of Young and his associates certainly did not help to forge new alliances: Jon Pepper, "Contrary to Popular Beliefs, Business and Mayor Coleman Young Did Get Along," *Detroit Free Press*, September 29, 1996.

88. John McCarthy, "Revitalization of the Core City: The Case of Detroit," *Cities* 14, no. 1 (1997): 4–5.

89. Half of the opinion poll respondents expected a further deterioration of the city's neighborhoods, and over half expected a further exodus of the middle class: Judy Diebolt, "Most Plan to Move Out of City," *Detroit News*, November 9, 1987.

90. Project Detroit Strategic Planning, *Report of the Detroit Strategic Planning Project, November 1987: Choosing a Future for Us and for All Our Children* ([Detroit]: Project Detroit Strategic Planning, 1987); Chauncey Bailey and N. Scott Vance, "The Plan," *Detroit News*, November 15, 1987; "Strategic Plan Highlights," *Detroit Free Press*, November 13, 1987; Patricia Chargot, "Study Finds Detroit Is Worst Hit of 10 Big Cities," *Detroit Free Press*; Mark E. Neithercut et al., "Detroit Twenty Years After: A Statistical Profile of the Detroit Area since 1967" (Michigan Metropolitan Information Center, Wayne State University Center for Urban Studies, 1987).

91. Oliver Joy, "Robocop Creator: Detroit Shows the Film's Fictional Future Is upon Us," *CNN*, July 25, 2013.

92. Betsey Hansell and Rick Ratliff, "A History of Sprawl, an Eclipsed Downtown," *Detroit Free Press*, December 11, 1983. Two years later, Gilb resigned in frustration from her position as planning director to return to Wayne State University and teach: Bruce Alpert, "Detroit's Planner Quits for WSU Job," *Detroit News*, July 22, 1985.

93. "Socializing the 'Pontch,'" *Detroit News*, April 26, 1987.

94. Robert H. Giles, "Detroit: A 20-Year Search for Renaissance," *Detroit News*, June 28, 1987.

CHAPTER 11: THE LEISURE CITY: 1988–2001

1. Ze'ev Chafets, "The Tragedy of Detroit," *New York Times*, July 29, 1990.

2. In one account, a restaurant owner indicates he waits for bad weather so loitering gangs will go away. The police department suggested that merchants accommodate gang members and "set up places to make money off them in a way where they would not harass other patrons": "Take Back the Streets," *Detroit News*, September 4, 1991.

3. David Barkholz, "Downtown Lost 18,500 Jobs in '80s: SEMCOG," *Crain's Detroit Business*, July 23, 1990.

4. "Empty Hulks Scar Detroit," *Crain's Detroit Business*, May 21–27, 1990; "Our Empty Downtown," *Detroit News*, May 27, 1990. The downtown hotel market in particular had deteriorated due to a lack of demand and the construction of newer hotels on the riverfront, leaving older hotels like the Tuller, Statler, Book-Cadillac, and Fort Shelby empty, fighting for their lives through a flurry of rotating owners and failed development dreams. The drastic cuts in historic preservation tax credits had only made the situation worse: David A. Markiewicz, "Vacant Hotels Still Haunt Downtown Detroit," *Detroit News*, August 14, 1988; "A Scramble for Tenants—Downtown Firms Play 'Musical Buildings,'" *Detroit News*, March 6, 1989.

5. Camilo Jose Vergara, "Detroit Waits for the Millennium," *Nation* 18 (1992).

6. More detailed proposals included People Mover spurs to Detroit Edison's office buildings, the aim to "re-establish Woodward Avenue as a major shopping street in the city," the persistent "no. 1 priority" of a Woodward rail line to the suburbs, and an electric cable car to Windsor: City of Detroit, "Master Plan of Policies" (Detroit, 1992). Drafts of the plan were derided by the *Detroit News* as creating a "romantic and total showpiece environment … [which] smacks of the grandiose": "Strategic Dream vs. Reality," *Detroit News*, April 11, 1990; Pete Waldmeir, "'Master Plan' Is All Mouse, with No Roar," *Detroit News*, April 19, 1990. Perhaps most importantly, Coleman Young paid little attention to the plan, and his successor Dennis Archer disregarded it altogether: "Growth First, Planning Later," *Detroit News*, February 18, 1994.

7. "Downtown Outlook—Can the People of the Motor City Learn to Walk Again?," *Detroit News*, July 26, 1990.

8. In 1992, for every 50-cent fare the city spent $3.44 in subsidies: "People Mover, Once Detroit's Symbol of Hope, Has Become a Symbol of Waste," *Detroit News*, July 22, 1994. Two years after opening, ridership was a third lower than the already decreased 1987 estimate, and only 14 percent of the original estimate—a nationwide issue: "The People Mover Deficit," *Detroit News*, May 12, 1989; Dan Gillmor, "Transit Errors Were Predicted—Study: Mover's Cost, Rider Estimates Were Off Base," *Detroit News*, January 18, 1990. *Detroit News* columnist and longtime People Mover opponent Pete Waldmeir likened the loop to an amusement ride: Pete Waldmeir, "The People Mover Isn't Crucial for City's Mass Transit. But at 50 Cents a Trip, It Beats Amusement Parks," *Detroit News*, October 19, 1990. Young continued his quest for regional rail in the 1990s, to no avail: Louis Mleczko, "Young's Priority: Woodward Rail Line to Suburbs," *Detroit News*, April 6, 1990. Young was able to keep the Mover running: Avram Goldstein, Diane Weiss, and David Pierce, "The Shape of the City," *Detroit News*, July 26, 1990; Jon Peter, "Mover Needs Money Fast, Official Says," *Detroit Free Press*, November 17, 1992; "Decision OKs $4.2 Million to Support People Mover," *Detroit Free Press*, November 19, 1992. The next year, City Council approved a $2.5 million 50/50 match with federal funding to study a People Mover extension to Midtown: "Study Funds OK'd for People Mover," *Detroit Free Press*, January 15, 1993. By the end of the 1990s, fewer than 1,000 people a day rode its loop: Mark Puls, "People Mover Campaigns for More Riders," *Detroit News*, June 16, 1999.

9. Denise L. Smith, "Surviving Downtown," *Detroit News*, July 10, 1989. A 1993 retrospective on the tenure of Coleman Young had calculated that he was responsible for $13 billion of new development, the vast majority of which had taken place downtown. The head of the Downtown Development Authority rhetorically asked: "what would the city look like without the $13 billion that has occurred and without Coleman Young as mayor during this time?": John Gallagher, "His Efforts to Rebuild City Brought Mixed Results," *Detroit Free Press*, June 23, 1993.

10. For example, the *City Journal* praised Detroit's comeback in 1995, citing the return of several larger corporations and a general upswing in the investment climate with Coleman Young's "antagonistic and self-destructive politics gone from City Hall": "Motor City Racing toward a Comeback, Journal Says—Magazine Cites the New Political and Economic Climate under Archer as the Keys to Resurgence," *Detroit News*, July 9, 1995. A new Planning and Development Department was created by the merger of the Planning Department and

Community and Economic Development departments. By 1996, planning staff had increased almost tenfold since 1984, although the economic upswing caused a surge in workload as well: R. J. King, "Detroit's Planning Department Losing Chief," *Detroit News*, August 15, 1997.

11. "Rebuilding Detroit: Projects, Large and Small, Add to $5.5 Billion," *Detroit News*, April 13, 1997.

12. Sociologist Hannigan notes that in 1994 alone, $13 billion in entertainment projects were in the pipeline, many of which were located downtown: John Hannigan, *Fantasy City: Pleasure and Profit in the Postmodern Metropolis* (London: Routledge, 2010), 60.

13. Personal interview with Mark Nickita and Dorian Moore, April 2016.

14. Asked about the forced sale to Ilitch, Forbes sighed: "you can't fight city hall." Allegedly, the city threatened to use its power to declare his holdings condemned if he wouldn't agree to sell them to the city, which would then sell them to Ilitch at a vast discount. Ilitch had purchased the Red Wings team in 1982 and was on good terms with Coleman Young—including a campaign donation after the deal was done: David A. Markiewicz and Bruce Alpert, "Little Caesars' Ilitch to Buy the Fox Theatre," *Detroit News*, July 8, 1987; Bernie Shellum, "Out-Foxed—Theater Is Sold, but Developer Still Has Big Plans," *Detroit News*, August 24, 1987. This paragraph was also informed by an interview with Mark Nickita and Dorian Moore of Archive/DS Architects in April 2016. Young's desperation to keep corporations in Detroit was also reflected in his offer for Comerica Bank to take the prime riverfront site of the Ford Auditorium when they threatened to leave the city: Vivian S. Toy and Liz Twardon, "Bank Headquarters: A Beauty of a Beast?," *Detroit News*, October 5, 1990.

15. Bruce Alpert, "Ilitch Plans Parking, Restaurants near Fox—Security Is Priority of Theater Project," *Detroit News*, July 9, 1987. Ilitch also renovated some residential buildings, and Forbes continued to expand his holdings: David A. Markiewicz, "Ilitch Plans to Restore Buildings," *Detroit News*, December 17, 1988; Susan Whitall, "The Fox Flocks—Theater District Born Again Is Investors' Dream Come True," *Detroit News*, October 22, 1989.

16. David A. Markiewicz and N. Scott Vance, "Fox Deal Worth Cost, Moten Says," *Detroit News*, July 20, 1987; George Cantor, "Downtown Glitters—but Neighborhoods Die," *Detroit News*, December 18, 1988.

17. Robert Ourlian, "Emerging Theater District Wants Tigers to Join the Act," *Detroit News*, October 1, 1991; David A. Markiewicz and David Sedgwick, "Ilitch Plans Mall near Fox Theatre," *Detroit News*, February 23, 1988. Interestingly, Ilitch and Forbes had one ally in common: the highly energetic theater planner Ray Shepardson, who was a driving force behind the renovation of almost all the theaters in the district. His formula was to offer constant, low-priced entertainment to maintain a steady flow of patrons from all classes and races, who could benefit restaurant and retail business as well: Jon Pepper, "'Lunatic' Has the Energy and Ideas to Finish Revitalization of the Theater District," *Detroit Free Press*, February 16, 1992.

18. Before the Ilitch purchase, the Tigers had indicated they wanted to move out of their Corktown locale, but were unsure of where to go. The city had already pushed for a downtown location but failed to convince the team's owner, Tom Monaghan of Domino's Pizza—even though the state had agreed to put a special downtown stadium tax on the ballot: Ourlian, "Emerging Theater District Wants Tigers to Join the Act"; Vivian S. Toy and Valarie Basheda, "Tigers Consider 4 Stadium Sites, None Downtown," *Detroit Free Press*, December 12, 1991; Mitch Albom, "White Knight Gives Tigers a Ray of Hope," *Detroit Free Press*, August 27, 1992. Ilitch was of course considerably more enthusiastic about the stadium's move to Foxtown: Bill McGraw, "Ilitch's Dreams Focus on the Fox—He Hints of Wings, Tigers near Theater," *Detroit Free Press*, August 27, 1992.

19. With the 1982 purchase of the Red Wings franchise, Ilitch had also gained significant control over the Joe Louis Arena and nearby Cobo Hall and Cobo Arena as their main leasing tenant: "Joe Louis Plan Piques Interest, but Paying for It Is Big Question," *Detroit Free Press*, September 21, 1992.

20. Ilitch's grandiose 1994 vision relied on $200 million of state support. The first phase would just contain the stadium and parking: Tina Lam and Jeanne May, "The Ilitch Vision," *Detroit Free Press*, March 24, 1994; Vivian S. Toy, "Ilitch Envisions a Detroit Rebirth," *Detroit News*, March 24, 1994; Ruby L. Bailey, "Design Firm Has Visions of Revitalizing Woodward Avenue— New Tiger Stadium Will Be a Spring Board for Development," *Detroit News*, September 8, 1994; R. J. King, "Stadium Adds Momentum to Grand Circus Park Projects," *Detroit News*, November 1, 1995; Pete Waldmeir, "Spooky Fiscal Magicians Turn Tax Trick into Stadium

Treat," *Detroit News*, October 29, 1995; Tina Lam, "A New Baseball Stadium? Detroit Voters Say … Build It," *Detroit Free Press*, March 20, 1996.

21. The Lions' stadium would be partly financed with a special tax on rental cars and hotels. A shared stadium for both teams was also briefly considered: Tina Lam and Daniel G. Fricker, "Stadium Plans Heat Up after Final Court OK—Downtown Site Could Shift; Lions Tax Sought," *Detroit News*, August 15, 1996; Pete Waldmeir, "Proposition S Aside, Lions Stadium in Downtown Detroit Is a Sure Thing," *Detroit Free Press*, October 20, 1996; Tina Lam, "Plan Would Link Lions, Tigers—All Sides Take Hard Look at Downtown Project," *Detroit Free Press*, August 16, 1996.

22. The city had learned to set up a special authority to purchase land from the arduous purchase of land to build General Motors' Poletown plant in Detroit. Signs of similar issues with holdouts and speculators quickly emerged when the stadium plans were published: Dan Holly and Zachare Ball, "Buying Land Could Pose Problems," *Detroit Free Press*, March 24, 1994. Many building owners who lived in the path of the stadium agreed to leave: Heidi Mae Bratt, "Merchants Say They'll Move if It Helps Revive Downtown—Waiting Game: Most Businesses in Project Area Claim to Be Behind Stadium Development Plan," *Detroit News*, March 24, 1994.

23. Forbes lobbied intensively to maintain his remaining downtown holdings, and earlier stadium plans avoided their locations: Cheri Y. Gay, *Lost Detroit* (London: Pavilion Books, 2013), 130; Michael Hauser and Marianne Weldon, *Detroit's Downtown Movie Palaces* (Charleston, SC: Arcadia, 2006); R. J. King, "Stadium Plan Could Spare Gem, Elwood Grill," *Detroit News*, January 8, 1997; Mark Puls, "Gem Theatre Move Begins: Mammoth Downtown Relocation Project Gets under Way," *Detroit News*, September 12, 1997.

24. Mark Puls, "Community Hits Homer in Tigers' Lease Deal—Expert: City, County Benefit as Team Puts up a Lot of Private Money," *Detroit News*, January 24, 1997.

25. Mark Puls and Shawn D. Lewis, "Reinventing Downtown—Again: New Tiger Stadium—the Architects Went Back to the Drawing Board and Say Fans Will Be Pleased with the Results," *Detroit News*, February 18, 1998. Over 50 percent of respondents had "no feeling" about the Joe Louis Arena's exterior appearance in a 1982 *Detroit News* poll: Gerry Storch, "There, Doesn't This Look Better?," *Detroit News*, May 21, 1982.

26. Patricia Montemurri, "Ilitch Chips in $35 Million as Stadium Loan Deal Closes," *Detroit Free Press*, August 26, 1998; R. J. King, "Lions Are Fired Up over Role in Rebuilding City's Hub, Image," *Detroit News*, November 17, 1999.

27. Matt Fiorito, "Levy Vows Variety, Quality at All Levels," *Detroit Free Press*, August 11, 2002; Mark Puls, "Detroit Lions Try to Snare Old Hudson's Warehouse—Proximity to Stadium Makes It Valuable, but Team Has No Firm Plans," *Detroit News*, January 24, 1997.

28. Curt Guyette, "Render unto Caesar," *Metro Times*, April 23, 1997.

29. The land west of Woodward Avenue continued to be a focal point for a Red Wings stadium but suffered from its proximity to multiple casinos, which Mayor Archer wanted to shield from sports activities: King, "Stadium Plan Could Spare Gem, Elwood Grill." Under the stadium agreement signed for the Tigers and Lions stadiums, any land that had already been condemned for any of the stadium options would still be handed over to Ilitch: Puls, "Community Hits Homer in Tigers' Lease Deal." The stadium authority ultimately bought up the western land to turn it into stadium parking, which prompted a massive spike in land speculation, as well as protest from landowners. Ilitch had an option to buy the land after nine years, which he ultimately did for many parcels: "Land near Stadiums Explodes in Value: Formerly $220,000 an Acre, It Now Goes for Three Times That," *Detroit News*, August 8, 1997.

30. "What a View! Tigers Offer First Glimpse inside Park," *Detroit News*, March 19, 1999; Guyette, "Render unto Caesar."

31. Young had attempted to legalize gambling during his first budget crisis in the 1970s. He attempted a few more times before he decided "to hell with it. The opposition was so damn righteous that I was punishing myself": Coleman Young and Lonnie Wheeler, *Hard Stuff: The Autobiography of Coleman Young* (New York: Viking, 1994), 217, 313; David Silverman, "Casino Ban Cleared by Attorneys," *Detroit News*, July 8, 1987. Casino gambling was defeated in ballots in 1976, 1981 and 1988: Jon Pepper, "All Bets Are on Again: Indian Casino Proposed for Greektown," *Detroit News and Free Press*, November 29, 1992; N. Scott Vance and David A. Markiewicz, "Blighted Woodward Area Called Best Bet for Casinos," *Detroit News*, April 12, 1988. Since 1992, Native American tribes had proposed a casino to be constructed in Greektown in 1992, but faced resistance from the governor: Heidi Mac Bratt and Melinda Wilson,

"Engler Won't Rush Casino Decision," *Detroit News*, August 19, 1994; Pepper, "All Bets Are on Again"; Vivian S. Toy, "Reject Indian Casino, Engler Tells Feds," *Detroit News*, April 7, 1993.

32. John McCarthy, "Entertainment-Led Regeneration: The Case of Detroit," *Cities* 19, no. 2 (2002). In the end, two local groups were chosen for the Greektown and Motor City casinos, and the Las Vegas-based MGM casino was selected as it offered the city several incentives for local investment: Melinda Wilson, "It's Greektown, Atwater, MGM: Mirage Is the Loser as Archer Sticks with Local Groups," *Detroit News*, November 21, 1997; Suzette Hackney, "Political Fallout: Archer, Council Avoid Showdown," *Detroit News*, November 21, 1997.

33. Tina Lam, "Archer Wants Casinos Off River—He Lays out Site Process," *Detroit Free Press*, November 8, 1996; "Detroit: New Casinos Will Be Limited to Downtown," *Detroit News*, February 14, 1997; Judy DeHaven, "New Casino Location: Urban Experts Fear That Mayor Archer's Flip-Flop May Hinder Downtown Detroit Development—Shift Leaves Land West of Woodward Stagnant," *Detroit News*, February 18, 1998; Tina Lam, "Archer Rerolls Dice on Casinos—Greektown Restored as Site Despite Panel," *Detroit News*, June 17, 1997; Bill McGraw, "7 Remain on List of Casino Bidders," *Detroit News*, August 23, 1997.

34. The area east of the Renaissance Center had become known as the Warehouse District, including a growing array of entertainment venues that were popular in Detroit's gay scene: Marlon M. Bailey, *Butch Queens up in Pumps: Gender, Performance, and Ballroom Culture in Detroit* (Ann Arbor: University of Michigan Press, 2013), 1; Bill McGraw and Darci McConnell, "Archer Takes Gamble on Riverfront Casinos," *Detroit News*, February 17, 1998; "On the Waterfront," *Detroit News*, February 18, 1998; Cliff Russell, "Winners and Losers Emerge before Casinos," *Detroit News*, March 30, 1998. The Council-led City Planning Commission strongly criticized Archer's change of plans, which reversed years of planning work for other downtown sites. General Motors was also not pleased, as it had its own plans for revitalizing the riverfront site. Bill McGraw and Darci McConnell, "Archer's Casino Plan Criticized by Commission," *Detroit News*, March 12, 1998. *Detroit News* journalist Jon Pepper speculated that the riverfront move showed Detroit's weak negotiating position with the casino owners, who had preferred a riverfront location from the onset: Jon Pepper, "Archer Casino Picks Put More of Detroit Dreams on Hold Again," *Detroit News*, February 22, 1998; Tricia Serju, "East Side Resurgence—Businesses Sprout on E. Jefferson," *Detroit News*, October 6, 1994; Suzette

Hackney, "Revised Renaissance: Move to East Reshapes Riverfront: Plans for Gardens, Bustling Clubs on Hold," *Detroit News*, February 18, 1998; Judy DeHaven, "Archer Mends Fences: He Appeals to Rivertown Property Owners, Residents to Support City's Casino Plans," *Detroit News*, July 17, 1998.

35. City Planning Commission, "1996–1998 Biennial Report" (Detroit, 1998).

36. The decision of Marian Ilitch to enter the casino business was prompted by plans for a sports arena and theater in Windsor, which could compete with her husband's holdings. Mr. Ilitch was not legally allowed to own a casino, as he owned two sports teams. Tina Lam, "Gamblers Are Lining Up at Motorcity—High Hopes Surround Opening of the Second Casino in Detroit," *Detroit Free Press*, December 15, 1999; Jon Pepper, "Marian Ilitch Joins Casino Group Seeking Gaming License," *Detroit News*, May 28, 1997.

37. Tina Lam, "Greektown Aglow for Opening—3,000 on Hand as 3rd Detroit Casino Finally Springs to Life," *Detroit Free Press*, November 11, 2000; Melinda Wilson, "Trappers: A Rough Go for Retailers," *Crain's Detroit Business*, February 19, 1990; Matt Roush, "Trappers Alley Advice: Consider It for Offices," *Crain's Detroit Business*, September 11, 1995; Julie Hinds, "Well-Dressed Secret—an Elegant, Upscale Design Center Tries to Make a Go of It in Downtown Detroit," *Detroit News*, December 8, 1994.

38. In the end, the city was only able to secure riverfront land for two casinos. In a bid to save face, Archer briefly wanted only the MGM Grand to stay on the riverfront, but it too was ultimately located inland: Mark Puls, "Archer May Fold on Riverfront Casinos," *Detroit News*, February 2, 2001; Bill Johnson, "Here's Story Behind Detroit's Riverfront Casino Switch," *Detroit News*, April 6, 2001.

39. "Detroit Should Salvage What It Can from Flawed Casino Plan," *Detroit News*, August 9, 2001; Darren A. Nichols, "Casinos' Fate up to Next Mayor—Riverfront Gambling Proposal Likely to Die with Archer's Outgoing Administration," *Detroit News*, July 6, 2001.

40. Stephen Henderson, "On Gambling, Detroit Is Rolling Snake Eyes," *Detroit Free Press*, May 13, 2012; Phil Linsalata, "Casinos' Impact: Some Restaurateurs Are Worried About Freebies for Gamblers," *Detroit News*, March 12, 1997; Mark Puls, "In Greektown: Long Struggle Finally Pays Off," *Detroit News*, November 21, 1997.

41. The latter two survived due to a lack of funding for demolition or redevelopment on their sites: Vivian S. Toy and Heidi Mae Bratt, "Detroit's Historic Book-Cadillac Faces Demolition," *Detroit News*, May 21, 1993.

42. A 1993 survey found 92 vacant buildings of the roughly 500 in the central business district: John E. Mogk and Central Business District Association, "Revitalizing Detroit's Central Business District: A Report and Five Year Strategic Plan to Eliminate Vacant and Deteriorated Commercial Building Conditions" (Detroit, 1993). A 1994 *News* article mentioned that downtown Detroit had 16 "operating office buildings" with an occupancy rate of 79.61 percent. This does not include completely vacant buildings: Tricia Serju, "Times Get Tough for Old Detroit Buildings," *Detroit News*, May 26, 1994. Interestingly, conversion of office stock to apartments was not commonly accepted in the mid-1990s: Rick Hampson, "Old Skyscrapers Endangered," *Detroit News*, October 24, 1995; R. J. King, "Stadium Adds Momentum to Grand Circus Park Projects," *Detroit News*, November 1, 1995; Madison J. Gray, "Restoring the Glory—Finding Old-World Materials, Skills a Challenge for Repairs," *Detroit News*, November 10, 1999.

43. With Detroit's economic uptick and the increasing complexity of federal programs to administer, the growing Planning and Development Department soon became understaffed: R. J. King and Daniel Howes, "The 1997 Mackinac Conference: City Developers Urge Bureaucratic Reform: Detroit Planners Say That Archer's Downtown Plan Faces Numerous Obstacles," *Detroit News*, June 1, 1997; Jon Pepper, "Road to Renaissance: Red Tape Stands in Way of Detroit Development," *Detroit News*, September 10, 1997; Valarie Basheda and Phil Linsalata, "City Hall Staff Shortages, Red Tape Slow Projects," *Detroit News*, July 16, 1996; David Migoya, "Detroit Department Ignores Calls and Loses New Business," *Detroit News*, September 26, 1995. Understaffing became such an issue that even basic information like building ownership wasn't always available: R. J. King, "Confusion over Owner Stalls Plans to Renovate," *Detroit News*, December 13, 1995.

44. Vergara, "Detroit Waits for the Millennium."

45. Initial board members consisted of executives of three local banks, the Big Three automakers, Detroit Edison, Michigan Consolidated, Marian Ilitch, the UAW president, a former basketball star, and both the Hudson-Webber and Kresge Foundations.

46. Jon Pepper, "Power Elite Designing a New Downtown," *Detroit News and Free Press*, March 10, 1996.

47. John Gallagher, "Planner Envisions (Just One) Downtown—Greenberg Enjoys Support Unseen since the '60s," *Metro Times*, June 4, 1997.

48. R. J. King, "Archer Unveils Design Strategy for Downtown: Blueprint Will Spur New Development While Renovating Buildings.," *Detroit News*, May 28, 1997; personal interview with Ken Greenberg, Toronto, December 2015.

49. With some public support from the DDA, developer David Schervish bought up a small cluster of buildings near the park and renovated them as a mixed-use strip of offices, dwellings, restaurants, and retailers: Marla Dickerson, "Two Part Harmonie Park," *Detroit Free Press*, August 9, 1992; Bill Vlasic, "Broadway Revival—a Subtle Mix of Musical and Artistic Attractions Start Drawing People to the Once-Desolate Street," *Detroit News*, July 15, 1994. The area's revival had a slow start due to wavering private interest and the negative halo of nearby vacant structures such as the large Madison-Lenox Hotel—which was too expensive to renovate: R. J. King, "Harmonie Park District Promises Three Restaurants, Coffee Bar, Lofts," *Detroit Free Press*, October 1, 1995; Judy Rose, "Tuning Up Harmonie Park," *Detroit Free Press*, March 26, 1996; R. J. King, "Club Owner Fights to Save Detroit's Madison-Lenox Hotel," *Detroit News*, November 30, 1995; "Vibrancy Returns to Harmonie Park—Restaurants, Concert Hall, Apartments Add to Lively Urban Village," *Detroit News*, October 23, 1998; John Bebow and Valarie Basheda, "Rush to Redevelop Downtown Carries a Price," *Detroit News*, January 29, 1996; R. J. King, "Saving Harmonie Park—Historic Theater District Is Downtown's Hottest Ticket: Developers Complete Vision for Architectural Renaissance," *Detroit News*, August 22, 1999.

50. "New Developments Bring Lower Woodward to Life," *Detroit News*, January 4, 2000. In the mid-1990s, the demand for apartments even created waiting lists: "Apartment Dwellers Rediscover Downtown," *Detroit News*, August 9, 1995.

51. "The New Downtown: Woodward Landlords Encouraged by Rebirth," *Detroit News*, March 30, 1997. By 1998, eight different loft projects totaling 1,500 units were slated for downtown's Necklace District by various developers. Santiago Esparza, "'Necklace' Lofts Could Help Downtown to Regain Sparkle: $5-Million Upscale Project Is Latest in Woodward District,"

Detroit News, February 4, 1998; R. J. King, "More Lofts Predicted in Downtown," *Detroit News*, February 27, 1998; Madison J. Gray, "City's Necklace District Coming Alive," *Detroit News*, December 29, 1999. The downtown residential growth hinged on the historic character of buildings, as the relatively new Trolley Plaza had actually gone into receivership by 1997: R. J. King, "Trolley Plaza Complex for Sale: Detroit Building Has 351 Units, Pool, $14.5m Price Tag," *Detroit News*, March 19, 1999.

52. Jon Pepper, "Building on Heritage Works for Detroit," *Detroit News*, April 11, 1999; R. J. King, "With Rebirth, Detroit Jewels Get a New Sheen: Investors Are Bringing Back Historic Buildings," *Detroit News*, June 16, 1999; "Downtown Buzzes near Comerica Park—Old Buildings Are Refurbished into Restaurants, Lofts," *Detroit News*, July 16, 1999. Many downtown residential developments were inspired by the success of the revitalization of Detroit's Midtown area under the leadership of Susan Mosey. Mosey positioned Midtown as an arts and cultural center, using its cultural capital to spur reinvestments. Midtown's smaller buildings allowed smaller investors to test the market, finding a large pent-up demand that was later met in larger downtown projects like Merchants Row: Jennifer Dixon, "Rebuilding History," *Detroit Free Press*, November 8, 1999; Gary Graff, "Candidates Take Cultural Stands," *Detroit Free Press*, October 24, 1993; R. J. King, "Developing the Woodward Corridor—Risky Plan Pays Big Dividends for Detroit Renovator," *Detroit News*, September 10, 1995; interview with Mark Nickita and Dorian Moore, April 2016; John Gallagher, "Hopes Blossom on Downtown's Woodward Ave.," *Detroit Free Press*, January 5, 2000. Besides younger residents, downtown also became a magnet for empty nesters: Barbara Hoover, "Downtown Defenders—They Live with Crime and High Taxes, but These City Residents Say Theirs Is the Best of Worlds," *Detroit News*, June 19, 1988; Tricia Serju, "A Growing Appetite for Diverse Cuisine—Downtown Is Turning into a Melting Pot of Ethnic Restaurants," *Detroit News*, March 23, 1995; Madison J. Gray, "Party Motown Style—Hip-Hop to Alternative Music, Clubs Jam to the Walls as City Revives Its Image," *Detroit News*, April 7, 1999.

53. The Hudson's store was the Partnership's first purchase: Lekan Oguntoyinbo, "Group Targets Detroit Blight—Woodward Corridor to Get Help First," *Detroit News*, March 12, 1996.

54. "Raze Old Building, Taubman Says," *Detroit News*, September 28, 1990; Lynn Waldsmith, "Archer Task Force Says Site Is Vital for Development of Downtown," *Detroit News*, August 3,

1994. Renovation costs soared as the Hudson's building had significantly deteriorated due to vandalism and parasitic ownership. Owners had included several developers, a Canadian company accused of stripping the building, a clergyman who failed to pay his taxes, and the State of Michigan which took the building as a result: Lekan Oguntoyinbo, "Destined for Dust—Downtown Hudson's Demolition Approved," *Detroit Free Press*, February 6, 1997; Jean Maddern Pitrone, *Hudson's: Hub of America's Heartland* (Franklin, MI: Altwerger and Mandel, 1991), 187–188.

55. This message echoed the recommendations made by his boss Alfred Taubman over the previous decades. Councilmembers were not fully convinced, especially since there were no private proposals for new construction if the site was cleared and the demolition would cost $12 million to $15 million: Suzette Hackney, "Downtown Blueprint to Focus on Woodward: Planners Urge Council to Approve Proposal to Demolish Hudson's," *Detroit News*, January 24, 1997.

56. Pitrone, *Hudson's*; Curt Guyette, "The Partnership Puzzle—the Methods of Shaping Detroit Are Largely Secret," *Metro Times*, June 10, 1997.

57. Ron French, "It's History—the Hudson's Building: 1911–1998," *Detroit News and Free Press*, October 25, 1998; Michael Hauser and Marianne Weldon, *Hudson's: Detroit's Legendary Department Store* (Charleston, SC: Arcadia, 2004), 126. The designation of 23 nearby buildings as the Lower Woodward Historic District, lobbied for by the same Greater Downtown Partnership that had ordered the Hudson's demolition, seemed only the more ironic: R. J. King, "23 Buildings Get Historic Tag," *Detroit News*, October 5, 1998.

58. Mark Puls, "Campus Martius Draws Interest: Developers Have Plans for Reviving Lower Woodward Area," *Detroit News*, February 6, 1998; "Project Reshapes Heart of Detroit," *Detroit News*, May 19, 1998; Mark Puls, R. J. King, Suzette Hackney, and James Tobin, "Firm Wins Chance to Reshape Detroit—Archer Picks Developer to Transform 9 Acres in Heart of Downtown," *Detroit News*, May 21, 1998.

59. Daniel G. Fricker, "Office Optimism," *Detroit Free Press*, May 15, 1998; "Campus Martius Still Lacks Tenants—Confidence Remains High Despite Development's Slow Start," *Detroit Free Press*, April 13, 2000.

60. "Dreams and Dust," *Detroit News*, October 10, 1998.

61. Jon Pepper, "Pieces Moving into Place for a Downtown Revival: So Much Hope, So Much Still to Be Done," *Detroit News*, April 18, 1999; R. J. King, "Bold Move: Compuware to Polish City's Old Core: Campus Martius Main Office Complemented by Riverfront Complex Linked to Rencen," *Detroit News*, April 18, 1999. The "bold, fresh start" is cited from the headquarters project description by Rossetti Architects, accessed September 23, 2014 via http://www.rossetti.com.

62. "Archer Envisions Central Park Downtown: A Restaurant Like New York's Tavern on the Green May Be Built," *Detroit News*, April 23, 1999.

63. The winning development team had originally proposed offices and restaurants on the Kern block, a massive hotel on the Hudson's site, a department store on the Crowley's blocks, and stores and offices on the southern Monroe Avenue block. Only the Compuware offices on the Kern block materialized, as Detroit's office market was nonexistent, its hotel market already oversaturated, and retailers wary of entering a downtown devoid of a critical mass of residents and workers: Puls et al., "Firm Wins Chance to Reshape Detroit"; Jon Pepper, "Partnership Hopes to Regroup, Keep Downtown Detroit Dreams Alive," *Detroit News*, May 31, 2000.

64. R. J. King and George Hunter, "Hudson's Demolition Lifts Downtown Hopes: Old Gives Way to New Projects, People," *Detroit News*, October 5, 1998; R. J. King, "Office Boom Revives Downtown Detroit—Observers Say GM's Purchase of Rencen Sparks Interest in Commercial Properties," *Detroit News*, September 11, 1998; Judy Rose and Deborah Solomon, "GM Purchase of Rencen Startles Some," *Detroit Free Press*, May 16, 1996; R. J. King, "Rencen Upgrade to Glitter," *Detroit News*, December 21, 1997. Development company Hines also proposed a new office and parking complex on lower Woodward Avenue, with the help of DDA gap financing and federal loans: David A. Markiewicz, "$16 Million U.S. Loan Sought for City Project," *Detroit News*, July 13, 1988; R. J. King, "GM to Create a Village on Detroit Riverfront: Rencen Lots to Be Developed into Lofts, Offices, Eateries," *Detroit News*, June 6, 1999.

65. "Studies Aim to Reshape Downtown: Planners Consider Revamping Traffic Flow for Influx of Residents, Business, Visitors," *Detroit News*, June 21, 1998; "Detroit Gets $6.2-Million State Grant: New Promenade to Be Built between Rencen and Cobo," *Detroit News*, August 5, 1999.

66. Gina Damron, "Detroit to Get Taste of Asian Flair," *Detroit Free Press*, January 2, 2007. Corruption was involved in the failure: Jim Schaefer, Dave Ashenfelter, and M. L. Elrick, "Ex-Kilpatrick Aide Faces Corruption Probe," *Detroit Free Press*, August 19, 2008.

67. Between 1983 and 1990, no less than four plans had been made for the Brush Park area, with no definite outcomes: Judy Rose, "Locked Out of the Mansions," *Detroit Free Press*, October 21, 1990; "Brush Park—at Last, a Plan That May Help Save a Part of City's Past," *Detroit News*, September 30, 1990; Claudia Capos, "Brush Park Residents Giving up Hope," *Detroit News*, April 3, 1988; McCarthy, "Entertainment-Led Regeneration."

68. Jennifer Dixon, "Fire Gets Mansions before Rehab Starts," *Detroit News*, April 5, 1999; "Brush Park Work May Start in March," *Detroit News*, February 2, 1999; R. J. King, "Archer, Developers Want Mansions Moved to Allow Condos in Brush Park Neighborhood," *Detroit News*, February 5, 1995; John Gallagher, "Condo Ready—Brush Park Likely to Get Major Housing Project," *Detroit Free Press*, November 19, 1994. In the original 1992 proposals for a stadium, the southern portion of Brush Park was designated as a parking lot for Ilitch's new Tigers Stadium development. The city never was a big proponent of this idea: Bill McGraw, "Ilitch's Dreams Focus on the Fox—He Hints of Wings, Tigers near Theater," *Detroit Free Press*, August 27, 1992; Vivian S. Toy, "Council: Stadium Parking Plan Wastes Valuable Land," *Detroit News*, September 26, 1991.

69. Arthur Bridgeforth Jr. and Robert Ankeny, "Developer Cruises Woodward for Retail Land," *Crain's Detroit Business*, September 13, 1999; Robert Ankeny, "More Development in the Works for Comerica Park Area," *Crain's Detroit Business*, May 15, 2000; James Tobin, "Blighted Area Shows Signs of Promise: Planners, Developers Believe Most Successes Hinge on Cass Corridor," *Detroit News*, April 13, 1997; George Hunter, "Long-Ignored Cass Corridor Comes Alive with Development," *Detroit News*, October 3, 1997. Developer Robert Slattery was a significant pioneer in renovating buildings just north of Cass Park from the mid-1990s onward. His success was amplified under Susan Mosey's leadership, and others began to invest in the area: Jess McCuan and Joseph B. White, "If Detroit Rebounds, Robert Slattery Should Receive Some of the Credit," *Wall Street Journal*, September 13, 1999; R. J. King, "Renewal Draws from Past in Call for Detroit Bus Lanes—New Transit Spur Will Link 'Midtown' with Downtown," *Detroit News*, September 15, 1998.

70. Laura Berman, "Masons' Move to Suburbs Could Doom Another Detroit Palace," *Detroit News*, June 13, 1999; Joel J. Smith, "Shelter for Vets, Poorly Run, Tenants Claim," *Detroit News*, June 27, 1993.The foundation that ran the Eddystone shelter ran out of money and was forced to close it in the late 1990s: United States Department of the Interior, "Michigan Sp Eddystone Hotel" (Washington, D.C., 2006). On the work of the Cass Corridor Neighborhood Development Corporation, see Vivian S. Toy, "Nonprofit Development Group Brings Self-Respect Back," *Detroit News*, March 17, 1994; William Kleinknecht, "Building into the City—Nonprofit Groups Provide Housing," *Detroit Free Press*, January 27, 1992.

71. The Enterprise Zone designation benefited Corktown with property tax abatements for new construction: "Corktown to Get New Townhouses," *Detroit News*, March 19, 1995.The neighborhood hired University of Michigan students for a community redevelopment plan: June Manning Thomas, *Redevelopment and Race: Planning a Finer City in Postwar Detroit* (Baltimore: Johns Hopkins University Press, 1997), 195.

72. Madison J. Gray, "Surviving in the Canyon—Merchants Hope They Are around to Reap the Benefits from Future Projects Along the Woodward Corridor," *Detroit News*, March 10, 1999.

73. George Cantor, "Competing for Metro Renewal: Detroit Pursues Entertainment Strategy, but Suburbs Continue Reinventing Themselves," *Detroit News*, February 22, 1998; "Birmingham Adapts," *Detroit News*, June 24, 1998.

74. Roberta Brandes Gratz, "Putting Casinos on Waterfront Threatens to Kill Detroit's Rebirth," *Detroit News*, October 9, 1998. Gratz frequently reiterated her criticism in journal articles and conferences: Maureen McDonald, "Author Faults Detroit's Lack of Grass-Roots Drive for Its Revitalization," *Detroit News*, April 25, 2001.

CHAPTER 12: A ROARING END: 2001–2011

1. *Detroit Free Press* architecture critic John Gallagher warned Detroit urban planners that downtown's demise wasn't "necessarily because our physical planning has been poor. It's because the derelict buildings in the way no longer present any market opportunity. If there was a genuine way to make money from downtown investments, people would make those investments. Much of our worry over our lack of street life would take care of itself." John Gal-

lagher, "Planner Envisions (Just One) Downtown—Greenberg Enjoys Support Unseen since the '60s," *Metro Times*, June 4, 1997. Wayne State urban scholar Elaine Driker had very similar sentiments: Lynn Waldsmith, "Facelift Urged for Woodward," *Detroit News*, November 11, 1994.

2. Most of the litigation concerned the purchase of riverfront casino land, as well as the operator selection process that a higher court later deemed unconstitutional. Kilpatrick allowed casinos to scale down their plans and decide their own final locations: Cameron McWhirter and Darren A. Nichols, "Casino Plan Downsized—Kilpatrick Seeks License Extension; Latest Plan Envisions Smaller Hotels, Less Revenue," *Detroit News*, March 21, 2002; Tina Lam, "Detroit Wins Big with Casino Deal—City Will Keep Riverfront Land, Get Windfall of $102 Million," *Detroit Free Press*, March 27, 2002; City Planning Commission, "2000–2002 Biennial Report" (Detroit, 2002), 18.

3. R. J. King, "Separated Casinos Will Limit Spin-Off," *Detroit News*, March 27, 2002.

4. Mary E. Kremposky, "Making the Desert Bloom—Enchanting Changes at DTE Energy's Downtown Campus," *CAM Magazine* (Fall 2009); Raymond Curtis Miller, *The Force of Energy: A Business History of the Detroit Edison Company* ([East Lansing]: Michigan State University Press, 1971); June Manning Thomas, *Redevelopment and Race: Planning a Finer City in Postwar Detroit* (Baltimore: Johns Hopkins University Press, 1997), 186.

5. Open letter by Marshall Weingarden in Dan Austin, Sean Doerr, and John Gallagher, *Lost Detroit: Stories behind the Motor City's Majestic Ruins* (Charleston, SC: History Press, 2010), 33–38.

6. Despite protest from the city's own historic commission, Mayor Kilpatrick agreed with the demolition and even provided an interest-free loan to subsidize it: Cheri Y. Gay, *Lost Detroit* (London: Pavilion Books, 2013), 138; Louis Aguilar, "Reshaping Downtown Detroit. Gilbert, Ilitches: 2 Strategies, 1 Goal for City—Developers Amass Swaths, Aim to Revitalize Core," *Detroit News*, March 6, 2014.

7. R. J. King, "Super Bowl Spruce-Up: $100m," *Detroit News*, April 4, 2002; Micheline Maynard, "Detroit Polishes, and Demolishes, for the Super Bowl," *New York Times*, January 22,

2006. While the Super Bowl was supposed to single-handedly turn the fate of downtown Detroit, the 2007 recession minimized structural economic spinoff.

8. Judy Lin, "Urban Park Draws High Hopes—Many See the New Downtown Square, with Its Ice Rink and Cafe, as the Key to City Revival," *Detroit News*, November 18, 2004.

9. Daniel G. Fricker, "Woodward Stretch Could Be Renewed as Merchant's Row Partnership Proposes 163 Loft Apartments," *Detroit Free Press*, September 11, 2001; "Woodward's Voices Tell of Hard Work, Wild Ideas—Bowling Alley, Orchestra Hall, Flower Shop Survive, Thrive," *Detroit Free Press*, July 10, 2001; R. J. King, "Another Downtown Detroit Building Gets Make-over," *Detroit News*, August 8, 2004; "Ernst to Move 400 to New Detroit Office Towner—Accounting Firm, Visteon Corp. Will Be Main Tenants at $54 Million One Kennedy Square," *Detroit News*, May 15, 2005.

10. "Historic Trolleys Are History," *Detroit News*, October 24, 2003. Quite contrary to the consensus in the 1980s on the Washington Boulevard transformation into a pedestrian-friendly setting, the Washington Boulevard Business Association criticized the red "erector set" that obscured the view of businesses and "never looked finished": Lynn Waldsmith, "Group Wants No Part of Giant 'Erector Set'—Washington Boulevard Framework Called a Barrier That Keeps People Away," *Detroit News*, February 8, 1995.

11. Louis Aguilar, "Restored Fort Shelby Hotel Opens," *Detroit News*, December 16, 2008; Louis Aguilar, Susan Whitall, and Maureen Feighan, "Restored Book Cadillac Hotel Reopens with Glitz, Glamour and Memories," *Detroit News*, October 26, 2008.

12. The plans for a trail had hatched two years before through the work of the Greater Detroit Heritage River Initiative, following a 1998 EPA designation of the Detroit River as an American Heritage River, overseen by the Metropolitan Affairs Coalition, a regional economic development nonprofit: Metropolitan Affairs Coalition, "Building the Riverfront Greenway—the State of Greenway Investments along the Detroit River" (Detroit, 2001).

13. The SOM plan has been commissioned by the Detroit Riverfront Conservancy and the newly revived City Planning Department under the leadership of Maurice Cox: James David Dickson, "Detroit's Riverfront Becomes Regional Magnet," *Detroit News*, February 25, 2017.

14. Ben Solis, "An Abridged History of Movement, Detroit's Electronic Music Festival," *Michigan Live*, October 24, 2017; Tamara Warren, "More Than a Movement: The Evolution of Detroit's Legendary Techno Festival," June 2, 2016, https://www.theverge.com/2016/6/2/11840650/movement-festival-detroit-demf-electronic-music-techno.

CHAPTER 13: A NEW BEGINNING: THE PAST AS FUTURE

1. The video series was created for Palladium Boots, eager to connect Detroit's grassroots revival to their brand: Thalia Mavros, Brendan Fitzgerald, and Johnny Knoxville, "Detroit Lives" (Palladium Boots, 2010).

2. David Segal, "A Missionary's Quest to Remake Motor City," *New York Times*, April 13, 2013.

3. The "creative class" refers to workers in the creative fields, a term coined by economist Richard Florida, *The Rise of the Creative Class: And How It's Transforming Work, Leisure, Community and Everyday Life* (New York: Basic Books, 2002).

4. Daniel Duggan, "Frontier Spirit—Urban Redeveloper Has Ideas to Remake Detroit," *Crain's Detroit Business*, August 21, 2011; "Lost Potential: Remembering Tony Goldman, the Developer Who Wanted to Change Detroit," *Crain's Detroit Business*, September 14, 2012.

5. Louis Aguilar and Lauren Abel-Razzaq, "Five Years, 78 Properties Later—Dan Gilbert's 'Detroit 2.0' Plan Still Going Strong," *Detroit News*, August 18, 2015.

6. Jennifer Chambers, "City's Ford Foundation Aid Flowing—Group to Step up Grants after $125m 'Grand Bargain,'" *Detroit News*, January 19, 2015; Randy Kennedy, "'Grand Bargain' Saves the Detroit Institute of Arts," *New York Times*, November 7, 2014; Matthew Dolan, "In Detroit Bankruptcy, Art Was Key to the Deal," *Wall Street Journal*, November 7, 2014; Chad Halcom, "Kresge Pledges $150 Million to Detroit Future City Project," *Crain's Detroit Business*, January 9, 2013. More information in Brian Doucet, *Why Detroit Matters* (Bristol: Policy Press, 2017).

7. The citation comes from the vision statement in Opportunity Detroit, "A Plan for Our Time" (Detroit, 2012), 23. See also David Segal, "A Missionary's Quest to Remake Motor City," *New York Times*, April 13, 2013; Opportunity Detroit, Project for Public Spaces, and D:hive Detroit, "A Placemaking Vision for Downtown Detroit" (Detroit, 2013).

8. Laura Berman, "Vision, Past Make Detroit Tale of 2 Cities," *Detroit News*, April 24, 2012.

9. Downtown Detroit Partnership, "Business Improvement Zone Plan" (Detroit, 2014).

10. Federal support was withdrawn for a 9-mile streetcar corridor from downtown to the edge of the city: Matt Helms, "Woodward Rail Plan Rolls Ahead," *Detroit Free Press*, April 23, 2013; Tom Greenwood and Leonard M. Fleming, "Route OK'd for Light Rail Project," *Detroit News*, June 30, 2011.

11. Daniel Duggan, "Dan Gilbert: There's No Reason to Go off the Rails on M1," *Crain's Detroit Business*, December 14, 2011. The rebranding was a result of a report sponsored by the Greater Downtown Partnership in alliance with the Hudson-Webber Foundation, DEGC, Midtown Detroit Inc., Invest Detroit and Data Driven Detroit: Abir Ali et al., "7.2 Sq Mi—a Report on Greater Downtown Detroit" (Detroit, 2013).

12. John Gallagher, "Gilbert Hopes to Recapture Hudson's Magic with New Iconic Woodward Structure," *Detroit Free Press*, November 25, 2013; J. C. Reindl, "Gilbert Seeks Ideas for Developing Hudson's Site in Detroit," *Detroit Free Press*, February 28, 2013; John Gallagher, "Dan Gilbert's Z Garage Opens," *Detroit Free Press*, January 29, 2014; Louis Aguilar and Michael Martinez, "Gilbert Set to Buy Greektown Casino," *Detroit News*, January 17, 2013; Christine Ferretti and Charles E. Ramirez, "Stadium Plan Reignites Jail Debate," *Detroit News*, April 28, 2016.

13. John Gallagher, "Dan Gilbert Is Doing More Than Buying, He's Leaving Design Mark on Downtown Detroit," *Detroit Free Press*, January 2, 2014.

14. Segal, "A Missionary's Quest to Remake Motor City."

15. Aguilar and Abel-Razzaq, "Five Years, 78 Properties Later."

16. Well-published cases of displacement include the displacement of over 100 low-income seniors from the Griswold Building by a local developer to convert the building into "The Albert," an upscale apartment complex, and the displacement of artists from the Farwell Building: Louis Aguilar, "Rent Moving Up—Downtown Market Nears Magic Number," *Detroit News*, June 18, 2014. "The Albert" developer Richard Broder responds in David Muller, "Downtown Detroit Development Offers Lessons for Displacing Low-Income Residents for Market-Rate Housing" (Michigan Live, online, last updated August 21, 2014). Violet

Ikonomova, "Detroit Officials Aim to Prevent Displacement at Midtown Apartment Building Slated for Upgrade," *Metro Times*, May 31, 2017; Nancy Derringer, "In a Gentrifying Detroit, an Uneasy Migration of Urban Millennials," *Bridge*, August 21, 2014; Doucet, *Why Detroit Matters*, 88–90.

17. Christine Ferretti, "Annual Detroit Count Shows 'Progress' on Homelessness," *Detroit News*, May 18, 2017. The ACLU filed a complaint with the city in 2013 about the regular displacement of the homeless from Greektown: Sarah L. Mehta, "Re: Unlawful Detroit Police Practice of Abducting Homeless People from Greektown and Deserting Them in Remote Areas of the Detroit Metro Area," personal communication, 2013.

18. Aguilar, "Rent Moving Up."

19. Dan Austin, Sean Doerr, and John Gallagher, *Lost Detroit: Stories behind the Motor City's Majestic Ruins* (Charleston, SC: History Press, 2010), 24.

20. Louis Aguilar, "Whitney Rolls out High-End Apartments," *Detroit News*, September 13, 2014; "Historic Whitney Glitters after $92 Million Makeover," *Detroit News*, December 16, 2014.

21. Ian Thibodeau, "Building Revivals Broadway Bound—Restaurants, Apartments Part of Plans for 3 Sites near the Paradise Valley Project," *Detroit News*, December 9, 2016; Louis Aguilar, "Paradise Valley Could Rise Anew within a Few Years," *Detroit News*, June 30, 2016.

22. The term was coined in Corktown by a realtor who noted that the neighborhood had come on the radar for investors who could no longer afford downtown due to Gilbert's holdings. "The 'Dan Gilbert Effect'—Downtown Building Sales Corktown Buying Spree," *Detroit News*, November 6, 2013.

23. Louis Aguilar, "Reshaping Downtown Detroit. Gilbert, Ilitches: 2 Strategies, 1 Goal for City—Developers Amass Swaths, Aim to Revitalize Core," *Detroit News*, March 6, 2014.

24. The stadium project is part of a 45-block vision for most of Cass Park and northwestern downtown Detroit. Olympia Development of Michigan, "Ilitch Organization Exploring Development of New Residential, Retail, Office and Events Center District in Downtown Detroit," news release, December 4, 2012.

25. Description from the District Detroit website, http://www.districtdetroit.com, accessed July 15, 2017.

26. Louis Aguilar, "Ilitch Plan: Save 1 Historic Hotel, Raze Another—Residential Use Proposed for Eddystone, Wrecking Ball for Park," *Detroit News*, January 31, 2015; Dan Austin, "Detroit's Past Can Play Role in Future Arena District," *Detroit Free Press*, May 20, 2014.

27. Kirk Pinho, "Map Reveals New District Detroit Details," *Crain's Detroit Business*, February 4, 2018.

28. Through various tax constructs, just under 40 percent of the stadium construction costs were borne by public funds—less than for the Comerica Park deal of the 1990s. The city used no general funds to finance the stadium, the support instead coming from a mixture of DDA assessments, TIF funds, and state-backed bonds. Controversially, some of these sources would otherwise have gone to fund Detroit's ailing public school system. The DDA owns the stadium and will lease it to Ilitch's organization for free, but will receive money to pay back $200 million of the DDA construction bonds. The land under the stadium was sold to the DDA for a symbolic $1. The old Joe Louis Arena is to be torn down with public funding. For more information on the stadium's complex financing arrangement, see Bill Shea, "Latest Little Caesars Arena Project Construction Cost: $862.9 Million," *Crain's Detroit Business*, May 23, 2017. For a critical analysis of the legal process preceding the stadium's construction, see Ryan Felton, "How Mike Ilitch Scored a New Red Wings Arena—Hockeytown's Caesar Gets a Sweet Deal. But What's in It for Detroit?," *Metro Times*, May 7, 2014.

CHAPTER 14: CONCLUSION

1. Quoted in Dolores Hayden, *The Power of Place: Urban Landscapes as Public History* (Cambridge, MA: MIT Press, 1995), 46.

2. Arthur Johnson, Camilo Jose Vergara, Donald Moss, Dan Hoffman, Richard Plunz, and Patricia Phillips, "Detroit Is Everywhere" (StoreFront Art and Architecture, Columbia University Urban Design Studio, and Cranbrook Academy of Art Architecture Studio, New York, 1995); Constantinos A. Doxiadis, *Emergence and Growth of an Urban Region: The Developing Urban Detroit Area*, Developing Urban Detroit Area Research Project (Detroit: Detroit Edison Co., 1966); Douglas Kelbaugh, Roy Strickland, and Eric Dueweke, "Adding Three Dimensions

to Downtown Detroit," in *Detroit Design Workshop 2007* (Ann Arbor: University of Michigan, Alfred A. Taubman College of Architecture and Urban Planning, 2007).

3. For more information, see figure 14.1.

4. John Hannigan, *Fantasy City: Pleasure and Profit in the Postmodern Metropolis* (London: Routledge, 2010).

5. Alison Isenberg, *Downtown America: A History of the Place and the People Who Made It* (Chicago: University of Chicago Press, 2004); Sharon Zukin, *Landscapes of Power: From Detroit to Disney World* (Berkeley: University of California Press, 1991).

6. Hyperreality, a term coined by postmodern philosophers including Umberto Eco and Jean Baudrillard, refers to the blurred boundary between reality and simulation. For more information, see Jean Baudrillard, *Simulacra and Simulation* (Ann Arbor: University of Michigan Press, 1994); Umberto Eco, *Travels in Hyper Reality: Essays* (San Diego: Harcourt Brace Jovanovich, 1990).

7. Paul Goldberger, "The Rise of the Private City," in Julia Vitullo-Martin, ed., *Breaking Away: The Future of Cities: Essays in Memory of Robert F. Wagner, Jr.* (New York: Twentieth Century Fund Press, 1996). For more on risk mitigation in urban reinvention, see Hannigan, *Fantasy City*, 71–74.

8. This argument mirrors historian Susan Fainstein's view, against the perceived loss of downtown authenticity in American cities, that downtowns always carried a heavy element of simulation and disconnect from most people's reality. Susan S. Fainstein, *The City Builders: Property, Politics, and Planning in London and New York* (Cambridge, MA: Basil Blackwell, 1994), 230–233.

9. Coleman Young and Lonnie Wheeler, *Hard Stuff: The Autobiography of Coleman Young* (New York: Viking, 1994), 2.

INDEX

Demolition (cont.)
270–272, 279. *See also* Urban renewal:
clearance for

Department of Street Railways, 92, 134.
See also Streetcars; Transit

Department of Streets and Traffic, 137

Detroit Athletic Club, 54

Detroit Bank and Trust Building, 154

Detroit Economic Growth Corporation,
213, 240, 249, 259

Detroit Edison Company, 183, 196, 197, 203,
205, 221, 233, 250, 260, 266, 280, 282

Detroit Housing Association, 64

Detroit Housing Commission, 108, 127,
129, 130. *See also* Housing

Detroit Industrial Expressway, 122, 136–137

Detroit Renaissance, 197

Detroit River, 11, 19, 22, 40, 47, 244, 253
port, 13, 25, 40, 98, 180
riverfront, 1, 10–11, 19, 23, 27–30, 34–36,
40, 44–48, 54, 90, 138–141, 152–154, 169,
178, 196–197, 202–205, 212, 217, 225,
236–238, 243–244, 249, 253, 280
tunnels, 48, 107, 216

Detroit Stove works, 22. *See also*
Manufacturing: stove

Detroit Terminal Railroad, 54

Dime Building, 58–59, 262

Dodge, John, 39

Donaldson and Meier (architects), 58, 84

Downtown Detroit Partnership, 259

Downtown Development Authority,
212–217, 221, 240

Doxiadis, Constantinos, 183

Drugs, 63, 203–204, 244. *See also* Crime

Durant, William C., 39

Eastern Market, 28, 44, 47, 60, 98, 205, 224

Economic development, 121, 213, 257

Economy, 18, 63, 84, 92, 101, 107, 117, 121,
168, 221, 258. *See also* Employment

Eddystone Hotel, 244, 263. *See also* Hotels

Edsel Ford Freeway, 137, 156, 164

Emery, George, 131–132

Employment, 19, 34–36, 47, 64, 107,
121–122, 125–127, 147, 160, 168–169,
176, 189–190, 194, 231–232, 236.
See also Economy; Unemployment

Entertainment, 3, 18, 21–23, 39–40, 62–64,
81–84, 89, 125–128, 133, 141, 148, 152,
155, 177–180, 202–204, 217, 223–224,
233–237, 241, 245, 250, 260, 263, 266,
274, 286. *See also* Ballrooms; Prostitution; Restaurants; Saloons; Theaters

Erie Canal, 15

Expressways. *See* Freeways

Farmer Street, 39, 60

Federal buildings
McNamara Building, 192, 250
1897, 39

Federal department store, 81, 148, 177